WOMEN IN A CHANGING WORLD

WOMEN IN A
CHANGING WORLD

The dynamic story of the
International Council of Women
since 1888

LONDON
ROUTLEDGE & KEGAN PAUL

First published 1966
by Routledge & Kegan Paul Ltd.
Broadway House, 68–74 Carter Lane
London, E.C.4

Printed in Great Britain
by Richard Clay (The Chaucer Press), Ltd.
Bungay, Suffolk

FOREWORD

By Marie-Hélène Lefaucheux
President of the ICW 1957–63, Honorary President 1963–64

The final wording of this text was still under consideration by Mrs. Lefaucheux at the time of her tragic death on February 25th, 1964.

BOTH TESTIMONY OF THE PAST and encouragement for the future, this history of the International Council of Women is particularly opportune at a time when different human communities are coming to recognize, with varying degrees of satisfaction, the 'evolution of women' accomplished in the twentieth century, and, indeed, are all too apt to consider this evolution as complete.

The reader of the coming pages will see how, for seventy-five years, the ICW has striven for the abolition of discrimination not only on grounds of sex, but also on grounds of race, class and creed, and how, through National and Local Councils, its efforts have reached into village, city and nation on every continent. And wherever it has worked for the recognition of human rights and duties, the ICW has also worked, ever since its foundation, for the essential condition of human progress—peace by the arbitration of international disputes: its first official delegation was that received by the International Peace Conference at the Hague in 1907.

Our century has seen important advances on these fronts: yet in certain areas of the world the needs and rights of men, and especially of women and of children are still unrecognized, if not in law, in custom and in application. In the case of women, even in those countries where most has been achieved, much remains to be done. Despite the almost universal right to exercise the vote, despite access to greatly improved, if not yet equal education, women are still excluded from many public offices, and, although their work is becoming more and more important a factor in national economies, opportunities for sufficiently varied vocational training are still lacking, and the principle of equal pay for equal work by men and women is not applied. Moreover, the fundamental problem—that of the legal status of woman in the family—has been satisfactorily settled only in very few legislatures. The rulers not only of developing countries, but also of highly industrialized societies still refuse to consider the institution of marriage as a union of partners equal in duties and in rights.

The ICW stands ready to pursue the work on which it has so long been engaged: defending in a context broader than that of the advancement of women those principles whose value, sixty years after the foundation of the Council, has been solemnly proclaimed in the Universal Declaration of Human Rights.

The scope of action of the ICW is constantly extending, as the experience of older Councils is reinforced by the clearly-expressed determination of Councils formed in newer states to play their part also in the world of tomorrow. Our organization serves efficaciously to bring the contribution of women—their courage, wisdom, generosity and prudence—to the search for peace and to the building of a more just, more stable and a happier world.

CONTENTS

HISTORIES OF
NATIONAL COUNCILS OF WOMEN

APPENDICES

INTRODUCTION

THE PREPARATION of a condensed history of the International Council of Women for the occasion of the 75th anniversary of its foundation was first proposed in a letter of June 25th, 1960, addressed to the ICW President, then Mrs M-H. Lefaucheux, by Mrs L. Dreyfus-Barney, who has served as ICW Liaison Officer to both the League of Nations and to the United Nations and its Specialized Agencies.

This suggestion was welcomed and formally accepted by delegates gathered from National Councils in 46 countries over the five continents at the Council Meeting held at Istanbul in August 1960. Shortly afterwards a representative *ad hoc* Committee of sponsors for this project was established, on which the following members of the ICW Board of Officers (1960–63) consented to serve:

Mrs M-H. Lefaucheux	President	France
Eva, Marchioness of Reading	Vice-President	Great Britain
Miss R. Gibson	Vice-President	Australia
Mrs Saraladevi Sarabhai	Vice-President	India
Mrs P. Kisosonkole	Vice-President	Uganda
Miss E. B. ten Bruggen Cate	Treasurer	
Mrs M. C. Schuller-McGeachy	Liaison Officer to the United Nations	

Assistants agreeing to work on this project included Dr R. Girod, Miss F. Baetens, Miss L. C. A. van Eeghen, Miss L. Marx, Mrs E. E. Monro, Miss M. Shaw, Mrs A. DeWitt Stetton and Miss E. A. van Veen. Assistance was also given by Mrs C. Pomonti, Administrative Secretary of the ICW.

In December 1960, an ICW Circular (NC/17) (see Appendix, 12, p. 351) was sent to all National Councils, requesting their cooperation in sending to ICW Headquarters by April 1961, their answers to specific questions concerning the history of their respective Councils. A second request followed in June 1961 and a subsequent communication extended the time limit for certain information to November 1962.

Delay in receiving replies from a number of Councils made it impossible to complete the project in time to publish this historical résumé for the 75th anniversary Council Meeting in Washington in 1963, as had originally been planned. However, with the assistance first of Mrs H. Schneider-Gmür, Ph.D., of Brown University, Executive Secretary of the ICW from 1949–57, and later of Mrs K. M. Delavenay, editor and translator experienced in work for the British Broadcasting Corporation and the United Nations, the book has now been completed and is here presented.

The original plan of work, as approved by the Board of Officers in 1961, has been closely observed, the main divisions being as follows:

1. A condensation of ICW activities over seventy-five years, divided into three periods of twenty-five years, each corresponding to a major period of world events and of ICW history: 1888–1913; 1914–38; 1939–63. This is followed by a short account of relations between the ICW and Intergovernmental Institutions (pp. 141–51).

2. The purpose, growth and accomplishments of ICW Standing Committees, based on the publication: *Standing Committees of the ICW*, 1957, prepared by Miss F. Baetens, Convener of the ICW Standing Committee on Laws and Suffrage (pp. 155–200).

3. Résumés of the work of the National Affiliates of the ICW, largely contributed by National Councils themselves in response to the above-mentioned ICW questionnaire. Also included are brief histories of Councils formerly affiliated to the ICW, condensed from the reports of their work appearing in the ICW publication *Histories of Affiliated Councils*, 1888–1938 (pp. 203–324).

The Appendices (pp. 327–54) contain additional material of special significance, such as excerpts from the original ICW Constitution of 1888, certain Declarations and Resolutions of the ICW, an account of the ICW Archives Project, a list of a number of important libraries containing ICW documentation, a list of publications by National Councils and a note on the finances of the ICW.

Throughout this work a consistent effort has been made to use only documented sources: Annual, Biennial, Triennial and Quin-quennial Reports, ICW books, brochures and periodicals, as well as publications by National Councils. Unfortunately, limitation of space, as well as an inevitable disparity in the material available, has made it impossible to do equal justice to all aspects of ICW work. While research has necessarily been restricted to material published in French and English (the present working languages of

the ICW) supplementary information on Councils using other languages may be found in the accounts of the activities of these Councils
contributed by them to Section 3 of this history (pp. 203–324).

It is sincerely regretted that it has not been possible, in the limited
space available, to record the outstanding work and achievements of
many Council members whose competence, devotion and tireless
effort have meant so much to the ICW and its affiliated National
Councils. It has, however, been necessary to restrict the mention of
names to those of persons closely identified with the specific activities
reported in the text.

*   *   *

The United Nations practice of employing English forms of
address—*Mr, Mrs, Miss*—for all nationalities in English language
publications has been followed throughout those sections of this
history dealing with the ICW and its Standing Committees.

In order to bring out the varied academic distinctions of Council
Members, it has been thought desirable, in those pages of the history
dealing with the period from 1945 onwards, to adopt the principle,
also current in UN publications, of reserving the use of the appella-
tion *Dr* for doctors of medicine, while specifying in the text, wherever
possible, the exact nature of other doctorates held. In view of the
lengthy research which would have been required to establish the
exact academic titles held by Council members named in earlier
periods of the history, the title *Dr* has, up to 1945, been employed
whenever the person in question was so designated in ICW records,
whether the doctorate was in medicine, law or another academic
subject.

EVOLUTION OF THE INTERNATIONAL
COUNCIL OF WOMEN

PROLOGUE

THE DATE WAS 1888, the scene was Albaugh's Opera House in Washington, DC, the occasion a Convention of women leaders from eight different countries gathered for the foundation of the International Council of Women.

What makes the establishment of this Council so important a milestone in the history of the emancipation of women? The fact that it marks a vital moment in the history of ideas—the moment when, for the first time, women asserted a collective right to play their full part in the forward march of humanity towards those goals proposed in the previous century by the forerunners of the French Revolution: 'the greatest happiness of the greatest number'.

Never before had the representatives of organized bodies of women banded themselves together, in the words of the original ICW Constitution, into 'a confederation of workers committed to the overthrow of all forms of ignorance and injustice'. Never before had women, collectively and internationally, determined upon 'an interchange of opinion on the great questions now agitating the world' in the conviction that such an interchange would 'rouse women to new thought . . . intensify their love of liberty . . . and give them a realizing sense of their power of combination' (*Council Idea*, p. 10).

Thus it was in the closing decades of the nineteenth century—and in America—that an international group of women first determined to 'throw the influence of united womanhood in favour of better conditions for humanity' (See Part I, Foundation and First Years of the ICW, p. 14).

To understand how this came about it is necessary to return to the earlier years of the century and examine, for a moment, the profound transformation of society, both in Europe and North America, resulting from the onset of the industrial revolution.

1800–48

In the great new urban centres of these continents—in countries priding themselves on being in the forefront of civilization and of progress—men, women and children came to live and work in

3

conditions of appalling hardship often close to slavery and on the borders of starvation. To women, already deprived of their most elementary legal rights—entirely subservient to husbands who, without infringing any law in the majority of countries, could not only dispose of property and earnings of their wives but also beat them, desert them and, in extreme cases, deprive them of their own children by giving, indenturing or willing them away—the early years of industrialization brought yet greater hardships. The wives and daughters of the rapidly-growing ranks of urban workers, suddenly removed from the relative satisfactions of life, however hard, in integrated rural communities, represented a welcome source of unskilled labour exactly of the type required for the most profitable exploitation of the new machines. Engaged at the lowest possible wages, hundreds of thousands of women and children entered the sweatshops, mills and factories of Europe and America to supplement the starvation wages of their menfolk, only to find themselves caught in a vicious circle in which their cheaper labour was used as a weapon to undercut male wages. Moreover, educationally barred from all opportunity to acquire those higher skills or learning which alone could lead to better jobs, women had yet less hope than men of any immediate betterment of their position.

Yet, at the same time that it created such conditions, the industrial revolution provided both the incentive and the means to overcome them, slowly opening up to both men and women entirely new horizons of social and economic progress. Markets could not be found unless the masses themselves were to rise above the prevailing margin of subsistence and enabled to spend money on the purchase of the goods they helped to manufacture. As the nineteenth century proceeded, it became obvious that the common man and woman had now to be something better than the drudge who had hitherto been found sufficient. Private exploitation of labour thus rapidly reached its economic limits, and the realization and organization of the growing economic power of the urban worker–consumer led not only to the extension of the franchise to new categories of male voter, to the beginnings of collective self-help represented by the first co-operatives and trade unions but also to those great democratizing movements towards parliamentary and legislative reform which were to end in increasing state intervention and regulation in both economic and social fields.

For the western world and its colonial dependencies, the nineteenth century was one of unprecedented expansion—of population, of wealth, of resources, of scientific knowledge, of mastery over nature and machine. It was also a century of increasing inter-communication not only on the physical level, but also on the plane of human consciousness. The railway, the steamboat, the spread of primary education and of literacy, and of the daily press, transformed the western world from a series of largely independent units at different levels of social and economic development, into an inter-dependent whole, with all the social and economic consequences this entailed, and still entails today. With the economic watchwords of the century—expansion and organization—came the corresponding social watchwords—interdependence and responsibility.

Nor was man's conscience disturbed and his anger stirred only by inequalities at home, within his own supposedly 'advanced' western world. For the first time in history, he became aware that the relative wealth of his own sector of society was based on exploitation instituted and maintained by him in those other quarters of the globe providing a major part of the new resources which contributed so greatly to his own material progress. The pioneers of this movement were the English emancipators who secured the abolition of the slave trade in British ships in 1807, and individual English women were among the first to proclaim not only women's rights (Mary Wollstonecraft, 1779) but also those of slaves throughout the world (Harriet Martineau, 1837). It was, however, in America that the collective voices of women first joined those of men in support of these same human rights.

The fact that so many men and women had come to the New World to seek freedom of religion or expression, as well as better material conditions, meant that both they themselves and the society they formed were more receptive to reform than many sectors of society in the Europe they had left behind. From the Old World to the New, particularly in the first half of the nineteenth century had migrated men and women reformers of the calibre of Francis Wright of Scotland, friend of Lafayette, and for some years co-worker in Robert Owen's socialist colony in Indiana, who during the 1820s wrote, spoke and aroused the conscience of Americans on problems of religion, labour, slavery and, indeed, almost every phase of intellectual and social life.

Moreover, in New England and elsewhere, important and influential protestant sects, and in particular the Quakers, had long been free of many of the trammels of theology and the still mediaeval concept of the rôle of women. The puritan condemnation of the sin of idleness, which had always applied not only to men but to women and to children, meant that Quaker women had long been used to work in craft industries outside the home, and to take an active and vocal part in the conduct and administration of both church and community affairs. Thus it is no surprise to find among the earliest and most vocal American supporters of the emancipators of the slaves and other humanitarian causes, such women as Margaret Fuller, Lucretia Mott and Susan B. Anthony who, like Elizabeth Fry in England, had been raised in such traditions. Moreover, it was in the ranks of the anti-slavery movement that such women not only learned to create and lead women's anti-slavery and other humanitarian societies, but also to brave public opprobrium and ridicule by compaigning for signatures for petitions, by raising funds, and by taking part in the business meetings and public debates, thus gaining invaluable experience and winning the respect of their male colleagues, many of whom became their strongest supporters in the subsequent campaign for the recognition of the human rights of women. It was no mere accident of fate that the two great pioneers of the public demand for women's rights in America—Lucretia Mott and Elizabeth Cady Stanton—should first have met as members of a small band of men and women reformers sailing to England to participate in the World's Anti-Slavery Convention called in London in 1840.

The significance of this Convention and of the historical link between the anti-slavery movement and that of women's rights can scarcely be exaggerated: the anti-slavery movement was the first great international manifestation of solidarity in defence of human rights, a movement to establish the freedom and equality of all men before the law, which could not fail to lead to an examination of the position of women and to an exposure of the elementary rights of which they too were deprived.

By 1840, the equal status of women within the Anti-Slavery Society of America was sufficiently well-established for Lucretia Mott and seven other New England women to be included as delegates to the London Anti-Slavery Convention, to which the young Elizabeth Cady Stanton accompanied her husband, an abolitionist lawyer and delegate to the Convention. The proposal that the

6

American women delegates should participate publicly in the discussions raised such an outcry even among progressive European delegates, that they were excluded from debate and forced to listen silently to the proceedings from a suitably-curtained balcony. That very night, Mrs Stanton has recorded, she and Mrs Mott resolved to hold a convention as soon as they returned home, and to form a society for the rights of women.

The indignation aroused by this affront 'to the most sacred rights of women' as it was described by Lloyd Garrison, the American abolitionist leader, gave great impetus to the cause of women's rights on both sides of the Atlantic, stirring into action many women of resource and talent and stimulating in several countries of Europe the appearance of the earliest women's rights journals and parliamentary petitions.

1848: SENECA FALLS

Eight years later, in 1848—year of short-lived liberal revolutions throughout Western and Central Europe, and of the proclamation of the abolition of slavery in the French Colonies—the American ladies fulfilled their promise, issuing a call to the First Women's Rights Convention, held at Seneca Falls, NY, on July 19th and 20th, 1848, to discuss the 'social, civil and religious condition and rights of women'. It is significant that the claims put forward by this Convention were clothed in what the authors themselves called 'a serious parody' of the words of the American Declaration of Independence:

> We hold these truths to be self evident: that all men and women are created equal: that they are endowed by their Creator with certain inalienable rights . . . that the history of mankind is a history of repeated injuries and usurpations on the part of man toward woman . . . To prove this let facts be submitted to a candid world.

This preamble was followed by a list of eighteen grievances, 'covering the whole field of women's inferior status—economic, political, social, domestic, religious'.

In the light of the future history of the women's movement it is interesting to note that all the resolutions put before the Convention were adopted unanimously, with the exception of the most daring of them all, that which declared that it was 'the duty of the women of the country to secure to themselves the sacred right of franchise'. This resolution was introduced on the personal initiative of Elizabeth

Cady Stanton, daughter and wife of lawyers, deeply convinced that 'the root of all our social and legal disabilities lies in our deprivation of the right to make laws for ourselves' against the advice of Mrs Mott and others who feared she would 'make the Convention ridiculous'.

1848–88

During the forty years which elapsed between this meeting and the foundation of the International Council of Women, great strides were made, through the efforts both of women and of many far-sighted men, as individuals and as groups, in many countries of Western Europe, as well as in North America, towards the goals publicly proclaimed, for the first time, at Seneca Falls.

Educated women were, of course, no novelty in world history. Quite apart from famous examples from antiquity of women of enterprise, learning or influence such as Nephertiti, Sappho or Hypatia, the letters and other writings of many individual women, from the early middle ages to the eighteenth century testify not only to the standard of education occasionally attained by the favoured few educated in the humanities within their family circle or by private tutors, but also to the accepted rôle played by such women in the intellectual life of their day. In the religious Orders of Germany and Italy and elsewhere, in the Guilds and Universities of the Italian Renaissance, in the great aristocratic households of Elizabethan, Georgian and Victorian England, at the Imperial Court of Russia, in the salons of seventeenth- and eighteenth-century France, highly-educated women had held positions of influence and importance in the thought of their day.

The new factor at work during the nineteenth century was once again that of democratization. The need for more skilled workers led to the spread of both primary and secondary education first for boys, and, slowly and much more gradually, for girls. Increasing numbers of women were able not only to acquire the 'three r's' on the benches of the primary schools, or the rudiments of a 'gentle' education in the convent, but to study a rapidly-expanding curriculum in the humanities and even in the sciences in those pioneer academies or private secondary schools for girls in which so many of the coming generation of women leaders were to receive their education.

While many of the women so educated turned to the one outlet

8

then available, that of teaching in their turn, others, particularly in England and America, began to force the gates of higher education, not only by resolutely making their way into universities or teaching-hospitals, but also by practising their professions once qualified, often in the face of almost unsurmountable difficulty. Others broke new ground by opening the first establishments of higher education for women—Queen's College and Bedford College in London, Mount Holyoke, Elmira, Vassar in the States. Such advances and concessions, most of them so hard-won, and of necessity still affecting only a privileged section of the population, convinced many women, both in Europe and America, that only when they had obtained the power to vote could they hope to exercise sufficient influence to persuade governments to grant to women the equal educational, professional and legal rights they wished to claim.

The organized movement begun at Seneca Falls had, of course, aroused echoes not only in America but in England, where Harriet Taylor, soon to become the wife of John Stuart Mill, declared in the *Westminster Review* in 1852 that 'there were indications that the example of America will be followed on this side of the Atlantic'. Sixteen years later appeared the great textbook of the English feminist movement, John Stuart Mill's *The Subjection of Women*, a work rapidly translated for the benefit of the increasing ranks of German feminists. In 1879, the new socialist doctrine of the future rôle of women was expounded in the work of the German Social-Democratic leader August Bebel: *Women and Socialism*—a book constantly reprinted and translated into many European languages, and which served to spread feminist ideals among many working women in Germany and other European countries. In France, where an unwritten Salic Law rather than legal barriers had long prevented women from entering Universities and professions, the Revolution, followed by the *Code Napoléon*, had brought about no improvement in the rôle of women. Despite the protestations of redoubtable French champions of female emancipation from Mme de Stael to George Sand, the majority of French women, less affected by industrialization than the women of Great Britain, Germany and America, were generally-speaking slower to claim their rights. Soon after Seneca Falls, however, the future organizers of the movement for women's rights in France were also making their first protests: Hubertine Auclert, future founder of the French

9

Women's Suffrage Movement allowed her household goods to be seized by bailiffs rather than pay taxes in obedience to laws she had not voted. In Sweden, the works of Frederika Bremer, and in Norway those of Camilla Collet, had been stimulating both men and women into a recognition of the injustice of women's position in progressive societies, and by 1888, Associations for women's suffrage or civic education had come into being in Canada, Finland, France, Germany, Great Britain, Norway, Sweden, the US as well as in other areas of continental Europe and the British Empire.

Partial suffrage—municipal or school-board—had been obtained in many localities on both sides of the Atlantic and some of the very worst abuses of the former total subjection of married women were gradually removed. Factory legislation and inspection were improving the lot of women and children in factories and sweatshops. In America, the Civil War had provided an opportunity for women to enter many formerly closed fields, assuming new and varied responsibilities with a courage and ability which did much to shatter the old ideas of 'the woman's sphere'.

In France, Germany, Belgium, Holland, the US and other countries then in course of rapid industrialization, more and more women were entering factories and workshops, some of them, particularly in the highly-organized cotton industry of Lancashire and the textile mills of New England—even beginning to organize Trade Union activities in defence of their own interests.

At the same time a whole new field of 'white collar' employment was opening up: thanks largely to the use of the typewriter (first marketed in the 1870s), thousands of young women of the formerly 'sheltered' classes were entering the shops and offices of commercial undertakings and municipal and government offices.

All these new opportunities for education and employment, the new sense of independence conveyed by the 'feel' of the pay envelope, however slender, were helping to overcome the hesitation of ever greater numbers of women to claim the right to participate in civic life and to accustom their menfolk to seeing them so participate without the prophesied disastrous results on home and family.

Among women of the upper and middle classes a new trend had long been evident in the gradual creation in almost every country of Western Europe, in North America and throughout the British Empire, of those local societies—literary, artistic, musical or cultural —organized by small groups of women for the occupation of their

10

increased leisure and the improvement of their minds. Meanwhile, to the anti-slavery societies of earlier days had succeeded innumerable groups devoted to good works among the less-favoured sectors of the population, whether at home or abroad, activities in which, the gentleman of the latter half of the nineteenth century seems to have been willing and even proud to have his womenfolk engage. By 1888, women's societies for temperance, for social purity, for missionary work in China, India and Africa, for penal reform, prisoners' and orphans' aid, for the rescue of 'fallen women' and help to 'friendless girls', were active on the local and national level in countries from Canada to Australia, Russia to the Argentine, Scandinavia to the Cape. The stage was set for the next step—international co-ordination and collective effort.

In 1883, in the course of a visit to her son in France and her daughter in England—both staunch supporters of the women's movement—and as a result of conversations with 'distinguished publicists and reformers of different countries', Elizabeth Cady Stanton, pioneer of Seneca Falls and now President of the National Women's Suffrage Association of the US, decided that the time had come to organize an International Woman Suffrage Movement (*Genesis of the ICW*, p. 1). An occasion for launching the proposal was almost immediately afforded by a meeting of 'friends of women's suffrage' convened in Liverpool on November 15th, 1883, in order to honour Mrs Stanton and her friend and lieutenant in the US Suffrage Movement, Miss Susan B. Anthony, before their return to America—a meeting attended by forty-one men and women including Mr and Mrs Jacob Bright of Manchester, Isabella Tod of Ireland, and Hubertine Auclerc of France. A Committee of Correspondence was appointed at this meeting, but while letters of mutual encouragement passed between its members, no further action was taken until 1887, when Miss Anthony set forth Mrs Stanton's plan before the Annual Convention of the National Women's Suffrage Association of the US. At this point the plan underwent a transformation which resulted in the eventual formation, not of an International Women's Suffrage Movement, but something much wider and more far-reaching, the International Council of Women.

The records of this Convention had already disappeared before an official history of the ICW could be written (*ICW Records 1899*, pp. 83–4) but the change in inspiration underlying the foundation of the ICW seems to have been as follows. Whereas the original plan as proposed by Mrs Stanton, 'favourably received' by the Liverpool meeting, and discussed between 1882 and 1887, was for an International Women's Suffrage Meeting, the Convention decided 'to extend the invitation to all associations of women in the trades, professions and reforms as well as those advocating political rights' (*Council Idea*, p. 9). The original suggestion for broadening the basis of the Convention is generally agreed (*ICW Records 1914*, p. 237) to have come from Susan B. Anthony—pioneer worker in the anti-slavery, social purity and temperance movements, and early apostle of equal pay for women teachers, as well as leader of the state-by-state American struggle for the women's vote. Immediate and strong support seems to have been forthcoming, particularly from Frances Willard, advocate of modern educational methods, eminent temperance leader, and woman of exceptional organizing ability, and from May Wright Sewall, educator, and worker for peace, social hygiene, dress reform, and women's clubs. In the first officially accepted history of the ICW (*Genesis of the ICW and the Story of its Growth 1888–1893*) compiled by Mrs Sewall in 1913, the following account is given:

> Many of the older women, or pioneer suffragettes, at first desired the proposed international meeting to be limited to the advocacy of equal political rights. The younger women, who belonged to women's clubs, to the Association of Collegiate Alumnae and to various other progressive movements in which conservative women and even anti-suffragists were associated with them, wished the plan to be extended to workers along all lines of human progress.

It was Mrs Sewall who subsequently introduced the following resolution:

> That the National Woman's Suffrage Association, to celebrate the approaching fortieth anniversary of the first meeting called in behalf of equal rights for women (at Seneca Falls, NY, in the year 1848) shall convene an International Council of Women to which women workers along all lines of social, intellectual, moral or civic progress and reform shall be invited, whether they be advocates of the ballot or opposed to women's suffrage (*Genesis*, p. 6).

The NWSA of the US assumed the financial obligations, while Susan B. Anthony, May Wright Sewall, Rachel Foster and others undertook the preparation of the meeting, inviting a wide range of 'literary clubs, art and temperance unions, labor leagues, missionary and industrial associations' as well as specifically suffrage groups. Mrs Sewall recounts in *Genesis* how, in the course of preparing for this meeting, there gradually matured in her mind 'a new concept of organization which took to itself the name of the Council Idea' (*Genesis*, p. 10). Correspondence with the representatives of many groups revealed timidity in accepting an invitation from a suffrage society and convinced Mrs Sewall that, since many groups appeared interested 'only either in women of their own class or in the legitimate recipients of their own charities', the time had come for a distinctly new departure in organization, the establishment of a permanent International Council of Women, composed of permanent National Councils 'not only for the United States of America, but for every country in the world, on the most democratic basis for the largest interests' (*Genesis*, p. 10).

PART I: 1888–1913

1888—FOUNDATION AND FIRST YEARS OF THE ICW

WHEN THE WOMEN MET in Washington, DC, in March 1888, with Susan B. Anthony in the chair, it was immediately clear that Europe had been ready and eager to respond to the call issued by the women of America: 53 different national organizations of women were represented, and 49 delegates had gathered from England, France, Denmark, Norway, Finland, India, Canada and the USA. Discussion centred upon education, philanthropies, temperance, industries, professions, legal and political conditions, social purity. The Council unanimously proclaimed itself in favour of the free opening of all institutions of learning to women, of industrial training for both sexes, for equal wages to be paid for equal work and for an identical standard of personal purity and morality for men and women.

At the request of the Chairman, Mrs Sewall presented her plan for forming 'as a fitting result of the present council' two permanent bodies, national and international. A Committee, presided by Frances Willard, and including Clara Barton, Mrs Sewall and Miss Foster, of the US, Baroness Gripenberg of Finland, Isabelle Bogelot of France, Mrs Keefer of Canada, Mrs Ormiston Chant of England, and Mrs Magelsson Groth of Norway, drew up draft Constitutions, embodying the idea evolved by Mrs Sewall—constitutions which have proved models of their kind, retaining their basic form today, despite the tremendous changes which have taken place in the status of women and in international organization since 1888 (see Appendix I, p. 329).

The delegates immediately adopted both these Constitutions—identical in form save for the title and frequency of meetings prescribed—in the belief that the establishment of such bodies would 'incalculably increase the world's sum of womanly courage, efficiency and esprit de corps' (*Genesis*, p. 15). According to the Constitution adopted for the ICW, any National Council might become auxiliary to the International Council by its own vote and by the payment of $100 every five years (Art. IV). In point of fact, however, since none of the non-American delegates present

14

were in a position to found NCWs before returning to their respective countries to negotiate the necessary affiliations, the newly formed NCW of the US was for the moment the sole affiliated member of the International Council.

The first task of the ICW was therefore the creation of further Councils. An international Board of Officers was elected: the proposed President being Mrs Millicent Garrett Fawcett of Great Britain. Elected *in absentia*, Mrs Fawcett unfortunately proved too occupied with her work for the women's rights movement in Great Britain, then in a crucial process of reorganization, to accept the post of President at this time. The Vice-President elected was the equally-busy Clara Barton, famous founder of the American Red Cross Society, the Hon. Corresponding Secretary Rachel Foster of the USA, the Hon. Recording Secretary Kristine Frederiksen of Denmark, and the Hon. Treasurer Isabelle Bogelot of France. Thanks to these women, and to the strong support of the American NCW, whose first President, Miss Williard, agreed from the outset that 'the international aspect of the council work was and would remain the most important part of the work of the American Council until a Council should be formed in at least one other country' (*Genesis*, p. 24), the project evolved in Washington was gradually nursed into reality.

1889–90

The next move was in France. In July 1889, the first *Congrès des Oeuvres et Institutions féminines* was held in Paris under the auspices of the French Government on the occasion of the *Exposition Universelle*, in celebration of the first centenary of the Revolution. To this Congress the NCW of the US was invited to send a representative. Miss Willard appointed Mrs Sewall, then Corresponding Secretary, to undertake this journey. In a masterly speech Mrs Sewall expounded to the women of France her idea of an International Council composed of National Councils similar to the already existing NCW in the United States: 'Is it not possible that what a National Council may do toward advancing the common welfare of any one people, an International Council may do toward advancing the common welfare of all the peoples of the world?' (*Council Idea*, p. 18). After the Congress, Mrs Sewall continued to spread the Council Idea in the course of many private visits and 'drawing-room meetings', in Switzerland and in France.

1891–92

Back in the United States, the NCW had set to work on the practical organization of their own Council. In November 1889 it issued a call to organizations of women in the US, explaining the modalities of organizing a National Council, from the local to the state and national levels. Their first Triennial Meeting was held in February 1891, by which time many important national women's organizations were already affiliated to the Council (*Genesis* p. 44). In the same year the US government had, through Congress, made provision for celebrating the 500th anniversary of the discovery of America by organizing a World's Columbian Exposition scheduled for Chicago in 1893, during which would be held a series of important congresses organized by the World's Congress Auxiliary. The NCW of the US was invited to hold its 1893 annual meeting in Chicago during this Exposition. With the agreement of Mrs Potter Palmer, President of the Women's Branch of the World's Congress Auxiliary, the American National Council proposed to the 'foreign officers' of the ICW that its first Quinquennial Meeting (as provided for in the Constitution) should also be held on this occasion, instead of in London as originally intended (*Genesis*, p. 48). This recommendation having been accepted, there gradually evolved, in collaboration with the Women's Branch of the World's Congress Auxiliary, a much more ambitious plan for organizing a World's Congress of Representative Women as one of the series of World Congresses to take place in the great Permanent Memorial Art Palace, Chicago, during the Exhibition (*NCW of US*, pp. 97–109). Mrs Sewall was appointed Chairman for the Committee of Organization for this Congress and Rachel Foster—now Mrs Foster Avery— its Secretary. In the summer of 1891 and again in the following year Mrs Sewall once more journeyed to Europe to arouse interest in this plan among leading women's groups.

Among the 'distinguished women' with whom Mrs Sewall conferred in the course of these visits were many who subsequently became conspicuous figures in the history of the ICW: among them Miss Marie Popelin of Belgium, Mrs Hedwig Heyl of Germany, Mrs Jules Siegfried and Miss Sarah Monod of France and Mrs Callirrhoe Parren of Greece. Thanks to these and other leaders, 'wide publicity was given to the plans for the Council's Congress through the press of France, Germany, England, Belgium, Canada,

16

Russia, Italy, Greece, Scandinavia, Switzerland and Sweden' (*Genesis*, p. 54).

Meanwhile, in the States, the indefatigable Mrs Foster Avery planned and carried out 'a voluminous and searching correspondence with a view to making complete lists of National Organizations of women in all countries where such existed and of securing their enrolment as members of the approaching Congress'. On Mrs Sewall's return to America in September 1892, the preliminary Address was issued. Thousands of copies in both French and English were distributed in 'every country of the civilized world' (*Genesis*, p. 56). In all, 126 formal organizations from 33 countries were invited to the Congress scheduled for May 15th to 22nd, 1893.

1893—WORLD CONGRESS OF REPRESENTATIVE WOMEN AND FIRST QUINQUENNIAL COUNCIL MEETING OF THE ICW—CHICAGO

The result was overwhelming: many thousands of persons of different races and nations, including American coloured women 'participating on equal terms with white women at all proceedings', attended the sessions of the World Congress of Representative Women, over 600 of them contributing to the different discussion groups, which studied similar fields of interest to those of the 1888 ICW gathering in Washington (*Council Idea*, p. 24, *Genesis*, p. 61).

On May 19th and 22nd, under the presidency of May Wright Sewall, now President of the NCW of the US, the business meetings of the First Quinquennial Conference of the ICW were held and attended by the officers of the ICW, of the NCW of the US and by official delegates from foreign countries. Reports were received of tentative steps for the formation of NCWs in Canada, France, Finland and the three Scandinavian countries, then acting together. In France, the *Fédération féministe*, grouping 37 societies and the *Solidarité des Femmes* already formed the nucleus of an NCW and had formally delegated Miss Isabelle Bogelot as their representative to this first Quinquennial (*Genesis*, p. 66).

The last items on the agenda were Council aims and methods and the election of a new Board of Officers. The election of a President was most important. As it was intended that the next Quinquennial should be held in London, it was thought opportune to choose a British President. Many prominent names were put forward, among them that of the Countess of Aberdeen, wife of the newly-appointed

Governor-General of Canada. At length the Countess of Aberdeen was elected 'with 12 yeas and 9 nays' (*In the Nineties*).

To Lady Aberdeen, the cable telling her of her election came as a complete surprise, but she accepted what seemed to her a splendid opportunity. Outstanding intelligence, family tradition, a position of particular responsibility as the wife of a high Government official, as well as her own interest and that of her husband in social and humanitarian problems, had fully prepared Lady Aberdeen, then aged 36, a happy wife and mother, for such a post of leadership and responsibility. Time was to show how fortunate the choice of the Chicago delegates had been.

'From the individual working alone, along one line of work, to the National Council and outward to the International,' said Mrs Foster Avery at the conclusion of the World Congress of Representative Women on May 22nd, 'women had perfected a strong and flawless chain'. Looking forward to the next Quinquennial meeting of the ICW, she prophesied that

> Five years hence, there will exist materialized that which now exists in the brain of the woman who has managed this Congress, (May Wright Sewall), 'a great International Congress of Women composed of delegates from all civilized countries, sitting for a part of each year, considering all questions between nations, throwing the influence of a united womenhood in favour of better conditions for humanity, greater educational opportunities for the world's children and in favour of that equality between man and woman which shall give to man the high privilege of living, not with his social and political inferiors, but with his social and political equals, which shall lend its influence towards peace and the healing of the nations' (*Genesis*, p. 63).

As the first links in this chain, the meeting nominated twenty-eight Hon. Vice-Presidents (*ICW Records 1899*, p. 85) to carry back the Council Idea to their respective countries and 'through whose aid the organization of Councils could be pushed' (*Genesis*, p. 69).

1894–99

While not all Hon. Vice-Presidents were equally active, the growth of the ICW in the years between the Chicago Congress and the second Quinquennial meeting of the ICW was amazing. Lady Aberdeen's official duties prevented her from travelling at this time, but her private secretary, Miss Teresa Wilson, who became Hon. Corresponding Secretary of the ICW in 1896, travelled to Europe on behalf of the ICW in 1895 and again in 1896, visiting France, Germany, Switzerland, Belgium, Holland, Norway, Sweden and Finland. Her letters to the President convey some idea of the difficulties and complications of contemporary travel, and contain a vivid account of her endeavours to promote collaboration between violent feminists 'who, in their effort at independence, shook off all convention' and aristocratic, orthodox and 'devout doers of good works' (*A Bonnie Fechter*, p. 133).

Despite such problems, nine National Councils of Women were formed before the next Quinquennial meeting: Canada—founded in 1893 by a group of Canadian women present at Chicago, and under the Presidency of Lady Aberdeen—was the next Council to affiliate in 1897. In later years, Lady Aberdeen was to pay tribute to the lessons learned in the establishment and growth of this early Council. 'It was from experience in the Canadian Council, and in watching its development through a chain of local councils between the Atlantic and the Pacific, that I began to understand this idea of bringing together diverse people to work for common causes' (*Proud Heritage*, p. 5). In Germany, 34 women's groups interested in all branches of social work, in civic education, as well as associations of teachers, met in Berlin in 1894 to found the *Bund Deutscher Frauen Verein*, which affiliated with the ICW in 1897, shortly followed by Sweden, where the well-known Frederika Bremer Association, actively campaigning since 1884 to 'unite experienced men and women all over the country to work for the raising of women morally and intellectually as well as socially' joined with other Swedish groups to affiliate with the ICW in 1898 (*History of Affiliated NCWs*, 1938, p. 53).

In Great Britain, where women's associations had been growing in strength and number since the 1850s, women's groups had begun to feel the need for co-ordination at about the same time as those in America. In 1888, Lady Aberdeen had called in Scotland a 'Women's Conference on Women's Work', while 1889 saw the first of a series of Conferences in various industrial centres. These Conferences organized by the Local Unions of Women Workers, originally formed to co-ordinate the work in favour of friendless girls begun by Miss Ellice Hopkins in the 1850s, drew together a remarkable concourse of organizers and voluntary workers from all over England and Scotland. In 1895, a further step was taken by the formation of a National Union of Women Workers which, under

19

the Presidency of Mrs Creighton, wife of the Bishop of Peterborough, convened its first national conference in Nottingham in October of that year, at which Mrs Sidney Webb made a passionate appeal for the overworked and underpaid women in industrial employment, and Mrs Fawcett gave a comprehensive exposé of women's claims, corresponding closely to the aims and objects of the ICW:

> The claim of women for sound education; their desire for wider opportunities of work and wages; their entry into the medical profession; their increased activity in public affairs, in missionary and church work—are all, with the demand for parliamentary suffrage, parts of one and the same movement of social evolution. In each of these directions, and in others, women are asking for and obtaining a share of things which our past history shows to have been an ennobling influence in the lives of men. We wish to serve . . .
> (*Women in Council*, p. 13).

After prolonged negotiations, the National Union of Women Workers agreed in 1898 to adapt its Constitution to qualify for affiliation to the ICW as a National Council.

The year 1899 saw the affiliation of four new Councils: in Europe NCWs had been formed in Denmark (at the joint instigation of Miss Frederiksen, first Hon. Recording Secretary of the ICW, and of Miss Ida Falbe Hansen, Hon. Vice-President for Denmark) and in Holland (largely as the result of an address delivered by Mrs Sewall at a National Exhibition of Women's Work held in the Netherlands in 1898). On the other side of the world, thanks to the encouragement of Mrs McLaren, Hon. Corresponding Secretary of the ICW from 1893 to 1896, the first and second Australian NCWs had been founded: New South Wales (on the initiative of Miss Margaret Windeyer, Representative of Australia to the Chicago Congress) and Tasmania (on that of Mrs Dobson, subsequently instrumental in the foundation of NCWs by other Australian States, and for many years the leader of the joint Australian delegation to ICW Quinquennials).

The first meetings of the Executive Committee (Voting members being the five international officers and Presidents of affiliated NCWs; Hon. Vice-Presidents being non-voting members) had been held in London in 1897 to adopt Standing Orders for this Committee. A second meeting, held in 1898, conducted the negotiations for the forthcoming Quinquennial in Great Britain (subsequently postponed for a year on account of prolonged negotiations for the affiliation of an NCW in that country) and a third in March 1899 to complete the preparations for this Quinquennial.

1899—SECOND QUINQUENNIAL COUNCIL MEETING OF THE ICW

Thus, at the Second Quinquennial Council Meeting the representatives of ten NCWs met in London under the presidency of Lady Aberdeen as the guests of the NCW of Great Britain under its first President, Mrs Alfred Booth. The Hon. Vice-Presidents turned up in force and, in all, women from 28 countries were represented at this meeting. Many more would have liked to come, but were held back for personal or financial reasons. Husbands did not always allow their wives to leave home for such long, and sometimes even dangerous journeys, and few women at this time had means of their own, independent of husbands or fathers. From the very beginning the ICW extended a welcome to other 'internationally organized' societies: on this occasion fraternal delegates from eight such groups, including the World YWCA and the General Federation of Women's Clubs, attended the Council Meeting.

Looking back from where we now stand, the most far-reaching decision taken at this meeting by the ICW was to pledge the support of the members of its NCWs in all countries to the new movement in favour of the arbitration of international disputes. Both the American and Canadian Councils had been extremely active in their respective countries in the furtherance of this movement and, in 1899, both submitted separate but similar resolutions on this subject, finally adopted by the ICW in the following form:

> . . . that the ICW do take steps in every country to further and advance by every means in their power the movement towards International Arbitration.

A public meeting on International Arbitration was held on June 27th, under the chairmanship of Lady Aberdeen. The leading members of the ICW fully realized that it was entering on a 'new phase in its existence' (*ICW Records 1899*, p. 216): 'up to now it has never been identified with any one movement, for by its Constitution it cannot further one propaganda at the expense of another'. With the exception of Sweden, whose delegates abstained on the grounds that they 'were not free to discuss political questions', all NCWs present agreed that 'this great movement' had 'passed beyond the stage of controversy' (*ICW Records 1899*, p. 217). The ICW heartily welcomed and supported the Peace Conference then in session at the Hague and expressed firm hopes for its success. A Standing Committee on Peace and International Arbitration was formed, with Lady Aberdeen as its first Convener, and Baroness Von Suttner of Austria as its Secretary.

On the question of women's political rights no resolution was proposed at this meeting, since, in accordance with the principles of the ICW, 'both sides of any controversy must be heard'. Ardent suffragists among NCWs were disappointed and, as a compromise, the National Union of Women's Suffrage Societies of Great Britain organized, outside the framework of the Quinquennial, a public meeting on the Political Enfranchisement of Women, at which Miss Anthony, Mrs Fawcett and other suffrage leaders were invited to speak (*Women in Politics*, pp. 115–27).

As the result of this independent meeting a new International Committee was shortly afterwards established with the specific objective of securing the recognition of political rights for women (*ICW Records 1899/1904*, II, p. 173).

The political rights of women remained, however, only a small part of those rights as individuals which the ICW desired to obtain. Their legal position remained deplorable almost everywhere. An ICW Standing Committee was established under Baroness Von Beschwitz of Germany, on Laws concerning the Domestic Relations, entrusted with the task of assessing the efforts made towards the abolition of the legal subjugation of married women and of strengthening the courage and confidence of women in the struggle for the recognition of their legal rights. In 1903, the name of this Committee was changed to Laws concerning the Legal Position of Women.

A Press Committee was formed at this Quinquennial with the aim of securing wider coverage of ICW and NCW news, and, at the suggestion of the NCW of Canada, National Councils were recommended to establish a Bureau of Information:

> where statistics regarding the women of the country shall be collected and kept up to date . . . to gather together and to give accurate information regarding the position, employment, education, pursuits, etc., of the women of the country and to collect any further information required (*ICW Records 1899*, p. 188).

By 1904, NCW Information Bureaus were functioning usefully in Canada, Germany, Great Britain, Sweden and Holland. A Finance Committee was also established in 1899.

The business transacted by this Council Meeting, subsequently published in six printed volumes (*Women in Education, Women in Politics, Women in Industrial Life, Women in Social Life, Women in Professions* (2 vols.), provides a unique picture of the position of women at the turn of the century, and of the remedies proposed by the ICW. Here are the main planks in the programme proposed by the second Quinquennial:

Equal pay for equal work.

Access to all professions according to aptitude and not to sex.

Radical improvement of conditions in the nursing profession.

State-paid maternity maintenance.

Appointment of female factory inspectors.

Participation of women in trade unions in order to defend their rights.

Protection of women and men workers (with the proviso that protective legislation in favour of women must never go so far as to exclude them from work).

Development of modern household machinery to relieve women from household drudgery.

Training of housewives and of domestic workers; better working conditions for the latter.

For the first time, each NCW presented a formal Report on the work it had accomplished since the last Quinquennial or the date of its affiliation. These reports, which were to prove a major feature of future Quinquennial meetings, are of the utmost interest. From them, and from them only, can be formed a picture of the tremendous volume of practical work accomplished slowly but surely by individual NCWs and their specialized affiliates in all the domains of humanitarian endeavours and of women's rights. They also show the gradual concentration of these efforts on those objectives which, by mutual agreement at the meetings of the ICW, were accorded priority in the work of all Councils through the agency of the appropriate International Standing Committee. In 1899, reports were presented not only by formally constituted NCWs, but also by the Hon. Vice-Presidents or representatives of women in Finland, Belgium, Italy, Russia, France, Norway, India, South Africa, the Argentine, Palestine and Persia.

A 'final seal' was set upon the 'complete success' of this Quinquennial by the gracious welcome accorded to its members by

Queen Victoria. A special train conveyed 300 delegates to Windsor to enjoy 'the crowning triumph of the approval of Her Majesty' (*ICW Records 1899*, p. 288).

1899–1904

May Wright Sewall was elected ICW President for the next Quinquennial period. Under her administration the Council Idea was spread to greater numbers of women in many countries. Between 1899 and 1904 the ICW set up important offices and held public meetings at the main international fairs which were such a feature of the 1900s—the Exposition Universelle, Paris, 1900, the Pan-American Exhibition, Buffalo 1901 (where the first Latin American contacts were established), and the Louisiana Purchase Exhibition in St Louis in 1904. Executive meetings of the ICW were held in Paris (1900), the Hague (1901), Copenhagen (1902) and Dresden (1903). At this last meeting final arrangements were made to hold the next Quinquennial in Berlin, as invited by the German NCW in 1899. On this occasion Mrs Sewall, who had the question of internationalism very much at heart and was temporarily assuring the Convenership of the Standing Committee on Peace and Arbitration, insisted that a public meeting be held in Berlin 'for the exposition and advocacy of our Peace principles', despite the warnings of members of the German NCW—themselves ardent supporters of propaganda for peace—that if peace were discussed in Berlin there would be 'but few auditors that night' and those few 'probably unsympathetic and silent' (*ICW Records 1899–1904*, II, p. 108).

Another of Mrs Sewall's aims was to co-ordinate and concentrate the women's movement. Unfortunately, already during her administration, the signs of an opposite tendency became increasingly apparent in the growing cleavage between those to whom suffrage was the all-important aim to which others should be subordinated, and those to whom it was but one of many vital aims. Among the reasons for this trend was the fact that many ardent suffragists in various countries regretted that the ICW was unwilling to concentrate wholly on this issue. In February 1902 the International Committee established in London in 1899 at the conclusion of the ICW Quinquennial had convened an International Suffrage Conference in Washington at which the decision was taken to set up a separate permanent international organization for women's suffrage (*ICW Records 1899/1904*, I, p. 126), and on June 3rd, 1904, two days before the next ICW Quinquennial, the first meeting of the Alliance for Suffrage, 'resulting from these preliminary steps and devoted to permanent organization', took place in Berlin (*ICW Records 1899/1904*, II, p. 174).

1904—THE SECOND TEN YEARS OF PROGRESS

THIRD QUINQUENNIAL COUNCIL MEETING, BERLIN

At the invitation of the German NCW under the presidency of Mrs Marie Stritt, the Third Quinquennial Council Meeting of the ICW was thus held in 1904 in Berlin—capital of a country then dominated by militarist ideas, and allegedly unreceptive to the questions of international peace and arbitration which occupied such an important part in the programme of the ICW.

Nine further NCWs had been affiliated since 1899: the new Council of France, now fully constituted thanks to the efforts of Mrs Sewall during the *Congrès Féministe* held in Paris during the 1900 Exposition, was represented by its President, Miss Sarah Monod, and by Mrs Avril de Sainte-Croix. In Italy, with the active encouragement of Mrs Sanford of the NCW of Canada, the Roman Federation had become affiliated to the ICW in 1900 and had subsequently been joined by the Piedmontese and Lombard Leagues. Switzerland, represented by Mrs Chaponnière-Chaix, its Proxy-President, reported the formation of the *Alliance des Sociétés Féminines Suisses* at a meeting of four major local groups and 19 individual societies held at Berne in 1899. Norway joined Sweden and Denmark among the Scandinavian NCWs, while South Australia and Victoria brought up to four the total of affiliated Australian Councils. In New Zealand, where women had been granted the suffrage in 1893, the NCW formed in 1896 had become affiliated to the ICW in 1900.

For the first time two Central European NCWs joined the ranks of the International Council: Austria, represented in Berlin by Mrs Marianne Hainisch, Hon. Vice-President for that country since 1893, and Hungary, represented by Miss Augusta Rosenberg. The Constitution of the Hungarian NCW, said Mrs Sewall, 'most perfectly reflects the spirit which animated the founders of the (International) Council': the fact that it was the first NCW constitution written in a language 'outside the official languages and equally alien to them all' provided an excellent demonstration of 'the wide applicability of the Council Idea' (*ICW Records 1899–1904*, II, p. 35). This wide applicability was further illustrated by the affiliation of the first Latin-American NCW, that of the Argentine Republic, which received a special welcome in Berlin despite the fact that no representative had been able to make the long journey to Germany. Mrs Sewall spoke particularly highly of the hopes entertained for this Council, which under its remarkable President, the former Hon. Vice-President for the Argentine, Dr Cecilia Grierson, first woman doctor of medicine in the country, was already collaborating actively with the government in many social fields and even participating in a 'friendly mission' of voluntary mediation sent by that government to Uruguay—a remarkable manifestation of the influence of this Council, which, said Mrs Sewall, 'ought to encourage women everywhere' (*ICW Records 1899–1904*, I, p. 222).

Reports of preliminary steps towards the foundation of NCWs in Finland, Belgium, Russia, Cape Colony (South Africa) and China had been received from the Hon. Vice-Presidents for those countries, and nominations had been made since the last Quinquennial for Hon. Vice-Presidents in Mexico, Peru, Chile, Venezuela, Japan and Turkey.

Mrs Sewall proved to have been right in her optimism, while the leading members of the German NCW had failed to appreciate the mood of many of their compatriots: the Philharmonia hall, in which the public meeting of Peace and International Arbitration was to be held at 8 p.m. on June 10th was almost instantly filled as soon as the doors were opened, and the courtyard was immediately packed by hundreds of people unable to enter the hall. Officers and speakers had to be escorted to the platform by policemen because the normal ushers were not able to make their way through the crowd. 'Never have I witnessed,' wrote Mrs Sewall, 'at any other Peace Meeting such sympathy, such eagerness, such longing, as were expressed by that audience.' Not only women were present but also professors and workers and even social-democrats 'of the agitator type'—an audience whose very presence seems to say, 'The people of this military empire want peace' (*ICW Records 1899–1904*, II, p. 109). Baroness von Suttner of Austria, tireless worker for peace, and future Nobel Peace prizewinner, Miss Bogelot of France and Lady Aberdeen made much-applauded speeches expressing strong belief in the final triumph of the pacific settlement of international disputes, and urging all mothers in the audience to educate their children in the ideals of peace.

26

Opinion within the ICW had evolved considerably since 1899 when, to the disappointment of many members, it had not given the question of suffrage an exclusive place in the forefront of its programme. At Berlin, a full discussion took place, at the request of seven NCWs, and a resolution was adopted, with only two abstentions, advocating that 'strenuous efforts be made to enable women to obtain the power of voting in all countries where a representative government exists' (*ICW Records 1904/5*, p. 13), and a Standing Committee on Women's Suffrage was formed with Anna Howard Shaw, Doctor of Medicine, Methodist Protestant Minister, and eminent orator of the US Suffrage movement, as its first Convener. Such action was not only the direct result of pressure by individual NCWs—in particular on the part of Norway, and of South Australia (which pointed to the 'advantages of suffrage' in those countries of the southern hemisphere which already enjoyed it), but also the gradual outcome of a growing conviction on the part of many NCWs that, in order to influence legislation in their respective countries, the vote was a prerequisite. Another factor, as Mrs Sewall pointed out, had been the plans for the creation of the Alliance for Suffrage. 'From one point of view,' wrote Mrs Sewall, after the Berlin Council meeting, 'this Alliance is really a direct fruit of the spirit of Internationalism whose culture is the specific function of the ICW. Reciprocally, it became the encourager and stimulator of the Council and was one factor in the uncompromising action which the Council took on this question in 1904' (*ICW Records 1899/1904*, II, p. 174).

The creation of the Alliance for Suffrage meant, however, that the forces of the international Women's Movement were now divided, strategically, into two main streams: the suffragists and those who, while agreeing on the vital importance of women's suffrage, were not prepared to place this issue before all others.

Mrs Sewall herself, and other leading figures in the ICW, would have liked to see a revision of the ICW Constitution permitting the affiliation not only of national but also of international societies, such as the new Alliance for Suffrage, but Lady Aberdeen's proposition to this effect placed on the Berlin agenda was not adopted by the Council.

To the majority of the ICW it appeared that work on other issues should not be relegated to the background until the women's vote, however vital, was achieved, and in Berlin a Standing Committee on the suppression of the White Slave Traffic was established at the same time as the new Committee on Women's Suffrage. A resolution was passed requesting the ICW and its NCWs to 'keep this question on its programme until its end be accomplished' and its distinguished first Convener, Mrs Avril de Sainte-Croix (France) was to lead the strenuous work of this Committee in the field of moral welfare for over thirty years.

The newly-affiliated NCW of Norway took the initiative in urging the ICW to concentrate its efforts towards the suppression of this traffic in women and children against which so many voluntary societies in different countries were finding that laws provided no effective help. 'We cannot alter the laws and we cannot exterminate immorality,' said its first President and founder, Mrs Gina Krog. 'But we can create an opinion so strong and so commanding that laws will have to be made, and if we cannot succeed in lifting the moral standard higher than it is at present, then we have no right to blame the men.' At the insistence of the French delegates it was further recommended that NCWs should unite to obtain the suppression of the 'odious system' of state regulation of vice, which makes it 'impossible to combat the White Slave Traffic and encourages the maintenance of a double moral standard for men and women' (*ICW Records 1899–1904*, I, p. 174).

To Mrs Sewall, the most original feature of the Berlin Council Meeting was the part played by young women. For several years past, the German NCW had held annual Congresses, first in Berlin and later in several major German cities, to which were invited young girls over 14 then in their last school years. At such Congresses these girls were introduced to various forms of social work and encouraged to take up that most suited to their tastes and qualities. Those who chose to take up such social service were invited to serve a part-time theoretical and practical apprenticeship in their own localities before determining upon their final choice of a career. During the 1904 ICW Conference, a meeting was held under the presidency of Miss Alice Salomon, then working for her Doctor's degree in Political Economy, attended by 3,000 young girls between the ages of 14 and 20, who were addressed by leaders of different departments of social service. Many of these young girls also worked, under Miss Salomon's leadership, in the material organization of the Congress, as interpreters, hostesses and ushers (*ICW Records 1899–1904*, II, p. 184).

Delegates were entertained at many official functions organized by a Committee of Arrangements presided by Mrs Hedwig Heyl, and the International Officers were received by the Empress of Germany who confessed that 'so long as I had only sons I did not think so much about the education of women, but now that my little daughter is almost twelve years old, I am much interested in knowing what the position of women is to be' (*ICW Records 1899–1904*, II, p. 160).

The Countess of Aberdeen was again elected President, and being now resident in Great Britain, was able to travel herself to the different NCWs and prospective Councils, at least until 1906, when Lord Aberdeen began a second term of office as Lord Lieutenant of Ireland. She was fortunate in that the 1904 Quinquennial had elected an outstanding Hon. Corresponding Secretary, Mrs (later Dame) Maria Ogilvie Gordon, musician, geologist, Gold Medallist of zoology and anatomy at London University, Ph.D. of the University of Munich, founder of the Women's Citizens Association in Great Britain and later one of the first women Fellows of the Linnean and Royal Physical Societies. In 1905, Mrs Ogilvie Gordon introduced a system of printed Annual Reports of ICW and NCW activities, which helped to strengthen the ties between National Councils, for whom they constituted 'a sure stream of information and inspiration'.

1905

The fourth Quinquennial period introduced new problems. In 1905, the breaking of the Union of Norway and Sweden by popular vote in Norway faced the ICW, for the first time since its foundation, with a political controversy between two countries whose women were members of the ICW. The Norwegian Council sought to explain its case within the ICW, while the Swedish Council protested against any attempt to make the ICW a forum for political controversy.

1906

As a result, the Executive Committee meeting in Paris in the following year decided to revise Article II of the ICW Constitution specifically to exclude from the programme of the Council 'political and religious questions of a controversial nature affecting the inter-relationship of two or more countries', though leaving National Councils free to 'make any communication as individual Councils one to another'. Norway opposed this change, considering that 'The Golden Rule would be better observed by frankness and mutual understanding than by shirking discussion on some points' (*ICW Records 1905/6*, p. 161). Lady Aberdeen pointed out that the revision of the Constitution was animated only by the conviction that the first aim of the ICW should always be 'to find out what united the women workers of the world'.

During this Quinquennial period the urgent question of public health and the care of children, long since major concerns of many NCWs, were taken up collectively by the ICW at the request of Lady Aberdeen, whose first-hand experience in Ireland and in Canada had convinced her of the urgency and feasibility of combatting tuberculosis and high rates of infantile mortality, and of educating the public in the elementary principles of hygiene. Although a Standing Committee on Health was not established until 1909, studies were undertaken by NCWs on the subjects of public health, the housing of the poor and the care of infants and children, and progress reports from the various councils were made on these subjects in every annual report. A large public meeting on Health was held in Geneva in 1908, and in 1909 an important report entitled *Health of the Nations* was published by the ICW, compiled from contributions made by individual NCWs. Further inquiries were conducted into special insurances for women, old age pensions and sickness insurance.

It was to the Paris Executive meeting in 1906 that Mrs Ogilvie Gordon presented a scheme whereby, with the help of affiliated NCWs, an international system of Educational Information Bureaus might be organized where 'expert advice and information would be available in the careers open to young men and women and the best means of training boys and girls for the selected lines of work'; a scheme foreshadowing the modern 'vocational guidance centre'. The proposal was adopted and the following resolution also voted:

> ... that this Executive recommend to the ICW to place the interests of Girls' Education upon its programme of work and propaganda.

Mrs Ogilvie Gordon was, at her request, given powers to 'conduct correspondence on education affairs pending full discussion of the subject at a future meeting of the ICW' (*ICW Records 1905/6*, p. 170).

1907

The outstanding public event of the period was the Second Peace Conference at The Hague in 1907. Peace and Arbitration had been the very first subject taken up by the ICW and, although the First Peace Conference in 1899 had decided that no deputations were to be received, the ICW was determined now to make its voice heard in the cause of Peace. A deputation was therefore set up, consisting of the First Vice-President, Mrs Marie Stritt of Germany, Mrs Ogilvie Gordon, and Mrs Chaponnière-Chaix, as representative of the NCW of a traditionally neutral country, Switzerland. Lady Aberdeen was prevented by illness from presiding the deputation, which was one of the only two received by the Conference, the other being a delegation 'from the Churches' (*ICW Records 1906/7*, p. 35). The ICW presented an address, drawn up by Lady Aberdeen in agreement with NCWs, promising the Peace Conference to use all its influence on women to 'infuse a higher ideal of what patriotism and national duty may mean', to lead them 'to teach their children that "what is wrong for the individual cannot be right for the State", and that arbitration between countries is the best way to settle disputes' (*ICW Records, 1906/7*, p. 36).

In the same year the ICW welcomed the initiative taken by several voluntary international organizations with headquarters in Brussels in founding the Bureau of International Associations, aimed at converging the efforts of private international associations throughout the world 'towards the organization of international life on a foundation as stable and as regular as those of national life' (*International Associations*, 1961, I, p. 42). Through the intermediary of Miss Lafontaine, an active member of the newly-formed NCW of Belgium and sister of Senator Henri Lafontaine one of the co-founders of this Association, the ICW became one of its earliest members and collaborators, and has consistently promoted its co-ordinating activities and availed itself of its collective services since this time.

1908

It had been decided in Berlin that the next Quinquennial should be held in Canada, at the invitation of the Canadian NCW. Since it was evident that relatively few women from each European NCW would be able to undertake such a long and expensive journey (neither

31

France nor Switzerland were in fact able to send any delegation), it was decided to hold a special Council meeting in Geneva in 1908 'to take stock of our position in Council assembled' (*ICW Records 1907/8*, p. 17), to determine the question of the revision of the Constitution and Standing Orders, and to discuss the urgent questions of public health and the formation of Educational and Employment Information Bureaus.

This Special Council Meeting in Geneva, called mainly for organizational purposes, was destined to be the first of many ICW gatherings in that city. Lady Aberdeen, Mrs Sewall and Mrs Ogilvie Gordon had done remarkable work in combining with their other activities the editing of the voluminous tri-lingual *Transactions* of the ICW from 1899 to 1907. The time had now come when this work, combined with the increasing burden of administrative work for the ICW, made it impossible to carry on the duties of President and Hon. Corresponding Secretary without professional secretarial assistance; all NCWs agreed to this necessary change in organization, and rendered unanimous tribute to the excellent work of Mrs Ogilvie Gordon as Hon. Corresponding Secretary.

It was suggested at Geneva that each NCW be asked to draw up a report on existing unequal laws relating to the position of women, to be collated for submission to the various governments with a request for women's suffrage. 'It was the general feeling of the ICW,' said Lady Aberdeen, 'that a simple and lucid explanation of the inequality of laws affecting women in their relations to the home, the family, the municipality and the state would better explain than any other method the reasons on which the ICW bases its demand for the suffrage of women' (*ICW Records 1909*, p. 3). This Report was published in 1911, a second edition appearing in 1912, as the first had been immediately exhausted. The ICW Board drafted a letter for NCWs to present to their governments together with this document, and many NCWs took the necessary action at once.

1909—FOURTH QUINQUENNIAL MEETING OF THE ICW, TORONTO,

On the invitation of the NCW of Canada, under the presidency of Lady Edgar, the Fourth Quinquennial Meeting of the ICW was held in the University of Toronto, Canada, in 1909. The ICW now had 22 affiliated NCWs: Belgium (largely owing to the efforts of Miss Marie Popelin, Doctor of Law and pioneer in the struggle for the admission of women to the Belgian Bar, Hon. Vice-President for Belgium since 1888), Greece (largely through the work of Mrs Callirhoe Parren and of Baroness Gripenberg of Finland) and Bulgaria, all having been affiliated since 1904. This figure includes the five separate Australian NCWs who had recently informed the Geneva Executive of their agreement to combine for the purposes of representation, as requested at Berlin (*ICW Records 1905/6*, p. 167) and to send to Toronto a delegation consisting of a President and ten members, the number prescribed for each NCW in the revised Constitution adopted at Geneva. Efforts to found new Councils further afield were reported: the enterprising Mrs Sanford of Canada, Hon. Treasurer of the ICW, having taken a trip through 'India and Japan, returning via Siberia and Russia in time to attend the Hague Conference', while Baroness Gripenberg, recently elected to a 'responsible position in the Finnish Diet', continued her efforts to constitute a Finnish Council, and to second the efforts of Mrs de Philosophoff in Russia.

For the first time in the history of the ICW, an affiliated NCW announced its withdrawal from the Council. This was New Zealand, on the grounds that it had practically 'ceased to exist' owing, mainly, as the Secretary had reported in 1906, to the fact that since New Zealanders 'so promptly and easily obtained universal suffrage', many women were now 'inclined to rest upon their oars'. At Toronto the ICW regretfully registered this withdrawal, and, in accordance with a suggestion from New Zealand, appointed Mrs Sheppard Hon. Vice-President for that country in the hope that it would one day be in a position to re-affiliate. (This it did, thanks to the efforts of Mrs Sheppard and others, in 1920.) (*ICW Records 1909*, p. 100.)

In Canada, still a pioneer country, the atmosphere was propitious to women in general and to the ICW in particular. The many questions treated by this parliament of women roused great interest in the Canadian public. Committee, Council and public meetings were lively and well-attended.

At a special evening session 'respectable' women everywhere were urged to campaign for changed conditions in the world of morals: without their help, traffic in girls and women would never be abolished. The American delegate insisted that only suffrage would give women sufficient power to create the conditions essential to the suppression of the evils of prostitution. It was felt that the old name of this Committee, White Slave Traffic, failed to cover the whole question and the Committee was renamed Equal Moral Standard and Traffic in Women.

A Standing Committee on Education was also established at Toronto, with Mrs Ogilvie Gordon as its first Convener. 'We of the ICW,' said Mrs Ogilvie Gordon, stressing the lack of educational facilities for women in many countries, 'have always to remember that it is our duty to interest ourselves in the wants of the countries that are not so happily situated; they derive courage and information from the reports that we give of the methods that are a success in some other country' (*ICW Records 1909*, p. 127). The aim of education, maintained Mrs Gordon, is not only to open the minds of boys and girls to their responsibilities in this world, but also to fit them for their various livelihoods, to develop in them the finer instincts and ideas of human life. To this end she urged the ICW to study means of supporting the teachers, so many of them women, in their task, to give particular attention to the lack of Middle or High Schools for girls and to the need for an 'adequate counsel service to cope with the difficulties which beset young people' at the critical age of 14 to 17 when they are 'taking the responsibilities of life upon them'. The final resolution establishing the Standing Committee on Education contained a rider recommending the 'formation of a national system of Educational and Information Bureaus under Public authority' (*ICW Records 1909*, p. 11).

It was also at Toronto that the ICW broached a question to which it was later to devote much time and attention: practical means of educating children on lines of international understanding and peace. Mrs Sewall proposed and the Council adopted a resolution urging:

> all NCWs to promote the use of such text books and reading books in schools as will present historical facts with the least possible bias, and to endeavour to arouse a living interest in the modern methods of peaceably settling international difficulties (*ICW Records 1909*, p. 133).

Another problem of deep concern at this time was that of Emigration and Immigration, at a period when large numbers of people were streaming overseas or from one continental country to another in search of new opportunities, or relief from misery or persecution at home. A Standing Committee on Emigration and Immigration was established in 1909, not to promote emigration but to safeguard immigrants, particularly women and children. In 1910, Lady Aberdeen suggested to the medical adviser of the Board of Health in New York that a leaflet on the conditions of life and work in the US should be prepared for the use of immigrants, which could then be translated and distributed through the Standing Committee of the ICW to prospective emigrants from their countries. In 1911 the Executive approved an extension of this plan, asking NCWs to 'put at the disposal of women emigrants a leaflet giving particulars of the principal laws of the country to which they are emigrating' (*ICW Records 1912/13*, p. 178).

During a public meeting on Health, Lady Aberdeen spoke of the work of the ICW in this field since 1906, and proposed the formation of a Standing Committee on Public Health. The formation of this Committee was agreed and Lady Aberdeen became its first Convener, more than half the members listed for 1909 being Doctors of Medicine.

The Committee on legislation had carefully collected data regarding women's legal position and all new laws concerning women and children, while the Suffrage Committee had undertaken to ask countries where women had enjoyed the vote for some years, whether suffrage had influenced women's position in general. The Rev. Anna Shaw, its Convener, who had been disappointed that the plan to affiliate internationally-organized societies had not been adopted at Berlin, and that the Alliance for Suffrage, created in 1904, was developing separately from the ICW, now recognized that 'external propaganda may well be left to suffrage organizations, but education and information within the Council must be carried on by Council members themselves' (*ICW Records 1912/13*, p. 127). The necessarily divided views of many NCWs on the suffrage question at a time when the militant tactics of one wing of the movement were alienating many sympathizers with women's rights in this and other domains was well illustrated by the position of the NCW of Great Britain: in 1911 the National Union of Women's Suffrage and the National League for Opposing Women's Suffrage were both affiliated to the NCW.

At Toronto the Suffrage Committee also turned its attention to other citizenship rights and their exercise, passing a resolution to the effect that:

> the ICW strenuously endeavour to place women on all Boards now open to women and to secure the inclusion of women on all other authorities or special committees dealing with public work.

In proposing this resolution, the Canadian delegate urged that women press for positions on the 'governing boards of schools, on County and City Councils, on all hospital and public charity boards' because of the 'educational value' of such positions to the woman herself and 'the higher status it will give her in the eyes of the men and boys of her family and community' (*ICW Records 1909*, p. 205).

Linguistically, the ICW was already running into some of the difficulties later encountered by other international organizations. At Toronto, a Danish delegate, herself conversant with, but not fluent in any of the three official languages (English, French and German) asked that consideration be given to the use of an international language for official purposes. Her proposal was rejected, despite the far-sighted arguments of those who looked forward to the future membership of NCWs from many non-European countries, and a plea from Mrs Sewall that 'the national pride' of those countries whose languages now served as vehicles of communication should not stand in the way of an experiment in the use of an accepted auxiliary language (*ICW Records 1909*, p. 135).

It is of interest to note that, as the result of a resolution passed at Toronto, the ICW tried to appeal directly to the World Postal Union, an early inter-governmental organization, asking them to introduce a penny postage 'answer prepaid' form to facilitate international correspondence (*ICW Records 1909/10*, p. 153). The reply received indicated that any such petition must come from a member government. The ICW therefore requested NCWs to appeal to their respective governments to sponsor this request, and this was promptly done by many Councils.

At the close of the Conference about 100 delegates, representing 12 countries, travelled by Pullman coach to the Pacific Coast, under the guidance of Mrs Willoughby Cummings, Secretary of the NCW of Canada, who had done so much to assure the successful organization of the Toronto Quinquennial Meeting. A number of local Councils were visited en route to the coast, the travellers returning via the International Fair at Seattle, and attending the Triennial Meeting of the NCW of the US.

1910–11

A notable event in the following year was the First Congress of Women to be held in Latin America, under the auspices of the NCW of the Argentine, under the Presidency of Mrs Van Praet de Sala, as part of the official Centenary Celebrations of the Republic of the Argentine. This four-day meeting, though conceived mainly as a 'purely patriotic effort' revealed the growing interest of the women of the Argentine in broader subjects such as 'joint action of the home and the school on the formation of our future citizens' and 'a study of woman's action in the progress of the world'.

1912

In 1912 an Executive Meeting took place in Stockholm, preceded by an official visit by members of the Executive and Standing Committees to the NCWs of Denmark and Norway. At the Stockholm meeting, Mrs Sanford, Hon. Treasurer, reported on a visit to the Balkan countries to promote the extension of the ICW. Besides visiting Councils in France, Italy, Greece, Bulgaria, Hungary and Austria, she had worked hard to promote Councils in Serbia (affiliated in 1911), Rumania, and Turkey. Important news from the faithful Hon. Vice-Presidents for Finland and Russia was also received at this Executive. Baroness Gripenberg of Finland, one of the drafters of the original ICW Constitution and Hon. Vice-President for Finland ever since that date, was able to report that 'the prospect of a meeting on the threshold of our country' had precipitated the formation of a NCW of Finland, long delayed owing to the difficult political situation of that country. Baroness Gripenberg had worked unceasingly with the powerful existing Women's Groups in Finland for the achievements of women's rights and in the work of educating women for the exercise of these rights once they had been granted in 1906. Her death, only a short time after her election as President of the new Council, was a sad blow both to her fellow-countrymen and to the ICW. The news from Russia was once more disappointing. Mrs de Philosophoff, appointed by Mrs Sewall as Hon. Vice-President for Russia in 1893, regretfully reported that permission to found a NCW of Russia had been refused, just as a Constitution had been prepared and the nucleus of a Council formed. Her report—summarizing the work already achieved by various women's organizations in Russia— makes most interesting reading. Among the societies ready to form the NCW were the organization founded by Mrs de Philosophoff herself, for the encouragement of cheap housing; a Students' Help Society; professional or mutual help associations of women doctors and teachers; a legal aid society; three women's political rights

organizations; an association for the training of women architects, and a fund-raising group for the Higher Polytechnical School
for Women (one of whose alumnae had recently completed the
construction of a bridge over the Volga). The headquarters of most
of these groups appear to have been in St Petersburg or Moscow,
but in some cases branches existed, in the words of Mrs de Philosophoff, 'in all the cities of our vast country' (*ICW Records 1910/11*,
p. 161).

In June 1912 the ICW Board of Officers met at Vice-Regal Lodge
in Dublin and in May 1913 an important Executive meeting took
place at The Hague, at which the announcement of the creation of
an NCW of South Africa was made in a letter from Claire, Lady
Molteno, Hon. Vice-President for that country, where the Act of
Union had been followed by the fusion of the Standing Committee
of Welfare Organizations of Johannesburg and the South African
Council of Women Workers in Cape Town. Much time and care
were expended at this Executive on resolutions to be placed on the
agenda of the next Quinquennial meeting, and four public meetings
were organized (*ICW Records 1912/13*, p. 183).

1913

In 1913 the NCW of France, under the Presidency of Mrs Jules
Siegfried, organized an important Congress on Women's Rights,
held in the Grand Amphitheatre of the Sorbonne, inaugurated by
the Minister of the Interior and attended, as was customary at
Congresses of the NCW of France, by Frenchmen eminent in many
of the domains discussed. 'We know we have much to learn from
our French sisters and brothers,' said Lady Aberdeen in her opening
address, and indeed the report of this meeting 'summoned by the
women of France with the idea of showing colleagues in other lands
to what extent their work had developed in the twelve years of their
federation with the ICW', reveals the highly practical nature of the
work undertaken by the NCW of France in social welfare, in health,
in education, legislation, employment, suffrage, sciences, arts,
letters and in the cause of peace. Discussions ranged from old
problems such as alcoholism to new ones such as the desirability of
sexual instruction in the terminal classes of primary schools, the
provision of adequate play space, pre-school and parent education
and identity of curricula for girls and boys.

As recently as 1849 a French dramatist had proclaimed himself 'revolted by the idea of a woman doctor, amused by that of a woman solicitor and terrified by that of a woman barrister'. Yet only sixty years later the delegates gathered from all over France in the Sorbonne included not only many such women doctors and barristers, but also women Trade Union Leaders, senior Government Officials, headmistresses and journalists as well as the future first woman Cabinet Minister of France, Mrs Léon Brunschwicg. Foreign delegates had gathered from as far afield as Tasmania, Argentina, Bulgaria, South Africa, Turkey, India and Persia. These delegates were received by President and Mrs Poincaré, and at a farewell banquet Mr d'Estournelles de Constant, recalling the brief but moving address made by Mrs Avril de Sainte-Croix in the course of an official visit paid by 50 delegates to a session of the French Senate, spoke the following words:

> If you had heard our comments after your departure, you would have understood that we were touched by your action and by your courage, because you are achieving things of which we have all done no more than vaguely dream, because while you work no doubt for the cause of women, you work also for the cause which is closest to the hearts of all of us, that of the children—of all our children (10e Congrès International des Femmes, Paris, 1914).

An attempt by the Board to evaluate the approximate membership of the ICW after twenty-five years existence, resulted in the rough figure of 6 million women in 23 countries (ICW Records 1913/14, p. 133). Thus, by 1913, the ICW was a well-established organization, with a broad but clearly-defined programme, affiliated Councils or contacts in all five continents, concentrating the efforts of women of different backgrounds, with differing temperaments and opinions, towards the goals set by its founders. Already at the Paris Congress, one of the keynotes of the next stage in their struggle had been sounded by a delegate from Bombay, representing the women of both India and Persia: 'Take us by the hand,' she begged the many western delegates, 'give us your understanding, your ideas and your energies' and 'help us to work for the progress, liberation and the future' of the women of the East. Looking back on the progress achieved since its foundation, the leaders of the ICW had good grounds for hope that the future would indeed eventually bring to all the women of the world those equal rights with men in citizenship, law, education, work and moral standard ceaselessly advocated by the ICW and its National Affiliates since 1888.

BIBLIOGRAPHICAL REFERENCES

PROLOGUE AND PART I

The Council Idea, Anna Garlin Spencer, ICW, 1930.

Genesis of the ICW and the Story of its Growth, 1888–1893, May Wright Sewall, ICW, 1914.

ICW Records 1899—*International Congress of Women, '99 Transactions of the Second Quinquennial Meeting of the ICW*, London, 1899. Ed. Countess of Aberdeen, Unwin, London, 1900.

NCW of US: History and Minutes of NCW of US: 1888–1898. Ed. L. B. Robbins, Boston, 1898.

In the Nineties, Marjorie Pentland. Caxton Press Ltd., London, 1947.

A Bonnie Fechter: Life of Ishbel Marjoribanks, Marchioness of Aberdeen, Marjorie Pentland, Batsford, London, 1952.

Proud Heritage: A History of the NCW of Canada, Rosa L. Shaw, Ryerson, Toronto, 1937.

History of Affiliated NCWs, 1888–1938, ICW, 1938.

Women in Council: Jubilee book of the NCW of Great Britain, Oxford University Press, 1945.

Women in Politics, ICW, 1900. One of the seven volumes of the transactions of the Second Quinquennial Meeting of the ICW, London, 1899.

ICW Records 1899/1904—*Transactions of the Third Quinquennial Meeting of the ICW in Berlin, 1904, including transactions of the period, 1899/1904*. Ed. May Wright Sewall, ICW, 1910.

ICW Records 1904/5, 1905/6, 1906/7, 1907/8—*Annual Reports of the ICW*. Ed. Mrs Ogilvie Gordon, D.Sc., Ph.D., Aberdeen.

ICW Records 1909—*Transactions of the Fourth Quinquennial Meeting of the ICW in Toronto, 1909*. Ed. Countess of Aberdeen, Constable, London, 1910.

Health of the Nations, ICW, Aberdeen, 1909.

International Associations—Monthly Review of International Organizations and Meetings, Union of International Associations, Brussels.

ICW Records 1909/10, 1910/11, 1911/12, 1912/13—*Annual Reports of the ICW*. Ed. Alice Salomon, Ph.D., Berlin.

Dixième Congrès International des femmes, Compte rendu des travaux, Mme Avril de Sainte-Croix, Giard, Paris, 1914.

PART II: 1914–38

1914—THE END OF AN ERA

1914—FIFTH QUINQUENNIAL COUNCIL MEETING OF THE ICW, ROME
ON THE EVE OF THE FIRST WORLD WAR, which was to plunge the world
into misery and stir up bitter hatred among nations, the ICW
gathered in Rome for its Fifth Quinquennial Meeting, as guests
of the NCW of Italy, under its President, Countess Spoletti Rasponi.
The affiliations of Councils in Serbia, Finland and South Africa
were confirmed, and that of Portugal provisionally accepted.

The Council had now become a larger and more representative
organization, proud of progress achieved and full of determination
for the future. Lady Aberdeen, presiding over a Quinquennial
Meeting for the third time, expressed the conviction that 'a great
advance of understanding of the idea underlying the work of the
ICW' was perceptible (*ICW Records 1914*, p. 10), while Dr Alice
Salomon, Hon. Corresponding Secretary since 1909, considered
that the last five years had been 'a time during which the sense of
responsibility of women for the public welfare has increased . . . and
the social value of women's work has received recognition and
found expression in the changed position of women in the community' (*ICW Records 1914*, p. 68).

It has been, and still is, the privilege of the President to reformulate
at each Council Meeting the aims and ideals of the ICW, thereby
renewing the 'Council Idea' for each generation of newcomers to
the Council, and recalling those fundamental principles which
must guide them in confronting the fresh challenges and new
problems of succeeding years. 'People . . . cannot understand how
practical results can follow an organization composed of women
belonging to so many different forms of creeds and political opinions,'
said Lady Aberdeen on this occasion. 'Our Council has been proved
to possess the most potent influence that exists, mainly because the
tie which unites us is essentially a spiritual one, which binds us to
follow the ideal in all the various relations of life'.

First on the agenda was Peace, in the form of a practical demand
that treaties be concluded by which governments would pledge

41

themselves to enter into negotiations for mediation in case of disputes. The Peace Committee also returned to the need to revise history books in use in schools—a question subsequently treated by the International Institute of Intellectual Co-operation, and still an important item on the programme of the United Nations Educational, Scientific and Cultural Organization. The Committee had decided to work for:

> the revision of school histories used by pupils in the advanced grades, in high schools, in academies, etc., to secure the following ends:
>
> (a) A decreased emphasis upon the military achievements of their respective countries;
> (b) A larger attention to the progress and development secured by industry, commerce and the arts;
> (c) An increased attention to existing social wrongs and miseries, and also to sociological progress;
> (d) To inculcate respect for other peoples and to abate the influence now exerted by the majority of school histories to eulogize vanity and arrogance in the name of patriotism.

Several NCWs reported taking this matter before organizations of teachers, historical societies and the writers of national histories for school use in their respective countries. The NCW of the US, in particular, reported some success in the acceptance of the recommendation by 'several authors of popular school histories who have already revised their text books' (*ICW Records 1914*, p. 410).

The Committee on the Legal Position of Women asked for equal rights of parents over their children; for an extension of Juvenile Courts (or other system of separate courts for juvenile offenders), and for international agreements to protect the legal rights of women and children and ensure their maintenance.

The Education Committee proposed that classes on laws affecting women and children be taught in girls' schools. The Committee on Equal Moral Standard recommended the establishment of licensed employment offices, the protection of girls travelling on trains and steamers, and again strongly protested against the state regulation of vice as constituting an encouragement to traffic in women. The Migration Committee suggested the establishment of information centres for prospective migrants. The Public Health Committee, under the Convenership of Lady Aberdeen, reported on its work for the prevention of tuberculosis and the payment of maternity insurance. The Histories of National Councils (see pp. 203–324) show how many of these practical recommendations made by the ICW in 1914 have since been carried out in many countries.

Child Welfare had, of course, been a subject of preoccupation to the ICW, its National Councils and many of their specialized Affiliates, for many years past. At Rome, it was placed in a new and important perspective in the President's opening speech: 'The views which we now hold as to the rights of the child and the duties of the present generation to that which succeeds it have undergone a radical development.' Whether at home, or at school, each child should have the 'right to be happy and to have the chance of expressing spontaneously the joyousness of childhood . . . to be so trained that it will be prepared to take part in the world of life with joy and dignity, not crushed by excessive hours and unproductive labour, but able to make a due contribution to the life of the community' (*ICW Records 1914*, p. 139).

As is customary, public meetings were held during the Conference, drawing a large number of interested listeners. Such meetings have always been a means of bringing the ICW's ideas and work before a greater audience—every possible occasion being used to interest public opinion in the subjects at issue. In Rome, these included (1) the life of women in rural areas, (2) juvenile delinquency (Mrs Ogilvie Gordon, Vice-President of the ICW, reporting the results of an exhaustive inquiry by all NCWs into the causes of such delinquency, subsequently published as an ICW pamphlet) (*Juvenile Delinquency*, 1913–14), and (3) the economic aspects of women's work, particularly equal pay, women's participation in trades unions and the professional training of women. As a result of this last meeting, a new Committee on Trades, Professions and Employments for Women, under the Convenership of Dr Altmann Gottheiner of Germany, was established.

Lady Aberdeen, without whose personality it is difficult to imagine the young ICW, had presided for sixteen years (with the exception of 1899–1904) and now wished to resign. The Executive appealed to her to 'let herself be nominated again as their honoured and beloved leader'. Lady Aberdeen accepted: 'Whether you are right,' she commented, 'is another matter. I could point out many drawbacks in your present President from personal knowledge of the same, in spite of what you so kindly say to the contrary' (*ICW Records 1914*, pp. 175–8).

43

1914–18—THE FIRST WORLD WAR AND AFTER

The women of the ICW gathered in Rome in May 1914 were inspired by a spirit of optimism and belief in the progress of mankind, undertaking every new task with high hopes for the future. Only three months later, even before the resolutions of this Council Meeting were committed to print, the outbreak of 'the fiercest conflict in the history of mankind' burst upon Europe, shattering many of these hopes, so that, as the *Foreword* to the Rome Report published in August sadly recorded, the very 'principles for which the ICW stands appear for the time being to have passed into oblivion' (*ICW Records 1914*, p. iii).

Although international relations were severed, Lady Aberdeen and the members of her Board tried to maintain contact with one another. NCWs of both belligerent and neutral countries rendered service to their respective countries in whatever ways they judged best, biding their time for 'the stupendous task of reconstruction'.

1919

Although the ICW met again 'as an unbroken family' in 1920 (*ICW Records 1920*, p. 13), an entirely new period had begun, for since 1914 great changes had taken place in the position of women in almost every country affected by the conflict. Economic, legal and social barriers which women had for years struggled to overcome, fell before national necessity in time of war. Women had been called to fill responsible positions, to perform men's jobs at men's wages, and after four years had proven their devotion, skill and capabilities, in innumerable fields hitherto partially or entirely closed to them. The restoration of peace therefore saw many new rights and responsibilities willingly and permanently accorded, including, in many cases, those suffrage rights still so hotly contested on the very brink of war. The outlook and maturity of women themselves had also inevitably altered. Throughout the war years, with their sufferings and added load of responsibilities, said Mrs Chaponnière-Chaix, soon to be elected post-war President of the ICW, 'women have developed and broadened in thought and action and are realizing better than ever before their power for helping forward the welfare of the world, and its reconstruction on a new and better basis' (*Bulletin, Vol. I, No. 6, 1923*).

As soon as the war was over the ICW came out of its enforced silence and made its voice heard again in the international field. The President of the ICW wrote to the Paris Peace Conference requesting an audience for a deputation to present women's views on the Covenant of the League of Nations then being drafted. Meanwhile the ICW participated in a deputation from a Suffrage Conference convened by the former Alliance for Suffrage (now renamed the International Women's Suffrage Alliance) which presented to the Labour Commission of the Peace Conference a programme covering the 44-hour week, compulsory schooling until 15 years of age, equal pay and a minimum wage for home work. Lady Aberdeen's specific purpose, however, was to secure an audience for the ICW before the special Commission for the establishment of the League of Nations, in order to request the inclusion of certain clauses in the Covenant itself. She therefore renewed her application to its Chairman, President Wilson. The Commission agreed unanimously to grant an audience to an ICW delegation which, in the words of President Wilson, represented 'the mothers of the world', and on April 10th, 1919, a Joint Delegation formed by the ICW and the Inter-Allied Conference of Women Suffragists, headed by Lady Aberdeen, appeared before a Plenary Session of the Commission. One by one they presented arguments 'laudable' —again according to President Wilson—for their 'lucidity and brevity' (*ICW Records 1920*, p. 71):

1. Eligibility of women to occupy posts in all bodies of the League (this was written into the Covenant).

2. Nations entering the League to agree to suppress traffic in women and children and licensed houses. (First step was the subsequent establishment of an Advisory Committee of the League on Traffic in Women and Children.)

3. Recognition of the principle of women's suffrage, with equal consultation of women and men whenever a referendum was taken in regard to changes of nationality. (The second point was immediately accepted.)

4 and 5. Creation of International Bureaus of Education and of Public Health. (Both subsequently achieved.)

6. A final statement in favour of the control and reduction of armaments.

(For a more complete account of this delegation see Appendix 7, p. 344.)

1920—SIXTH QUINQUENNIAL COUNCIL MEETING OF THE ICW, OSLO

More than 300 delegates from 26 countries met at the first post-war and Sixth Quinquennial Council Meeting of the ICW held in

September 1920 in Christiania (now Oslo). The hosts were the National Council of Women of Norway under the Presidency of Mrs Betsy Kjelsberg. The shadow of the war years still lay heavily upon the delegates, but Mrs Ogilvie Gordon later recorded her impression that 'feelings of sympathy with other war sufferers rose above differences of race or nationality'. The main causes advocated at this Quinquennial, which gave the ICW 'a strong push forward in public recognition' were, firstly, peace and arbitration and, secondly, equal political, industrial, legal and educational rights for men and women. New NCWs were affiliated in Russia, Ukrainia, Iceland and Mexico.

The ICW had already been so long engaged in international collaboration towards the ideals of peace and human welfare that three eminent statesmen—General Smuts of South Africa, Prime Minister Edward Beneš of Czechoslovakia and British Foreign Minister Sir John Simon—were on different occasions each subsequently to salute it as the 'mother' or forerunner of the League of Nations. Naturally the ICW felt strongly reinforced by the existence of the new permanent inter-governmental institution, and the first steps in a long and fruitful co-operation between the ICW and the League of Nations were taken in Oslo, where a public meeting was devoted to the aims and objectives of the League.

Unhappily, the ICW itself was unable entirely to escape all experience of post-war bitterness. The German NCW sent no delegates to the Meeting in Norway because it felt that, as long as Germany was not accepted as a League member, there could be no true equality among nations and no true basis for internationalism. In order to support the German Council, the ICW adopted a resolution recommending that 'all fully self-governing States' be accepted as League members, and, in spite of the fact that the German Council did not permit any of its members to seek office, Dr Alice Salomon was nominated as Vice-President in her absence and subsequently elected by acclamation to this office (*ICW Records 1920*, p. 146). The German Council reappeared at the ICW Executive meeting at the Hague in 1922 where it was represented by Dr Marie Elizabeth Lüders. The Hungarian and Austrian National Councils, though in the same position as the German Council, both came to the Oslo meeting and accepted nomination.

No new Standing Committees were established at Oslo, but resolutions were submitted by the NCWs of Italy and the US asking the ICW to draw up a Children's Charter, indicating the minimum rights which the ICW would desire to claim for the children of all nations. A Special Committee on Child Welfare, under the Convenership of Lady Aberdeen, was appointed for the purpose of drafting such a Charter, to be circulated to NCWs to obtain suggestions and amendments and subsequently to be submitted to the next Executive. The decision was made to create, within the framework of the Education Committee, a Sub-Committee on the Cinema which, however, did not begin active work until 1925.

Lady Aberdeen presided over the meeting at Oslo, but did not stand for re-election, feeling that she should withdraw in favour of a personality from a neutral country. Mrs Chaponnière-Chaix, President of the NCW of Switzerland, was then elected Third President of the ICW.

Relations with the League of Nations began on the very day the meetings in Oslo came to a close. Before separating, the chief officers sent to Sir Eric Drummond, Secretary-General of the League, a list of all resolutions passed at Oslo on behalf of the League, and a few weeks later all ICW publications were deposited in the Library of the League. The President of the ICW received an invitation to all the plenary meetings of the League Assembly, at which 'she had the very great satisfaction of witnessing the presence as deputies of their respective countries of Miss Henni Forchammer of Denmark, Vice-President of the ICW, Dr Kristine Bonnevie of Norway and Mrs Anna Wicksell of Sweden, Vice-President of the IWSA' (*ICW Records 1920/22*, p. 32). On December 15th, 1920, Miss Forchammer, President of the Danish NCW and technical adviser to the Danish Delegation to the League, spoke before the First Plenary Session of the League Assembly on the subject of traffic in women and children.[1] This was the first time a woman addressed a Plenary Meeting of the League Assembly and her intervention was greeted with marked applause. More than 20,000 women and children, said Miss Forchammer, were held in captivity worse than slavery, and while expressing satisfaction that the Assembly had recognized its responsibility in dealing with the problem of traffic in women and children, she asked for the establishment of a committee of inquiry

[1] The personal records of Miss Forchammer having unfortunately been dispersed, it is to the ever-ready co-operation of Mrs E. Merete Ross, former President of the NCW of Denmark, a Council still prominent in work in favour of refugees, that we are indebted for information on this historic occasion.

to investigate not only the conditions of women and children deported to Armenia and Asia Minor, but also to cover other areas of the world: 'Gentlemen, I appeal to you to ask your Governments to introduce a legislation which prevents traffic in women and children. This traffic is a blot to civilization and is often criticized by nations which we call uncivilized' (*League of Nations Records, First Session of the Assembly*, 1920, p. 546).

1921

During the Second Session of the League Assembly a Board Meeting of the ICW was held in Geneva and a letter was sent to the President of the Assembly and to all Delegations pressing for the inclusion of a woman doctor in the proposed Health Organization. Several ICW members represented their governments at the first Conferences of the International Labour Office: among them were Mrs Carmichael, President of the Canadian NCW, and Mrs Betsy Kjelsberg, President of the NCW of Norway, Mrs Thorburn, also of Canada, and Miss Hesselgren of Sweden. At the request of the Secretary-General of the League and in agreement with other women's organizations, Mrs Avril de Sainte-Croix was nominated to serve as the representative of the major women's organizations on the Advisory Committee established by the Assembly on Traffic in Women and Children. Requests were also made to the women's international organizations for the designation of women candidates for nomination to other Advisory Committees of the League (*ICW Records 1920/22*, p. 35).

A new feature of the post-war world was the rapid proliferation of national and international women's organizations in fields where, prior to 1914, the ICW had often worked alone or with but few collaborators. As has been seen above and will be frequently noted from the following pages, the ICW consistently welcomed the growth of these sister associations and on many occasions during the ensuing decade assumed the initiative in promoting active co-operation and concerted action between the different international groupings, concerned only that their several efforts should, where useful, be combined in the interests of efficiency, and that duplication of effort should not lead to wastage.

Women's organizations were faced with many material problems in the post-war world. Before the war it had been an accepted practice for delegates and office holders to bear their own expenses:

in the changed conditions of the 1920s this obligation would have proved a serious barrier to the participation of many of those very women whose services were essential to the work of the ICW, which, therefore, found itself faced with the necessity of paying part of its officers' expenses and of supplementing its voluntary officers with professional assistants. In 1920 it had proved impossible to find a woman disposing of the increasing time and means necessary to undertake and execute all the responsible work of Honorary Corresponding Secretary as performed in pre-war days by Mrs Ogilvie Gordon and Dr Alice Salomon, in addition to their own important professional activities and obligations in other fields. Mrs Anna Backer of Norway was elected Hon. Corresponding Secretary, and with the generous financial support of the NCW of Norway, and the assistance of the ICW's first professional secretary, Miss G. M. Günther, the business of the ICW was conducted from the small town of Fredrikstad in Norway of which Mrs Backer was an honoured member of the Town Council. Meanwhile National Councils had their own post-war financial problems: widespread unemployment, particularly among women, was prevalent, and some NCWs had a hard struggle simply to exist.

1922—THE ICW AND THE LEAGUE OF NATIONS

Despite its financial difficulties, the ICW had taken up its work with vigour and published the first issues of the new *Bulletin* (separate editions in French, English, German), shortly after the Executive Meeting held in The Hague in 1922. It was at this meeting that Lady Aberdeen was once more elected President of the ICW, when ill-health necessitated the resignation of Mrs Chaponnière-Chaix, who was appointed 'Special Representative of the Council in connection with the great international movements that have their headquarters in Geneva' (*ICW Records 1920/22*, p. 262). Before retiring Mrs Chaponnière-Chaix was able to report new Councils affiliated in Chile, Estonia and Rumania.

It was also in 1922 that the ICW began regularly to send representatives to meetings of certain other major international organizations. Attention was given to the question of close collaboration with the International Women's Suffrage Alliance, which, since the war and the achievement of political equality for women in many countries, had turned to questions outside suffrage. In 1922 a joint meeting of the Boards of Officers of the two organizations was held in London under the chairmanship of Lady Frances Balfour, President of the NCW of Great Britain (*ICW Records 1922/24*, p. 167) to consider the possibility of federation. Proposals for a federation, and future joint action were drawn up in time for inclusion in the agenda of the IWSA Congress held in Rome in 1923. While the joint proposals were not approved by the IWSA Congress, this body voted to invite the ICW to send three delegates with voting rights to attend all future Congresses of the IWSA, at the same time expressing the hope that the ICW would insert a reciprocal clause in its own Constitution (*ICW Records 1922/23*, pp. 30–1).

The years 1922–24 marked an important step forward in the question of children's rights. The Special Child Welfare Committee of the ICW had drawn up a Children's Charter as proposed in 1920. This was submitted to the ICW Executive at The Hague, which authorized it to be printed and distributed to NCWs with the request that after adaptation to the needs of their respective countries it should be brought to the notice of their governments with the purpose of stimulating child welfare legislation.

> This Charter is based on the principle that every child is born with the inalienable right to have the opportunity of full physical, mental and spiritual development.
> It is the privilege, no less than the duty of parents, to provide such opportunities for their children. In the event of parents not being able, for whatsoever reason, to discharge this duty, the community is bound to secure the fulfilment thereof (*ICW Records 1920/22*, p. 324).

This preamble was followed by provisions covering the life of the child from pre-natal care to employment, including special clauses on the subject of juvenile delinquency. Yugoslavia was the first NCW to report acceptance of the Charter as the basic child welfare programme of its government.

1923

In 1923 the International Save the Children Fund adopted the *Declaration of Geneva*, a charter of children's rights embodying almost every provision of the ICW's charter, and the national auxiliaries of the Fund were asked to draw up national children's charters. 'To avoid overlapping' between the two forms of Children's Charter, the ICW Executive formally endorsed the Declaration of

Geneva and asked all its NCWs to collaborate with the national committee of the Save the Children Fund in preparing for each country a Children's Charter adapted to national needs and conditions.

1924

In 1924, at the ICW Executive held at Copenhagen, the Special Committee on Child Welfare asked that, in view of the general and increasing interest manifested in all parts of the world in all that concerns child welfare, a Standing Committee on Child Welfare be formed within the ICW. This proposal was accepted (*ICW Records, 1922/24*, pp. 333–6).

This meeting of the Executive was held in the Aula of the University of Copenhagen and was welcomed by Mrs Nina Bang, first woman Cabinet Minister of Denmark, and by the Municipality of Copenhagen. The King and Queen of Denmark honoured the ICW by receiving all delegates at their Summer Palace of Sorgenfri.

Lady Aberdeen reported that six new Councils had applied for affiliation: Latvia, Cuba, Czechoslovakia, Guatemala, Poland and Ireland. Good progress was also reported towards the establishment of a NCW in India.

The question of peace was, as always, foremost in the minds of the ICW leaders, now fully conscious that, unhappily, the end of the First World War had not brought about the peace the women of all nations longed to see. A Call to the Women of the World to try to understand the causes which lead to war, issued in 1922, had been followed by the formation of a Committee of seven women's organizations with headquarters in London, which had mandated the ICW to convene a Conference on the Prevention of Causes of War. This important Conference was organized by Miss Elsie Zimmern, Hon. Recording Secretary of the ICW since 1920, on behalf of the ICW, the World Alliance for Promoting Peace through the Churches and the World's Temperance Union. It was held in conjunction with the British Empire Exhibition at Wembley in 1924, during which the NCW of Great Britain operated a highly successful pavilion for the purpose of propagating the aims and activities of the ICW. Speakers included representatives of the major women's organizations, of the League of Nations and of the League of Red Cross Societies.

'It was wonderful because from it pealed forth the clarion note of the new age,' wrote a fraternal delegate whose impressions were quoted in the President's subsequent report, 'the clarion note of international co-operation and help to all weaker states and peoples' (*ICW Records, 1922/24*, p. 91).

1925—SEVENTH QUINQUENNIAL COUNCIL MEETING OF THE ICW, WASHINGTON, D.C., 1925

The Seventh Quinquennial Meeting of the ICW was held in Washington, DC, in May 1925, thanks to the efforts of the NCW of the US, under the Presidency of Mrs Philip North Moore, which raised a contribution of $20,000 towards the travelling expenses of ICW officers and delegates. Lady Aberdeen recalled the 'all-impelling motive of the ICW, the Golden Rule', and reminded delegates that the tasks of the ICW, while still the same as in 1920, should now include the 'right of all children . . . to have equal opportunities for full physical, mental and spiritual development' (*ICW Records 1925*, p. 238). While the range of the ICW activities broadened from meeting to meeting, its *raison d'etre* remained, as Lady Aberdeen expressed it, 'to form a centre round which all women's societies and movements can gather, confer and make the voice of organized womanhood heard regarding various subjects of world interest'.

In pursuance of its policy of active collaboration with the IWSA, a footnote was added to the ICW Constitution to the effect that the Alliance be invited to send three voting delegates to the Quinquennial meetings of the ICW, thus reciprocating the invitation voted at the Rome Congress of the Alliance in 1923 (*ICW Records 1925*, p. 142). The Council then welcomed three IWSA representatives: Mrs Corbett Ashby, President, Mrs Chapman Catt and Dr A. Jacobs.

No fewer than 29 International societies had accepted invitations to send fraternal delegates to Washington, including the International Union of League of Nations Associations, the International Red Cross, the International League of Youth and all the major women's associations. As at Berlin in 1904, the ICW Board placed before the Council Meeting certain amendments to the Constitution which, if adopted, would have permitted the ICW to affiliate international women's organizations as well as National Councils. The ICW, however, preferred not to amend the Constitution at this juncture and voted to continue the practice of inviting fraternal delegates to Council Meetings with the right to take part in discussions on matters not affecting the Constitution, but, except for the IWSA, without a vote (*ICW Records 1925*, p. 203).

Poland, Chile, the mandated territory of Palestine and (provisionally) India were affiliated at Washington, but the Russian NCW formed in 1920 had ceased to function and the question arose as to whether, in the absence of any responsible government in the Ukraine, the NCW of that country could remain a member.

Important public meetings, at which the practice of colour segregation was not admitted, were organized dealing with 'Recent Developments in Citizenship', and 'Social Ideals in International Life'. Three hundred delegates were received at the White House by President and Mrs Coolidge.

Standing Committees had full programmes and busy meetings. The Migration Committee was working towards the admission of the dependent families of immigrants already admitted by receiving countries. Steps taken in Washington, where an ICW delegation was received by the US Department of Labor, subsequently contributed, in 1927, to an amendment of the US Immigration Act to allow the entry (within the quota system) of wives and children of aliens who had legally entered the US since July 1924. The Education Committee urged that NCWs give special attention to educational conditions in regions where groups of different nationality were living together, urging that the character and genius of all minorities be fully respected. The Balkan NCWs took important steps in this direction, the Rumanian NCW in particular co-operating closely with the minority women's associations.

In 1925 the ICW welcomed the fact that 'teaching of youth about the existence and aims of the League' had been placed on the Agenda of the League (as the result of an intervention made by Dame Edith Lyttleton, Delegate of Great Britain, in the Assembly of 1924). At Washington Mrs (later Dame) Elizabeth Cadbury, Convener of the ICW Peace Committee since 1914, reported that her Committee now 'found itself increasingly drawn towards and into constructive educational activity'. After the Washington meeting Lady Aberdeen asked all NCWs to obtain from their affiliates as much information as possible regarding efforts being made in their country to interest children and young people 'in all that tends to promote peace and goodwill amongst the nations' (*Bulletin*, October 1925; *ICW Records 1925*, p. 536).

The Washington Meeting confirmed the establishment of a

Standing Committee on Child Welfare, with Lady Aberdeen as its first Convener. A Sub-Committee on the subject of 'recreation and the provision of adequate playing space' was also established.

Another step taken at Washington was to reorganize the Secretariat of the ICW to keep pace with the increasing volume of work. Headquarters were subsequently transferred from Norway to London, and while Miss Louise C. A. van Eeghen (Netherlands) succeeded Mrs Backer as Hon. Corresponding Secretary, Miss Elsie Zimmern was appointed General Secretary, Miss E. van Veen Assistant Secretary and Miss Günther, Editor of the *Bulletin*.

For the first time representatives of the League and of the ILO attended an ICW Council Meeting. Miss Martha Mundt of the ILO, and Princess Gabrielle Radziwill of the League were the first of a line of distinguished delegates regularly sent to participate in ICW Council Meetings by the ILO, the League, and its successors. 'The League needs the work of women,' said Princess Radziwill, then at the beginning of her long collaboration with the ICW, 'and we women need the League of Nations' help, because the work that we are doing can only bear fruit if it is really sanctioned by our Governments and we women must help this sanction to be given' (*ICW Records 1925*, p. 331).

The ICW President was able to report to the Washington meeting a number of steps already taken to promote such collaboration with the League. During each session of the Assembly, an ICW deputation had been received by the Secretary-General of the League and by the President of the Assembly, to whom were presented personally ICW resolutions related to the work of the League. A similar deputation had also been regularly received by the Director-General of the ILO, who was thus informed of ICW resolutions falling within the ILO sphere of activity. At Washington, the Council Meeting decided on the establishment of an ICW Liaison Committee with the League of Nations and the ILO, which subsequently met regularly in Geneva immediately before the annual session of the League Assembly (*ICW Records 1925*, p. 223). Mrs Guthrie D'Arcis, of the World Union of Women for International Concord, was kind enough to place at the disposal of the ICW, office space in the Geneva Office of that association, as well as secretarial assistance. The Committee (appointed as a 'consultative and not executive' body) was composed of Mrs Kjelsberg of Norway, Mrs Brunschwicg of France, Dr Altmann Gottheiner of

Germany, Mrs Chaponnière-Chaix, Mrs D'Arcis and Mrs Romniciano of Rumania, Hon. Recording Secretary of the ICW since 1922, who acted as Hon. Secretary of this Committee (*ICW Records 1925*, p. 223). Mrs L. Dreyfus Barney (France), Vice-Convener of the ICW Standing Committee on Peace and International Relations was appointed as Liaison Officer to the newly-founded Institute of Intellectual Co-operation in Paris (*ICW Records 1925*, p. 17). When the League announced its intention of enlarging its Committee on Traffic in Women and Children to include child welfare, the ICW and four other women's organizations intervened, requesting a separate Committee of the League for Child Welfare to deal with the training and education of the normal as well as of the abnormal, poor or illegitimate child, and also that the women's organizations should be represented on such a Committee (*ICW Records 1925*, p. 531).

Meanwhile, throughout the 1920s the ICW was strongly represented among governmental delegates to the ILO as well as to the Assembly and Committees of the League. Among prominent Presidents or Vice-Presidents of NCWs representing their countries in Geneva during this period were Mrs Moss of Australia, Miss Carmichael of Canada, Miss Forchammer of Denmark, Mrs Hainari of Finland, Dr Gertrud Bäumer of Germany, Countess Albert Apponyi and Miss Augusta Rosenberg both of Hungary, Mrs Kjelsberg of Norway and Princess Alexandrine Cantacuzène of Rumania (*ICW Records 1922/24*, p. 471; *1925*, p. 22; *1925/30*, p. 339, etc.).

The ICW was also naturally concerned to ensure the co-ordination of the efforts of the various women's organizations in relation to the League. At Washington, it voted to propose the establishment of 'an International Standing Committee of Women, whose object shall be to work unitedly for the appointment of suitable women on Commissions or other bodies in the League of Nations where women's opinion should be represented' (*ICW Records 1925*, p. 199). This proposal was welcomed by other women's organizations and the first meetings of this Committee were held later in 1925 at the new ICW headquarters in London. Seven International Women's Organizations, including the IWSA, the International League for Peace and Freedom, and the International Federation of University Women collaborated with the ICW on this Committee (known as the Joint Standing Committee of Women's International

Organizations), of which Miss Elsie Zimmern, General-Secretary of the ICW, acted as Hon. Secretary until 1946 (*Bulletin*, July/ October 1954). Monthly meetings were held in London and an annual meeting took place in Geneva in September to coincide with the sessions of the League Assembly. By 1930, Mrs Ogilvie Gordon was able to report successful results in having women members appointed to the following Committees or Commissions of the League and of the ILO: Health, Infant Mortality, Child Welfare, Forced Labour, and Mandates. Strong recommendations had been made to the Secretary-General of the League to renew the contract of Dame Rachel Crowdy (Chief of the Social Section) and to appoint suitably qualified women to other posts on the Secretariat (*ICW Records 1925/30*, p. 336).

1926

In order to strengthen ties with South America, Miss L. C. A. van Eeghen, Hon. Corresponding Secretary of the ICW, visited Peru, Bolivia, Chile, Brazil, Argentina and Uruguay, helping to found NCWs in Bolivia and Brazil. In 1926, Lady Aberdeen, Mrs Sanford, Hon. Treasurer, and Miss van Eeghen visited Bulgaria, Rumania, Yugoslavia, Hungary and Austria. Later, Mrs Sanford and Miss van Eeghen went to Czechoslovakia, the latter continuing to Estonia, Latvia and Lithuania (where a new NCW was created). In Rumania, the NCW opened a remarkable Women's Centre (including a Workers' Canteen, free Medical and Legal Advice Clinics and a Crafts School) and Lady Aberdeen recommended all Councils to consider creating similar centres. Meanwhile, the immediate financial position of the ICW had been greatly improved since Washington by the 'energetic action' of the Hon. Corresponding Secretary, who, with the aid of a strong Committee in the Hague, and the co-operation of NCWs throughout the world, had organized an International Fancy Fair in that city which contributed an important sum to the ICW treasury (*ICW Records 1925/27*, p. 25). The post-war situation had by now improved in most countries and Councils once more seemed flourishing, particularly those in Eastern Europe. The two Councils with the largest membership were Great Britain, with almost two million members, and Germany with one million.

The year 1926 also marked the beginning of close and regular co-operation between the ICW and the Committee and Institute of Intellectual Co-operation, now formally charged with the task of promoting the education of youth in the spirit of peace. The Vice-Convener of the ICW Peace Committee, who had been designated by the Council of the League to serve on the Sub-Committee of Experts set up by the League Committee on Intellectual Co-operation on this subject, prepared and arranged for the printing of a leaflet giving concise information on the Constitution of the League and its various activities during the first five years of its existence. In France, where instruction on the League was already being given in the schools, the Minister of Education arranged for the distribution of several thousand copies of this leaflet among French student bodies. This leaflet was also recommended to NCWs for distribution at meetings, to affiliated societies and in schools. In the same year, the ICW organized a competition on 'How to facilitate the teaching of the aims and work of the League of Nations in schools'.

The year 1926 also saw the beginnings of the important activities of the Joint Committee of Major International Organizations interested in education for peace, or '*Comité d'Entente*', founded largely at the suggestion of the ICW in December 1925. This Committee was given a headquarters and secretariat in the Institute of Intellectual Co-operation in Paris and worked in the closest collaboration with that body. It also held one annual meeting at the headquarters of the League on the occasion of the annual session of the League Committee of Intellectual Co-operation. It began its work with a Declaration of Principles (approved by the ICW Executive in Geneva in 1927), which formed the basis of much of the pioneer work subsequently undertaken by these associations in the fields of education for international understanding, student and teacher exchange, teaching of history and geography, revision of school textbooks, etc. (*Joint Committee: Ten Years' Activity*, Paris, 1936). The work of this Committee continued until immediately after the Second World War and is described in the official history of the Institute of Intellectual Co-operation published in Paris in 1946 (pp. 561 ff.).

1927

An Executive Committee meeting held in Geneva in 1927 proved 'a landmark in the history of the ICW' for 'it brought the representatives of NCWs for the first time into close contact with the actual work of the League and with those responsible for its conduct' (*ICW Records 1925/27*, p. 21). A deep sense of responsibility was awakened by the official recognition which the ICW received from the League authorities on this occasion. In a series of six lectures 'able exponents' from the League and the ILO dealt with international problems of interest to the ICW: among them Dame Rachel Crowdy on the Humanitarian Activities of the League, Mr Madariaga on Arbitration and Security, Professor Alfred Zimmern on Intellectual Co-operation, Mr Albert Thomas on the Protection of Working Women and Sir Arthur Salter on the forthcoming International Economic Conference. Each lecture was followed by open discussions.

The close and cordial relationship existing between the ICW and the League was further demonstrated by a reception held by the Secretary-General of the League, Sir Eric Drummond, for members of the Executive and Standing Committees, followed by a dinner offered by the ICW to the President and members of the League Council. Sir Austen Chamberlain, British Foreign Minister, replying to Lady Aberdeen's toast to the League, modestly recalled the youth of the League as compared to the experience of the ICW, and emphasized the rôle of women in forming public opinion, on the support of which the League relied so greatly. Other speeches were made by Mrs Avril de Sainte-Croix, Mr Paul Boncour, representing Mr Briand, and Mr Beneš, Prime Minister of Czechoslovakia, who expressed the view that, especially in education, the work of women, less dominated than men by ideas of 'strength, power and vanity' was essential for the raising of a 'new generation for peace' (*ICW Records 1925/30*, p. 203).

No new Standing Committees were created in Geneva, but an *ad hoc* Committee of Experts on Economic Problems was set up, in view of the growing recognition of the importance of these problems to world peace, and three major women's organizations were invited to co-operate. The Public Health Committee drew up plans for the collaboration of NCWs in the execution of the programme of the newly-established International Health Organization of the League.

In Washington the Trades and Professions Committee had adopted a resolution recommending that 'the prohibition to work in the weeks before and after confinement be accompanied by a maternity provision' (*ICW Records, 1925*, p. 25). In 1927, Miss Margaret

Bondfield (who became British Minister of Labour in 1929) insisted that working women must be further protected, pointing out that women's organizations opposing over-protection generally had few working women members. The committee then discussed the matter again and submitted a new resolution asking that no action be taken regarding protective legislation without prior consultation of working women's organizations (*ICW Records 1925/27*, p. 47).

Also in 1927 the ICW convened a representative Conference to consider the question of Forced Labour. This Conference met at the ICW office in London and a Memorandum was drawn up for submission to the Director-General of the ILO with the signature of the six major women's international organizations participating (*ICW Records 1925/27*, p. 447).

1928–30

At the meeting of the Executive Committee held in London in 1929, Dr Salomon spoke on the 'Future of the ICW', saying that, although the Council Idea should be preserved under all circumstances, the internal organization should be revised if the ICW wanted to remain influential and really alive. This suggestion among others led to the subsequent establishment of a Committee, chaired by Dr Salomon, to draw up recommendations for the revision of the ICW Constitution and Standing Orders, on which served Dr Maria Verone of France, Convener of the Standing Committee on Laws and Suffrage, the Hon. Corresponding Secretary Miss L. C. A. van Eeghen and the President of the NCW of Sweden, Miss Ingegerd Palme, Doctor of Political Science and History.

In 1929, Lady Aberdeen, convinced that the ICW was 'not complete without the co-operation of countrywomen' took the initiative of organizing a Committee charged with studying groupings of rural women. This Committee subsequently called a Conference of representatives of rural organizations, held under the auspices of the ICW in London in May 1929, at the same time as the ICW Executive Meeting. Lady Aberdeen presided this Conference, which was attended by 60 delegates from 24 countries, who determined the immediate formation of a permanent Liaison Committee of Rural Women's Organizations (*ICW Records 1925/30*, p. 95).

Also in 1929, the ICW and the IWSA again formed a Joint Committee to work on plans for co-operation between the two organizations. They decided to hold joint demonstrations and meetings, and to develop co-operation between their Standing Committees. In the next few years the Peace Committee of the ICW and the IWSA in particular worked in close and useful collaboration. The International Committee of the IWSA arranged to hold their forthcoming Congress at the same time and place as the Eighth Quinquennial Meeting of the ICW—the Hofburg Palace, Vienna, 1930 (*ICW Records 1925/30*, pp. 88 and 352).

Meanwhile a Liaison Committee of Women's International Organizations was formed to complement the work of the Joint Standing Committee of eight such organizations formed in 1925 to secure the appointment of women to the Committee of the League. (These two committees were subsequently amalgamated in 1934.) The first action of the new Committee was an appeal by the World's Women to the World's Statesmen, declaring 'work for peace to be the most urgent task before the world today'. Noting that the nations 'stagger under an unprecedented burden of armaments in the midst of commerical depression and economic warfare', they demanded 'energetic action' and exhorted statesmen to increase their efforts to make the observance of the Briand–Kellogg pact a 'safeguard of humanity'. A delegation was sent to the President of the League Assembly to support this appeal (*ICW Records 1930*, pp. ix and 450).

In the same year, at the suggestion of Dr Lüders of the NCW of Germany, delegate of her country to the League Conference for the Codification of International Law held in the Hague, a Joint Conference and Demonstration was organized by the ICW and the IWSA to support the resolution that 'every woman, whether married or unmarried, shall have the same right as a man to retain or to change her nationality' (*1925/30*, pp. 183, 366). 210 national branches from 35 different countries were represented, and after a public meeting so successful that it overflowed the hall, a deputation, including Miss Chrystal MacMillan of Great Britain, Mrs Maria Vèrone of France and Mrs Georgette Ciselet of Belgium presented a Memorandum to the Chairman of the Codification Conference. Despite the fact that the women's immediate requests were not granted, this demonstration and deputation were largely responsible for the fact that the Codification Conference recommended to governments the embodiment of the principle of equality between man and woman in their respective laws in regard to nationality (*ICW Records 1925/30*, p. 366).

THE TROUBLED THIRTIES

1930—EIGHTH QUINQUENNIAL COUNCIL MEETING OF THE ICW, VIENNA

At the Eighth Quinquennial Council Meeting of the ICW held in Vienna in 1930, as the guest of the NCW of Austria, under the Presidency of Mrs Hertha von Sprung, the ICW was officially welcomed in the Festsall of the Hofburg Palace by Chancellor Schober, the Burgomaster of Vienna and Dr Michael Hainisch, First President of the Austrian Republic and son of Marianne Hainisch, founder of the NCW of Austria and Hon. Vice-President of the ICW. Mrs Hainisch herself, then aged 91, was accorded an ovation when she rose to speak of her memories of the early activities of the ICW in the Peace Movement, and of her own close collaboration with Baroness Bertha von Suttner in this same cause. During the Conference a private economic meeting was held under the presidency of Dr Michael Hainisch, in the course of which Sir Arthur Salter, head of the Economic Service of the League, addressed the delegates.

Besides those members of the Secretariats of the ILO and of the League regularly charged with relations with women's voluntary organizations, the League was represented at Vienna by Mr G. Oprescu, Secretary of the Committee of Intellectual Co-operation, and by Miss Colin of the Child Welfare Section.

In her speech of welcome to the Council Meeting, Lady Aberdeen emphasized that the chief strength of the ICW rested on the 'elasticity and adaptability of the ICW Constitution. . . . Its rules and regulations can easily be changed to fit changing times, but its central idea remains. . . . It can never grow out of date.' Quoting criticism of the Council as 'old-fashioned and out of date as compared with some of the younger international societies' created to promote certain specific aims, Lady Aberdeen observed that while this was 'their right and proper business', it was not that of the ICW, whose purpose was, through its NCWs, 'to bring into personal contact in every country all women's organizations which are seeking the welfare of others' (*ICW Records 1930*, p. 53).

The Resolutions passed at Vienna covered many fields: requests to the League to establish an Institute of Public Nutrition, to draw up an International Convention to provide for the recovery of alimony and maintenance obligations in foreign countries, and to work for removal of customs duties on educational films. Other resolutions pledged the ICW to work for minimum wage legislation, the incorporation of women in national police forces, and the raising of the age of consent to 16 years, or legal age of marriage, whichever was the higher.

The Council adopted the Charter of the Rights of Mothers proposed by the ICW Standing Committee on Public Health under the Convenership of Dr Thuillier-Landry (France). The following rights were claimed for all mothers:

1. Pre-natal care and medical care during and after childbirth.
2. The right to be able to nurse and care for her child.
3. The right to education and maintenance of the child.
4. Equal rights with the father over the children.
5. The right to take part in the public affairs of her country 'as the destiny of her child depends thereon'.

A shortened text was submitted to NCWs 'for their consideration and adaptation to their own conditions' (*ICW Records 1925/30*, p. 641). The text of this Charter was reviewed and modified several times before being adopted in final form in 1934 (*Bulletin*, April 1935).

Several other important steps were taken at Vienna:

1. The decision to create a separate permanent international organization of rural women. Miss Elsie Zimmern, able General Secretary at ICW headquarters in London since 1925, was released to assume the direction of the Secretariat of the new Organization of Rural Women, which subsequently developed into the Associated Country Women of the World, an organization which Miss Zimmern later presided for a term and with which the ICW has always maintained and still maintains excellent and close relations (*ICW Records 1925/30*, p. 50).

2. A study of the possibility of representation on the ICW of non-independent countries resulted in the creation of Councils of Women in various non-self-governing territories, of which South-West Africa became the first to affiliate in 1938.

3. The decision that, in the future, Council Meetings should become Triennial instead of Quinquennial (*ICW Records 1925/30*, p. 393).

Several new NCWs were officially affiliated: Peru, Brazil, Bolivia and Lithuania, as well as provisional Councils in Southern Rhodesia, Japan and Turkey. Attempts to form an Albanian NCW had failed. The affiliation of Guatemala was terminated as neither reports nor fees had been received. In deference to the eight Latin American Councils, Spanish was adopted as a semi-official language and the question of a Spanish edition of the ICW *Bulletin* was discussed, but left in abeyance for financial reasons.

As in Berlin in 1904, a special effort was made to interest young people in the work of the ICW. At a meeting 'crowded with young girls', and presided by Dr Salomon, speeches were made by Mrs Pichon-Landry, Dr Maria Schauer and Mrs Corbett Ashby in the course of which 'youthful hearers were urged to make the most of the opportunities which had been won for them by women pioneers and to build truly and nobly on the foundations which had been laid' (*ICW Records 1925/30*, p. vii).

After the Council Meeting, a number of delegates made a tour of the NCWs of Rumania, Hungary and Czechoslovakia. In Rumania they were welcomed to the Women's Centre by Princess Cantacuzène; in Hungary, 300 delegates were received by the Prime Minister; in Czechoslovakia both President Masaryk and his Foreign Minister, Mr Beneš, emphasized their long-standing interest in the women's movement by receiving delegates of the ICW.

1931–32

The Sub-Committee on Cinematography and Broadcasting, established in 1925, under its Convener Mrs L. D. Barney, demonstrated its growing activity in 1931. At the request of the President of the International Educational Cinematographic Institute established by the League, Mrs Barney organized a Conference held in the building of this Institute in Rome, at which Mr Coeuroy-Bellime, Secretary of the Institute of Intellectual Co-operation, spoke on the development of broadcasting, and papers on various aspects of the cinema were presented by highly-specialized delegates of fifteen NCWs. The Secretariat of the League Committee on Intellectual Co-operation was represented at this Conference by Miss Kallia. Foremost among the subjects discussed (which included censorship, the exemption of educational films from customs duty, regulations for the safety of spectators) was the promotion of international understanding through the use of films and radio. In 1933, this Sub-Committee became an independent Standing Committee and its Convener prepared memoranda for each of the other Committees indicating how the cinema might help their work.

Economic depression and unemployment were now widespread, and difficult times lay ahead for the ICW. From 1930 on, many NCWs had been unable to pay their affiliation fees, and the task of the Treasurer, Lady Trustram Eve, became more and more difficult. Miss Günther, Editor of the *Bulletin*, and Miss van Veen, Executive Secretary of the ICW, the headquarters of which had been moved to Paris in 1930 for reasons of administrative convenience, generously worked long hours outside office time in order to save the ICW additional professional expense. Various fund-raising activities had been adopted by different NCWs to raise sums necessary for fees and travelling expenses.

During the 1930 Assembly of the League, an ICW Centre was opened in the Athénée in Geneva, proving so popular and useful that it was decided to continue this practice during successive Assemblies of the League, the permanent representation of the ICW in Geneva being assumed by Miss van Eeghen, also re-elected Corresponding Secretary in 1930 (*ICW Records 1925/30*, p. viii).

In September 1931, the Liaison Committee of Women's International Organizations established a Special Committee in support of the Conference for the Limitation and Control of Armaments called for the following year. The ICW was a foundation member of this Committee, of which Mrs L. D. Barney was elected a Vice-President. On February 6th, 1932, several truckloads of petitions bearing the signatures of over 8 million individual men and women from all parts of the world were presented in solemn procession to the Conference by the representatives of women's organizations from 56 countries whose spokesman was the President of the Committee, Miss Mary Dingman of the WYWCA, and a common programme approved by member organizations was drawn up and submitted to the Conference. A Memorandum concerning the recent efforts of individual NCWs in support of the limitation and control of armaments was later sent to the Secretary-General of the League (*Bulletin*, Feb. 1932).

1933

In May 1933 the German Frauenfront had ordered the NCW of Germany to accede to the following demands:

1. Unconditional submission to the Fuehrer.
2. Recognition of the special tasks assigned to women by the Nazi State (i.e. mainly social welfare).

3. Exclusion of Jewish members from the national Board of Officers as well as from the boards of all affiliated associations and local councils.

4. The imposed appointment of Nazi women to leading positions in the NCW.

Since the acceptance of these requirements would have violated its most sacred principles, the NCW of Germany decided to disband.

The dissolution of the German NCW saddened the delegates to the meeting of the Executive of the ICW held in Stockholm later in 1933, but the loyalty of the German Council demonstrated that the 'Golden Rule' was no empty formula to the members of the ICW.

Peace was naturally still the main preoccupation of this Executive and resolutions urged NCWs to press their governments to support all measures to strengthen the League, to observe the Covenant, and to ratify the Convention against the use of poison gas; also to ask their governments to take the necessary measures 'to prevent private interests from interfering with the common good notably in all that concerns the manufacture, sale and export of arms' (*ICW Records 1936*, p. 13).

Also uppermost in all minds at Stockholm was the problem of unemployment. A public meeting was held on Unemployment and Youth and resolutions adopted were concerned with the following: the danger of the curtailment of national budgets for education; the protection of children from the dangers resulting from long unemployment of parents; the formation of educational and recreational clubs for the unemployed.

An emergency resolution was taken on the right of married and unmarried women to determine their own nationality, and in the following year the ICW welcomed the Montevideo Treaty 'according to which the signatory States engage themselves not to establish any distinction based on sex in their legislation and regulations in matters of nationality' (*Bulletin*, July 1934, p. 7).

The year 1933 also marked the fortieth anniversary of the World's Congress of Representative Women held in Chicago in 1893, and, to celebrate this occasion, the NCW of the US, under the presidency of Miss Lena Madesin Phillips, organized in that same city, then celebrating 'a century of progress', an important International

65

Congress of Women on the theme, 'Our Common Cause, Civiliza-tion'. A series of Round Table discussions was held on subjects such as Security through Employment, and Opportunity through Education, and speakers included the Hon. Florence E. Allen, Jus-tice of the US Supreme Court, David Lilienthal, Director of the Tennessee Valley Authority, the historians Charles and Mary Beard and many distinguished delegates from outside the US. To Mrs Carrie Chapman Catt, who with Miss Jane Addams represented the generation of the pioneers of 1893, the 'greatest enjoyment' afforded by the meeting was to compare the bearing of the women of 1933 with that of those of forty years before—'no longer petitioners', but possessing 'a poise, a self-reliance . . . a knowledge' far in advance of anything the pioneers could have imagined. Mrs Catt appealed to the present generation to use their new power and confidence to seek solutions to the two great shadows overhanging the US and the rest of the world in 1933, despite all progress—namely economic depression and renewed threat of war (*Our Common Cause*).

1934—NINTH COUNCIL MEETING (FIRST TRIENNIAL) OF THE ICW, PARIS
The next meeting—the first Triennial of the ICW as decided at Vienna—took place in Paris in 1934. Mr Henri Bonnet, then Director of the International Institute of Intellectual Co-operation, had offered the ICW the use of its historic building in the Palais Royal for this Conference, and it was in this distinguished setting that the ICW held its Ninth Council Meeting, as guest of the NCW of France under the presidency of Mrs Pichon-Landry. Financial conditions were such that the Records of this first Triennial Meeting were restricted to a Special Number of the ICW *Bulletin* (July 1934). The NCWs of Iceland and Brazil had been temporarily dissolved. Since neither news nor fees had been received from Mexico, Bolivia or Uruguay, these councils were removed from the list of NCWs. No new councils were affiliated, though there was some hope for affiliations from Japan and Spain.

Once more unemployment and its effect on the right of women to work was the dominant theme. Jointly with 13 other women's organizations, the ICW held a public meeting in the Sorbonne which turned out to be 'an impressive demonstration'. It was resolved by all that 'a woman, whether married or unmarried, shall have the same right as a man to retain and obtain paid work, and (this meeting) strongly protests against any attempt to deprive her of that right'. The principle of equal pay for equal work was proclaimed an essential 'means of combatting unhealthy competition between men and women workers' (*Bulletin*, July 1934, p. 3).

This Council Meeting requested the League of Nations to appoint a Commission on the treatment of prisoners and itself undertook further investigation regarding prisons, reformatory houses and penitentiary institutions for women and children.

1935–36

By 1935 many NCWs felt compelled to demonstrate their increasing anxiety at the rapid deterioration of international relations. 'Silent peace processions' and other demonstrations were organized by NCWs in a number of cities ranging from Aberdeen to Johannesburg. Together with other women's organizations, the ICW appealed to Mussolini to halt the invasion of Abyssinia. The Peace Committees of the ICW and of the IWSA held joint open meetings in support of collective security, moral disarmament, the reduction and control of armaments and traffic in arms, and the education of youth in a spirit of international goodwill. At the IWSA Congress held at Istanbul in 1935, new proposals presented by Mrs Ogilvie Gordon on behalf of the ICW for an amalgamation of the two organizations were rejected in favour of a continuation of joint action in specific fields (*Bulletin*, May 1935).

Despite all difficulties, 1936 was a particularly active year for the ICW. A welcome new departure was the invitation of the NCW of India to a Joint Conference in Calcutta opened by the Maharani of Baroda. Among those attending this Conference were Lady Pentland (representing her mother, Lady Aberdeen), Dame Elizabeth Cadbury of Great Britain, Princess Cantacuzène of Rumania, Dr R. Girod of Switzerland, Miss J. de Buchère of Belgium and delegates of a number of other NCWs including those of Ireland, Australia and Greece. 'Never before had India had in her midst such a great gathering of renowned women' (*Calcutta Conference Souvenir*, p. 7). Discussions were held on many subjects of concern to women, particularly in India (rural welfare, the rôle of the social worker, housing, health, with special stress on maternal and infant mortality). As a result of the Conference a Rural Committee of the Indian NCW was initiated for the extension of the 'much-needed work in rural districts' already undertaken by the NCW of India. In the course of a memorable tour at the conclusion of the

Conference, delegates were able to discuss many problems with Indian leaders throughout the country (*ICW Records 1936*, p. 2).

Later in the same year, the ICW was represented by Lady Nunburnholme and Miss van Eeghen at an important Women's Dominion Conference in Johannesburg, addressed by General Smuts and organized on the occasion of the Empire Exhibition in that city by Mrs C. D. Scandrett, veteran leader of the women of the NCW of South Africa, unflinching then as now in their efforts to surmount the many social and inter-racial problems of their country.

NEW THREATS TO PEACE

1936—TENTH COUNCIL MEETING (SECOND TRIENNIAL) OF THE ICW, DUBROVNIK

Also in 1936, the ICW held its Tenth Council Meeting in Dubrovnik, at the invitation of the NCW of Yugoslavia under the presidency of Mrs Leposava Petkovitch. At this meeting, Lady Aberdeen, then aged 78, resigned as President of the ICW after 36 years of office. She now gladly handed over sceptre and gavel to Baroness Pol Boël, President of the NCW of Belgium, elected fifth President of the ICW at this meeting. Throughout the long period of her leadership, said Baroness Boël, Lady Aberdeen had given 'without stint and without limit all her abundance of personal charm, of great ability, of high station, of good health and of happy life and surroundings' (*Bulletin*, October 1938), and with her continued invaluable counsel as Hon. President Baroness Boël and the ICW prepared to set to work immediately upon the many problems then facing the Council and its 35 affiliates.

The Hon. Treasurer, Miss Karen Glaesel, had been able to set the ICW's financial arrangements on a more satisfactory basis (*ICW Records 1936*, p. 8), and it was decided at Dubrovnik that a *Lady Aberdeen Fund*, to be used for special projects, should be raised by all NCWs before the Golden Jubilee meeting due to be held in Scotland in 1938.

At Dubrovnik the long and outstanding services of Mrs Avril de Sainte-Croix and of Dame Elizabeth Cadbury were acknowledged both by their own Standing Committees (Moral Welfare and Peace respectively) which owed so much to their Convenership, and by the Council as a whole when they were elected Hon. Vice-Presidents with long applause. Tribute was also paid to Dr Alice Salomon of Germany, not, of course, present at the meeting, but re-elected Hon. Vice-President of the ICW, after 27 years of service on the Board of Officers.

A new Standing Committee was established on Housing and Rural Planning, with Lady Pentland as its first Convener, and an *ad hoc* Committee on Home Economics. The Cinema and Broadcasting Committee was divided into two separate Committees. Public meetings were held on 'Rural Problems', 'Housing' and 'Women in Industry'.

Under the chairmanship of Lady Nunburnholme (Great Britain), the revision of the Constitution and Standing Orders of the ICW was completed at two special meetings in Dubrovnik, coming into force at once (*ICW Records 1936*, p. 8).

Members of the ICW were received by Queen Marie of Yugoslavia and her mother Queen Marie of Rumania, at the former's summer residence, several hours outside Dubrovnik.

The only new candidate for affiliation was a National Committee of Women formed in Japan, but a NCW of Burma had been formed which requested permission to affiliate as soon as the British administration of Burma became separate from that of India. A group of Philippine women had announced their intention of forming a Council, on achieving independence. The civil war in Spain had provisionally ended the ICW's hope for the affiliation of a Spanish Council, and Lady Aberdeen reported ICW participation in a joint 'Message of Entreaty' to all concerned in this conflict. Representations had also been made to the Secretary-General of the League, in the hope that 'the Humanitarian Section of the League might render assistance to the suffering people of Spain, irrespective of the parties to which they belonged' (*ICW Records 1936*, pp. 7–8).

The resolutions adopted at Dubrovnik demonstrated the increasing range of ICW interests: the problems of nutrition, of a more equitable distribution of the world's resources, the place of women in the administration of broadcasting and in drawing up radio programmes, children's libraries, and the technical training of crippled children. Determined work continued on the search for solutions to such long-term problems as slavery, the suppression of the exploitation of prostitution, an international convention on the nationality of married women, equal working conditions for men

F 69

and women. Two excellent pamphlets had resulted from the recent work of ICW Committees: one by Mrs Ogilvie Gordon on *Civil and Political Status of Women* and another on the *Economic Status of Women*, by Miss C. Matheson of Great Britain, Convener of the Standing Committee on Trades and Professions.

1937–38

Two years remained for the new President to prepare for the Jubilee Meeting in Edinburgh. ICW Headquarters were removed from Paris to the President's home—the city of Brussels—where the ICW was happily able to retain the services of both Miss van Veen and Miss Günther.

Emigrants and refugees from Nazism and Fascism were now streaming across the frontiers, among them ICW Vice-President Dr Alice Salomon, who emigrated to the US. In 1938 another early Council—Austria—disappeared as a result of the German Anschluss.

Meanwhile the ICW continued its co-operation with and support for the League of Nations. In Geneva a small permanent ICW office was established in 1936 in the Palais Wilson, former home of the League, now an International Centre housing many international organizations (*ICW Records 1938*, p. 30). Dr Renée Girod (Switzerland) was appointed ICW representative in Geneva. The year 1937 saw an intensive effort on the part of the Liaison Committee of Women's International Organizations in favour of the adoption of a Convention granting equality of rights with respect to women. In 1937 the First Committee of the League, whose Rapporteur was Miss Hesselgren, President of the NCW of Sweden, proposed to the League Assembly the establishment of a Committee of Experts of both sexes to undertake an extensive study of the legal status of women. Mrs Paul Bastid, of the NCW of France (distinguished Professor of Law, later to serve as President of the Administrative Tribunal of the United Nations), was appointed a member of this Committee of outstanding jurists. During its first session in April 1938, the Committee held a meeting to hear the views of the representatives of the various international women's organizations, at which those of the ICW were expressed by Dr Girod (*ICW Records 1938*, pp. 30 and 44).

1938—ELEVENTH COUNCIL MEETING (THIRD TRIENNIAL) AND GOLDEN
JUBILEE OF THE ICW, EDINBURGH, 1938

For the third time in six years the ICW met in July 1938, to hold
its Eleventh Council Meeting and Fiftieth Anniversary in Edinburgh,
in Lady Aberdeen's home country, Scotland. The meeting place
was, most appropriately, the Assembly Hall of the Church of
Scotland, built with money raised by women members of the Free
Church of Scotland and inaugurated in 1859 by a meeting of the
Free Church Ladies Society for Female Education in India and
Africa. The hospitality of the NCW of Great Britain, under the
presidency of Lady Ruth Balfour, and of the civic authorities and
women of the City of Edinburgh contributed greatly to making this
Jubilee Council Meeting a historic occasion for ICW delegates. Two
hundred delegates also visited the Empire Exhibition in Glasgow,
where they were received by Lady Aberdeen and the Committee
responsible for the construction of the Peace Pavilion devoted to the
work of the League of Nations and of the Voluntary Peace Societies.

Fifty years had passed since the day when a few women from
eight nations had the vision to found a permanent International
Council of Women. The position of women in these countries had
altered out of all recognition since 1888. What, asked Baroness Boël,
would these pioneers who, in that year, already 'rejoiced in the
progress made by the women's movement' have said, had they been
present at the meeting on New Careers for Women, held at Edinburgh? At this meeting leading Councilwomen (including Mme
Léon Brunschwicg, French Under-Secretary of State for Education,
Miss Florence Horsburgh, British Member of Parliament and
Mrs Woytovicz, Judge of the Polish Courts) were able to speak
encouragingly of the many openings now available to women in the
fields of government, politics, magistrature, business, housing,
medicine, engineering, tourism, etc. (*ICW Records 1938*, p. 104).

Two aims, said Baroness Boël, in her opening address, had been
put before the ICW by its founders: to eliminate all inequalities
from which women suffer and to establish a women's international
point of view. For fifty years, the ICW had worked steadily towards
both these aims in a continuous endeavour to 'raise our highest
aspirations as women on to a universal plane, above the turmoil of
conflicting ideologies' (*ICW Records 1938*, p. 7). The almost world-
wide membership of the ICW, said the President, demonstrated a

71

'quasi-universality' which was its most precious possession, even though it might at times 'restrict or slow down our action'. This world-wide membership now comprised 22 NCWs in Europe, 6 in the Americas, 4 in Asia, 2 in Africa, 2 in Australasia and 3 corresponding members (Iceland, Egypt and Southern Rhodesia). Most of these Councils, very different in organization and in membership were represented on the 16 Standing Committees to which a seventeenth was now added: Home Economics, with a Polish Convener and Yugoslav Vice-Convener.

Among the problems to be studied by this Committee, that of nutrition was given particularly close attention at Edinburgh. At the public meeting on Health and Nutrition, Sir John Boyd Orr, later (1949) awarded the Nobel Peace Prize, suggested that each NCW should issue a pamphlet on nutritional standards, as established by the League, applicable in its own particular country, and see that it reached the hands of every housewife and mother in that country.

The Peace Committee was planning to celebrate its fortieth anniversary in the following year, and was determined to redouble its efforts in favour of international comprehension. A resolution reaffirmed the ICW's 'wholehearted opposition to war' and belief that the 'sanctity of international obligations is the most effective safeguard of collective security', and called for 'energetic efforts to obtain economic justice between nations' (*ICW Records 1938*, p. 88). Reaffirming its most sacred belief in the Golden Rule, the ICW unanimously adopted a resolution against persecution of persons on account of race, religion or political views.

The fate of young people in times of unemployment, poverty, war and persecution again occupied the thoughts of ICW delegates gathered in Edinburgh. Councils were asked to intensify relief work to alleviate 'famine and mental depression among children in countries which are at war and among refugee children' (*ICW Records 1938*, p. 95), a task upon which many NCWs were already actively engaged.

The League of Nations and the ILO were represented at this meeting by Miss Craig McGeachy (later Mrs Craig Schuller-McGeachy) and Mrs Thibert respectively and 'the presence of both these experienced international workers at the business sessions and Committee meetings was greatly valued' (*ICW Records 1938*, p. 103).

Baroness Boël presided over her first full Council Meeting with 'clarity, firmness and good grace'. Never at a loss to clarify and sum up discussions, she won the sympathy of many delegates by the modesty with which she deferred to Lady Aberdeen—the 'Grannie' of the ICW—whose 80th birthday was being celebrated at the same time as the Council Meeting. Many NCWs had made a special effort to send strong delegations to this Jubilee Meeting.

Referring to the virtual disappearance of the NCW of Austria, the President urged delegates not to be cast down by any vicissitude: 'We are convinced that the future belongs to those who, like ourselves, believe that active collaboration between women, whatever their way of thinking, or the colour of their skin, can alone provide more happiness, more stability and therefore more peace in a world which is momentarily unsettled' (*ICW Records 1938*, p. 21). Political conditions made it impossible for the ICW to decide where the next Triennial should be held, but tentative plans were made to hold in 1942 a Conference in Australia, similar to that convened in Calcutta by the NCW of India in 1936.

Such was the ICW on the eve of the Second World War—a still-growing organization with a wise and eminent leader, experienced in suffering and endurance, convinced of the great rôle of the International Council as a world-wide women's forum aiming 'not to obtain the speediest results, but always to pursue the highest aims' (*Bulletin*, October 1938).

BIBLIOGRAPHICAL REFERENCES

PART II

1914-38

Bulletin—Periodical Publication of the ICW (English, French, German editions) —1922-38.
ICW Records—*Juvenile Delinquency: its causes and methods of prevention and correction*, ICW, 1913-1914.
ICW Records 1914—*Report of the Fifth Quinquennial Meeting of the ICW in Rome, 1914*. Ed. Countess of Aberdeen, Karlsruhe, 1914.
ICW Records 1920—*Transactions of the Sixth Quinquennial Meeting of the ICW in Kristiania, 1920*. Ed. Marchioness of Aberdeen and Temair.
ICW Records 1920/22, 1922/23, 1923/24—*Annual Reports of the ICW*. Ed. Mrs Anna Backer.
ICW Records 1925—*Report of the Seventh Quinquennial Meeting of the ICW, Washington, 1925*. Ed. Marchioness of Aberdeen and Temair.
ICW Records 1925/27—*Biennial Report of the ICW*. Ed. Miss Elsie Zimmern.
ICW Records 1925/30—*Record of Quinquennial Period 1925/30 and Transactions of ICW Eighth Quinquennial Meeting in Vienna, 1930*. Ed. Marchioness of Aberdeen and Temair.
ICW Records 1936—*President's Memorandum regarding the Council Meeting of the ICW held at Dubrovnik, 1936*.

ICW Records 1938—*President's Memorandum regarding the Council Meeting of the ICW held in Edinburgh, 1938.*

Joint Committee—Ten years activity 1926–1936. Palais Royal, Paris, 1936.

Our Common Cause: Civilization: Report of the International Congress of Women, Chicago, 1933. NCW of US, New York, 1933.

Calcutta Conference Souvenir, January 1936. Art Press, Calcutta.

PART III: 1939–63

1939—SECOND WORLD WAR AND RECONSTRUCTION

AFTER THE EDINBURGH JUBILEE, NCWs and Standing Committees set to work on the far-reaching plans established at that meeting. The care of the increasing numbers of refugees driven from their homes by the advancing tide of Nazism and Fascism became, however, the prime concern of many NCWs, for the illusory hope of 'Peace in our time', born at Munich in the autumn of 1938, soon gave way to preparation for war on every side.

The first six months of 1939, a year which was to prove the end of an era in so many ways, saw the death of three of the early leaders of the ICW; Lady Aberdeen, Mrs Avril de Sainte-Croix and Dame Maria Ogilvie Gordon, thus spared the storm which destroyed so many of their hopes.

Meeting in Belgium in the spring of 1939, as Czechoslovakia followed Austria under Nazi domination, the ICW Board of Officers chose this tragic moment—to reaffirm the basic principles of the ICW:

Recognition of right based on justice, respect of the human personality, moral and physical, reprobation of all violence, both as a means and as an end (*Bulletin*, April 1939).

A dramatic highlight of the meeting was the unhoped for—and unhappily last—appearance of Senator Plaminkova of Czechoslovakia, whose courageous leadership of the women of her country was shortly to lead to her imprisonment and execution.

In September 1939, the outbreak of the Second World War shattered the last hopes of maintaining peace. Baroness Boël at once sent out the following message to ICW members:

At a time when the world is plunged in gloom, we must have more faith than ever in our collective effort; we must reaffirm our unshaken will to build up a world from which violence will be forever banished (*Bulletin*, October 1939).

1940–44

Those members of the Board of Officers still able to leave their countries met once more in Brussels, in February 1940. Contact with

75

Czechoslovakia and Poland was already severed, while from the faithful NCW of invaded Finland, anxious to communicate once more with the ICW before the ways were closed, came a moving message and financial contribution.

Baroness Boël, convinced that the so-called 'phoney-war' was no more than a respite, took steps to ensure the continuation of the ICW should Belgium—once more in the front line of defence against the German armies—be invaded. 'We shall all be involved,' she said, 'Switzerland alone may escape,' and, turning to Dr Girod, asked her if she might count upon her to take her place as President in case of need. 'The ICW must go on; we must maintain contact with one another, however tenuous.'

Three weeks after the invasion of Belgium on May 10th, 1940, Dr Girod received a copy of a message from Baroness Boël asking her to take over the Presidency of the ICW. The little ICW office on the Quai Wilson in Geneva sprang into life as the temporary centre of the ICW. Not only was censorship a major obstacle, but funds were inevitably lacking. Only the generosity and devotion of friends in Switzerland and of those Councils still able to convey their contributions to Geneva enabled Dr Girod to continue. As early as June 1940, assisted by Miss van Eeghen, who acted as Hon. Treasurer, Dr Girod was able to despatch an emergency 4-page issue of the *Bulletin*, in the hope that it might serve as 'the connecting link between those women of goodwill who wish to maintain, in spite of everything, the ideas of the ICW' (*Bulletin*, September 1940).

Few official records are available of the work of most NCWs during the war years. In Europe many Councils were dissolved, obliged to meet in clandestinity or to cease all activity. Others were busy with the reception of new flows of refugees and urgent war relief—the terrible proportions of which did not, however, blind them to the problems of post-war reconstruction.

As early as July 1940 it was evident that London was becoming the main international centre. The governments of nine invaded countries were functioning from that city, and thousands of refugees, among them officers and members of the ICW, managed against increasing odds to make their way to Great Britain to continue the struggle. The Liaison Committee of Women's International Organizations, set up an Inter-Allied Advisory Committee which organized courses for Allied women wishing to prepare for relief work in their own countries on the cessation of hostilities, and consulted with Allied Governments in Exile on the question of equal rights for women in plans for post-war national legislations.

After the total occupation of France in November 1942, contacts between Dr Girod in Geneva and Lady Nunburnholme, First Vice-President of the ICW, in London, were finally severed. With the encouragement of the Hon. Mrs Home Peel, President of the NCW of Great Britain, Lady Nunburnholme opened a Supplementary Office of the ICW in her own home in London, where the *Bulletin* was subsequently edited (1944–46), with the collaboration of Miss Retchford, Vice-President of the ICW Press Committee, and other volunteers of the NCW of Great Britain.

1944–47—POST-WAR RECONSTRUCTION OF THE ICW

In September 1944, Brussels was liberated. 'Slowly, very slowly, the silence which had surrounded us disappeared and we were able to renew contact with other parts of the world,' Baroness Boël recounted later (*ICW Records 1947*, p. 85). As soon as possible she got into touch with Dr Girod and Lady Nunburnholme, but Belgium was still too much in the front line for work to be resumed at once in Brussels.

Immediately after the cessation of hostilities in Europe, an unofficial Board Meeting was held in London in June 1945 attended by the President, Lady Nunburnholme, Miss Madesin Phillips (US), Miss Fernande Baetens (Belgium) and Miss Cecile Mathesen (Great Britain). It was decided that ICW Headquarters should return from Geneva to Brussels, but that the *Bulletin* should continue to be published in London. In June 1945, Miss van Veen, faithful ICW Executive Secretary, returned to Belgium and the ICW once more took possession of the office it had occupied until 1940. Part of the furniture was recuperated, but all archives and documents had been taken by the occupying forces (*Bulletin*, June 1946, p. 9). Baroness Boël later described as 'real detective work' the task of getting into touch once more with former ICW members and collaborators.

In September, the President was able to travel to Geneva to renew international contacts with Dr Girod and others. A Board Meeting held in London in October, on the occasion of the fiftieth Jubilee Conference of the NCW of Great Britain, was attended also by the Conveners of a number of Committees. A survey of the position of

NCWs was made and the possibilities of work for Standing Committees reviewed.

Next came the meeting of the Executive Committee in Brussels in June 1946. Thirty-three members were present, representing 13 Councils out of the remaining 21. The war had taken a heavy toll. Vice-President Plaminkova, President of the NCW of Czechoslovakia, had been imprisoned and executed by the Nazis, leaving to the women of her country and of the world a precious legacy of 'courage, fortitude and faith' (*ICW Records 1947*, p. 67). The President of the NCW of Rumania, also Vice-President of the ICW, Princess Cantacuzéne, had died imprisoned in a room of her own home. Rosa Manus of the NCW of the Netherlands, Mrs Siemienska of the Polish Council and other members of European Councils had suffered and died in concentration camps (*Bulletin*, June 1946, p. 2). The Baltic Councils were lost, and no news was available from Bulgaria, Yugoslavia or Portugal. The NCW of Hungary had been dissolved. Some hope was, however, entertained of renewing contacts with Poland and Czechoslovakia, and an organizer was already at work in Austria.

FIRST CONTACTS WITH UNITED NATIONS AND SPECIALIZED AGENCIES

Faithful to its principle of international co-operation, and strong in its experience with the League of Nations, the ICW lost no time in entering into contact with the new international governmental organization, the United Nations. At the San Francisco Conference in 1945 the ICW had been represented by Mrs Egerton Parsons of the NCW of the US. In February 1946 a written communication was sent to Mr Paul-Henri Spaak, President of the first UN Assembly in London, while Baroness Boël participated in a delegation from the Liaison Committee of Women's International Organizations to Sir Ramaswami Mudaliar, Chairman of the First Session of the Economic and Social Council, offering the collaboration of the principal women's organizations to this body, as authorized under Article 71 of the UN Charter (*Bulletin*, June 1946, p. 7).

The ICW Liaison Officer with the League of Nations International Institute of Intellectual Co-operation, Mrs L. Dreyfus Barney, was asked to assume similar responsibilities in relation to the United Nations and the Specialized Agencies then in process of formation, and the years 1946–48 saw the establishment of working relations between the ICW and the ECOSOC, the UN Food and Agriculture Organization, the UN Educational, Scientific and Cultural Organization, the World Health Organization and the International Refugee Organization.

As early as June 1946, a resolution adopted by the ICW Executive concerning the problems of refugees and displaced persons was submitted to the Second Session of the ECOSOC which was also requested to transform the recently created Sub-Commission on the Status of Women into a full Commission (*ICW Records 1947*, p. 87), and in March 1947 the ICW was one of the first group of 31 NGOs granted Consultative Status B with the ECOSOC, offered to NGOs 'concerned with matters within its competence'. This was to be the starting point of a very close and fruitful co-operation with the ECOSOC and its principal Commissions which has since become an integral part of the work of the ICW.

Early in the same year, a Conference of International Non-Governmental Organizations (NGOs) was convened at Lake Success with a view to establishing working channels for information on UN to all parts of the world and to all types of organized public opinion. In addition to the Liaison Officer, a strong ICW delegation included Mrs Bodil Begtrup, President of the NCW of Denmark and Chairman of the Status of Women Commission, Mrs Edgar D. Hardy of Canada, Vice-President of the ICW, and Miss D. Lewis and Miss H. Havener, Conveners of the ICW Standing Committees on Broadcasting and the Cinema respectively (*Bulletin*, March 1947).

In September 1946 the ICW was represented by Mrs Carlton Smith at the Copenhagen Conference of the new Food and Agriculture Organization (FAO). In Washington in June 1947, on the strong recommendation of the Director-General of this body, Sir John Boyd Orr, the ICW was granted Consultative Status as one of twelve international NGOs 'interested in the promotion of one or more of the specific aims of FAO', thus giving recognition to the long and active interest of the ICW in the preservation of natural resources and sites, of rural welfare and housing, in the promotion of agriculture and in education in nutrition and home economics (*ICW Records 1947*, p. 87; *1951*, p. 30).

Relations with UNESCO had the advantage of being a direct continuation of the long and close collaboration of the ICW (both as an individual organization and as a member of the *Comité d'Entente* of Major International Organizations) with the former

Institute of Intellectual Co-operation. Since UNESCO preferred to co-operate with NGOs on an individual basis, the *Comité d'Entente* was dissolved in 1946. In the same year the ICW Liaison Officer together with Mrs Pichon-Landry, President of the NCW of France, and Mrs Puech, Convener of the ICW Standing Committee on Education, represented the ICW at the first General Conference of UNESCO. Early in 1947, Baroness Boël attended the meeting for the organization of a Temporary International Council for Education Reconstruction (*Bulletin*, March 1947, p. 88). The following year the ICW was granted consultative status (Category B) with UNESCO.

With the United Nations Children's Emergency Fund, established by the General Assembly in 1946, the ICW together with a very small number of NGOs active in the field of child welfare, collaborated from the very beginning, when its efforts were primarily directed to the emergency supply of food and milk to children in war-devastated countries. The active participation of a number of NCWs (in particular that of Greece) in the field work of UNICEF gradually increased as this organization, partly at the insistence of NGOs, extended its activities to combating and preventing disease among children in all parts of the world.

The ICW had never ceased to maintain relations with the International Labour Organization and had been represented at International Labour Conferences held during and immediately after the war in Philadelphia, Montreal and Geneva (*ICW Records 1947*, p. 88)

In 1947, the ICW welcomed the World Health Organization Interim Commission in the hope that when it became a Specialized Agency it would develop 'vital service' in the fields of 'children's health, maternal care and the protection of the health of the industrial worker' in which the ICW had an 'historic and inherent interest' (*ICW Records 1947*, p. 40).

1947—TWELFTH COUNCIL MEETING (FOURTH TRIENNIAL) OF THE ICW, PHILADELPHIA

In September 1947, nine years after the memorable Jubilee Conference in Edinburgh, the Twelfth Council Meeting of the ICW was held in the University of Pennsylvania, Philadelphia, US. The NCW of the United States, under the Presidency of Mrs Ambrose N. Diehl, had not only invited the ICW to hold its first post-war Triennial in its country of origin, but also offered generous financial assistance to delegates of NCWs from war-devastated countries who would not otherwise have been able to attend. The ICW, said Baroness Boël in her Presidential Report, had survived a critical period in its history. Thanks to the wisdom of its Constitution, 'the Council has kept its appeal, that of an organization capable of voicing the opinion of free women' (*ICW Records 1947*, p. 90). Membership had been reduced from 36 NCWs in 1938 to 21 in 1947. In Europe alone 12 NCWs had disappeared.

Many familiar faces were, however, to be recognized, though marked by years of suffering. But many gaps were deeply felt by all the delegates, and tributes paid to Senator Plaminkova of Czechoslovakia and other Nazi victims. Nevertheless the Golden Rule remained the keynote of the Council meeting, and the first contacts with the women of post-war Germany were reported. Mrs von Zahn Harnack, President of the NCW of Germany at the time of its dissolution in 1932 and Mrs Theanolte Bähnisch, Doctor of Law, President of the Government District of Hanover, were at work organizing local groups of German women. Already in 1946 they had been invited to England by the International Relations Committee of the NCW of Great Britain under the Chairmanship of Lady Nunburnholme, and a German observer from the Western Occupation Zones had subsequently been invited to attend the Philadelphia Meeting (*Bulletin*, December 1946; July 1950, *Review*, January 1959). An organizer for Austria was also present, while applications for new affiliations had been received from NCWs in Southern Rhodesia, and Nyasaland, as well as from the Women's Advisory Council of the New Life Movement in China.

The Philadelphia meeting was in many respects reminiscent of the Quinquennial Council Meeting at Oslo in 1920. Held shortly after the conclusion of a great world war, both ushered in an entirely new period of work for the ICW; new personalities came forward, a new President was elected, new and urgent tasks required the elaboration of a new programme. During both wars NCWs had been active serving their countries in different ways, often under the greatest difficulties, particularly in zones of enemy occupation, with the subsequent need to re-adapt to post-war needs. Standing Committees had not met for many years and their terms of reference required fresh definition. Like 1920, 1947 was a crucial year for the ICW, once more required to prove itself flexible enough to adapt to new conditions, yet stable enough to adhere to its fundamental principles in a rapidly evolving world.

At Philadelphia a group system of discussion first tried out in Brussels before the war was adopted whereby several Committees met together to hear reports and discuss urgent questions from the different points of view of their Committees, and the work plans of individual Committees were drawn up only after a thorough review of all sides of the problems involved.

To reaffirm the position of the ICW, a formal Declaration was adopted to precede the Resolutions voted at Philadelphia, recapitulating the ICW standpoint on many issues and restating

> its faith in the idea which it has upheld for nearly 60 years: to unite women of the whole world without distinction of race, nationality, faith or class in order to promote the welfare of the individual, the family and humanity (*ICW Records 1947*, p. 33).

The first Resolution adopted at Philadelphia was an expression of 'unequivocal' support for the proposed agreement for a Convention for the Prevention and Punishment of Genocide by an International Criminal Tribunal. The second urged the drafting of an international Convention on the Condemnation of War Crimes affecting the civilian population in occupied countries, with special reference to those affecting women.

Other Resolutions pledged the support of the ICW to the UN Appeal for Children (UNAC), and to the newly-created International Refugee Organization (IRO) and asked NCWs to 'urge the signature and ratification of all those Conventions drafted by the UN and its Specialized Agencies as well as those of the League of Nations still in vigour that meet the aims of the ICW'. Noting that 'in spite of war devastation, destruction, retardation, an educational revival is apparent throughout the world', the ICW urged

> that a full and adequate education should become available to every human being even in the remotest rural areas, thus assuring the maintenance of culture and the full development of personality, and that instruction in citizenship should cover responsibilities for home life as well as for the life of the community (*ICW Records 1947*, p. 43).

Equal pay for equal work, equality of opportunity for the training and retraining of girls and women, the provision of home assistance for mothers in need, improved housing conditions and the inclusion of women on housing committees and in national police forces were also recommended. In the field of culture it was urged that women as well as men should be assured of free time 'to share in the intellectual, spiritual and artistic life of their country'. The arduous task of Hon. Recording Secretary, vitally important to the proper conduct of the Council and to the constitution of its archives had, from the very beginning of Council history, been entrusted to distinguished members of the ICW Board of Officers. The first post-war team of Hon. Recording Secretaries, elected at Philadelphia and led until 1954 by the Hon. Mrs Home Peel, Magistrate, and former President and Parliamentary Secretary of the NCW of Great Britain, was, like others before it, to render tireless and valued service to the ICW, sometimes in difficult circumstances, for many years to come.

This meeting was Baroness Boël's last Council Meeting as President of the ICW. She now felt she should pass the office to a younger woman while still able to be of assistance to her successor. In her opening speech on 'Power and Responsibilities of Freedom', the retiring President, who throughout her life had always insisted on women's responsibilities and duties rather than on their rights, foreshadowed the new spirit of assistance to under-developed countries: 'The education of women who have not yet reached your standard,' said Baroness Boël, 'is your responsibility.' As long as somewhere in the world woman is still treated as a slave, 'the rights we have fought for may be called in question, and the emancipation of women is but a word. The position of women anywhere affects their position everywhere' (*ICW Records 1947*, p. 58).

For some time past, Baroness Boël had been impressed by the qualifications of Mrs Jeanne Eder-Schweitzer, Ph.D. of the University of Zürich, Switzerland, a woman of great intelligence and authority, of keen scientific mind, whom she consequently invited to her home to meet the Board at its last meeting prior to the Philadelphia Conference. As a result of this meeting, Mrs Eder was officially proposed as Presidential candidate, and at Philadelphia was elected fifth President of the ICW.

1947–49—THE ICW IN THE POST-WAR WORLD

Immediately after Philadelphia, Mrs Eder began her heavy task with the efficiency and energy known of her in international circles. Not only must Headquarters be found in her home city of Zürich, and the ICW office transferred there from Brussels, but, owing to the resignation of Miss van Veen, Executive Secretary, after twenty-two years of service, a new Executive Secretary had to be found and trained. Happily Miss van Veen was able to go to Zürich to help establish the new Secretariat and subsequently continued to serve the ICW first as Convener of the Finance Committee and later as Hon. Treasurer. When succeeded in this onerous task in 1957 by her compatriot Miss ten Bruggen Cate, financial expert and President of the NCW of Holland, Miss van Veen became an Hon. Vice-President of the ICW.

The administrative period 1947–50 was of necessity a time of re-adjustment for the ICW and many of its Standing Committees and NCWs. Not only were the President and the Executive Secretary new to their tasks, but only four Conveners and Vice-Conveners had previous experience of these positions.

In all difficulties, Mrs Eder was able to turn to her predecessor in office, Baroness Boël, who, as Hon. President, continued to attend meetings of the Board, of the Executive and of the Council for several years. In the summer of 1953, a memorable Board Meeting took place like many before it, but for the last time, in Baroness Boël's country estate of Le Chenoy.

From 1948 the *Bulletin* was published in Zürich. Financial considerations unfortunately precluded the production of a publication as outstanding as the French, German and English issues edited in pre-war years by Miss Günther. The tasks of editing and proof-reading were shared by Mrs Eder and her small office staff, and a single edition with articles in French and English had to suffice to renew links between NCWs and to keep ICW members informed of the rapidly multiplying activities of the international organizations.

Mrs Eder fully appreciated the importance of regular and efficient co-operation between the ICW and the UN. An ICW delegation was received by Mr Bramuglia (Argentine) President of the UN Assembly held in Paris in 1948, and steps taken to reinforce contacts between ICW Headquarters and the UN Secretariat. Mrs Coleman, a professional librarian was engaged as Assistant Executive Secretary, and a catalogue of all relevant UN publications and documents established. Meanwhile Miss Helen Gmür, Ph.D. of Brown University, (US), the young Swiss Executive Secretary, was encouraged by Mrs Eder to apply for one of the UN internships designed to give NGO personnel first-hand experience of UN work.

In 1949 a tribute was paid to the ICW as senior women's international organization by the election of its President to chair the important meeting of experts organized by UNESCO on the subject of Obstacles to the Equality of Educational Opportunity for Women. The ICW submitted a report and proposed a resolution sponsored by the NCW of Egypt (newly affiliated by written vote) regarding the urgent need for special fundamental education programmes for women (*Bulletin*, March 1950).

In January 1948, the NCW of Greece issued an urgent protest against the abduction of children from Greece to Yugoslavia, Bulgaria, Albania, Rumania and Hungary, which was immediately forwarded by the ICW to the UN. This was followed, in May, by a second appeal from Greece, and in July the ICW proposed the following addition to Article 14 of the Declaration of Human Rights:

> Both parents shall have the same rights over their children. Children are not to be forcibly removed from their parents except in the special cases regulated by law (*Bulletin*, July 1948).

This addition was not accepted for inclusion in the Declaration and the urgent problem of the abducted children was one to which the ICW was to devote much time and energy during the next few years.

1949–50

The first meeting (other than those of the ICW Board of Officers) chaired by the new President took place in Lugano (Switzerland) where the Executive and several Standing Committees met in June 1949.

Lugano stands in the history of the ICW as the occasion on which the NCWs of Austria and Italy were readmitted to the ICW, and when Mrs Bähnisch, now President of a small but active group of German women in the British zone of occupation, was appointed Hon. Organizer for a NCW in Germany. This group soon expanded all over Western Germany and, as the *Deutsche Frauenring*, became the second National Council of German Women in 1951. Austria's *Bund Oesterreichischer Frauenvereine*, dissolved in 1938, was re-affiliated without difficulty at Lugano. In Italy, however, the situation was complicated by the fact that two different groups of women desired affiliation as the NCW of Italy. After serious consideration of the claims of both groups, the Board proposed and the Executive adopted a resolution granting provisional recognition as NCW of Italy to the organization founded by the recent Congress of Milan (1949) whose methods of work corresponded closely to those of the ICW, at the same time recommending both parties to hold a joint Assembly and unite their forces.

Resolutions on current international problems called on NCWs to help in the settlement of refugees and displaced persons, and protested against the prolonged detention of men and women in forced labour camps.

Another important resolution protested against the separation of parents and children, with special reference to the Greek children, and was followed in January 1950 by a direct appeal to Marshall Tito of Yugoslavia and to the Prime Ministers of other countries assumed to be harbouring Greek children, urgently requesting them 'to reunite the Greek children and their parents or relatives' (*Bulletin*, January 1950). A favourable reply was received from Yugoslavia. In the course of the next few years many Greek children were returned from that country to Greece or to join their families in other countries. Meanwhile the ICW continued to press for UN action to secure the return of the abducted children and to follow closely the admirable work of the Red Cross, through whose efforts some 5,000 of the 28,000 children were eventually repatriated.

Early in 1950 a new blow fell upon the women of Czechoslovakia. Almost eight years after the execution of her friend and co-worker Senator Plaminkova, Milada Horakova, who, after liberation from years of suffering in the Nazi fortress of Terezin had reorganized the NCW of Czechoslovakia in 1945, was arrested and condemned to death by the government of that country. Despite an appeal by the ICW to the Secretary-General of UN and of direct approaches by many NCWs to the Czech government, Milada Horakova was executed in the last days of June 1950.

1951—THIRTEENTH COUNCIL MEETING (FIFTH TRIENNIAL) OF THE ICW, ATHENS

The next Council Meeting of the ICW was held in Athens in March 1951—the first large Congress held in that city since the war. In her opening speech Mrs Eder thanked the NCW of Greece, under the Presidency of Mrs Elmine Pantelaki, for their 'courageous' invitation to meet in a country so recently torn by civil war. 'We have come to your country,' she said, 'not because of its ancient monuments and glorious past, nor because of its beauty and its sunshine, but because we know your country has suffered beyond imagination, but not beyond your fortitude.' The organization of the Council

Meeting, despite certain material difficulties, was remarkably successful, and the linguistic and diplomatic gifts displayed by Mrs Eder enabled her to preside with calm and efficiency over debates in which feelings were often forcefully expressed.

At the brief opening ceremony held on the Acropolis on March 29th, delegates heard a moving speech by Baroness Boël on the theme of the contribution of Greek civilization to the dignity of the individual and the rights of man (*Bulletin*, May 1951).

At the first public meeting Queen Frederika of Greece honoured the ICW by a short address of welcome to delegates as 'messengers of a new faith', expressing the hope that 'the tragic fate of the abducted Greek children' might become 'a symbol to rouse the dormant spirit of our modern civilization into at last fulfilling its mission' (*ICW Records 1951*, p. 11).

After the heavy losses of the ICW as a result of the war, it was heartening to see the delegates of eight new or reaffiliated Councils walk into the Conference Hall to take their places to the accompaniment of loud applause: Austria, the Dominican Republic, Egypt, Germany, Italy, Lebanon, Hong Kong and Uganda. Though still sadly depleted in Europe, the ICW was gradually expanding its membership and gaining ground in other continents.

'Woman as Custodian of Life' was the theme of Mrs Eder's opening address at Athens, in which she defined as follows the task of modern woman: 'to make her own values in due measure recognized in family, community and country, and to place the fields of human activity that to her are important in their right and equitable place within society . . . respect for individual needs, love for the sufferer, gentleness and understanding' (*ICW Records 1951*, p. 7).

Meeting in Athens, it was natural for the ICW to return once more to the problem of the Greek children, and a resolution was passed asking the UN to study the means, 'if necessary through moral, economic or other sanctions', of inducing Member States of UN to respect integrally their international obligations. The threat implied by the use of words 'and other sanctions' caused much discussion and led to 60 abstentions in the final vote, some NCWs and individual members feeling that this clause infringed the non-political proviso of the ICW Constitution. This experience, among others, subsequently led to a change in Article II Paragraph 2 of the Constitution. To the sentence excluding ICW intervention in 'political and religious questions of a controversial nature affecting the inter-relationship of two or more countries', the following phrase was added in 1954 'excepting those affecting fundamental human rights and freedoms'.

Wishing to introduce younger women to the international work of the ICW, Baroness Boël proposed at Athens the addition of four non-voting members to the Board of Officers. One of the first of these Junior Board members was Mrs Mary Craig Schuller-Mc-Geachy, former member of the Secretariat of the League of Nations, recently Director of the Social Welfare Division of the United Nations Rehabilitation and Relief Administration, and at this time Chairman of the Peace and International Relations Committee of the NCW of South Africa.

Peace was again the subject of the first resolution voted at Athens: recognizing 'in the light of terrible experience that the once wide-spread belief in disarmament as a means to peace is a fallacy unless the UN has both the moral authority and the material and physical power to maintain peace and protect human liberty', the ICW welcomed the recognition of the General Assembly that 'striving for social and economic justice' was inseparable from 'striving for a lasting peace' and called upon its NCWs to:

1. Support and develop the moral authority of the UN in all countries.

2. To help assure the UN the power to forestall and overcome aggression.

3. To maintain ceaseless vigilance over such power in order to ensure its use only in the cause of peace and liberty.

This Resolution was followed by another urging NCWs to press their governments to accept effective international control of atomic energy under the UN and requesting the latter to draft 'a Convention condemning the use of all weapons of mass destruction'.

The report of the Liaison Officer to the UN, which had recently been transferred from Lake Success to New York, showed that the ICW was meanwhile intensifying its co-operation with UN and the Specialized Agencies in accordance with the resolutions adopted at Philadelphia. After the early months of exploratory experience, reported the Liaison Officer at Athens, it had become evident that one person could no longer conscientiously fulfil all the requirements of this position. She had therefore enlisted the valuable aid of Mrs William Barclay Parsons, Vice-Convener of the International

Standing Committee on Peace and International Relations. Further assistance soon became necessary and Mrs Parsons had introduced to work at UN Mrs Eunice Carter and Mrs Frances Freeman. Thanks to the work of this team during this pioneer period of UN/NGO relations the ICW had been able to cover UN meetings of importance to Council work, to emphasize ICW viewpoints to UN officials and delegates, and to draw the attention of ICW Headquarters to essential UN decisions and projects, as well as to opportunities for appropriate ICW intervention or action.

It was also at this time that Mrs A. DeWitt Stetten, Vice-Convener (later Convener) of the ICW Standing Committee on Peace and International Relations, suggested and developed an extensive and much-needed hospitality plan, carried out by the Hospitality Committee of the NCW of the US, for welcoming and guiding women attending UN conferences or visiting the US to study questions of social or cultural interest.

In addition to the regular 'briefing' sessions for NGO representatives at UN Headquarters, at which current UN projects were the object of a free exchange of views between the Secretariat and NGOs, the UN Department of Information had in 1949 extended the range of its activities to organize Regional Meetings of NGOs with the aim of interesting public opinion in various areas of the world in the work of the UN and its Agencies and the ICW had been represented at those held in Geneva (1949), Bangkok (1950) and Bali (1951).

Collaboration between NGOs in Consultative Status had proved desirable both in the interests of the NGOs themselves and those of the UN and its Agencies and in 1947/48 the ICW Liaison Officer was instrumental in creating the Conference and Committee of NGOs in Consultative Status with the ECOSOC, and the ICW subsequently encouraged the formation of similar groups of NGOs in Consultative Status with the FAO, UNESCO and UNICEF.

Since the foundation of the League of Nations, inter-governmental and non-governmental organizations had evolved considerably in their relationship with one another: starting out with a certain diffidence, continuous co-operation throughout the years of the League and of the UN had resulted in a relationship based firmly on mutual confidence, and on a common recognition of the fact that, as the Liaison Officer told the ICW 'the voluntary organizations touch people in an intimate way which cannot be done by official institutions'. Thus, on the one side, UN and its Agencies periodically requested NGOs to provide information not always readily available from government sources, and encouraged them to inform public opinion on subjects upon which the voice of the people could facilitate national ratification and implementation of UN Conventions, Recommendations and Resolutions.

The ICW, on the other hand, and the rapidly increasing number of NGOs in Consultative Status, could and did avail themselves of the facilities offered under Article 71 of the Charter to present their views to the Economic and Social Council. A close and permanent relationship was thus built up between the ICW and the various Commissions of the ECOSOC, notably the Social Commission, the Commission on Human Rights and the Commission on the Status of Women.

Mrs. Frances Freeman, now ICW Consultant with UNICEF, was currently serving as Vice-Chairman of the Advisory Committee of NGOs which the ICW had been instrumental in creating at Geneva in 1949. She reported to the Athens Council Meeting that the work of this Committee in helping to plan the extension of UNICEF activities in child and maternal welfare and in stimulating the co-operation of national branches of NGOs in the field work of this organization, had been a contributory factor in the recent decision of the General Assembly to prolong indefinitely the life of the original 'Emergency' Fund, which had now become a permanent UN activity.

At Athens (as at succeeding ICW Triennials at Helsinki and Montreal), the UN was represented by Mrs Mary Tenison Woods, since 1950 Chief of the Status of Women Section of the Secretariat, expert in the legal aspects of child welfare and former advisor to the NCW of Australia. The Specialized Agencies (notably ILO, FAO, UNESCO) as well as UNICEF were also regularly represented at ICW Council Meetings.

A number of important resolutions adopted at Athens, resulted from the careful work of the Laws and Suffrage Committee, under its Convener, Miss Fernande Baetens of Belgium, Doctor of Law and Barrister of the Brussels Appeals Court, whose sound judgment and profound knowledge of international law was of inestimable value of the ICW during her years as Convener, and as Hon. Vice-President. These resolutions drew the attention of international bodies then engaged in drafting Conventions to important points concerning women's political, civil, inheritance, marriage, nationality, pension and taxation rights. Another resolution welcomed the long-awaited ILO proposal for an International Convention on Equal Pay and urged prior consultation with women workers' organizations. The Migration Committee was particularly concerned with the work of NCWs towards the settlement of 'hardcore' refugees, and other Committees presented resolutions on the need for instruction on the dangers of the misuse of narcotics, alcohol and other stimulants, as well as with means of improving living conditions in rural areas, and the use of broadcasting in the service of adult education (*ICW Records 1951*, pp. 106–16).

Thirty-five out of 37 Resolutions passed at Athens dealt with subjects of concern to the UN or its Agencies and special measures were taken to see that these resolutions reached delegates to the Commissions on Human Rights and Status of Women, in session in Geneva and New York respectively at the conclusion of the Athens meeting of the ICW. As soon as published these resolutions were circulated in the normal manner to members of the July session of the ECOSOC and to the appropriate high officials of UN, ILO, UNESCO, FAO, UNICEF, WHO, and to the High Commissioner for Refugees. In November, a delegation of Board Members presented these resolutions to Mr Padillo Nervo of Mexico, President of the UN General Assembly held in Paris (*Bulletin*, January 1952, p. 24).

1951–52

For Mrs Eder, the year 1951 was to be the climax of her period of office. Shortly after the successful Conference at Athens, she was invited by the Australian Government to attend the Commonwealth Jubilee Celebrations in Canberra, after which she was flown on a tour of the whole country, visiting every State Council federated into the NCW of Australia, meeting Council members informally in many local branches as well as addressing public meetings in Perth, Adelaide, Melbourne, Brisbane, Hobart and Sydney. This visit, the first made by an ICW President to Councils which, though in a continent far removed from ICW Headquarters, were among the oldest, most energetic and internationally-minded of NCWs, proved a great experience for Mrs Eder, who also had the advantage of visiting the NCW of New Zealand and a number of its local branches and, on her way home round the world, the NCWs of Canada and the USA.

In September 1952, the Executive Committee met at Reading, England, where they were welcomed by the Marchioness of Reading, then Vice-Convener of the ICW Standing Committee on Child Welfare. Since most delegates were housed in one of the women's Halls of Residence of the University, contacts were particularly close and constant, and Reading proved to be an excellent meeting-place for an Executive Committee, the object of which has always been to concentrate on the development and execution of ICW work programmes. The reports of the eight Standing Committees meeting at Reading show intensive work on the following subjects: Child Welfare—a study of relative merits of placement of homeless children in institutions or in family care, undertaken at the request of the Social Affairs Division of UN; Housing—the need to educate women concerning the control and restriction of rents; Trades and Professions—opportunities of work for older women. The Broadcasting Committee considered a report on television by Mrs E. Sprott of Great Britain, one of its Vice-Conveners, presented at a time when, as the Canadian Convener of this Committee, Miss E. Long, pointed out, few countries could speak with authority on the effect of television on the family and on the home (*Bulletin*, April 1953). The Migration Committee had exchanged extensive information on the adaptation of refugees to their country of immigration. The Arts and Letters Committee examined a report on the prejudicial effects of 'horror comics' on young readers and reviewed the work of the Music Section established in 1951, which had conducted inquiries into the position of women as students, performers, teachers and composers of music. Miss Mary Shaw (Great Britain), Vice-Convener, also informed the Committee of the work of the International Council of Music and urged NCWs to support the creation of Music Councils in their respective countries.

At Reading the question of steps for the preservation of ICW archives—national and international—was raised before the Board of Officers, which agreed that measures to this end should be undertaken before it was too late. (For an account of the development of the ICW Archives Project see Appendix 4, p. 337).

At the public meeting which closed this Executive, delegates were honoured by an address by Lord Reading, and heard talks on the position of women in India and Greece by Mrs Tarabai Premchand and Mrs Elmina Pantelaki respectively, followed by an analysis of the Attitude of International and National Women's NGOs and Politics by Mrs Sigrid Stray of Norway.

1953

In 1953, following the establishment by UN of a Committee to draft a Convention on the Recovery of Maintenance Obligations Abroad, a subject long on the agenda of the ICW, Dr Girod organized in Geneva a joint meeting of the Child Welfare and Moral Welfare Committees, under the presidency of Mrs Eder, at which the text of this Convention was carefully examined to determine whether it gave satisfaction on all points of interest to the ICW. A commentary on the Convention was published in the *Bulletin*, April 1953, and ICW members were urged to press nationally for its ratification and implementation. A Resolution to this effect was adopted at the next Council Meeting and many NCWs took action on the national level in support of this Convention.

The question of the participation of NCWs in Technical Assistance programmes received special attention at this time, and a survey was made by Headquarters of the activities of NCWs in this domain and in that of fundamental education. The newly-affiliated NCW of Egypt reported a pioneer project in fundamental education of interest to UNESCO's expanding programme in this field. Experimental adult literacy classes in towns and villages had been carried out as a result of which 75% of pupils had passed official tests supervised by the Ministry of Education (*Bulletin*, July 1953).

In 1953 the ICW welcomed the election of Mrs Pandit of India as the first woman President of the General Assembly of UN. Ever since 1946, when it supported the appeal of the few women delegates to the First Session of the Assembly, in favour of a more extensive participation of women in international life, NCWs had been urged to ask their governments to include more women in national delegations to the UN Assembly and other international meetings. Since this time, women delegates, alternates and advisers (including many members of NCWs) had become more numerous and in 1951, Mrs Ana Figueroa, delegate of Chile and member of the NCW of that country, had been elected President of the Third (Social) Committee of the Assembly, on which Mrs R. J. Marshall, Doctor of Law, of the NCW of Canada was the delegate of her country.

Among the increasing number of women delegates to other major Conferences of UN and its Specialized Agencies had been distinguished council members such as Miss E. Pikhala-Beaurain, sister of Miss A. M. Beaurain, Hon. ICW Vice-Recording Secretary, appointed delegate of Finland to the General Conference of the FAO and Miss Geronima Pecson, delegate of the Philippines to that of UNESCO and the first of three members of NCWs to serve on the Executive Board of that institution between 1951 and 1960.

THE ICW FACES THE PROBLEMS OF THE ATOMIC AGE

1954—FOURTEENTH COUNCIL MEETING (SIXTH TRIENNIAL) OF THE ICW, HELSINKI

The Fourteenth Council Meeting of the ICW took place in Helsinki. The NCW of Finland, under the presidency of Mrs Margit Borg-Sundman, had invited the women of the ICW and in June 1954 they gathered in the land of the midnight sun.

'Women's response to the opportunities and dangers of the atomic age', was the theme of the Conference and of the President's opening address. As a scientist, Mrs Eder was well-equipped to speak on this subject and to review the development of atomic research and the rôle played in it by women. Insisting on the responsibility of the individual in all free countries in the use made of knowledge on atomic fission, the President referred to the 'cold' fear of atomic warfare. 'Why should a Women's Congress be built around this theme?' asked the President. 'It has ever been the rôle of woman to be a source of strength and calm among her people. All things concerned with life . . . are our closest interests, so inevitably peace and understanding are our concern, be it in the souls of men or in the uses of the atom.' Today's generations, continued Mrs Eder, 'face a future destined to be very different from the past, into which the atom will bring enormous new good or evil, depending on the use made by humanity of its new powers. Has the woman of the twentieth century her own response to make to this challenge thrust upon humanity?'

The leading Resolutions adopted at Helsinki naturally dealt with the Conference theme—women and the potential uses of atomic energy:

The ICW wishes to unite women to work against the destructive and aggressive use of these energies, for their international control and for their pacific uses.

94

Foreseeing great sociological changes as a result of the development of atomic power, it urged NCWs

> to foresee and take steps to prevent economic and social upheavals and to strive to solve these problems in a spirit of responsibility, mutual comprehension and concern for the individual human being.

It was also interesting to note a new trend in discussions evident at Helsinki, a fear that the acquisition of legal rights for women in many countries might be leading in certain cases to a relaxation of vigilance concerning the full implementation of these rights. The second Resolution voted at this meeting reflected this apprehension, calling on NCWs

> to persevere in the struggle to obtain in fact as well as in law, full equal rights for all women in all countries.

At the Public Session held on June 11th, Mrs Marie-Hélène Lefaucheux, President of the NCW of France, many times delegate of her country to the General Assembly of UN and the Status of Women Commission (which she presided for five years), presented a panorama of the situation of women in under-developed areas in Asia, Africa and Latin America, indicating ways in which NCWs in more privileged countries could help these women to advance rapidly on the road to emancipation and social progress.

Besides the regular Committee meetings, group meetings were arranged at Helsinki for the rank and file of Conference participants to discuss subjects connected with 'women and the home'. These discussions were much appreciated by those Finnish visitors and other participants who, though neither official delegates nor Committee members, felt they had nevertheless a contribution to make to the debates. It was decided to repeat this venture at future Council meetings, especially as the final joint meeting, brilliantly chaired by the Marchioness of Reading, was acclaimed an outstanding success.

The decision, taken at this Council Meeting, to omit German as an official language of the ICW was naturally a great disappointment to German delegates, members of one of the oldest NCWs. Financial considerations, however, made it impossible for the moment either to maintain German or to envisage the addition of Spanish, despite the need to facilitate contact with Latin American Councils.

The affiliation of the All Pakistan Women's Association as the NCW of Pakistan was confirmed at Helsinki.

Five Helsinki Resolutions dealt with the UN and its Agencies. A complete report compiled by Headquarters on consultative activities during the period 1949–53 had been submitted to the ECOSOC together with an application for renewal of Consultative Status B which had been granted.

At UN itself the principal channels of collaboration continued to be the NGO sections of the Department of Public Information and of the Secretariat of the ECOSOC.

At UNESCO the NGO group had been consulted in a series of meetings to consider the draft future programme, the ICW being represented on the Education group by Mrs Pichon-Landry, while Mrs L. D. Barney chaired the group on Mass Communication. Co-operation with the FAO, now in its Rome Headquarters where the ICW was regularly represented by Professor Antonietta Orrù, eminent Italian biologist, continued in many vital fields—preservation of forests and other natural resources, rural welfare, nutrition, etc. Two Vice-Presidents—Dr Girod and Miss van Eeghen—continued to represent the ICW at meetings of the ILO, the WHO and at the Geneva Headquarters of the High Commissioner for Refugees (*ICW Records 1954*, pp. 34–42).

At all previous Council Meetings it had been customary for NCWs to present an oral report on their activities since the last Conference. At Helsinki, NCWs had agreed that as an experiment the Executive Secretary should present a single synthetic report covering important activities of NCWs grouped by subject and based on replies to a special questionnaire. In addition, each NCW was to have the opportunity to speak briefly on outstanding recent activities of special interest to other NCWs. The report presented at Helsinki provided an interesting analysis of the variety of methods and activities of individual NCWs and allowed delegates to obtain, in the limited time at their disposal, a good overall picture of the work recently accomplished by their co-affiliates.

1955–56

The presence of Baroness Boël, still active Hon. President, had been greatly missed at Helsinki, and in January 1956 the ICW was saddened by the news of her death. A Memorial Issue of the *Bulletin* (April 1956) included tributes from many of those privileged to have worked with her in Belgium and in the ICW, and Mrs Eder recalled in deep-felt words the 'wise and vivid personality' of

Baroness Boël, who had led the ICW through so critical a period in its history.

For the 1956 meeting of the Executive, the NCW of Italy invited ICW delegates to meet in the Cini Foundation, the former monastery standing on the Venetian island of San Giorgio, a short boat ride from the Piazza San Marco.

The Venice meeting brought its quota of new problems: one of the most debated questions was the difficulties raised by two Arab Councils to the affiliation of the Council of Women's Organizations of Israel, a representative body of women set up in conformity with the Council Idea and a formal applicant for affiliation to the ICW. Thanks to the mediation of the Begum Ikramullah of Pakistan, Vice-President of the ICW, these countries finally agreed upon abstention on this issue. The spirit of the Golden Rule thus prevailed over political divergencies, and Israel was received with applause as a new member of the sisterhood of NCWs. The affiliation of the important group of Women's Organizations federated into the Civic Assembly of Women of the Philippines (already accepted by unanimous written note) was also confirmed at Venice.

In addition to the regular Standing Committee meetings, four Committees joined in discussing the problems of working women with family responsibilities. As an outcome of this meeting, an extensive survey was undertaken, dealing not only with the problems of working mothers but also with the difficulties of unmarried working women responsible for parents, brothers, sisters or other dependents.

An interesting informal meeting was held on Trades and Professions, dealing with vocational and technical training for women and the question of women's employment in countries in process of rapid industrialization.

The Press Committee discussed the future of the *Bulletin*, and of the *Monthly News Sheet* for urgent items edited by Mrs Barzin (Belgium), Convener of the Press Committee. Some members still hoped to revive the excellent pre-war *Bulletin* or even to create a first-rate international women's magazine. The major obstacle remained lack of funds: the pressure of work at Headquarters was continually increasing and despite the efforts of a competent staff at modest salaries, less time and money than in earlier days could be devoted to publications inevitably requiring specialist editing and preparation.

97

CONCERN FOR THE FUTURE OF THE WOMEN'S MOVEMENT

1957—FIFTEENTH COUNCIL MEETING (SEVENTH TRIENNIAL) OF THE ICW, MONTREAL

Mrs Eder, whose health had been failing ever since Helsinki, reached the end of her constitutional three terms of office at the Fifteenth Council Meeting held in Montreal in June 1957, at which the ICW delegates were the guests of the NCW of Canada presided by Mrs Rex Eaton. The ICW President elected at Montreal was already well known to delegates: Mrs Marie-Hélène Lefaucheux, President of the NCW of France, highly esteemed in international circles both as an excellent President of the UN Commission on the Status of Women, and as an indefatigable delegate remarkably well-informed on the problems of women in newly-developing countries throughout the world.

When Mrs Eder opened the Conference at Montreal, her many friends present were deeply moved by the sight of a very sick woman making a supreme effort to give her audience what was destined to be her last speech and, indeed, her testament to the ICW. The President spoke of the Women's Movement which had played so important a rôle in her life: 'Have we been loyal to what our pioneers expected of us, to uphold the human rights of women, the great importance of justice in the world, the work towards freedom and a more perfect justice in the future?' (*ICW Records 1957*, p. 6). If we examine the situation in the world today, said Mrs Eder, we perceive that most of the old problems still exist, though often in different forms and in new parts of the world. She quoted a heartfelt appeal from a woman of an eastern country, in which women still lacked 'even the most elementary freedoms'. 'Is not the same degree of dedication as that of the pioneers of the Women's Movement still required to do away with such old evils,' asked Mrs Eder, 'as well as to combat the new evils constantly arising in countries where so much has already been achieved?'

Significantly enough, the report of the NCW of France to this Council Meeting sounded another note of warning against complacency in countries where women's rights had largely been achieved: by failing to exercise their rights and regarding studies or employment as purely transitory while waiting to marry, 'women endanger the status they have gained' (*ICW Records 1957*, p. 117).

A written message from Mrs L. D. Barney, ICW Liaison Officer with UN and the Specialized Agencies, retained in Paris by ill-health, stressed the importance of the 'new channels' being opened up by the expansion of UN, which might lead to 'the solution of grave problems on which the ICW and its Affiliates had worked for many years'. Mrs Barney paid tribute to the work of the growing team of ICW representatives with UN and its Agencies now active in Geneva, Rome, Paris and New York.

At UN Headquarters Mrs W. B. Parsons, Mrs E. Carter and Mrs F. Freeman had for nearly ten years 'excelled in making the most difficult post dependable and progressive'. The two last-named had been elected Chairmen of the Committees of NGOs in Consultative Status with the ECOSOC and UNICEF respectively.

Mrs Schuller-McGeachy, who had recently come to live in New York, had lent valuable assistance to this group, and at Montreal the ICW Board of Officers invited her to serve as Liaison Officer to coordinate the increasing volume and diversity of the work of ICW representatives at UN Headquarters.

In Rome, at the Headquarters of the FAO, Mrs Barney reported continued close relations with FAO Divisions of Information and Education, Nutrition, Agriculture and Forestry. At the Paris meetings convened by the FAO Agriculture Division to coordinate efforts on agricultural needs in Europe, the ICW had asked and obtained that rural welfare and housing conditions should be a permanent subject of study (*ICW Records, 1957*, pp. 36–40).

Resolutions adopted at Montreal drew the attention of NCWs to the 'paramount importance' of International Conventions on the status of stateless persons, the nationality of married women, traffic in persons, equal political rights, the recovery of maintenance obligations. Resolutions adopted called for new efforts to persuade governments to ratify these conventions, if this had not yet been done, and to insist on scrupulous implementation where ratification had already been effected.

NCWs were also asked to urge their governments to provide the necessary funds for the realization of the UN four-year programme for the settlement of 'hardcore' refugees, and to encourage them to receive as many handicapped refugees as possible. Full support was expressed for the work of UNICEF, and NCWs were urged to continue to stimulate interest among citizens and governments in the world-wide needs of children, and to press for the provision of adequate funds for UNICEF.

The Council Meeting strongly supported the UN proposal for a Supplementary Convention on the Abolition of Slavery and requested the appropriate UN authorities to draft agreements on the advance registration and international observation of nuclear test explosions, and on protection against atomic fall-out.

A special feature of the Montreal meeting was the conclusion of the international competition organized with the support of the Music Sub-Committee of the NCW of the US by Miss Grace Spofford (Doctor of Music, New York College of Music), Vice-Convener of the ICW Standing Committee on Arts and Letters. A total of 184 works from 32 countries was received, the winning composition being *Air de Syrinx*, a four-part chorus by Mrs Lucie Vellère of Belgium, based on a poem by Paul Claudel (*ICW Records 1957*, p. 48).

Only a few months after the Montreal meeting, Mrs Eder, now Hon. President, fell victim to the cruel disease which had undermined her strength for some years past. Mrs Majorelle (France), Hon. Recording Secretary of the ICW, representing the Board of Officers at her funeral in Zürich, recalled the lesson of Mrs Eder's speech at Montreal: 'The only thing that counts is to have lived for some great task.' 'Now that I can take the full measure of Jeanne Eder's work,' wrote her successor Mrs Lefaucheux, in the number of the *Bulletin*, devoted to the memory of Mrs Eder (October 1957), 'each day I understand a little more the debt of gratitude we owe to her.'

1957–60—A PERIOD OF GEOGRAPHICAL EXPANSION AND INTERNATIONAL DEVELOPMENT

Many changes in leading personalities and in administration had taken place in Montreal. Not only the President changed, but also a large part of the Board of Officers (on which 17 countries in 5 continents were now represented), and 17 Conveners and Vice-Conveners of ICW Standing Committees.

As it was the custom to have the ICW Headquarters in the city of residence of its President, office quarters now had to be found in Paris. Miss Dissard (France), Convener of the ICW Housing Committee, kindly offered the secretariat hospitality in her own apartment during the first difficult years, when the post-war Paris housing problem was still acute. The same difficulties experienced by

Mrs Eder at the beginning of her term of office now beset her successor. Moreover, her career in international affairs, with its multiple obligations outside France, while affording unique opportunities for the ICW to participate in international co-operation for the advancement of human rights, particularly among the women of the under-developed countries of the world, inevitably meant greatly increased work for her assistants. Since no member of the Zürich staff could come to Paris, once again all Headquarters personnel were entirely new to ICW work. After a number of appointments, including that of Miss J. Bougenot and Mrs C. Pomonti, Headquarters was removed to more suitable premises in 1962. To avoid future disruption in the work of Headquarters and to achieve greater continuity, the Council Meeting was soon to propose the establishment of a permanent Headquarters for the ICW, irrespective of the place of residence of its President.

Thanks to the constant efforts of Mrs Lefaucheux, and as a result of the extensive travels undertaken both by her and by her indefatigable Vice-President Mrs W. B. Parsons, the ICW was able to expand rapidly to new regions of the world.

At the Executive Meeting held in Vienna in May 1959, it was able to accept the provisional affiliation of six new councils in Latin America and Asia, thus becoming more and more a widespread 'federation of women of all races, nations, creeds and classes'. During the Vienna meeting, in order to give symbolic expression to this diversity in unity, Miss van Eeghen, Board Member of the ICW for almost forty years presented the President with a banner modelled on two previous ICW banners, both unfortunately lost in the course of succeeding wars.

A report was given on progress in the location, preservation and utilization of ICW archives. National Councils (in particular those of Belgium, Canada, Great Britain, South Africa and the US) were thanked for the co-operation which had made it possible to supply valuable and much-appreciated information to interested libraries, particularly that of the United Nations in Geneva (see Appendix 5, p. 339).

Another feature of the Vienna meeting was the establishment of an Eder Literary Prize for the best work of fiction written by a woman since 1956. Twenty Councils submitted entries, and after successive elimination by a series of bi-lingual juries, the prize was finally awarded to the Italian entry: *Isola di Artura* by Elsa Morante.

The NCW of Austria, under its President Mrs Henrietta Hainisch, had arranged visits to a number of social welfare projects of special interest to the Executive and to the many members of Standing Committees present in Vienna. To mark World Refugee year, a bungalow to house elderly refugees, offered in the name of the ICW by Miss van Eeghen, was built on the outskirts of Vienna, the first stone being laid during this meeting of the Executive.

The Vienna Executive also approved the publication, begun in December 1957, of an experimental *ICW Quarterly Review*, intended to appeal to a somewhat wider public.

1960—SIXTEENTH COUNCIL MEETING (EIGHTH TRIENNIAL) OF THE ICW, ISTANBUL

The next Council Meeting of the ICW was held on the borders of Europe and Asia, though still on European soil, in the fabulous city of Istanbul, Turkey, in August 1960. There were two reasons for holding a Council Meeting in this Middle Eastern country: to help launch a new Council in this region and to make it easier for Asian and African Council members to attend (*ICW Records 1960*, p. 149). In addition to the new host Council of Turkey, presided by Mrs Edibe Sayar, new Councils were affiliated in Bolivia, Colombia, Haiti, Iran, Korea and Singapore.

In the three years since Montreal, said Mrs Lefaucheux in her introduction to the Conference report, the ICW had achieved two important aims: it had expanded geographically and it had developed its methods of co-operation with international institutions. 'It sometimes happens, that in certain UN Commissions you may hear deplored the silence of the NGOs,' said Mrs Lefaucheux. Such reproaches cannot concern the ICW, which 'participates in investigations, sends representatives to the Economic and Social Commissions of the UN and to Study Circles held not only in New York and Geneva but in Africa, Asia and Latin America'.

After outlining ICW plans for collaboration with UNESCO and work with FAO, WHO, UNICEF and the Office of the High Commissioner for Refugees, the President welcomed the new link recently established with the ILO, which, as the result of a change of policy, had recently granted official status on its Special List to the ICW, after forty years of friendly co-operation. The presence at Istanbul of Mrs Grinberg-Vinaver, Chief of the Status of Women Section of the UN Secretariat, as well as of representatives of

UNESCO, ILO, WHO and UNICEF testified once more to the importance attached by UN and its Specialized Agencies to the deliberations of the ICW.

The President regretted the discontinuance of the *Quarterly Review* for financial reasons, and recorded her conviction that the work of the Standing Committees could be rendered more effective. As regards ICW publications, the Istanbul meeting decided on a *Monthly Newsletter* to be edited under the auspices of the Press Committee. Miss Cocks, an Australian journalist and member of the NCW of Great Britain, was subsequently appointed editor.

A Committee composed of Miss van Veen (Hon. Vice-President), Miss ten Bruggen Cate (Treasurer), Mrs E. E. Monro (Hon. Vice-Recording Secretary) of the NCW of South Africa and Mrs E. Merete Ross (President, NCW of Denmark) was established to review the administration of the ICW and the conduct of Executive and Triennial meetings, and an *ad hoc* Committee was appointed to consider amendments to the Constitution and Standing Orders.

It was at Istanbul that the Board of Officers welcomed and accepted the proposal of Mrs L. D. Barney that a condensed history of the first seventy-five years of the ICW should be prepared for publication under the sponsorship of an international *ad hoc* Committee of ICW Officers.

This meeting also saw a change in the valuable team of ICW Recording Secretaries led by Mrs Majorelle (France) and Miss Mary Shaw (Great Britain), the former being elected Hon. Vice-President of the ICW after thirteen years as a much-appreciated Hon. Recording Secretary. Her successor, elected at Istanbul, was Miss Nellie Wiener (President of the NCW of Belgium), who, together with Miss Lily Marx (Italy), Doctor of Law, had already contributed six years of assiduous service as Hon. Vice-Recording Secretary.

The theme of the Istanbul Conference was 'Women and the family in a changing world'. Four major groups discussed various aspects of this problem. At the plenary session, where reports of these group meetings were presented, a packed house agreed that it was necessary to ensure that women had the opportunity of developing to their full capacity at all levels of life and talents—'the choice between careers in and out of the home must be that of the individual' (*ICW Records 1960*, p. 186).

After the regular meetings, the nine Standing Committees most concerned with young people gathered under the Chairmanship of the Marchioness of Reading, Vice-President of the ICW since 1957, to discuss the problems of children's use of leisure time and its relationship to juvenile delinquency.

A recent disturbing recrudescence of racial prejudice in several countries inspired a resolution urgently requesting NCWs 'to press their governments to encourage active education to promote under-standing of racial and religious differences'. Other resolutions advocated preventive measures for dealing with the increasing problems of mental ill-health, education in home safety and in preparation for family living, the need for the co-operation of women in the conservation and improved utilization of natural resources and—an entirely new subject—the desirability of inter-national co-operation in the exploration and peaceful exploitation of outer space.

A written message from Mrs L. D. Barney expressed appreciation of the remarkable manner in which Mrs Schuller-McGeachy had taken over the demanding task of Liaison Officer to the UN. A detailed report by Mrs Schuller called attention to the emphasis now being placed by many UN technical bodies on the social aspects of their technical work, causing them to 'take a fresh' look at the important rôle of voluntary organizations in areas of rapid social change (*ICW Records 1960*, pp. 167–74).

Immediately after this Council Meeting, an ICW/UNESCO Seminar on the rôle of women in the UNESCO Major Project on the Mutual Understanding of Eastern and Western Cultures was held in Istanbul. As a result of this seminar, attended by 70 delegates from 33 countries, at which papers were presented by Mrs Dutt, Indian Vice-President of the Associated Countrywomen of the World, Mrs Lelièvre (Doctor of Letters) of the NCW of France, and Professor Hilimi Ziya Ulken of Turkey, it was decided to promote the 'twinning' of NCWs in East and West, who could then proceed to a more profound knowledge of their respective cultural traditions and ways of life. The first volunteer 'twins' included: Great Britain/Israel, Canada/Turkey, Denmark/Uganda and Thailand/Australia.

1961–62

During the twelve months following the Council Meeting at Istanbul, applications for affiliation were received from 3 new Councils in Africa: Kenya, Cameroons and Congo (Brazzaville).

The following table demonstrates the trend in geographical distribution of affiliated Councils between 1938 and 1962:

Affiliated Councils in	1938	1947	1954	1963
Europe	22	10	13	13
America	6	6	7	10
Asia	4	2	5	12
Africa	2	4	8	12
Australasia	2	2	2	2
Total	36	24	35	49

The loss of 10 Eastern and Central European Councils during and after the Second World War, followed by geographical expansion in other continents, had transformed the ICW from a predominantly European body (22 out of 36 NCWs) into a thoroughly inter-continental organization. In 1962 Mrs W. B. Parsons, Vice-President specially charged by the Board of Officers with the promotion of new affiliations, reported that a team of fifteen women was at present working in this field. She stressed the necessity for personal contacts in the various areas and listed 16 countries in Latin America, Asia and Africa in which good contacts had recently been established.

The increasingly inter-continental membership of the ICW, together with the wide experience of the ICW President in work with inter-governmental institutions augmented the regular links between the ICW and the various UN bodies and led to the establishment of new methods of collaboration, many of them based on the ICW's ability to integrate the work of national Affiliates in all five continents with that of the United Nations and its Agencies, now becoming more and more active on a regional basis.

One form of collaboration now on the increase was the participation of National Councils in national programmes benefiting from the aid of one or other of the inter-governmental organizations, under the heading of Participation Programmes. In the field of adult education, to take only one example, NCWs or specialist organizations forming part of such Councils were participating in large-scale literacy campaigns sponsored by their Governments and in a number of cases, undertaken with the financial and technical aid of UNESCO. In other fields NCWs in many countries played an active part in the national sector of international campaigns such as World Refugee Year and the Freedom from Hunger Campaign.

Meanwhile a number of NCWs had been also developing their own programmes of international contacts and bi-lateral aid. In New York, where the proximity of UN Headquarters increased possibilities for such contacts, the NCW of the US had considerably extended the work of its energetic Hospitality Committee. The National Councils of Germany and Israel were participating in the organization of training courses for African women in their respective countries and the NCW of Denmark (in collaboration with UN) was sponsoring a training centre in Africa in which women receive a twelve months training in community development prior to employment in regional centres for training local leaders and workers. The NCW of the US was initiating a series of scholarships for the secondary school education of girls in Nigeria.

Opportunities were also increasing for the organization of joint ICW/UN projects for the attainment of objectives common to them both, in various regions of the world.

Since 1957 the ICW had been engaged in a Pilot Project by which NCWs in Israel, India and Pakistan had been working with representatives of the Technical Assistance projects in their countries to interpret these programmes to their fellow-countrymen and women in order to facilitate and accelerate acceptance of these programmes. At the same time, wherever useful, these NCWs had been helping to integrate visiting experts and their families into the life of the local community.

A Study Circle was organized by the President of the ICW at Yaoundé, Cameroons, in July 1962, for the leaders of women's organizations in French-speaking countries of Tropical Africa. The newly-affiliated NCW of the Cameroons successfully carried out all the material arrangements and 13 African States and Madagascar were represented by 30 delegates whose travel expenses were covered by UNESCO. The agenda provided for an exchange of views on the position of African women's organizations and on the opportunities open to them for co-operation with UN and its Specialized Agencies as well as with NGOs such as the ICW, the International Federation of Business and Professional Women, the University Women and the Associated Countrywomen of the World, who collaborated with the ICW in presenting the women's NGOs to the women of French-speaking Africa.

Conscious of the need to concentrate the action of women's NGO's in relation to inter-governmental institutions (which are sometimes embarrassed by their number and diversity), the ICW had, in 1958, taken the initiative of calling the first of a regular series of meetings between the Presidents of several of the principal women's NGOs in order to concert their views on priorities for the immediate future.

Meanwhile, the Liaison Committee of Women's International Organizations, which, on ICW initiative, had helped to pioneer consultative relations with the League of Nations, had continued to closely work with United Nations in New York and Geneva since its admission to Consultative Status with the ECOSOC in 1947. In 1963, however, the Liaison Committee, recognizing the difficulties inherent in the fact that nine of its thirteen member organizations enjoyed Consultative Status in their own right, decided to renounce its Consultative Status and increase its effectiveness as a rallying point for mobilizing the efforts of women's international organizations for common aims.

Within the ICW, an increasing amount of regional co-operation was developing among Councils of similar cultural interests and levels of economic progress. The four nordic Councils had co-operated for many years, holding regular regional meetings and achieving excellent results with a common programme on many issues; and in 1961, 10 European NCWs met at Axenstein (Switzerland) to discuss closer regional co-operation and questions of common interest within the framework of new European institutions. With the agreement of the Board of Officers of the ICW, a centre of European NCWs was subsequently established in Brussels under the direction of Miss Marguerite Jadot of the NCW of Belgium, for the purpose of permanent liaison between these Councils. In 1963, this Centre was accorded Consultative Status (Category A) by the Council of Europe in Strasbourg.

In the General Assembly of the United Nations, as in the General Conference of UNESCO and other Specialized Agencies, the number of women delegates continued to increase. Newly independent member states in Africa were not slow to nominate women delegates and by the 17th Session of the UN Assembly in 1962 the number of countries including women in their delegations had risen to 53. As in previous years, these included a number of distinguished Officers of the ICW representing their respective countries: among them Mrs Lefaucheux, ICW President, delegate of France; Countess Flavia della Gherardesca, First Vice-President of the ICW, delegate of Italy; Presidents or members of NCWs in Belgium, Colombia,

Denmark, Israel, Greece and Sweden. Since 1952, women had on several occasions chaired main Assembly Committees and headed a number of national delegations both to the Assembly of UN and to the General Conference of UNESCO, where the Executive Board elected in 1962 included women from Great Britain, India and Panama.

During this same period women were also playing an increasingly important rôle in the foreign affairs of many nations. Since the appointment of the first woman to the diplomatic rank of Minister in 1933, women had served with distinction as Ambassadors in such influential posts as London, Washington, Moscow and New Delhi. In 1956 Mrs Golda Meir of Israel became the first woman to serve as Foreign Minister of any country, and in 1961 Mrs Sirimavo Bandanaraike became Prime Minister of Ceylon.

1962

An important meeting of the Executive Committee was held in Rome in May 1962. Many major administrative decisions were taken provisionally, subject to ratification at the next Triennial Council Meeting. The Executive discussed reports submitted by the Committee appointed in Istanbul to examine administrative methods of the ICW together with the organization of the Executive and Council Meetings, and reviewed revisions in the Constitution and Standing Orders proposed by the *ad hoc* Committee appointed for this purpose.

To ensure continuity in the administrative work of the Council, the Executive proposed that the Headquarters of the ICW remain permanently in Paris, independently of changes in the Presidency, which, it was recommended, on the proposal of the NCW of France, should not in future be held by any one person for more than two Triennial periods.

An urgent resolution proposed by the NCWs of Great Britain was adopted by the Rome Executive urging NCWs to renew pressure on their Governments for the ratification of the two existing International Conventions on the Abolition of Slavery which, though dating from 1926 and 1957 respectively, were in 1962 still unratified by 48 and 71 countries respectively, slavery remaining a legalized institution in certain UN Member States. This resolution further urged that an *ad hoc* Committee of Experts be set up by the ECOSOC at their next meeting to examine the world position in regard to slavery.

Invitations to the ICW to hold future meetings in India, Uganda and the Lebanon further illustrated the actively intercontinental nature of the ICW.

For its next Council Meeting which would also be the seventy-fifth anniversary of the foundation of the ICW, the Executive Committee accepted with great pleasure the invitation of the NCW of the US to meet once more in Washington, DC, the city in which both were founded in 1888.

In her report to the Executive Committee in Rome, Mrs Lefaucheux once again drew attention to the fact that 'present forms of international life' were resulting in new and important responsibilities devolving upon NGOs which, 'while without power of decision are not without authority'. Thanks to the sustained efforts of the team of ICW Liaison Officers and Consultants under the direction of Mrs Schuller-McGeachy, all headquarters meetings and projects of UN and its Agencies relevant to the work of the ICW had been closely followed in order that the programmes of the ICW should wherever possible support and further those of the inter-governmental organizations.

In addition, the ICW and its Affiliates stood ready to send qualified representatives to participate in inter-governmental meetings and seminars wherever and whenever subjects relevant to its programme were discussed. The ICW had been represented at every session of the Status of Women Commission, whether in New York, Geneva or Buenos Aires and had sent representatives to the Human Rights Seminars organized by the ECOSOC at Bogota, Bucharest and Tokio.

As a general principle the Presidents or other expert members of local or neighbouring NCWs were called upon to represent the ICW at these regional meetings. For the 1962 Tokio Seminar on the Status of Women in Family Law, the ICW group of observers, headed by Mrs Schuller-McGeachy had included authorities on various aspects of family law sent by the NCWs of Australia, India, Iran, Israel, Korea, Pakistan and Thailand, and a written contribution by the Council of Women of Hong Kong. Representatives of the ICW had attended meetings of UN Regional Commissions (Asia and the Far East, Latin America and Africa).

Since Istanbul, NCWs had also sent representatives to UNESCO Meetings or Seminars held in Germany, Canada, India, Thailand, Tanganyika, Dahomey and Senegal.

The NCW of the US which, by reason of its New York head-quarters was able to maintain particularly close contact with UN undertook the publication of a monthly UN Digest and Calendar, thus providing a most welcome service to the members of its own Council and those of other countries. Accurate advance information on UN meetings and activities of interest to the ICW was thus made available to NCWs, together with an indication of the relevant UN documentation and an account of the salient points of recent meetings pertinent to the work of the ICW.

Despite evidence of increasingly active and widespread co-operation between the ICW, National Councils and inter-govern-mental organizations on the international, regional and national levels, Mrs Lefaucheux drew the attention of the members of the ICW Executive gathered in Rome in 1962 to the 'note of inter-rogation' perceptible in recent discussions concerning 'the very meaning' of the ICW. 'Born three quarters of a century ago, does it still have a reason for existing today?' asked the President.

Much work remained to be done before the many substantial theoretical advances achieved towards the Council's objectives were transformed into reality. Indeed, all too often public opinion and governments alike appeared to the President 'to take refuge' behind such theoretical justice to delay practical action which alone can render it effective.

To Mrs Lefaucheux, nearing the end of her term as President of the ICW, confident in the international movement towards the goal proposed by the ICW pioneers in 1888—'the overthrow of all forms of ignorance and injustice'—the future rôle of the ICW was clear and 'in no way revolutionary':

> There is no question of branching off the long and beautiful road of the International Council of Women but of following a straight and, needless to say, up-hill course, with eyes fixed on the increasingly wide horizons which scientific and technical discoveries are opening up before us and the new possibilities of action now available to women. (*Speech to Executive Meeting, May, 1962.*)

PAST HERITAGE AND FUTURE RESPONSIBILITY

1963—SEVENTEENTH COUNCIL MEETING (NINTH TRIENNIAL) AND SEVENTY-FIFTH ANNIVERSARY OF THE ICW, WASHINGTON, DC

'Inheritance from the past, responsibility for the future', was the theme chosen by the ICW for the Seventeenth Council Meeting held in Washington in June 1963, seventy-five years after its foundation in that city.

The young Washington of 1888 had long since grown into a great world capital, and the theatrical setting of Albaugh's Opera House was succeeded by the streamlined efficiency of the Conference Floor of the Hotel Statler-Hilton.

Once again, the NCW of the United States was the generous host and sponsor of the ICW. Thanks to the hard preparatory work of its President, Mrs Sophia Yarnall Jacobs and of the team of able helpers led by her First Vice-President, Mrs Louis J. Robbins, the technical organization of the meeting, the arrangements for its effective coverage by press and other information media, as well as for the comfort, relaxation and cultural entertainment of the many delegates were all in the highest traditions of the ICW and of the American Council's own long-standing reputation for hospitality. Delegates were received at the White House and at Mount Vernon, and were entertained to lunch at the US Senate, as well as at afternoon receptions given by a number of different Embassies.

On June 19th, the very day on which ICW delegates gathered in Washington, the news from Moscow of the successful space flight of the first woman astronaut focussed the attention of the world not only on the spectacular transformation in the accepted rôle of women, but also on the infinite possibilities of the future for men and women everywhere. The Board of Officers of the ICW, at its first meeting held that morning, greeted the outstanding exploit of Valentina Tereshkova by conveying to her through official channels an immediate message of congratulation.

ICW delegates came to a city already occupied with one of the greatest problems of our time—the fight to free the world from hunger. Washington in June 1963 was already host to the World Food Congress of men and women of all nations—including members of many NCWs—actively engaged in the great collective attack on world hunger led by the FAO.

These same summer weeks found Washington also the focal point of a great nation traversing a period of extreme racial tension and adjustment. Greeting delegates at the opening dinner organized by her Council, the President of the NCW of the US assured them that the 'understanding presence' of women 'who had struggled all over the world for political and civil rights' was particularly welcome to her Council in 'such grave and serious days', which they must 'surely recognize as the inevitable precursors of the triumph of the rights of the individual'.

Turning to another subject of universal concern, which her Council wished to share with the ICW, Mrs Jacobs introduced the distinguished naturalist, Mrs Rachel Carson, cited by the US Council as an outstanding American 'Woman of Conscience' for her recent book *Silent Spring*, in which she warns the public of the risks of man's destruction of his own environment and possible mutilation of his own descendants by the misuse or abuse of modern chemicals and pesticides. Accepting the citation of the US Council, presented to her on their behalf by Dr Janet Travell, personal physician to President Kennedy, Mrs Carson told ICW delegates of the urgency of directing the attention of responsible opinion in their own countries to the need for safeguards to ensure only the judicious and appropriate use of these valuable technological aids to progress otherwise so potentially destructive to humanity.

At the close of this opening dinner, Mrs Lefaucheux, President of the ICW, expressed the gratification of ICW delegates for the opportunity provided by the US Council to celebrate in the city of its birth the seventy-fifth anniversary of the foundation of the Council—an important date in the history of the ICW and a notable occasion for taking stock of past progress and facing the opportunities and responsibilities of the future.

During the Plenary Sessions of the Council Meeting, which began on the following morning, ten new Councils were officially welcomed into the ICW. The provisional affiliation of the Cameroons, the Congo (Brazzaville), and Kenya was formally confirmed and new Councils affiliated in Ecuador, Gambia, Liberia, Luxemburg, Niger, Sierra Leone and Trinidad and Tobago. Observers from groups of women interested in establishing Councils in 16 other countries, from Japan to Mexico, and Western Samoa to Zanzibar, also attended Council Meetings to learn at first hand something of the work and methods of the ICW.

Thus the little band of delegates from eight nations meeting three-quarters of a century ago to found the ICW had expanded to include representatives from over 60 nations, many from the newly independent states of Africa, the brilliant costumes and splendid carriage of their delegates adding a proud new note to the spectacle of the ICW in Council. The fact that the women of African countries of gravely conflicting governmental policies were able to work together within the ICW vividly confirmed the conviction of the founders of the ICW that, without distinction of nationality, race or creed, women everywhere could usefully unite their efforts for the benefit of mankind.

Mrs Lefaucheux, to whose wise leadership the expansion of the ICW, particularly in Africa, was in such great measure due, retired from the Presidency of the ICW in Washington. As she explained to the Council Meeting, the decision taken at the Rome Executive and confirmed in Washington, establishing a permanent ICW Headquarters in Paris, irrespective of changes in the Presidency, should make it possible for this office to rotate more frequently among a wider range of countries—a development she herself felt to be essential for a truly international organization in present world conditions (*ICW Records, 1963*, p. 17).

Among the fundamental questions raised by Mrs Lefaucheux in her last report as President of the ICW was the rôle of a voluntary organization such as the ICW in a world in process of a transformation so rapid that their efforts sometimes seemed doomed to insignificance. In the first place, said Mrs Lefaucheux, until the status of women everywhere attains to true equality in law and in practice, the work of the ICW is still unfinished. A second uncompleted task is that of the promotion and defence of human rights, particularly vital at a time when, despite the undoubted progress represented by the establishment, through the United Nations, of a nucleus of international legislation guaranteeing human rights, the divergency of interpretation of such rights represents the most important idealogical conflict in the world today. As a freely-constituted nongovernmental international organization the ICW must work not only for the implementation and extension of Human Rights as guaranteed by International Conventions, but also for the preservation of their full significance—so clearly understood by its founders seventy-five years ago—as the rights of men and women everywhere, not only in their social context, but as individuals.

The President also spoke of the important work of the Federation of Democratic Women, in many respects so near to that of the ICW.

Returning to the question of the future of the ICW, Mrs Lefaucheux hoped that the Council meeting would adopt those recommendations of the Rome Executive which would permit an extension of the Council's efforts. The ICW had proved an excellent instrument, now stronger than ever and highly capable of adaptation. The problem was not to assess or reassess its utility in the modern world, but to choose wisely from among the all-too-numerous tasks which lay before it.

The subsequent election of Mrs Lefaucheux as Honorary President of the ICW was enthusiastically received, and delegates were thus assured that the remarkable variety of her talents and devotion to the freedom of the human spirit would remain at the service of the ICW.

The new President elected was Mrs Mary Craig Schuller-Mc-Geachy of Great Britain. Mrs Schuller's experience of the League of Nations and of the United Nations, her pioneer work for UNRRA in war-devastated countries, her close and active contacts with voluntary organizations in Europe, South Africa, Canada and the US eminently qualified her to lead the Council in a time of rapid expansion and increasing international responsibility.

In view of the growing demands made upon the ICW secretariat, as a result both of the growing number of NCWs and of the increased range of opportunities for co-operation with inter-govern-mental institutions in more and more areas of the world, the Council confirmed the decision of the Rome Executive to reinforce the secretariat by creating the new professional post of Executive Director. The appointment to this new post of Mrs Sonia Grinberg-Vinaver, Doctor of Law and former Chief of the Status of Women Section of the UN Secretariat, was a source of satisfaction to the Council Meeting. This post would be in addition to that of the Administrative Secretary, held since 1959 by Mrs C. Pomonti who, in the words of the retiring President, had in often difficult circum-stances shown valued qualities of intelligence, perseverance, and loyalty (*ICW Records, 1963*, p. 12).

The Assembly also decided on a re-examination of the financial structure of the ICW and on a determined effort to expand financial resources to enable the Council to fulfil its increasingly widespread international responsibilities. Changes to the Constitution as recommended by the Rome Executive were adopted and the revision of the Standing Orders deferred until the next meeting of the Execu-tive Committee.

The desirability of closer and more frequent contacts between National Councils to consider common problems was a recurrent theme at Washington. In addition to a one-day seminar of delegates and observers from Western Hemisphere countries, a lunch was held to discuss actual and projected regional groupings of Councils within the framework of the ICW. A second lunch meeting was devoted to the expansion of the project on East/West twinning of National Councils decided at Istanbul, in which 23 National Councils from five continents had now volunteered to participate.

The rôle of the ICW in the UN Decade of Development was a major theme of the Seventeenth Council Meeting. Representatives of the UN and Specialized Agencies welcomed ICW participation in this ten years of concerted effort on the part of UN Organs and Agencies, Member States and NGOs to accelerate the economic and social advancement of under-developed countries.

In her last report as ICW Liaison Officer to UN, Mrs Schuller-McGeachy stressed the special rôle of voluntary organizations in stimulating the invention of new methods to meet new needs, and in fitting material improvements to human and social purposes. The long and varied experience of National Councils, said Mrs Schuller, provides the ICW with a great opportunity to respond to the moral challenge of the Decade of Development. Not only do National Councils work continuously towards the alleviation of hunger, the elimination of ignorance and injustice, the adaptation of men and women to new patterns of life, they also cherish and encourage the enrichment of personal life by art in all its forms, and foster the utilization of the great information media—press, cinema, radio and television—as means of broadening human communication and understanding. In the resolutions subsequently presented and in the work plans established by Standing Committees (see Histories of Standing Committees, pp. 155–200) the ICW demonstrated its conviction that, thanks to the impetus of the UN Decade of Development, almost every facet of Council experience can be brought to bear more intensively on the problems of developing countries.

The rapid evolution of ideas within the ICW was strikingly demonstrated by the resolution on education for responsible parenthood adopted at Washington. The 1960 Triennial, hesitating to take a stand, had merely asked NCWs to consider the advisability of an inquiry into this complex problem. The 1963 Council Meeting, largely at the instigation of delegates from African and Asian countries, adopted by a large majority a resolution advocating community education on the medical, ethical and moral aspects and dangers of the world population increase, and recommending

115

that qualified and acceptable child-spacing instruction be provided to all parents who desire it, as part of the regular medical services to the community.

Other specific problems to which attention was directed at Washington were: the need for renewed efforts to secure the effective implementation of International Conventions on the Abolition of Slavery; the urgency of further work towards legislation guaranteeing equal parental rights; the encouragement of art education by radio, television and in the programmes of all secondary schools; and the importance of the preservation and proper use of natural resources. An *ad hoc* Committee was established by the Board of Officers to investigate the potential rôle of NCWs in awakening and educating public opinion concerning this last and vitally important contemporary problem.

After a series of group Committee Meetings, a plenary evening session, chaired by Eva, Marchioness of Reading, was devoted to the discussion of the rôle of NGOs in the training and education of young people of both sexes for the exercise of civic responsibility.

At the last Plenary Session on June 29th, Presidents of National Councils determined to mark the ICWs own seventy-five years of work for the promotion of human rights, and the Fifteenth Anniversary of the Universal Declaration. A statement was issued, signed by every President present, pledging their respective Councils 'to seek vigorously to influence all branches of government, civic and other institutions to join in the fight to end discrimination in all its forms and all violations of Human Rights, so that the principles enunciated in the Declaration may become a reality'.

For the final meeting of this Anniversary Conference, the ICW was honoured by a farewell dinner in the dignity and beauty of the State Department dining rooms, at which delegates were welcomed, in the absence of her husband, by Mrs Dean Rusk, wife of the Secretary of State and addressed by Mrs Katie Louchheim, Deputy Assistant Secretary of State for Public Affairs. This distinguished American Government official recalled how, during the last hundred years, 'the voluntary contributions of women have changed the faces of their communities, urged reforms which could have waited for the passage of law and fought long and hard for laws that made such reforms permanent'. Now that the world has 'become the kind of place where events in our own community affect all of humanity, even those at the other ends of the earth', concluded

116

Mrs Louchheim, the growing influence of women in so many spheres should serve to create an atmosphere in which peace and progress are possible for all mankind.

Thanking the State Department for the encouragement afforded to the ICW by the welcome and support given on this historic occasion, the new President of the ICW told her listeners that, in her opinion, the most startling feature of this Seventy-fifth Anniversary Council Meeting had been the clarity with which it had revealed the modernity of the ICW: the exact relevance of the purpose of 1888 to the needs of life today. An abiding concern with human values has always been the touchstone of the ICW, said Mrs Schuller-McGeachy: 'In our tradition lies our opportunity. In this time of unprecedented change it remains the great privilege of the ICW to express its belief in the integrity of the human spirit.'

ICW delegates and observers leaving Washington for their homes in every continent carried back with them not only vivid impressions of this Jubilee meeting, of work accomplished and responsibilities faced, but also the firm conviction of the continued validity of the Constitution, the objectives and the methods of the Council and of its determination and ability to rise to the challenges and opportunities of future years.

.   .   .   .   .

Only eight months later, on February 25th, 1964, the Honorary President of the ICW, Mrs Marie-Hélène Lefaucheux was tragically killed in an aircraft accident on her way from Mexico to New York to attend a session of the UN Commission on Human Rights. It seems fitting to share with readers of this history the homage paid to her memory by the members of this Commission on the day of her death.[1]

Twentieth Session of the Commission on Human Rights
Held at Headquarters, New York on
Tuesday 25th February, 1964 at 11.5 a.m.

Tribute to the Memory of Mrs M. H. Lefaucheux.

The Chairman (Mr Ponce Y Carbo, Ecuador) informed the Commission that Mrs Lefaucheux, who had been serving on the Human Rights Commission as Representative of the Commission on the

___

[1] The following summarized account is taken from *UN Document E/CN.4/SR. 783* of February 28th, 1964.

Status of Women, had just lost her life in an aircraft accident while returning from Mexico where she had been holding consultations with the Chairman of that Commission. He paid tribute to the exceptional qualities of Mrs Lefaucheux and to the importance of her work for Human Rights and, speaking on behalf of all members of the Commission on Human Rights, offered sincere condolences to the French Delegation, the French Government and to the family of Mrs Lefaucheux.

At the request of the Chairman the members of the Commission observed a minute of silence in memory of Mrs Lefaucheux.

Mr Seydoux (France) thanked the Chairman for his tribute which testified to the feeling of respect and affection which Mrs Lefaucheux had inspired in the great United Nations family, and more particularly in the Commission on Human Rights. Recalling the outstanding rôle of Mrs Lefaucheux in the Resistance, in the post-war parliamentary institutions of France and in the French Delegation to the United Nations, Mr Seydoux spoke of her active and burning interest in international problems, to which she had given of herself unsparingly. Her death was a great loss to the French Delegation, to France and to the United Nations.

The Rapporteur (Mr Ignacio-Pinto, Dahomey) expressed his deep emotion in undertaking the very painful task of speaking on the occasion of the tragic death of a sincere friend with whom, after the war, he had worked in the French parliament to pave the way for the French Union which was to lead the peoples of French Africa to independence. Mrs Lefaucheux had in those days shown deep affection and untiring devotion towards the ebony-skinned men who had been called upon to work in the parliamentary institutions of the metropolitan country. With a courage which all had admired and wondered at, she had supported them in all their just grievances. Travelling ceaselessly over the vast African continent, she had worked for the emancipation of Negro women and had always been seeking better ways of serving the cause of the status of women. Her life would set an example and the memory of her fine qualities and her virtues would be a source of strength and an encouragement to press on in the service of human rights.

Mr Hakim (Lebanon), speaking also on behalf of the Delegations of India, the Philippines and Turkey; *Mr Beaufort* (Netherlands), speaking also on behalf of the Delegations of Austria, Canada, the United Kingdom and the United States; *Mr Nedbailo* (Ukrainian Soviet Socialist Republic), speaking also on behalf of the Delegations of Poland and the Soviet Union; *Mr Sperduti* (Italy), speaking also on behalf of the Danish Delegation; *Mr Volio* (Costa Rica), speaking also on behalf of the Delegations of Chile, Ecuador and El Salvador; and *Mr Doe* (Liberia) expressed their deep sorrow and paid tributes to the memory of Mrs Lefaucheux. They felt immense grief at the passing of one of the greatest figures in the United Nations, who had devoted her life to the promotion of human rights. In Mrs

Lefaucheux, the United Nations and, with it, the noblest interests of mankind, were losing an outstanding person.

Mr Farman-Farmaian (International Labour Organization) speaking also on behalf of the United Nations Educational, Scientific and Cultural Organization and of the World Health Organization, associated the Specialized Agencies with the tributes paid to the memory of Mrs Lefaucheux, and *Mr Raphael* (International Commission of Jurists) expressed the profound grief of all the Non-Governmental Organizations.

BIBLIOGRAPHICAL REFERENCES

PART III

1938–63

Bulletin, ICW Periodical Publication, 1938–57.
Review, ICW Quarterly Publication, 1958–60.
Newsletter, ICW Publication, 1961.
ICW Records 1947—*Report of First Post-War Council Meeting, Philadelphia, 1947.*
ICW Records 1951—*Report of the Triennial Council Meeting, Athens, 1951.*
ICW Records 1954—*Report of the Triennial Council Meeting, Helsinki, 1954.*
ICW Records 1957—*Report of the Triennial Council Meeting, Montreal, 1957.*
ICW Records 1960—*Report of the Triennial Council Meeting, Istanbul, 1960.*
ICW Records 1963—*Report of the Triennial Council Meeting, Washington, 1963.*

BIOGRAPHICAL SKETCHES
OF ICW PRESIDENTS

BIOGRAPHICAL SKETCHES
OF ICW PRESIDENTS

MAY ELIZA WRIGHT SEWALL

Originator of the Council Idea

President of the World Congress of Representative Women and
First ICW Quinquennial Council Meeting, Chicago, 1893.

ICW PRESIDENT: 1899–1904

Through her father, a school teacher in Milwaukee, USA, May Wright Sewall (1844–1920) was from her earliest years closely associated with the world of education. A precocious child, said to be reading Milton at the age of 7, her early studies were with her father and in the local public schools. She herself first taught school in Wakesha, Wisconsin, in order to earn money for the college education she desired. Graduated from Northwestern University in 1860, she taught in Mississippi, in Michigan and in Frankfurt, Indiana. After her marriage to Edwin Thompson, the school Principal, she moved with her husband to Indianapolis where both taught until his early death in 1876. In 1880, she married Theodore Lovell Sewall, a graduate of Harvard, who had established a classical school for boys in Indianapolis. Together they founded an equivalent school for girls, of which Mrs Sewall remained the Principal for some time after the death of her second husband in 1885.

A feminist from her earliest years, Mrs Sewall's activity in the women's movement dates from her arrival in Indianapolis, where she set about gathering groups of like-minded women to work for public service. She was a charter member of many Indianapolis clubs and founder of the Indiana Association for promoting Women's Suffrage. The wide range of her interests is evidenced by the fact that, following the visit of Pandita Ramabai to the United States, she formed the Ramabai Circle 'to assist in freeing the women of India from their ancient bondage'. She was also one of the first members of the Association of Collegiate Alumnae and lived to see her vision of a World Federation of University Women realized in 1919.

123

It was through her work in the cause of women's suffrage—in the course of which she took part in campaigns for the women's vote in many of the middle-western states—and in her capacity as Chairman of the Executive Committee of the National Suffrage Association, that Mrs Sewall came to serve as Chairman of the Committee which, in 1888, organized the foundation of the National Council of Women of the United States, and of the ICW.

In 1889, Mrs Sewall travelled to Paris to expound the Council Idea at a meeting of an International Congress of Women convened under the auspices of the French Government on the occasion of the Great Exhibition, following this up with visits to Zürich and Geneva. In 1891 and 1892, undaunted by the difficulties of contemporary travel, the indefatigable Mrs Sewall returned to Europe to awaken interest in the World Congress of Representative Women of which she was the general organizer and President, held in Chicago in 1893, as part of the Columbian Exhibition. Mrs Sewall was subsequently active in the promotion of National Councils in Holland and other European countries, and her term as President of the ICW (1899–1904) saw the affiliation of many new Councils.

On resigning the Presidency of the ICW, Mrs Sewall actively pursued the programme of work for peace already launched under her inspiration by the National Council of Women of the United States. From 1904–14 she served as Convener of the first ICW Standing Committee on Peace and International Arbitration. In April 1907, she addressed the National Arbitration and Peace Congress held in New York under the presidency of Andrew Carnegie. She also organized and presided the International Conference of Women Workers for Permanent Peace held in San Francisco in July 1915.

Nor was the scope of Mrs Sewall's interests only in the fields of suffrage and of international relations. She was a strong believer in the need for 'moral education and social purity' and delivered one of the first lecture courses on what has since come to be known as the Social Hygiene Movement. She was also a personal pioneer in the movement for healthy and practical dress for women. A strong advocate of the Women's Club movement in the United States, Mrs Sewall realized their value in promoting cultural and social interest, and their beneficial effect on the mental development of mothers and housewives in an era promising increased leisure. She actively promoted the formation of the Federation of Women's

Clubs in 1889 and served as its first President. She died on July 22nd, 1920. Her published works include: *Higher Education of Women in the Western States of the U.S.A.; Women, World War and Permanent Peace; Neither Dead nor Sleeping,* a work on psychical research.

ISHBEL, MARCHIONESS OF ABERDEEN AND TEMAIR

ICW PRESIDENT: 1893–99, 1904–20, 1922–36

Youngest daughter of Sir Dudley Coutts Marjoribanks, Liberal M.P. for Berwick-on-Tweed, afterwards first Lord Tweedmouth, the future Lady Aberdeen was born in London in 1857. She herself has stated that the predominant influence on the formation of her character and ideals was that of her mother Isabella, daughter of Sir James Weir Hogg, M.P. of Lisburn, County Down, Northern Ireland, and sister of Quintin Hogg, founder of the London Polytechnic Institute. Educated privately in the finest liberal tradition, which aimed at the early inculcation of a sense of social responsibility, Ishbel Marjoribanks found in her own home, whether in Inverness-shire or in London, constant opportunity for contact with many of the political and religious leaders of the time, and her vocation for religious and humanitarian work was thus awakened at an early age. With Mr Gladstone, the young Ishbel formed a friendship which continued with increasing strength throughout the life of the great elder statesman and became, like her husband, an ardent Liberal, serving as President of the Women's Liberal Federation both in England and in Scotland.

In 1877 she married John Gordon Campbell, Seventh Earl of Aberdeen and subsequently First Marquess of Aberdeen and Temair, who from his own earliest days also showed a deep personal preoccupation with social welfare. Lady Aberdeen was by birth and education admirably fitted to second and support her husband in his diplomatic assignments, while Lord Aberdeen for his part, not only encouraged his wife to do her utmost in the service of humanity but—to quote her own words—'associated himself with me in all my undertakings and so made everything possible'.

Wherever it might be, the home of Lord and Lady Aberdeen became the centre of generous hospitality and the birthplace of fruitful social enterprise—one of the earliest being the Haddo House Association which, beginning as an educational and recreational

125

project for the young women on their Aberdeenshire estate, soon extended its membership in Great Britain and the Dominions as the Onward and Upward Association. Lady Aberdeen was also the founder of the International Lyceum Club.

In 1886, when Lord Aberdeen was appointed Lord Lieutenant of Ireland, Lady Aberdeen accompanied him on a tour of the disturbed southern counties and first interested herself in the promotion of those cottage industries which were subsequently to bring such practical advantage to countless Irish homes. The brief period of Lord Aberdeen's first tour of office in Ireland was eventful and historic and their departure was marked by a demonstration of singular good will and deep regret. In the same year, 1886, in the course of a world tour, Lord and Lady Aberdeen visited India, Australia and the United States. They travelled through Canada and, after visiting several emigration projects, founded an organization for the provision of literature to lonely settlers. In 1893 Lord Aberdeen took up his appointment as Governor-General of Canada.

The duties involved by her position as wife of the Governor-General might well have sufficed to occupy the energies of a woman also determined, as was Lady Aberdeen, personally to supervise the education of her three young sons and of her daughter who, as Lady Pentland, later became an active international officer of the ICW. Lady Aberdeen, however, not only willingly accepted the heavy duties involved by her election as President of the ICW during the first year of her husband's term of office, but also found time and energy in Canada both to organize and serve as first President of the National Council of Women of that country and to institute a nation-wide health service by creating, in 1898, the Victorian Order of Nurses.

In 1906, Lord and Lady Aberdeen returned to Dublin Castle where Lord Aberdeen served as Lord Lieutenant for nine years, the longest term in the history of this office. It was from Ireland that Lady Aberdeen served the major part of her second and third terms as President of the ICW; in Ireland that she and her guests, Baroness Gripenberg of Finland and Mrs Sanford of Canada, received in the night watches the cable bringing the momentous news of the first breakthrough in the struggle for the women's vote in Europe— Finland's granting of full political rights to women in 1906; in Ireland, too, that she founded the Women's National Health Association, with its crusade against infant mortality and tuberculosis, its

126

travelling exhibitions on preventive hygiene and on housing and other pioneer initiatives in the field of education for public health.

In 1919, Lady Aberdeen was the leader and spokesman of an ICW deputation to the League of Nations Committee established by the Versailles Peace Conference. From 1918 to 1920 Lady Aberdeen worked indefatigably to revive and regroup the ICW in the first post-war years. In 1920, she deliberately interrupted her long term as President by relinquishing her office to the citizen of a neutral country, Mrs Chaponnière-Chaix of Switzerland. In 1922, she was once more elected President and took up the task of directing the post-war reconstruction and programme of the ICW. In 1927, Lord and Lady Aberdeen celebrated their Golden Wedding Anniversary, unhappily followed, in 1934, by the death of Lord Aberdeen. In 1936, at the age of 79, Lady Aberdeen resigned from the Presidency of the ICW, though continuing to lend to her successor the strength of her invaluable experience and advice as Honorary President for her remaining years, which were as full as ever of unceasing action in the interests of peace and of those Scottish, Liberal and humanitarian activities with which she had been so long associated.

Early in 1939, Lady Aberdeen, incompletely recovered from an attack of influenza, insisted on journeying to Birmingham to speak at the opening of a new YWCA building. She suffered a relapse, but, lucid and tireless to the end, sent from her sick bed a message to the local branch of the League of Nations Society, deploring the ruthless invasion of Czechoslovakia and urging the rallying of the peaceful powers. She died on April 18th, 1939, and was interred in the private burial ground at Haddo House.

PAULINE CHAPONNIÈRE-CHAIX

ICW PRESIDENT: 1920–22

Pauline Chaix (born 1850), whose father was an eminent Swiss Professor of Geography, grew up in an atmosphere of great intellectual distinction. To supplement her knowledge of English acquired at home from a family friend, she was sent to school in Germany at the age of 15 to learn German. At 18 she married her cousin, Edouard Chaponnière, a Geneva banker. After only seven years of marriage, her husband's health suffered a complete breakdown, necessitating long hospitalization. During numerous stays in Paris to be near her husband, Mrs Chaponnière-Chaix made her first contact with women inspired by feminist ideals, among them Miss Sarah Monod, Mrs Avril de Sainte-Croix and Mrs Jules Siegfried.

Returning to Switzerland after her husband's death, she found herself alone and childless, and in 1880 entered the *Maison des Diaconesses de Reuilly* in Paris working for several years in connection with the shelter run by that institution which revealed to her a misery only to be found in the slums of a great capital. Feeling that it was the young who needed most help and care, Mrs Chaponnière-Chaix subsequently transferred to the reformatory centre, the work of which was primarily concerned with the protection of minors from moral danger. Here she not only taught, having passed the examinations necessary for the exercise of the teaching profession in France, but extended her care successively to the inmates of the Women's Prisons at St Lazare and Doullins, and to 'Les Ombrages' a rest home for women workers. Together with Miss Monod, Mrs Chaponnière-Chaix here organized the 'Conferences de Versailles'— a series of annual meetings of representatives of the various branches of social and philanthropic work with which they were concerned, which was to prove one of the main sources of the future National Council of Women of France.

Only a breakdown in her own health forced Mrs Chaponnière-Chaix to abandon active social work in France after fifteen strenuous years. Restored to health after careful treatment, she was able to resume contact with the Women's Movement, this time with the Geneva group responsible for the *Union des Femmes*. In 1896, year of the Swiss National Exhibition in Geneva, Mrs Chaponnière-Chaix was among the organizers of the First Swiss Congress of Women's Interests, which led to the establishment of the *Alliance des Sociétés Féminines Suisse* in 1900. In 1904 she was elected President of this body and headed the delegation to the ICW Triennial Council meeting in Berlin at which the Swiss Council was affiliated to the ICW.

From 1916–20, Mrs Chaponnière-Chaix again presided the Swiss Council and thus it was that at Oslo, in 1920, Lady Aberdeen, wishing to entrust the post-war reconstruction of the International Council to a citizen of a former non-belligerent country, requested her to assume for a time the Presidency of the ICW. After two years,

Lady Aberdeen once more took up the reins, Mrs Chaponnière-Chaix, now Hon. Vice-President, continuing until 1925 to represent the ICW with the new international organisations established at Geneva. Appointed a member of the International Red Cross Committee in this same year, she became Vice-President in 1930 and, despite her eighty years, continued, as Hon. Vice-President, to follow its work with unflagging interest until her death in 1934.

BARONESS POL BOËL

ICW PRESIDENT: 1936–47

Born in Ghent in 1877 of an aristocratic Belgian family, members of which had for many generations devoted themselves to public service, Marthe de Kerchove de Denterghem was educated in the primary, middle and upper classes of the Kerchove Institute founded by her grandfather. In 1895 she took her *Brevet Supérieur* in Paris, where she also continued her studies in drawing and painting at the Académie Julian. In 1898 she married Pol Boël, director of an important metal works at La Louvière. Her interest in social problems was immediately aroused, and she founded at La Louvière one of the earliest maternity centres in Belgium. In addition to her social work, Baroness Boël devoted active attention to the education of her daughter and three sons, as well as assisting her husband in his political career, as Deputy and Senator. Her home was for many years an active centre of Belgian cultural life.

In 1914, during the German occupation, Marthe Boël organized a secret correspondence service between soldiers and their families. Arrested in 1916, she was condemned to two years imprisonment. Even from her prison cell her strong moral influence inspired her fellow prisoners, radiating an atmosphere of tranquil hope despite a heart disease and constant anxiety as to the fate of her husband and her young son, who had secretly joined the Belgian army at the very moment his parents were sentenced. In 1917 she became seriously ill, and was exchanged for a German woman prisoner of high standing. She was not, however, permitted to return to Belgium, but remained in Switzerland until the Armistice. After the war, hearing of the difficulties experienced by some of those who had shared her imprisonment in Siegburg, Germany, Marthe Boël founded a Friendly Association of her ex-fellow-prisoners which she presided, and to which she remained devoted the rest of her life.

After liberation, Baroness Boël became more and more a leading figure in the women's movement, as well as in the political and social life of Belgium. She founded the National Federation of Liberal Women, over which she presided until 1937. She was also instrumental in the foundation of the Belgian branches of the Girl Guides and the YWCA and was active in many societies engaged in social or cultural work. In 1934 she was elected President of the National Council of Women of Belgium. The subsequent reorganization and development of this Council under her inspiring leadership so impressed the members of the ICW Executive Committee meeting in Brussels in 1935 that Lady Aberdeen, convinced that she had found in Marthe Boël an ideal successor, proposed her candidature as President of the ICW, to which office she was elected at Dubrovnik in 1936.

When the Germans invaded Belgium in 1940, the Gestapo demanded that, as an ex-political prisoner and president of an organization whose ideals and principles were incompatible with Nazism, Baroness Boël should immediately cease all national and international activity. This did not, however, restrain her from giving moral support and expert advice to all those who, around her and often very close to her, worked in the clandestine movement. She offered shelter to the persecuted and the suspect. It was under her roof that the Belgian National Council continued to meet periodically, despite its supposed suppression. Her wise prescience had prompted her, even before 1939, to arrange for the work of the ICW to be carried on by one of her Vice-Presidents in case of German occupation, so that, in May 1940, she sent a message to Dr Girod in Switzerland asking her to take over the Presidency.

As soon as freedom returned, Marthe Boël, scarcely out of the combat zone, began renewing ICW contacts and set to work on reconstruction. She presided the first post-war ICW Council Meeting in Philadelphia in 1947, at which she resigned from office, continuing, however, to serve as Honorary President of the ICW and as a member of the Belgian Committee for Co-operation with the United Nations. She died in 1956, after a life centred in service, not only to her husband, whose death in 1941 ended a remarkably happy union, and to her family, but also to her country and to humanity.

RENÉE GIROD

ACTING PRESIDENT OF THE ICW: 1940–45

Born in 1887 of an old Geneva family, originally seventeenth-century Huguenot refugees from France—just one year before the foundation of the ICW—Renée Girod grew up in a society in which University studies were not yet considered suitable for young girls. She therefore took up nursing, long since an approved feminine vocation. During the First World War she served as a nurse with Red Cross units.

After the war, feeling that her nursing training alone would not allow her to accomplish all the aims she had set for herself, Renée Girod, then aged thirty, decided to become a doctor. When her medical studies were completed, she became a skilled and well-loved practitioner, devoting herself above all to the care of women and children. Placing herself always at the service of those in need, she was for many years the honorary physician of *La Maternelle* established by the Salvation Army. She also helped to found the inter-denominational pre-natal welfare service known as *Aide et Conseil aux Futures Mères*, of which she was Vice-President for twenty years. Dr Girod also concerned herself actively with improving the situation of her former nursing colleagues, of whose professional association she became President in 1927.

A convinced feminist who wished to see women better informed concerning their rights, Dr Girod was primarily concerned that they should recognize the duties and responsibilities these rights entailed. Service to the Women's Movement was as important to her as her own profession, and she was an active worker on the cantonal, federal and international levels. Besides her long service with the Alliance des Sociétés Féminines Suisses, of whose Health Committee she was President for almost thirty years, Dr Girod, introduced into international work by her Geneva neighbour Mrs Chaponnière-Chaix, worked as representative of the Swiss National Council on the ICW Child Welfare Committee. Her Geneva home was always an international centre of hospitality to those who shared her many interests. Besides representing the ICW in Geneva, where a small permanent office had been established, Dr Girod served on the Committee of the Liaison Centre of Geneva Women's Associations, of which she was President for many years. In 1936, she was a member of the ICW delegation to Calcutta to attend the

Conference on Women's Problems called by the National Council of Women of India.

In 1940, it was naturally to Dr Girod, ICW Vice-President and citizen of neutral Switzerland, that Baroness Boël turned when it became impossible for her to continue to preside the ICW from occupied Belgium. In her capacity of Acting-President for five years, Dr Girod strove to maintain contact between Councils in the face of great difficulty, handing back her charge to Madame Boël at the conclusion of hostilities in Europe. In the spring of 1947, she organized at Montreux an informal meeting of French-speaking Councils, thus affording to many of their members their first opportunity of renewing contacts broken by the harsh years of isolation. In 1946 she was invited to speak before the National Councils of the US and of Canada in their respective countries.

To Mrs Eder, elected President of the ICW in 1947, Dr Girod was an easy-to-reach and ever-helpful Vice-President. Active and practical as always, she devoted much time in her later years to the establishment of the Dr Renée Girod Foundation which constructed in Geneva a residence, comprising 48 apartments for elderly women living alone and without further income from their work. Shortly before her death in 1962, she had the great joy of presiding at the opening ceremony of this building.

JEANNE EDER

ICW PRESIDENT: 1947–57

Born in New York in 1894 of Swiss parents, Jeanne Schwyzer's pre-college education was acquired in that city, where her father's work as a physician brought her into frequent association with people of many nationalities and social conditions. Her summers were spent travelling in Europe with her parents. Father and mother alike were firm believers in women's suffrage and in later years Dr Eder attributed her own feminist convictions to her early contact with pioneers in the women's movement.

After passing her college entrance examinations, Jeanne Schwyzer accompanied her family to Switzerland where they remained throughout the First World War. She studied chemistry at the University of Zürich, received her Ph.D. in 1919, and later worked for some time as research assistant to the future Nobel Prize winner, Professor

Paul Karrer. Shortly afterwards she married Robert Eder, Professor of Pharmaceutical Chemistry at the Swiss Federal Institute of Technology.

During the years which followed, besides closely supervising the education of her two scholarly daughters for their future careers and assisting her husband in his research work, mainly in synthetic drugs and drug control, Jeanne Eder became increasingly active in questions of suffrage and of university education and organization, assuming gradually a more and more important rôle in the activities of women's organizations both in her own country and in the international field. Besides serving for many years as a member of the International Relations Committee of the National Council of Women of Switzerland, she was elected successively local and national President of the Association of University Women, later serving on the Board of the International Federation as Vice-President and as Treasurer.

On the outbreak of the Second World War, Jeanne Eder took an active part in the organization of the Women's Auxiliary Service of her country, devoting herself particularly to work in refugee camps. Her wartime service also involved the promotion of moral resistance in the form of lectures designed to keep the women of Switzerland informed on current events and on the dangers threatening not only the existence of their country but the whole democratic way of life.

After her husband's death in 1944, Mrs Eder placed her experience of organization, her knowledge of languages and her deep interest in the future of western democracy entirely at the service of the women of her country, assisting in 1946 in the organization of the important Third Congress of Swiss Women's Organizations and becoming President of the Swiss Institute of Home Economics founded as an outcome of this Congress.

Elected President of the ICW at Philadelphia in 1947, at a moment when the future of the Council, truncated of many of its finest Affiliates, was preparing to gather up the broken threads and to face the new responsibilities of women in the post-war world Jeanne Eder devoted the last ten years of her life, despite the increasing ravages of illness, to the reconstruction of the ICW. In 1951, she was able to see for herself the work of a number of National Councils far removed from her headquarters: invited to Australia for the Golden Jubilee of that Council, she spent several weeks visiting Councils in every state and addressing members in many cities of Australia. She also visited the NCW of New Zealand and, on her way home, those of the US and of Canada.

Mrs Eder was a member of the Executive Committee of the Swiss National Commission for UNESCO, on which she served from the date of its foundation in 1949.

She died in 1957, only a few months after her resignation from the Presidency of the ICW: a woman whose scientific mind and sense of responsibility to the future made her particularly well-qualified to lead the ICW into the atomic age.

MARIE-HÉLÈNE LEFAUCHEUX

ICW PRESIDENT: 1957–63

Marie-Hélène Postel Vinay was born in Paris in 1904. After completing her secondary education, she pursued advanced musical studies and attended the *Ecole du Louvre* before becoming one of the first women students admitted to the *Ecole des Sciences Politiques*, where she studied until her marriage to Pierre Lefaucheux, Doctor of Law and civil engineer.

During the German occupation of France, Marie-Hélène Lefaucheux worked side by side with her husband and friends in the Resistance Movement. In 1944, when Pierre Lefaucheux, then Chief of the *Forces Françaises de l'Intérieur* for Paris and the surrounding area, was arrested by the Gestapo, she faced the greatest risks to obtain his release from Buchenwald. For her resistance work she was awarded the *Croix de Guerre* and the *Rosette de la Résistance*.

After the Liberation of France, when her husband became President-Director of the newly nationalized Renault automobile works, Mrs Lefaucheux was nominated Deputy of the Aisne Department in the First Constitutive Assembly (1945) and became Vice-President of the Paris Municipal Council, after the first election in which women were allowed to participate. From 1946–48, she served as member of the *Conseil de la République* (French Senate), where she devoted particular attention to the problems of Overseas France. In 1948, Mrs Lefaucheux left the Senate to represent Metropolitan France in the Assembly of the French Union, on which she sat for ten years, and of which she was elected Vice-

President in 1959–60. Apart from these official positions Mrs Lefaucheux was instrumental in the foundation of the *Association des Femmes de l'Union Française*, devoted to the problems of the women of the French Union as well as to the welfare of the many young African women coming to France to complete their studies.

Mrs Lefaucheux has also played a leading part in the work of the United Nations for the improvement of the status of women throughout the world. A member of the French delegation to the First General Assembly in 1946, she has represented her country at many subsequent sessions, at the UNESCO General Conference in New Delhi in 1956, as well as serving as an expert on the Trusteeship Commission. On the Status of Women Commission, she has represented France ever since the creation of this Commission, of which she served as President for five successive years (1947–51). She also represented the Status of Women Commission on the Commission of Human Rights and on the Sub-Commission on the Prevention of Discrimination and the Protection of Minorities.

Already President of the NCW of France since 1954, Mrs Lefaucheux accepted the Presidency of the ICW to which she was elected at Montreal in 1957. Under her leadership the ICW was enriched by the affiliation of many new Councils, in Latin America, Asia and in Africa, and extended its relationship with the United Nations. Mrs Lefaucheux served as President until 1963, when, at the seventy-fifth Anniversary of the ICW at Washington, she handed over the gavel to her successor, Mrs Mary Craig Schuller-McGeachy, but accepted election as Honorary President.

In the course of her dual career—national and international—Mrs Lefaucheux has travelled far and wide in Europe, Africa, Madagascar, Asia and North and South America—as expert, consultant or representative of France, of the UN or of the ICW. Marie-Hélène Lefaucheux has retained a remarkable freshness of approach and an enthusiasm not only for the many tasks confronting her, but also for art, for literature and, above all, for music, as well as a strong concern for the sound formation of the younger generation, in France, in Africa, throughout the world, in whose hands lies the future of those ideals of national and international equity, sanity and progress towards which she herself works with such unfailing energy and tenacity.

. . . . .

The foregoing biographical sketch was already in the hands of the publisher at the time of the tragic death of Marie-Hélène Lefaucheux in an aircraft accident near New Orleans on February 25th, 1964, on her way to attend a session of the UN Human Rights Commission.

MARY CRAIG SCHULLER-McGEACHY

ICW PRESIDENT: 1963–

Mary Craig McGeachy, daughter of a clergyman, was born of a Scottish pioneering family in Canada in 1904. She graduated from the University of Toronto with honours in History and Philosophy, continuing post-graduate work in Education, Pedagogy and Political Science.

After further studies at the Universities of Paris and Geneva, Craig McGeachy was, in 1930, appointed to the Information Section of the Secretariat of the League of Nations, where her work included relations between the League and international voluntary organizations (the ICW among them) at a time when the foundations of the present extensive collaboration between inter-governmental and non-governmental organizations were gradually built up. In 1938, she attended the Fiftieth Anniversary Council Meeting of the ICW in Edinburgh as representative of the Secretary-General of the League.

During her ten years in Geneva—a period when the hopes and aspirations embodied in the League made it a great international centre for students from all over Europe and America—Craig McGeachy also lectured both at the Institute of Higher International Studies and at the Summer School directed by Professor Zimmern, forming at this time many of those international friendships which, together with her musical studies and her love of literature and the theatre, were to play so important a rôle in her life.

When war broke out in September 1939, Craig McGeachy was asked to remain in Geneva as part of the small holding staff of the League, but after several months accepted a post in the newly-created British Ministry of Economic Warfare, which included among its functions the maintenance of contact with occupied Europe. The knowledge of and sympathy with the aspirations of voluntary organizations acquired in Geneva proved a constant guide in her work and served as the inspiration of many broadcasts aimed at supporting the faith and endurance of those suffering enemy

136

occupation. She was appointed a member of the first Inter-department-mental Committee established in London as early as September 1941 to consider plans for post-war relief.

Seconded to the British Embassy in Washington, also in 1941, at a time when the admission of women to the British Diplomatic Service was under consideration, Craig McGeachy was in 1942 appointed a First Secretary at the Embassy, thus becoming the first woman to be given British diplomatic status.

In the Economic Warfare Division of the Embassy she was still concerned with preparations for post-war relief and in 1944, on the creation of the United Nations Relief and Rehabilitation Administration—the earliest of all the international organizations to emerge from the war—she was made Director of one of its five Divisions, that concerned with social welfare in liberated countries. In this capacity she initiated the system by which voluntary service organizations were enabled to go abroad under the auspices of UNRRA to begin relief work even during the period of military occupation, thus encouraging the emergence of local leadership in the organization of relief and social welfare. During this period she was responsible for holding the first post-war meetings of women in Paris, Vienna and Prague.

Her marriage to Mr Erwin Schuller, an international banker who shared her humanist temper and interests, had taken place in December 1944. In 1946 Mrs Schuller resigned from UNRRA after completing the transfer of the long-term aspects of its welfare work to the Social Department of UN, and accompanied her husband to Johannesburg where he had been sent by his firm. Living for more than six years in South Africa, Mrs Schuller had the new experience of direct participation in voluntary work, instead of as a helper of voluntary organizations from the ranks of officialdom. She visited many parts of Africa, becoming particularly active in the Child Welfare Society of South Africa, which deals with children of all races in that country, and served for three years as its President. In 1948, Mrs Schuller became Chairman of the International Relations and Peace Committee of the NCW of South Africa. In 1951 she was elected to a term as non-voting member of the ICW Board of Officers. In 1954 she and her husband moved to Toronto, taking with them their family, the young daughter and son of friends who had died, whom they had adopted in South Africa. While living in Toronto she served as Liaison Officer at UN Headquarters for the NCW of that country. At the Montreal Council Meeting of the ICW in 1957, Mrs Schuller was once more elected to the Board of Officers, assuming and fulfilling with distinction the task of Liaison Officer in charge of the co-ordination of all ICW relations with UN in New York, where she has resided since 1959.

Extra-professional offices held by Mrs Schuller-McGeachy have included: Governor of the Institute of International Relations in South Africa; Vice-Chairman of the Institute of International Affairs in Canada and of the Women's Africa Committee in New York.

THE ICW AND INTER-GOVERNMENTAL INSTITUTIONS

THE ICW AND INTER-GOVERNMENTAL INSTITUTIONS

THE FOREGOING PAGES will have shown something of the valuable links gradually forged between the work of the ICW and that of the great twentieth-century inter-governmental institutions. The ICW wishes here to record its appreciation of the co-operation of the many officials of these institutions, thanks to whom has been built up a gradual understanding of what governments and voluntary organizations have respectively to offer to the solution of human problems.

BEFORE THE LEAGUE OF NATIONS

The First International Peace Conference held in The Hague in 1899 afforded the ICW its earliest opportunity publicly to pledge the support of its members for the aims of an inter-governmental meeting, namely the preservation of peace by international arbitration (*ICW Records 1899*, p. 216). Eight years later, in 1907, an important precedent was established when the President of the Second Peace Conference at The Hague consented to receive delegations from two private international organizations, namely the ICW and the Salvation Army (*ICW Records 1906/7*, p. 35).

1919—1939

THE LEAGUE OF NATIONS

Useful contact between the League of Nations and the ICW began at the Paris Peace Conference in 1919, when President Wilson, Chairman of the League of Nations Committee, permitted a delegation, headed by Lady Aberdeen of the ICW, to present to a Plenary Session of this Committee six major points which the Council wished to see incorporated into the Covenant of the League (*ICW Records 1920*, p. 71, and Appendix 7, p. 344).

The League Covenant included no specific provision for collaboration with private international organizations such as the ICW, nor, at first, was there any official attempt to inform public opinion or to enlist its support in favour of the ideals of the League, except by means of regular contact with the world press.

As early as 1920 the decision was taken, however, to include representatives of private international organizations on certain of the Advisory Committees of the Assembly in the field of social welfare. Thus in 1921 Mrs Avril de Sainte-Croix (France), Vice-President of the ICW, was appointed as the accredited representative of the major women's international organizations on the League Committee for the Prevention of Traffic in Women and Children. When a separate Committee on the Protection of Children was established a few years later, Mrs Avril de Sainte-Croix continued for many years to serve with distinction on the Committee on Traffic in Women, while Miss Eleanor Rathbone of the IWSA was appointed to represent the women's organizations on the new Committee (*ICW Records 1925*, p. 22).

Moreover, thanks to the active co-operation of Sir Eric Drummond, Secretary-General of the League, of Mr Pierre Comert, Director of the Information Section and of his principal colleagues, facilities were provided for a number of voluntary organizations, including the ICW, to follow the meetings of the League and to make their views on questions of mutual concern known to League authorities both officially and unofficially.

Opportunities for contact with such League officials as Dame Rachel Crowdy, Chief of the Social Section, and with those Sections of the League Secretariat dealing with subjects as varied as Child Welfare, Mandates, Minorities, Disarmament, Health, Narcotics, Housing, etc., enabled the ICW to follow closely the formulation of League Conventions on subjects on which ICW Standing Committees and National Councils had in many cases long been seeking to promote national and international action. NCWs were thus able to play an increasing rôle in alerting public opinion in member countries of the League to the importance of national ratification and implementation of these Conventions.

In 1922, the ICW named a permanent representative to the International Organizations in Geneva and by 1925 formal and informal relations had reached a stage where it was found desirable to establish a Liaison Committee, and an office in that city to facilitate contacts both with the Secretariat and with delegates to the Assembly and Committees of the League, among whom were numerous officers or members of NCWs representing their governments or serving in an individual capacity as experts or advisers (*ICW Records 1922/24*, p. 421, *1925*, p. 22, *1925/30*, p. 339, etc.).

From 1925 a member of the League Secretariat was specially charged with relations with voluntary organizations, and the comprehension consistently shown by these officers (Princess Gabriele Radziwill, followed by Miss Mary Craig McGeachy) proved most useful in facilitating regular contacts between the ICW and the increasing activities of the League.

In 1926, facilities were accorded for joint representations by the Liaison Committee of Women's International Organizations created as the result of an ICW resolution, which was on many occasions able to make useful interventions on behalf of the major women's international organizations (*ICW Records 1925*, p. 16, *1925/30*, p. 336, etc.).

A meeting of the ICW Executive and Standing Committees in Geneva in 1927 afforded many NCW members their first close contact with the work of the League and the official recognition and hospitality extended to the ICW by the League authorities on this occasion did much to strengthen the ICW's sense of responsibility and understanding of its potential rôle in relation to the League (*ICW Records 1925/27*, p. 21).

COMMITTEE OF INTELLECTUAL CO-OPERATION AND ITS INSTITUTE

In 1924, the Fifth Assembly of the League took the first important step towards officially soliciting the co-operation of certain voluntary international organizations by the adoption of a resolution requesting the Secretariat to investigate methods of developing and coordinating efforts to educate youth in the principles of the League and the ideals of world peace and solidarity.

With the understanding co-operation of Senator Inazo Nitobé, Under Secretary-General of the League responsible for the execution of this resolution, a series of practical recommendations on education in the service of peace was subsequently drawn up by a Sub-Committee of the League Committee on Intellectual Co-operation, continuously presided by Professor Gilbert Murray and on which the ICW was throughout the women's organization represented. This Sub-Committee continued work until the outbreak of the Second World War.

Meanwhile, in 1925, in response to this important League initiative, and largely at the suggestion of the ICW, a small group of interested voluntary organizations formed the Joint Committee of Major International Organizations, better known as the *Comité d'Entente*, with the aim of co-ordinating their individual efforts 'to train the public mind, and more particularly the mind of the rising generations, with a view to promoting better international collaboration' (*Joint Committee, Ten Years' Activity, Palais Royal, 1936*).

Thanks to the senior officials of the Institute of Intellectual Co-operation, established in Paris in 1924 as the executive organ of the League Committee on Intellectual Co-operation—and notably to Mr Julien Luchaire, Professor Alfred Zimmern, and, later, Mr Henri Bonnet—this Institute became the headquarters and focal point of the important work of the *Comité d'Entente*, which was presided with outstanding ability first by Mr. André Waltz, an expert of the Institute appointed by its Director, and, in later years, by an elected president, Monsignor Beaupin, representing *Pax Romana*.

Direct and close relations were also maintained between the *Comité d'Entente* and the League Committee on Intellectual Co-operation, through the good offices of the Secretary of the latter, Mr Georges Oprescu, and one annual Plenary meeting of the *Comité d'Entente* was held in the League Headquarters in Geneva immediately before that of the League Committee on Intellectual Co-operation. Thanks to Mr Montenach, who followed Mr Oprescu, the ICW and other interested organizations were able to work with Government representatives and radio specialists in preparing the important Convention on the use of broadcasting in the cause of peace.[1]

In addition to its work as an active member of the *Comité d' Entente* the ICW had in 1925 appointed a permanent Liaison Officer to follow the work of the Committee and Institute of Intellectual Co-operation in Geneva and in Paris and inform the relevant ICW Standing Committees (Peace, Arts and Letters, Education, etc.) of opportunities for useful work with the Committee and Institute. In 1934, the ICW was invited to hold its Triennial Meeting in the Palais Royal, Paris headquarters of the Institute of Intellectual Co-operation.

[1] For a fuller account of the work of the *Comité d'Entente*, see also the official history of the Institute of Intellectual Co-operation, published in Paris in 1936, p. 561.

INSTITUTE OF EDUCATIONAL CINEMATOGRAPHY

In 1931, the ICW was invited by the President of this Institute to organize, in collaboration with its Director, Mr De Feo, and in its Rome Headquarters, a Conference on the use of cinema and broadcasting in education (*Bulletin of the Institute of Educational Cinematography*, December 1931). This initiative led to active co-operation with this Institute, and the ICW was able to assist in preparing a Convention to facilitate the circulation of educational films.

INTERNATIONAL BUREAU OF EDUCATION

ICW collaboration with the International Bureau of Education dates from their joint work on the *Comité d'Entente*. Since 1929, when the IBE became inter-governmental, the ICW has thanks to the kindness of Mr Piaget, Director of the Bureau, and his colleagues, been granted facilities to send an observer to the annual Conference of Public Instruction, and to profit by the valuable documentation published by this organization.

INTERNATIONAL LABOUR ORGANIZATION

While the representatives of labour and employers were granted an equal voice with governments in the constitution and operation of the ILO, established by the Labour Commission of the Paris Peace Conference in 1919, non-professional organizations such as the ICW were given no official status. A deputation of Allied women's organizations, including the ICW, was, however, permitted to present to the Commission a number of requests concerning work hours, equal pay, minimum wages, etc. Their collaboration was subsequently often sought by the ILO on matters within their special competence. The ICW was subsequently able to make its views known, both officially and unofficially, thanks to the active policy of co-operation pursued by the Director-General of the ILO, Mr Albert Thomas, both personally and through the intermediary of those of his staff—notably Miss Mundt, and later, Mrs Thibert, who were mainly concerned with the protection of women workers.

ILO Conventions coinciding with the objectives of the ICW were actively supported by NCWs, which were encouraged to alert public opinion in their respective countries to the potential benefits of such Conventions and to work towards their ratification and implementation.

The Convener of the ICW Standing Committee on Emigration and Immigration was appointed to the ILO panel of experts on Migration (*ICW Records 1925/30*, p. 21).

1945–1963

THE UNITED NATIONS

The United Nations, by its own definition an organization of peoples as well as of governments, has from the outset made specific provision for the co-operation of non-governmental organizations both as allies in the propagation of its principles and as potential auxiliaries in the formulation and execution of certain sectors of its economic and social programmes.

At the first Session of the Economic and Social Council held in London in February 1946, the ICW took advantage of Article 71 of the Charter to place at the service of the United Nations its long experience in international co-operation (*ICW Records 1947*, p. 87). In the following March, the ICW took its place among the first thirty-nine organizations admitted to Consultative Status with this body. In conformity with the rights accorded to NGOs in Consultative Status (Category B) the ICW has thus since this date been able, whenever it deemed opportune, to present the views of the Council, orally or in writing, to the world forum constituted by the appropriate Commission of the ECOSOC.

Meanwhile as early as 1946, the Department of Public Information of the UN Secretariat was working to awaken public interest in the UN, providing organizations in Consultative Status, including the ICW, with facilities for attending UN meetings, and also organizing Information Sessions at which UN projects of interest to other voluntary organizations working towards the achievement of UN objectives were the subject of free discussion.

Official channels of contact for the representatives of NGO's thus became the NGO Sections of the Department of Public Information and of the Secretariat of the ECOSOC, and the ICW has received co-operation from the staff of both these sections, and in particular from Mr James Orrick, Mr Lyman White and Mr Charles Hogan. These two Sections also serve to facilitate NGO contacts with other Departments of the Secretariat and with the important work of the Trusteeship Council, the Security Council, the Technical Assistance Board and other UN Organs.

The ICW would also like to pay tribute to the growing comprehension shown by the staff of the technical sections of the Secretariat (particularly those dealing with the work of the Social, Human Rights and Status of Women Commissions of the ECOSOC) of the contribution which NGOs may bring to the work of these Commissions. From 1946 onwards, the growing team of ICW Liaison Officers and Consultants at UN has been encouraged to use the Consultative Status of the Council both to take part in the work of these Commissions in New York and Geneva, by means of written statements and oral interventions, and to arrange for increasing ICW and NCW participation in the valuable regional seminars organized by the ECOSOC in an increasing range of countries. The ICW counts it a privilege thus to have been able to work towards the adoption and subsequent ratification and implementation of the growing number of UN Declarations, Conventions and Recommendations which the Council regards as essential to the achievement of its own aims.

In 1947–49, the ICW was instrumental in establishing the Conference and Standing Committee of NGOs in Consultative Status with the ECOSOC, and has since then actively participated in the formation and operation of similar groups of NGOs in like status with the FAO, UNESCO and UNICEF.

THE SPECIALIZED AGENCIES

The work of the Specialized Agencies established by the ECOSOC corresponds so closely and in so many domains to that on which the Standing Committees of the ICW have long been engaged that the association of the work plans of the ICW Standing Committees with the programmes of the corresponding Agencies is a constant feature of ICW policy. ICW Committees are kept informed of Agency programmes through the intermediary of a Consultant appointed by the ICW Board of Officers to the Headquarters of the various Agencies. These Consultants regularly draw the attention of ICW Headquarters to opportunities for ICW or NCW participation in Agency programmes and campaigns as well as in the various Conferences, Meetings of Experts, Seminars, etc., organized by these Agencies both at home and in the field.

THE INTERNATIONAL LABOUR ORGANIZATION

With the ILO the collaboration of 1919–39, when the programme of this organization laid stress mainly on the protection of women workers against exploitation, continued even during and immediately after the war, in Philadelphia and in Montreal. This collaboration has since been extended to a broader programme aimed at equipping women with skills so that they may enjoy the same opportunities as men to participate to the full in the economic life of the community. Since 1954, the ICW has had the advantage of working with Mrs Ana Figueroa, a leading figure in the women's movement in Chile, first as Head of the ILO Section of Women and Young Workers and later as Assistant Director General. The ICW Standing Committee on Trades and Professions, as well as that of the Legal Committee, have wherever useful, associated their work with the appropriate sections of the ILO, and NCWs work towards the ratification and implementation of important ILO Conventions such as those on Equal Pay and Discrimination in Employment. Since 1960, the ICW has had a place on the ILO Special List of co-operating NGOs.

FOOD AND AGRICULTURE ORGANIZATION

The FAO in 1947 was the first of the Specialized Agencies to grant Consultative Status to the ICW, its first Director General, Sir John Boyd Orr, unhesitatingly recognizing the potential rôle of the ICW in mobilizing the support of women in the cause of the conservation and utilization of natural resources, in the improvement of living standards in rural areas, as well as in education, in nutrition and other aspects of domestic economy. Working relationships between the Standing Committees of the ICW and the appropriate sections of the FAO Secretariat began at its temporary headquarters in Washington and has continued in Rome. Both on the international and the national levels a number of NCWs work actively with the National FAO Committees established in their respective countries.

UNITED NATIONS EDUCATIONAL, SCIENTIFIC AND CULTURAL ORGANIZATION

Since UNESCO, the official successor to the International Institute of Intellectual Co-operation, preferred to treat with voluntary organizations individually rather than on a group basis, the Joint

Committee of Major International Organizations dissolved itself in 1946. UNESCO granted Consultative Status to the ICW in 1948, and has since encouraged the ICW to collaborate with the many divisions of UNESCO whose programme includes questions of concern to ICW Committees such as Education, Peace, Arts and Letters, Press, Cinema and Radio and Television. The advice and encouragement of Mr Jean Thomas, Assistant Director General, and of Mr Vladimir Hercik, for many years Chief of the Section of Relations with NGOs, has facilitated the many contacts of the ICW with this organization. UNESCO consults NGOs on the plans for its future programme, welcomes the aid of NGOs in work for the formulation, ratification and implementation of Conventions (such as those on Discrimination in Education and Free Flow of Information) and in recent years, has offered NGOs increasing opportunities for working directly with UNESCO in the execution of its programme in various regions of the world.

UNITED NATIONS CHILDREN'S EMERGENCY FUND

When UNICEF was established in 1946, primarily to provide emergency relief to children in war-devastated countries, many private organizations, including the ICW, which were engaged in similar work, sought to associate their efforts with those of the UN. When UNICEF subsequently extended its efforts to combating disease and improving the health and nutrition of children throughout the world, its Director General, Dr Maurice Pate, turned to the many voluntary organizations active in the field of child welfare. Thanks to the initiative of the UNICEF Liaison Officer Mrs Grace Holmes (now Mrs Barbey) the UNICEF Advisory Committee of NGOs (of which the ICW was a founder-member) was created in order to facilitate and concentrate UNICEF/NGO collaboration. Consultative Status with UNICEF was granted to the ICW in 1948, and the ICW Standing Committee on the Child and the Family, as well as many NCWs have been able to collaborate effectively with UNICEF on the international, national, and local levels.

THE WORLD HEALTH ORGANIZATION

The co-operation of the appropriate ICW Standing Committees with the Health Organization of the League of Nations continued with the new WHO which, however, grants Consultative Status only to highly specialized associations in the medical sphere.

OFFICE OF THE UN HIGH COMMISSIONER FOR REFUGEES

Since the earliest days of the League, the Migration Committee of the ICW, originally established in 1909 to deal with the welfar of voluntary migrants, has collaborated in the work of successive inter-governmental organizations for the welfare of all categorie of migrants, including refugees, displaced persons and stateless persons. An ICW Consultant at the Office of the UN High Commissioner for Refugees keeps the ICW and its NCWs informed of the regular work of this organization and of opportunities to partici pate in collective campaigns such as World Refugee Year, as well as in seeking solutions to the many long-term problems involved.

. . . . .

Some account of the gradual extension of collaboration between the UN, the Specialized Agencies and the ICW is contained in those pages of this history covering the evolution of the ICW from 1947 to 1963 (pp. 77–117). During these years, the continuous expansion of the work of UN in the economic and social spheres, thanks to the great financial resources offered to UN or its Member States through the Expanded Programme of Technical Assistance, the UN Special Fund, the International Bank for Reconstruction and Develop ment and its Affiliates, and by the International Monetary Fund, has been a constant source of encouragement to the ICW. The Council has also been satisfied to observe the growing realization that official action alone cannot hope to solve all the problems with which the UN and its Agencies are called upon to deal in the field of human relations, and that therefore NGOs such as the ICW have an important rôle to play in the effort of the United Nations to ensure that human rights and social adjustment keep pace with economic development. The ICW is convinced that, by virtue of its structur and its experience it continues to have a specific contribution to make to the increasingly close association of government and voluntary effort towards the solution of human problems, both nationally and internationally.

BIBLIOGRAPHICAL REFERENCES

ICW Records 1899—*Transactions of the Second Quinquennial Meeting of the ICW, London*. Ed. Countess of Aberdeen (Unwin, London, 1900).

ICW Records 1906—*Annual Report of ICW*. Ed. Mrs Ogilvie Gordon, D.Sc., Ph.D., Aberdeen.

ICW Records 1920—*Transactions of the Sixth Quinquennial Meeting of the ICW, Kristiania, 1920*. Ed. Marchioness of Aberdeen and Temair.

ICW Records 1922/24—*Annual Report of the ICW*. Ed. Mrs Anna Backer.

ICW Records 1925—*Report of the Seventh Quinquennial Meeting of the ICW, Washington, 1925*. Ed. Marchioness of Aberdeen and Temair.

ICW Records 1925/27—*Biennial Report of the ICW*. Ed. Miss Elsie Zimmern.

ICW Records 1925/30—*Record of Quinquennial Period 1925/30 and Transactions of ICW Eighth Quinquennial Meeting in Vienna, 1930*. Ed. Marchioness of Aberdeen and Temair.

ICW Records 1947—*Report of First Post-War Council Meeting of the ICW, Philadelphia, 1947*.

Standing Committees
of the
International Council of Women

STANDING COMMITTEES OF THE INTERNATIONAL COUNCIL OF WOMEN

In alphabetical order:

Arts and Letters
Child and Family
Cinema
Education
Finance
Health
Home Economics
Housing
Laws and Suffrage
Migration
Peace and International Relations
Press and Public Relations
Radio and Television
Social Welfare
Trades and Professions

In order of foundation:

Peace and International Arbitration (1899)
Laws (1899) and Suffrage (1904)
Press (1899)
Finance (1899)
Moral Welfare (1904)
Health (1909)
Education (1909)
Migration (1909)
Trades and Professions (1914)
Child Welfare (1925)
Cinema (1926)
Radio (1926) and Television (1951)
Arts and Letters (1927)
Housing (1936)
Home Economics (1938)

INTRODUCTION TO THE HISTORY OF ICW STANDING COMMITTEES

FORMATION OF THE FIRST COMMITTEE

THE EXPRESS HOPE AND INTENTION of the founders of the ICW was that the Council might eventually develop into a permanent Congress of Women, 'throwing the influence of a united womanhood in favour of better conditions for humanity' (Rachel Foster Avery, Chicago, 1893). During the first years of the Council's life, however, the energies of the leaders of the young ICW were naturally largely absorbed in promoting the creation of those National Councils without which the ICW itself could exist on paper only.

By 1897 it seemed to Lady Aberdeen, President since 1893, that the time had come for the ICW to take direct action towards the realization of the aims set out in 1888 and 1893, and to organize concerted international debate and action in specific fields. In view of the first inter-governmental Conference to promote peace and disarmament called at The Hague for 1899, she asked National Councils to give 'great prominence' in their programmes to the 'subject of International Arbitration'. At the Second Quinquennial Council Meeting of the ICW held in London in 1899, attention was deliberately focused on this vital subject by means of a great public meeting, with addresses by representatives of all National Councils then affiliated. The ICW unanimously resolved to take steps in every country to 'further and advance' by every means in its power 'the movement towards International Arbitration'.

In order to set about implementing this resolution, it was decided forthwith to form the first ICW Standing Committee: *Peace and International Arbitration*, which, under the dynamic Convenership of May Wright Sewall, inaugurated that series of International Standing Committees which gradually developed into an original and highly flexible method of permanent international non-governmental collaboration, and an effective instrument in the determination and execution of ICW policy. While the pioneer's dream of a permanent Congress of Women has remained utopian, it has nevertheless proved possible for members of the ICW throughout the world both to keep a constant watch on subjects of concern to women and to devote simultaneous practical attention to specific problems as and when they become urgent. Out of this first Standing Committee has grown the present Committee called, since 1957, *Peace and International Relations*, which, besides studying successive urgent problems in the field of international relations (from arbitration to the control of atomic energy and the exploration of outer space), has proved one of the most useful instruments of the ICW in its collaboration with the relevant bodies of the League of Nations and the United Nations.

NEW FIELDS FOR STANDING COMMITTEES

Besides creating the Committee on *Peace and International Arbitration*, the 1899 Council Meeting decided to establish three other Standing Committees: two designed to facilitate the technical work of administration and publicity—*Finance* and *Press*—and a third: *Laws concerning Domestic Relations*, to deal with a problem then foremost in the minds of many Councils—the complete legal subjugation of married women.

In 1902 the name and terms of reference of this last Committee were altered, to include *Laws concerning the Legal Position of Women.* In 1904 a separate Committee on Suffrage and Civic Education was added, remaining separate until 1947, when the two were combined in the present *Laws and Suffrage* Committee which deals not only with political rights, but also with such varied subjects as the laws concerning nationality of women and minors, marriage rights of African women, inheritance and civil rights of Muslim women, the reform of Indian Marriage laws, the affiliation of illegitimate children, pension rights, taxation of spouses, and the recovery of maintenance abroad.

In 1904, the ICW decided to found a Committee exclusively devoted to the problem of traffic in women and children, out of which has grown the present *Social Welfare Committee,* whose terms of reference, while still including this problem, and that of an equal moral standard for men and women, now covers a far wider field ranging from mental hygiene to the problems of the unmarried mother, sexual education of young people, the protection of minors, etc.

The year 1909 saw the formation of the *Education Committee* to concern itself not only with increasing educational opportunities for women and girls, but with women's vital interest in educational progress in every field, including education for literacy, citizenship and world-wide understanding. This Committee has naturally worked in close contact with the International Bureau of Education, the International Institute of Intellectual Co-operation and with UNESCO.

In the same year, the urgency of improving conditions for emigrants led to the creation of an ICW Standing Committee on *Emigration and Immigration.* Its name has since been changed to *Migration* Committee and its scope expanded to deal with the multiple post-war problems of refugees and stateless persons, particularly as they have affected women, children and family groups, their living conditions, rehabilitation and resettlement, etc., in close collaboration with the International Refugee Organization, the Office of the UN High Commissioner for Refugees and the Conference of Non-Governmental Organizations interested in Migrations.

Also in 1909 Lady Aberdeen assumed the first Convenership of the new *Public Health Committee*; which aimed at concerting women's energies in the fight against preventable disease and epidemics, and at the promotion of health and hygiene in the home. This important Committee became the present *Health Committee* in 1957.

The work of the Committee on *Trades and Professions*, established in 1914 to study the many obstacles still besetting the path of the woman worker, as well as the conditions of her employment, was naturally rendered even more urgent by the great increase in the numbers of women workers in industry during and after the First World War. The present terms of reference of this Committee cover a remarkably broad and complex field, from equal pay for equal work to maternity and pension rights, the combination of work and family responsibilities, part-time work, and means of influencing public opinion on the subject of the working woman.

In 1922, a Special Committee of the ICW, long active in the field of the protection of the child, was established to undertake the drafting of a *Children's Charter* the progenitor of the international *Declaration of Geneva*, and the subsequent *U.N. Declaration of the Rights of the Child*. To follow up this work, an ICW Standing Committee, on *Child Welfare*, under the Convenership of Lady Aberdeen, was formed in 1925.

The original *Press* Committee, created in 1899 to promote publicity for the ICW, and to act as liaison between the ICW and the Press Committees of National Councils, subsequently required expansion owing to the phenomenal extension of the scope, pressure and potential influence (for good or evil) of modern methods of mass communication; its terms of reference also include such problems as the free flow of information and the training of women journalists.

In 1926, the ICW, which was among the first International Organizations to appreciate the growing power of modern methods of communication, decided on the creation of a Committee on *Cinema and Broadcasting* which, as one of the few international bodies active in the field, was able to work in particularly close collaboration with those organs of the League of Nations subsequently created to encourage the constructive use of these new media. In 1936 it was felt necessary to divide this committee into separate committees on *Cinema* and *Broadcasting*, and, in 1951, the latter was renamed to cover the field of television and became the *Radio and Television Committee*.

Many National Councils had, of course, been active in the field of culture long before the formation of the ICW International Sub-Committees on *Arts* and *Letters* in 1927. The principal rôle of these Sub-Committees (merged into the new *Letters, Fine and Applied Arts Committee* in 1930) was therefore to co-ordinate and concentrate the work of National Committees which, in many cases, had been in existence almost as long as the Councils themselves. Thirty-one Councils currently participate in the work of this Committee, since 1947 called *Arts and Letters*, to which was added in 1954 a Sub-Committee on *Music*.

In 1936, the urgency of problems of post-war housing conditions, hitherto studied by the *Health Committee*, required the creation of a separate Committee on *Housing*. In the same year, an *ad hoc* Committee on *Home Economics* was set up primarily to study methods of helping the housewife to handle the increasingly complex task of home management. Two years later, this Committee was made permanent and its work progressively extended to include the study of nutrition, consumer protection, co-operative organization, dietetics, marketing and distribution, the education of both sexes for home and family life, as well as vital long-term problems such as the conservation and improved utilization of natural resources.

The short histories of each of the International Standing Committees which follow are based on the ICW pamphlet *Standing Committees of the International Council of Women* (Zürich, 1957) compiled by Miss Fernande Baetens, Doctor of Law, Convener of the ICW Standing Committee on Laws and Suffrage, and Vice-President of the ICW 1951–60. These histories have here been brought up to date to the close of the Seventy-fifth Anniversary Meeting of the ICW in 1963, and a sequel to the 1957 pamphlet is now available.

ARTS AND LETTERS

The *ICW Letters Committee*, founded as a Sub-Committee of the Press Committee in 1927, became independent after the Vienna Conference in 1930, with Mrs Jane Misme, a French writer, as its Convener. It fought against obscene literature and favoured intellectual co-operation as a means of international understanding.

The Committee helped to draw up an international panel of translators and contributed material to the International Press Exhibition in Cologne (1928). Countess Jean de Pange became

Convener in 1934. The Committee inquired into the position of women writers and organized exhibitions of books written by women: in Dubrovnik (1936), Paris (1937) and in Edinburgh (1938). It also studied the question of children's theatres.

The *Arts Committee*, founded as a Sub-Committee of the Press Committee at Geneva in 1927, also became independent after the Vienna Conference in 1930, when its name was changed to '*Committee on Fine and Applied Arts*'. Its first Convener was Mrs Mary Dignam (Canada), a painter of distinction who had taken a large share in the research for and preservation of the popular arts in her country. Many ICW members in various countries were interested in the promotion of popular arts, and contacts had been established with the Intellectual Co-operation organization of the League of Nations then convoking a Congress of Popular Arts in Prague (1928) at which the ICW was represented by Mrs Dignam who addressed the Congress. The International Society of Women Painters and Sculptors, which the Arts Committee had been instrumental in creating, arranged an exhibition of the works of women artists at the ICW Paris Conference in 1934.

The Committee worked towards the inclusion of literature on arts and crafts in public libraries; equal opportunities for women students in art schools, and art education for school children. It organized international exhibitions of works of women painters and sculptors in Paris (1937), Belgrade (1938) and New York (1939).

In 1936, Princess Alexandrine Cantacuzène (Rumania) succeeded Mrs Dignam as Convener, and in 1947 Countess Jean de Pange of France became Convener of the combined *Arts and Letters Committee*.

This Committee stressed the housewife's need for leisure time to allow her to take part in the artistic, intellectual and spiritual life of her country; urged women to become artistic and literary critics; studied the question of 'comics'; and supported the development of popular arts. In 1954, during the Helsinki Council Meeting, at which Miss Anna Lelli (Italy) was elected Convener of this committee (re-elected 1957 and 1960), an exhibition of Finnish handicrafts was organized by the Trades and Professions Committee.

From 1954 to 1957, the Committee focused its attention on the means of promoting art education; the recording of the names of women artists in each country; the exchange of artists' studios; the promotion of good literature for children; and the continuation of the fight against harmful 'comics'.

In 1957 the Committee voted to study the rôle of art in relation to increased leisure time due to automation, as well as the introduction of visual art programmes into factories and youth movements. The question of the protection of national monuments and natural beauty spots was treated in a number of reports from individual NCWs.

The activities of national Arts and Letters Committees vary considerably from country to country, the National Councils of Great Britain, the United States, Belgium and Pakistan being among those which have been particularly active in recent years. In 1960, for instance, Pakistan reported organizing cultural programmes covering music, drama, dancing, sketching, stencil painting and libraries; as well as a seminar with UNESCO aid for the women of South East Asia on 'The rôle of women in the preservation and development of culture in the community'. In Great Britain the Arts and Letters Committee has been particularly active in keeping a close watch on proposed parliamentary legislation concerning such matters as copyright, obscene publications or those harmful to children, sending recommendations for incorporation or deletion of certain clauses and influencing the government in favour of the preservation of historic sites and monuments.

After the death of the former ICW President, Mrs Jeanne Eder in 1957, the Committee was asked to organize a Literary Prize in her memory to be awarded for the best recent work of fiction by a woman writer. Twenty countries submitted entries, and after progressive elimination by bi-lingual juries, the novel finally selected was *Isola di Arturo* by the Italian author, Elsa Morante.

At Washington in 1963, the retiring Convener, Miss Lelli, reported encouraging results of efforts to improve the standards of literature written for children, as well as for improved facilities for the circulation of such literature. Mrs Sweet (Great Britain) was elected Convener, and the current programme includes an inquiry into the possible extension of the use (voluntary in Great Britain) of expired royalty rights as a fund for the encouragement of the arts; campaigns to press for the teaching of art as a regular subject in all secondary schools and for the inclusion of art courses in radio and television programmes; the encouragement of the display of works of art in schools and other public places; and the organization of more guided visits of students and schoolchildren to art galleries, museums and national monuments.

MUSIC SECTION

Following an extensive survey into women's place in music, conducted by Miss Mary Shaw (Great Britain) a special Music Section of the *Arts and Letters Committee* was set up in 1954, under the Vice-Convenership of Miss Grace Spofford, Doctor of Music of the New York School of Music (US), who had represented the ICW at the UNESCO Conference on Music Education in 1953. Music specialists from fourteen NCWs now contribute to the work of this Section. A composition contest launched by the Music Committee of the NCW of the US (long a leading NCW in this field) attracted 184 participants from 32 countries. Mrs Lucie Vellère of Belgium received the final award for her four-part chorus *Air de Syrinx* based on a poem by Paul Claudel. Among the subjects studied by the Music Section are the registration of music teachers to prevent those unqualified from teaching, the rôle of music in UNESCO's Major Project on the mutual appreciation of cultural values in East and West, the use of music in social work (music therapy in hospitals, prisons, etc.); and means of stimulating the interest of young people in serious music. The Music Section also collaborates in the work of the International Council of Music.

In 1961 an international contest was organized by the Music Section of the NCW of Germany for the best orchestral, chamber music and vocal work by women composers. At Washington, in 1963, Miss K. Bromham (Belgium) was elected Vice-Convener for music on the retirement of Miss Spofford, and the Committee voted to continue its current programme, and to intensify co-operation with the International Council of Music and UNESCO, particularly in connection with plans for the UN Decade of Development.

CHILD AND FAMILY

At the 1909 Council Meeting, the ICW resolved that National Councils should give special attention to questions affecting children. In Rome, in 1914, it decided to pursue the study of children's problems. In 1920, the NCWs of Italy and of the US proposed that the ICW formulate a Children's Charter defining the minimum rights which the women of the world would unite in claiming for all children. Since this subject was too wide and far-reaching in character to be dealt with in a single Council Meeting, it was 'remitted to a Special Committee to be formed of those NCWs especially interested in the subject, with Lady Aberdeen as Chairman'. A draft Children's Charter was drawn up by this Committee and submitted to the Executive Meeting held at The Hague in 1922, based on the principle that 'every child is born with the inalienable right to have the opportunity of full physical, mental and spiritual development'. In May 1923, the International Save the Children Fund adopted a Declaration of Geneva on almost identical lines, which was formally endorsed by the ICW at Copenhagen in 1924. All NCWs were asked to collaborate with the national branches of the Save the Children Fund in preparing a children's charter adapted to the needs and conditions prevailing in individual countries, and in urging the adoption and observance of such charters.

The Special Committee on Child Welfare then requested permission to study the question of alien children in various countries; and at Washington in 1925, the Committee was formally organized as one of the ICW Standing Committees, with a Sub-Committee on recreation and the provision of adequate playing space for children.

At Vienna, in 1930, Countess Daisy di Robilant (Italy) became Convener, and under her leadership the Committee continued work on the causes of infant mortality, the care of abnormal children, child guidance, the effects of rheumatism on children, the provision of playgrounds, the training of play leaders and the working conditions of child cinema actors. The Committee prepared reports to the League of Nations on the status of illegitimate children, blind children, the children of unemployed parents, the effects of pre-natal care on infant mortality, the nutrition of school children, the provision of day-nurseries and crèches, and on the care of orphans.

In 1947, under the Convenership of Mrs G. Barbizet (France) (re-elected 1951 and 1954) the Committee studied legislation concerning family allowances and its effect upon the family. At Athens, in 1951, it expressed its indignation at the kidnapping of Greek children and urged that the Children's Charter should be amended to contain a provision against such outrage. It welcomed the action of UNICEF and urged Councils to support its efforts. Collaboration with UNICEF has since been constant both on the international and national levels, notably in Greece and other countries with urgent problems in child welfare. A study of women police and their effect on juvenile offenders was also undertaken during this period and NCWs were urged by the Committee to press for the ratification of the Convention enforcing the recovery abroad of maintenance allowances, vital to the wives and children of men employed or resident in foreign countries.

From 1951–54, a detailed study of the placement of children in foster homes was undertaken, together with a comparison of the advantages of private foster-homes as opposed to institutional care. Facilities for pre-school education in various countries were also studied.

From 1954–57, the Committee investigated the problems of how mothers can reconcile their professional life with the care they owe their children. Special attention was given to the requirements of the very young child, to the need for psychological instruction for parents, and to the mother–child relationship. Other subjects investigated were painless child-birth, child care and welfare in rural districts, playgrounds and road-safety.

Miss L. M. Mackenzie (South Africa), who had recently completed an assignment in the Family Protection Section of the Social Affairs Department of the United Nations, was elected Convener at Montreal in 1957 (re-elected 1960). The Committee undertook a study of the emotional and intellectual development of the child from two angles: the influence of family relationships and the effects of modern inventions on children's use of leisure time. Particular attention was given to the possible impact of these two factors on juvenile delinquency.

In 1959, it was decided to change the name of this Committee from *Child Welfare* to *The Child and the Family*, which was considered 'more in line with the modern approach to the subject'.

At Istanbul, in 1960, the Committee welcomed the UN Declaration of the Rights of the Child in a resolution calling upon NCWs to do everything in their power to publicize the text of this Declaration, and expressing the hope that a Convention would be drafted in the near future to implement the rights and principles it proclaimed. Following a joint-meeting of several Committees at Istanbul, on the subject of Children's Leisure Time and Juvenile Delinquency, chaired by the Marchioness of Reading (Great Britain), this Committee investigated current forms of juvenile delinquency, with special reference to existing methods of treatment and possible preventive measures.

This study resulted in a comprehensive survey presented by the retiring Convener at Washington, summarizing national reports and emphasizing the importance of strengthening the family unit as a preventive to juvenile delinquency. The Committee also sponsored in Washington an important resolution on Education for Responsible Parenthood, proposed jointly with the Health and Social Welfare Committees, in the conviction that parents should be educated to recognize their responsibility to plan their families in such a manner as to be able to care adequately for every child.

The new Convener was Mrs Grace Holmes Barbey, her election to take effect upon her retirement from UNICEF after many years outstanding service as Liaison Officer, first with the United Nations Appeal for children, and later with voluntary organizations working in the field of child welfare all over the world. The major theme selected for the 1963–66 work programme was family stability in the Decade of Development, with special reference to the integration of families moving from rural to urban areas and to the rôle of Community Development programmes in helping to stabilize the family.

CINEMA AND BROADCASTING

The ICW was the first international women's organization to concern itself actively with the influence of cinema and radio on the minds of peoples and especially on those of children. In 1926, the Council established a Sub-Committee of the Education Committee to study modern means of disseminating ideas and promoting healthy recreation and culture. Under its initial Convener, Mrs Dreyfus-Barney (France), this Sub-Committee collaborated first with the Protection of Children Committee of the League of Nations, and the International Labour Organization, and subsequently with the International Educational Cinematographic Institute established in Rome by the League.

In 1931, at the request of this Institute, Mrs Barney organized a conference of the ICW held in the Institute building and attended by highly specialized delegates from 15 National Councils, and representatives of the League and of the Institute of Intellectual Co-operation. Subjects studied included hygienic conditions of cinema theatres, the safety of spectators, the work of actors, the regulation of the employment of children in film studios, the use of cinema and radio broadcasting as educational auxiliaries in schools, and the suppression of customs duties for educational films. The influence of bad films on youth and adults, the need for censorship and reliable control of film-producing were discussed, and much attention given to the use of both films and radio for the promotion of better understanding between nations. The Conference expressed satisfaction that the previous Assembly of the League had entrusted to the Institute of Intellectual Co-operation the study of the effects of broadcasting. The ICW recommended that National Councils should press for the inclusion of more 'qualified and competent women' on committees created to deal with broadcasting, and that national authorities be asked to agree to the creation of a specialists' committee for the handling on the radio of subjects of concern to women.

In 1934, the Sub-Committee on Cinema and Broadcasting was given full Committee status, and it was also represented at the first International Congress on Teaching and Educational Films. Reports were prepared for the League on the influence of cinema on youth (1934) and on recreational films (1935).

The Committee worked for better systems of censorship, better programmes, the adoption of a standard size for reduced films, the use of the cinema in schools, the establishment of listening circles for adults and children, etc., as well as for the application of the 1936 International Convention concerning the use of broadcasting in the cause of peace, Mrs Barney serving as an expert on the League Committee for the study of this subject in Geneva.

At the Dubrovnik Conference in 1936, the Cinema and Radio Committee became two separate Committees. (For subsequent history see also Radio and Television Committee, p. 188.)

CINEMA

The Convenership of the Cinema Committee was assumed by Mrs Germaine Dulac, a distinguished French film producer who devoted herself particularly to the encouragement and demonstration of techniques for the production of films for educational and artistic purposes.

In 1938, the Committee supported the ratification and implementation of the International Convention on the Circulation of Educational Films and prepared a report for the League on how to develop the taste of cinema audiences.

At Philadelphia in 1947, Mrs L. Thornton Archer (South Africa) was elected Convener. Practically all Committee members reported that previewing Committees of public-minded citizens, many of them women, were assuming responsibility for recommending or refusing to recommend film output. These Committees were showing special interest in material for children: all had expressed concern at the effect of cinema on children, and at the lack of appropriate films. The Committee welcomed the special films for children and for less developed peoples being made in Great Britain, and the increasing use of films as a means of education and of developing world-wide understanding.

At Athens, in 1951, Miss Mary Field (Great Britain) was elected Convener (re-elected 1954, 1957 and 1960). Miss Field's first report noted that whereas most National Council reports dealt primarily with educational and cultural films, these in fact play only a small part in any nation's film industry. She pointed out that it was the commercial film which should be influenced, and regretted that only a few Councils, e.g. Australia, Great Britain, Norway, U.S.A. had established any kind of co-operation with their film industries. She protested against the negative censorship which consists in forbidding entrance to certain age groups instead of developing discriminating audiences. In 1955 Miss Field attended the inaugural meetings of the International Centre for Films for Children, and she has continued to represent the ICW at the meetings of this organization, of which she subsequently served as Chairman.

In 1957, this Committee turned its attention to the impact of television on the cinema, and to an investigation of the constitution and working methods of the film and television industries in various countries. Members also conducted investigation on the possibilities of educating young people's taste in films (through film clubs, film appreciation in schools, etc.). The 1960–63 programme included a study on how far films are misused to foster national or racial discrimination, and how far they influence adversely, or otherwise, attitudes towards persons for whom the respect of the community is socially desirable.

At Washington Mrs Sohier-Brunard (Belgium) was elected Convener on the retirement of Miss Field. The work plan adopted at this

167

meeting includes the encouragement of educational and documentary films with emphasis on civic responsibility and a sustained effort to have selected films of this nature shown on television and exchanged with other countries. National Committees are to select the best ten family entertainment films produced in their country (which must be feature films of at least one hour shown on a commercial circuit) with the object of securing wider release or re-release of such films. A project for the award of an ICW prize for the best family entertainment film is also under consideration.

EDUCATION

The Standing *Committee on Education* was established in 1909. Mrs Ogilvie Gordon, D.Sc., Ph.D., its first Convener, reported in 1912 on National Systems of Education and in 1914 on Juvenile Delinquency.

When women gathered again after the war, it was to face a new world and new problems, as women took an ever-increasing part in the educational and civic life in every country.

In 1920, Professor Marian P. Whitney (US) became Convener, and until 1925 the Committee concentrated on studying the changes in education due to the growth in democratic spirit. From 1925 to 1930 the differences between the education of boys and girls from kindergarten through to university were studied. In 1933 the Committee studied overloaded secondary school programmes; the education of supernormal and subnormal children; the effects of the financial depression on education; and education for citizenship. Even in the early days, the work of the Committee was never narrowly feminist. It furthered the opening of every opportunity for women to study and to enter the learned professions, but it also recognized women's vital interest in educational progress in every field. Miss M. W. Kydd (Canada) became Convener in 1936 and Mrs Puech (France) in 1938.

When the Committee met in Philadelphia in 1947, education had been turning away from the classics and towards new techniques, towards arts, applied science, sport and home economics. Miss M. G. Cowan (Great Britain) was elected Convener and the studies of the next few years were concerned with the question of education in rural areas; the status of married women in the teaching profession; quota system restricting the number of women students in universities; special curricula for women students; adult education, etc.

The following period witnessed an awakening to new possibilities of development in mankind, to the relation of scientific research to material prosperity, to the need of fundamental and mass education and the teaching of international understanding. Newly discovered psychological techniques were put into effect and there was a great development in free secondary education. Access of women to education, family influence on education, status of women in the teaching profession, freedom and the life of the spirit were discussed in Athens in 1951, where the objectives of education were given as follows: 'Education should aim at the full flowering of personality, developing the physical, intellectual and spiritual capacities of the Individual. This implies insight, independence of judgment, courage to seek truth and the spirit to serve, in relation to the family, the community and the whole world.'

Under the Convenership of Professor Sophie Antoniadis (Greece), from 1951 to 1954, the Committee studied, among other subjects, the reading habits of adolescents and the impartial teaching of history.

Miss Luise Bardenhewer, Ph.D. (Germany), was elected Convener in 1954 and again in 1957. During this period the Committee studied the necessity for and the problems of vocational and technical training of girls; youth clubs; the great economic, social and spiritual changes to be expected from automation; adaptation of education to increased leisure; extension of compulsory schooling; education for citizenship and international comprehension; access of women to education at all levels; education to prevent cruelty to animals.

The Committee has been in close contact with the International Bureau of Education and UNESCO since their foundation and has sent reports to UNESCO on the access of women to education; teaching civics to women; education for international understanding; adult education; the barriers to the education of girls in Africa, and in rural areas; and the reasons for premature school-leaving by girls.

Two Committee members represented the ICW at the UNESCO Seminar on methods and teaching of Adult Education in Women's Organizations held at Twickenham, England, in 1959. From 1957–60, studies included the extension of compulsory schooling, and the promotion of the interest of girls in scientific and technical training. At the ICW Istanbul conference in 1960, prompted by a recrudescence of racial and religious prejudice in various countries, the Committee presented an important resolution (adopted unanimously) urging National Councils to 'confer with educational and other public authorities and private organizations in their respective countries to the end that the educational systems and programmes practised in their countries, from the earliest to the highest stages, be so designed and, if necessary, revised as to eradicate the racialist views and other prejudices reflected in these manifestations'. The new Convener, Mrs Marianne Grewe, Doctor of Law of the University of Königsberg (Germany), presided a Seminar organized at the conclusion of this Conference in collaboration with UNESCO, on the subject of the rôle of women in UNESCO's Major Project on the mutual appreciation of cultural values in East and West. This was followed by a plan for the 'twinning' of National Councils for the mutual exchange of cultural material and information. 1960–63 studies included an inquiry into parent education, methods of following up UNESCO's Convention against Discriminatory Measures in the field of Education, and the rôle of the educated woman in building up civic education in newly developing countries.

The report submitted by the retiring Convener in 1963 stressed the increasing rôle of parent education in many countries—NCWs reporting on comprehensive programmes including hygiene, psychology, family law, economic and social problems, handicrafts and domestic economy—and drew the attention of all NCWs to the useful work being done in a number of countries for the education of parents of mentally defective or retarded children.

Under its new Convener, Miss Helga Stene (Norway), elected at Washington, the Committee put forward a proposal designed to contribute towards the UN Decade of Development by urging governments and NGOs to encourage qualified teachers to include in their careers a period of teaching or service in a developing country. The work programme for 1963–66 includes participation in the Universal Campaign for the Eradication of Illiteracy; continuation of work in favour of the Convention against Discrimination in Education, together with renewed demand for identical school curricula for girls and boys, for equal opportunities for both sexes in higher education and research and for equal access to high administrative and policy-making posts in the educational field.

FINANCE

This Committee studies the finances of the ICW in relation to its programme of activities and to the finances of its member Councils, and advises the ICW on financial questions.

Major items in the history of this Committee have been: the assessment plan for annual contributions by NCWs prepared by Convener Karen Glaesel (Denmark) in 1936; the establishment in 1938 of the Lady Aberdeen Fund (administered by private trustees) in commemoration of the ICW Jubilee; the post-war assessment plan proposed by Convener E. A. van Veen (Netherlands) in 1951.

It should be noted that in addition to the fixed annual Affiliation Dues and Assessments, National Councils assume substantial voluntary expenditures when they are hosts to the ICW on the occasion of Executive or Council Meetings. Members of the Board of Officers, Conveners, Vice-Conveners and ICW Consultants to inter-governmental organizations pay their own travelling and other expenses which are often appreciable. This type of contribution does not appear in the accounts of ICW headquarters.[1]

In 1956, after the death of Baroness Pol Boël, her children made a donation to the ICW. Wishing to honour its past President, the ICW created with this donation a fund bearing her name which serves to finance enterprises for which ordinary resources cannot provide.

Shortly after the death of Mrs Eder in 1957, an Eder Memorial Fund was established to honour her memory, not to be regarded as an Endowment Fund but to be available for such special projects as should be considered desirable by the Board.

From 1930 to 1957, the Hon. Treasurer of the ICW had always been Convener of the Finance Committee, but at Montreal it was agreed to separate the two functions for a three-year trial period. Miss E. B. ten Bruggen Cate (Netherlands) was elected Hon. Treasurer (re-elected 1960) and Mrs Norman Griffiths (Great Britain) Convener of the Finance Committee. At Istanbul in 1960, on the recommendation of the retiring Convener, it was decided that the Convener of the Finance Committee should in future be either the Treasurer or Vice-Treasurer of the ICW. Mrs Rex Eaton, Hon. Vice-Treasurer, was elected Convener.

At the Seventy-fifth Anniversary Meeting of the ICW at Washington in 1963, Miss ten Bruggen Cate was re-elected Hon. Treasurer,

[1] For a note on the Finances of the ICW, see Appendix 9, p. 348.

and the Finance Committee, under its new Convener, Mrs D. Edwards (Australia), who is also Hon. Vice-Treasurer of the ICW, determined to explore every means of obtaining adequate finance for the increasing running expenses and expansion of the ICW, including the provision of travel funds to meet the widespread international responsibilities of the Council. A special Committee was established to examine the financial structure of the ICW with a view to drawing up a revised scale of annual assessments which would be fair to all Councils. The Committee also recommended that funds from the bequest of Dr Girod (Acting-President of the ICW, 1940–44) should be utilized for a special purpose.

HEALTH

Before the Quinquennial Council meeting held in Toronto in 1909, Lady Aberdeen, who had always kept before the ICW the claims of work for public health and had, by her campaign against tuberculosis and in favour of home hygiene in Ireland, provided a 'brilliant example' in this field, requested all Councils to prepare reports concerning public health in their respective countries. Under the title *The Health of the Nations* these reports—dealing with the care of infants, and conditions in industrial work, housing, and measures against tuberculosis—and edited by Mrs (afterwards Dame) Maria Ogilvie Gordon, appeared in printed form (Aberdeen 1909). The interest they evoked led the Toronto Council Meeting to establish a *Standing Committee on Public Health*, with Lady Aberdeen as its first Convener.

In 1911, the Committee undertook an investigation of different measures designed to prevent the spread of tuberculosis through infection transmitted by advanced cases, the results of which were again published in book form (Karlsruhe, 1913).

In 1913, the Committee compiled a report on maternity insurance, and, in 1920, it promoted co-operation with the young League of Nations' Public Health Organization, stressing the need for healthy housing in the post-war world. In 1922 at the Hague, Dr Thuillier-Landry, French Vice-Convener of the Committee, in collaboration with Dr Montreuil-Straus, presented a report on the fight against venereal disease and drew up with Mrs Maria Verone, Doctor of Law, a 'Mothers' Charter' which was presented to the League of Nations.

In 1927, Dr Elizabeth Thelberg, Professor at Vassar College (US), succeeded Lady Aberdeen as Convener but illness prevented her from carrying on her duties. In 1930 Dr Laura Turnau (Germany) was elected Convener and the Committee discussed maternal morbidity and mortality, prenatal care, infant mortality, training of mid-wives, playgrounds for children, rheumatism and its crippling effect on children, and marriage health certificates. From 1936 to 1938 nutrition was the subject studied by the Committee under the Convenership of Dame Janet Campbell (Great Britain).

In 1947 Dr Simone Laborde (France) became Convener and the name of the Committee became *Hygiene Committee*. As a consequence of the war, tuberculosis, syphilis and infant mortality had increased, but hygiene and medicine had so advanced as to be able to restore better conditions in a fairly short time. The Committee felt qualified women should take a more active part in the work of the UN World Health Organization and that education formed an important sector of health work. Its studies concerned alcoholism; mental hygiene; juvenile drug addiction; marriage health certificates.

In 1954, Dr M. Mitchell (Great Britain) became Convener (re-elected in 1957) and the Committee's name became the *Health Committee*. The studies made at this time concerned the mental health of children and adolescents; the harmful effect of noise on the individual; medical aspects of nuclear energy; rehabilitation of victims of poliomyelitis. The Committee collaborated with the Committees on Child Welfare, Home Economics and Trades and Professions to study the effect of employment on the lives of women and children, e.g. effect of factory work on pregnant women.

From 1957–60 new inquiries were made into mental after-care, local customs detrimental to the health of women, air pollution, and the habit of tobacco or marijuana smoking among young people. In 1960, Dr Rautgundis-Rotter (Austria) was elected Convener (re-elected 1963) and the Committee studied methods of cure and prevention of mental ill-health, the prevention of cancer and the care of the aged.

At Washington in 1963 a study of recent medical evidence determined the Committee to present a resolution urging NCWs to intensify educational efforts to inform the public in general and young people in particular regarding the health hazards of cigarette smoking. The Health Committee joined with the Social and Child

Welfare Committees in sponsoring a resolution on education for responsible parenthood, urging that 'wherever possible child-spacing information should be made available to all parents as part of the regular medical services to the community' and that 'a programme of education be encouraged concerning the medical, ethical and moral aspects and the dangers of the world population increase'.

The current programme includes a study of the problems of hunger and deficiency diseases, as well as education on home care of the sick in countries suffering from a shortage of hospital beds.

HOME ECONOMICS

Starting as an *ad hoc* Committee in Dubrovnik in 1936, the *Standing Committee on Home Economics* was established in 1938 and began to work actively after the Second World War with Mrs Chapman-Handley (South Africa) as its Convener. In 1947 she reported close collaboration with the Committees on Health, Housing and Child Welfare, and the Committee began studies on the teaching of domestic economy; training of domestic assistants; the raising of the status of domestic help; home help schemes; dietetics; marketing and distribution of food; consumers' associations; 'home consultants' to help solve the homemaker's problems; marriage guidance; education for home and family life. In 1949 the Convener attended an FAO meeting on soil and water conservation as an observer for the ICW. On this subject, as on many others, the Committee has remained in close contact with the FAO.

In 1951 the Convener became Mrs Etty Wood (Great Britain) under whose guidance the following new subjects were dealt with: trend of rural populations to move towards the towns; co-operation between town and country dwellers; means of popularizing new foods, improvement of domestic equipment; efforts to standardize the sizes of ready-made clothes; design and efficiency of household equipment and labour-saving devices, especially for rural households; training of both boys and girls in home-making and in the responsibilities of parenthood; training of women for careers in domestic work.

In Helsinki in 1954 a resolution was passed urging National Councils to collaborate with FAO in its vital effort for the improvement of nutrition, domestic economy, rural life and the safeguard of natural resources in order to better the lot not only of under-developed countries but also of those struggling with economic and social problems.

In 1957, Mrs George A. Klinck was elected Convener (re-elected 1960 and 1963). Between 1957 and 1960 Committee members reported at the request of the ECOSOC on progress in the provision of training in nutrition and all aspects of home-making for both boys and girls, on methods of improving the status of women doing paid domestic work, on the organization of part-time help both by government and by private schemes, and on measures designed to help the aged and infirm to maintain their economic independence.

In 1958 Councils were urged to support WHO's food and health programme. A joint meeting with the *ICW Health Committee* was held in Vienna on the occasion of the Executive Meeting. The Committee co-operates in the joint FAO–UNICEF programme on nutrition, and since 1960 has participated in the Freedom from Hunger campaign launched by the FAO.

The 1960–63 programme concentrated on the need for training for family living and the study of the production, distribution and preservation of food, in close collaboration with FAO and WHO. The work of FAO on water and soil conservation and the prevention of air and water pollution received the Committee's attention and NCWs have been urged to initiate programmes on these problems.

The Council Meeting in Washington in 1963 coincided with the closing days of the World Food Congress organized in that city by the FAO to assess progress in the Freedom from Hunger Campaign. This Congress was attended by the Convener and Vice-Conveners of the Home Economics Committee as well as by members of NCWs participating in this campaign. The Council Meeting adopted a resolution sponsored by the Home Economics Committee reaffirming the support of the ICW in the fight against hunger and resolving 'to mobilize its resources for awakening public opinion and for stimulating appropriate action to combat hunger, and malnutrition throughout the world'. The Committee decided on an intensification of its programme on education in nutrition both for underfed and overfed peoples and on measures to combat conditions adversely affecting family life and home management. Among the new problems which this Committee is currently studying within this framework is one raised at the opening dinner of the Washington Council Meeting by the American naturalist, Rachel Carson, namely the increasing hazards caused by the indiscriminate use of pesticides and other chemical products in agriculture and in the home.

An *ad hoc* Committee was established to study further means of educating the public on the importance of the conservation and improved utilization of natural resources.

HOUSING

The ICW had urged its Councils, following the First World War, to support convenient and healthy housing as an essential necessity arising from post-war conditions. The interest which women showed in this problem, nationally and internationally, led to the setting up of the *Housing Committee* in 1936 with Lady Pentland (Great Britain) as Convener. Work was directed towards community centres; nursery schools; housing for the aged; the rôle of women in housing administration; rent rebate schemes.

In 1947 the Norwegian architect I. Kraft became Convener of the Committee which felt that, although previously studied questions were still of interest, housing should be investigated on a broader basis. Housing is of great importance to all nations and women must play an important part in this sphere and be encouraged to equip themselves to do so. The housing shortage was world-wide and a problem of particular concern to women as mothers and housewives and one which required their united action. Qualified women would also be needed for regional town-planning and the disposition of residential zones and housing estates. The future would also require the training of women architects; the design of rational equipment; technical devices and communal facilities to lighten housework; and consideration for the needs of the family, the single person and the aged, with the ultimate aim of providing satisfactory housing for everyone.

From 1949 to 1956 Mrs M. Pleydell-Bouverie (Great Britain) was Convener. During this period, Councils endeavoured to secure more permanent housing but temporary dwellings still remained; and much State housing lacked individual atmosphere. Repairs and modernization were hindered by rent control. The Expanded Towns Act in Great Britain encouraged small towns to expand by absorbing people from overcrowded cities. Other problems discussed were the provision of open spaces in new housing projects; raising the standard of equipment to ease domestic work; collective facilities;

education of housewife in home-making under difficult circumstances such as overcrowding; workers' housing.

The Committee welcomed the foundation of the International Council for Building Documentation, implementing the ICW Athens resolution which called for the interchange of information and for research on housing and the building industry.

Individually the NCWs which have representatives on the *Housing Committee* or have national Housing Committees of their own have done outstanding work in obtaining evidence and channelling public opinion on various housing problems and, when necessary, making representation to the local, national or international authorities concerned.

Special attention has been paid in recent years to rural housing, and an important memorandum by Miss Françoise Dissard (France) on the 'Improvement of Housing Conditions and Better Working Methods' was presented to the FAO European Conference on Rural Life in 1957. At Montreal, Miss Dissard was elected Convener (re-elected 1960 and 1963), and under her direction the Committee has studied the work of women on local and municipal housing and town-planning boards, the access of women to the professions of architect and town-planner (for the UN Commission on the Status of Women), as well as basic national units of housing. During this period Committee members were instrumental in the promotion of important Women's Housing Exhibitions (designed by women architects) in Berlin and in Zürich. An outstanding feature of the latter—forming part of the SAFFA (Swiss Exhibition of Women's Work, 1958) and arousing world-wide interest, was the 9-storey Housing Tower, presenting housing units designed for various social categories and ages, large and small families, working couples, etc. From 1960–63, the Committee undertook study of methods for assuring the adaptation of families from slum areas to modern housing conditions, and the organization and financing of open spaces in large urban areas (trees, gardens, playgrounds, etc.).

In her Triennial report to the 1963 Council Meeting, the Convener noted the growing influence of NCWs with town-planning authorities in their respective countries. In view of the long-standing concern of the ICW with housing and town-planning, the high priority accorded to these problems in UN plans for the Decade of Development was a source of satisfaction and encouragement to the Committee. Close attention will be given to the work of the special committee set up by the ECOSOC and to those of other international or regional bodies dealing with these questions. The current work plan includes special housing problems in rural areas, particular attention being given to the provision of adequate housing for families with low incomes, and to planning for community facilities.

LAWS AND SUFFRAGE

Established in 1899, the *Laws Committee*, first called the *Committee on Laws Affecting Domestic Relations* and later *Committee on Laws regarding the Legal Position of Women* has always been faithful to its aim: 'Equal and full human rights for women all over the world.' This came at a time when women in many countries were unaware of the legal subjugation imposed on them and there were few women lawyers to put forward their claims. In 1904 another committee was set up to deal with *Suffrage and Civic Education* which remained separate until 1947, its Conveners including a number of outstanding women such as Senator Plaminkova of Czechoslovakia.

The Conveners of the *Laws Committee* have included many eminent barristers and Doctors of Law: Baroness Beschwitz (Germany) 1899–1908; Mrs d'Abbadie d'Arrast (France) 1908–13; Dr E. C. van Dorp (Netherlands) 1914–20; Mrs Edwin Gray (Great Britain) 1920–27; Mrs Maria Verone (France) 1927–36; Mrs Stael von Holstein (Sweden) 1936–47; Miss F. Baetens (Belgium) 1947–51 and 1960–62; Mrs Eunice Carter (USA) 1951–60; Mrs Mantzovlinos (Greece) 1963–66.

A survey of the work of these committees since their foundation was made at the ICW Jubilee Conference in 1938. The *Laws Committee* had studied affiliation orders for illegitimate children; women's right of guardianship; marriage and divorce laws; the removal of sex disqualification; the payment of alimony when the debtor had left the country. The First World War had brought to the fore the question of the nationality of married women and women's suffrage. By 1938 a number of European countries had granted women the right to retain their nationality on marriage and only 5 European countries still refused them any form of political suffrage. Since 1920 social questions had been brought before the League of Nations, thus bringing women's aspiration before the public. By 1938 women had recognized position in the community as acknowledged citizens. Most of the obstacles that had closed

Civil Service positions to women had been removed and in Scandinavia the status of the wife within the family was equal to that of the husband. Most illegitimate children could claim support from their father.

In 1947, a new survey revealed that equal political rights were recognized, at least theoretically, in most European countries, but that women in many other parts of the world still had not obtained the franchise. Though the Second World War had changed conditions of work, women still experienced difficulty in competing with men. Many, moreover, seemed to be satisfied with their lot, and not as ready to fight for their rights as the pioneers had been.

In 1945, the United Nations Charter proclaimed that the peoples of the United Nations are determined 'to reaffirm faith in fundamental human rights, in the dignity and worth of the human person, in equal rights of men and women . . .'. The shift from 'equal' to 'human' rights marks an important step in women's development and maturity and the ICW is determined to continue its fight until women the world over have achieved fundamental human rights.

The UN set up the Commission to Study the Status of Women (June 21st, 1946) and collaboration with this Commission became an important part of the ICW programme. Since 1947, the status of women has been influenced by several international agreements: Inter-American Convention drawn up at Bogota in 1948; Universal Declaration of Human Rights 1948; Convention on Equal Pay 1951; Convention on Political Rights of Women 1953; Convention on the Recovery Abroad of Maintenance 1956 and Convention on the Nationality of Married Women 1957.

By 1951, 21 new countries had granted women political rights and by 1954, 6 additional countries. By 1957 few nations remained in which women were not yet granted some form of suffrage.

At Athens in 1951, the Committee determined its position as to the status of women in civil and family law in favour of equality for husband and wife, of equal parental rights and, of course, for equal rights in all fields. The ICW would have preferred a UN International Convention on the Nationality of Married Persons instead of 'Married Women' but decided at Helsinki to support this last initiative as a step forward. At Montreal, in 1957, the Committee passed a resolution demanding equality of rights of spouses in the administration of family property.

The period 1957–60 was devoted to the study of the effects of

Retirement Laws on women, and the effect on the nationality of children of a change of nationality on the part of their parents. During the same period, the effects of various systems of taxation of married women were thoroughly studied. In Athens in 1951, the Committee had pronounced against the joint assessment of the separate incomes of spouses. In Istanbul in 1960, the Committee showed less conviction as to where justice lay, but agreed that men and women should be placed in an equally favourable position, and that taxation should not act as a deterrent to gainful employment.

In 1958, the Committee supplied replies to a questionnaire on Consent to Marriage, Age of Marriage and Registration of Marriage required for a study undertaken by the UN Commission on the Status of Women with a view to the drafting of a Convention on this subject.

In 1960, Miss Baetens, Honorary Vice-President of the ICW was entrusted by the Board of Officers with a comparative study on the position of women under private and family law in countries where Greek and Roman Law prevailed.

In Istanbul in 1960, Miss Baetens was once again elected Convener on the retirement of Mrs Carter. Between 1960 and 1962, the Committee enquired into the reasons why major International Conventions affecting the status of women were not ratified, and what influence such Conventions had, whether ratified or not.

A questionnaire on women's inheritance rights, especially as influenced in Anglo-Saxon countries by domicile, and in other countries by Muslim Law, brought significant answers which, when tabulated, were sent to the UN Commission on the Status of Women in November 1961.

Information about Muslim Law, gathered from UN documents and the press was circulated to relevant countries, drawing corrections, explanations and comment from women's organizations. A debate on polygamy in the UN Social Commission was submitted in the same way, drawing from African women the expression of strong opposition to polygamy.

In 1961 the Convener prepared for a gathering of European Councils of the ICW a summary of the conditions under which parental authority is exercised in the countries of Europe which have a National Council affiliated to the ICW.

At the Rome Executive in 1962, Miss Baetens found herself obliged to resign from the Convenership for reasons of ill-health, and was replaced by a Vice-Convener, Mrs Mantzoulinos, many times representative of Greece on the UN Status of Women Commission.

In 1963 Mrs Mantzoulinos was elected Convener and the Committee presented to the ICW Meeting in Washington resolutions urging NCWs to press for equality of inheritance and parental rights between men and women and for the ratification of the recent UN Convention on Free Consent to Marriage, Minimum Age of Marriage and Registration of Marriages. Reaffirming the long-standing concern of the ICW for the ratification and implementation of existing International Conventions on the Abolition of Slavery (League of Nations 1926, UN 1956), the Laws and Suffrage Committee also submitted to the Washington meeting a resolution calling upon NCWs to press upon their governments the urgent need to ratify or accede to these Conventions, and requesting the ECOSOC to establish a Standing Committee of Expert Advisers to maintain continuity of investigation of this problem and to make policy recommendations.

The current programme includes a study of social factors affecting the participation of women in public life (national assemblies, local government, other public office), and of the status of women in private law with particular reference to dissolution of marriage and to parental rights and duties.

MIGRATION

From the very earliest days the vast contemporary problem of migration was never far from the thoughts of the pioneers of the ICW. Under the presidency of Lady Aberdeen, the Canadian Council played a major rôle in the establishment of a national policy of immigration and the settlement of the tremendous influx of 'new Canadians'. Like other Councils in countries receiving large numbers of immigrants such as Australia and New Zealand, they campaigned locally and nationally against abuses of immigrant labour, particularly that of women and children, and in favour of proper health safeguards and placement systems.

Other Councils, while less directly concerned with the settlement of immigrants, were well aware of the problems raised by the migration of some 65 million persons from one continent to another within the space of a century, and in 1909 the ICW voted to create a Standing Committee on *Emigration and Immigration*. In its early years, under its first Convener, Countess Daniele Camozzi, the Committee concerned itself not only with settlement problems but also with the conditions under which emigrants travelled, and a first step was achieved when the ICW, together with other organizations, brought pressure on shipping authorities to appoint a matron aboard each ship to take care of girl emigrants. National Councils assisted emigrants by providing hostels at the chief ports of embarkation, helping women and children on arrival, and informing prospective emigrants in order to prevent misunderstanding and disappointment.

After the First World War the tide of voluntary emigrants was swollen to gigantic proportions by millions of involuntary refugees who had lost their homes during and after the fighting. At the same time emigration began to be hindered by regulations inspired by sanitary, economic and racial considerations. The ICW co-operated actively with the Permanent Conference for the Protection of Migrants established in Geneva, and with the Permanent International Conference of Private Migration Societies in seeking solutions to the new problem of stateless persons and homeless refugees. On the death of Dr Kate Waller Barrett (US), Convener from 1920 to 1925, Mrs Ogilvie Gordon (Great Britain) served as Convener until 1930, when she was succeeded by Mrs Anna Blanck (Germany). In 1936 the Convener elected was Miss Fanny Ulfbeck (Denmark) whose National Council had for many years been actively supporting both the resettlement of Armenian women and children and the work of Fritjof Nansen for the evacuation of destitute Russian women from Constantinople and the Far East.

Another major question which occupied the attention of the International Committee during the post-war period, in this case in close collaboration with the National Council of the US, was that of Central and Eastern European families separated by the introduction of quota restrictions in the US after the immigration of the head of the family. Other problems treated included the protection of girls working abroad *au pair* to learn another language; the training of women settlers; adequate social insurance for migrant families; the exchange of women workers; and openings for educated women migrants.

When the ICW met in Philadelphia in 1947, the Second World War had left behind it more than a million displaced persons still living in camps after enduring all forms of persecution. More than half of the D.P.s were women and children who could not return to their country of origin for racial, religious or political reasons. The United Nations and the newly established International Refugee Organization were tackling the problem. The ICW appealed to public opinion in receiving countries to accept refugees on a wider basis so that they could start a new life. National Councils were also making efforts to give displaced persons satisfactory living conditions while awaiting permanent resettlement.

At Philadelphia, Mrs Elie Chevalley (France) succeeded Miss Ulfbeck as Convener in 1947 (re-elected in 1951, 1954, and 1957).

By 1951, 800,000 persons had been resettled and the ILO was planning to alleviate unemployment in Central Europe and Italy through organized emigration and to revive the International Convention that it had advocated ever since 1932. Non-Governmental Organizations were asked to comment on the Draft Convention and the ICW expressed the opinion that, social conditions having changed so greatly, this proposed Convention was out of date.

By 1954 a new flow of refugees from Eastern European countries, and those displaced by war in the Near and Far East, or by the partition of India into India and Pakistan, in addition to Europe's surplus population still eager to emigrate, had increased the problem. A recent official estimate has put at over 50 million the number of migrants registered since the end of the Second World War. Holland's methods of preparing prospective emigrants for their new life proved of interest to many other countries, in particular to receiving countries such as Canada and Australia (calculated to have absorbed 2 million and 1,700,000 emigrants respectively between 1945 and 1962). In 1954 at the request of the ILO, a report was prepared on the need for informing and working for the welfare of migrants and on the effects of emigration on family life and the status of women. A further report was sent to the UN on the development of welfare work among migrants since 1945.

Since 1954 the exchange of social workers between countries of emigration and immigration has been realized. The ICW replied to a questionnaire of the Conference of NGOs interested in Migration concerning the rôle of administrative and non-governmental organizations in various countries. At Montreal in 1957 Committee resolutions were adopted on the following points: continued international help for refugees and expatriated persons; rehabilitation of difficult cases among refugees; reunion of migrant families. An extensive report on naturalization was presented also to the Montreal Congress, at which the Committee decided to embark upon a general study of conditions of the migration of women, together with a special investigation of the situation of young female refugees from Hungary. During the next Triennial period an inquiry into the rights of foreigners to leave their country of residence was undertaken at the request of the UN Commission on the Status of Women. In 1959, the Australian member, Mrs J. G. Norris (Vice-Convener) was able to report progress in obtaining Government acceptance of the admission of handicapped refugees and all NCWs reported concentrated work in favour of the UN campaign for World Refugee Year. To mark this campaign, thanks to the generous gift of Miss van Eeghen, an ICW bungalow for elderly refugees was built on the outskirts of Vienna.

At Istanbul in 1960, following the resignation of Mrs Elie Chevalley of France, indefatigable Convener of this Committee for thirteen vital post-war years (1947–60), Miss L. Corcos, Doctor of Political Science of the University of Rome, was elected Convener (re-elected 1963). Under her direction the Committee undertook a study of the return movement of migrants towards their country of origin, as well as working on the national plane for ratification and implementation of the UN Convention for the Recovery of Maintenance Abroad.

At Washington in 1963 the Committee welcomed an extensive report on feminine migration drawn up by Mrs Bousquet de Florian (France) as the result of the work of the previous Triennium and a resolution was presented urging NCWs to ensure fair contractual conditions and social benefits for migrants and refugees and their families. The current work plan includes an investigation of the special facilities and limitations (both legal and social) now in force in individual countries in regard to immigrants and refugees, together with a study of how such special conditions affect the adjustment, economic advancement and integration of refugees and migrants into the life of their adopted country.

PEACE AND INTERNATIONAL RELATIONS

The ICW was the first international women's association to identify itself with the Peace Movement. A resolution was passed at the

Council's plenary meeting in London in 1899 pledging the ICW to the promotion of peace through arbitration, and a message was sent to the First Peace Conference held at The Hague in the same year.

A Standing Committee for Peace and International Arbitration was formed in 1899, with Lady Aberdeen as its first Convener, followed by Mrs May Wright Sewall, Dame Elizabeth Cadbury, and Mrs L. Dreyfus-Barney, 'whose close connection with the League of Nations and the Institute of Intellectual Co-operation made her the ideal leader' in Lady Aberdeen's opinion. Mrs Barney resigned as Convener in 1947, to devote her full attention to her post as ICW Liaison Officer with the United Nations.

The work for better understanding among peoples and for international collaboration is too fundamental in the ICW for it to be the privilege and responsibility of any single Committee. The *Peace Committee* mainly provides the forum for discussions of ICW's international policy and support of intergovernmental institutions.

The ICW worked with other established international voluntary organizations to further its aspiration of Peace, and it was through its initiative, in 1925, that 'the Joint Committee of Major International Associations for peace through education and the organization of peace' was formed. A permanent secretariat was offered to this group by the Institute of Intellectual Co-operation of the League of Nations at its Headquarters in Paris. Twenty-nine outstanding associations of men and women were members, and held an official annual meeting at both Geneva and Paris. This was in effect the first recognized grouping of international NGO's in this domain.

When, in 1932 the League of Nations convened a Conference on Reduction and Control of Armaments, a member of the *Peace Committee* was designated to follow the long sessions and keep the ICW closely informed. At an early point a short paper on 'Moral Disarmament' was submitted to the Conference and appeared in the League Journal.

In addition to its work with the League of Nations, the Peace Committee was among the earliest bodies to concern themselves with the removal of harmful national bias from school textbooks, and with the encouragement of opportunities for young people to visit other countries.

Mrs C. Bakker van Bosse (Netherlands) was Convener from 1947 to 1951. Mrs Henrici (Switzerland), Convener from 1951 to 1956, defined the Committee's aim as follows: 'To work for Peace, not through fear of war, but for the love of mankind; not only to ensure the survival of our present institutions, but with the will to build a better future.' Committee members also exchanged information on political action disguised as work for peace.

After the UN established its Headquarters in New York, Mrs DeWitt Stetten, one of the Vice-Conveners of the Committee, formed an active International Hospitality Committee of the NCW of the US to welcome women delegates, wives of delegates, scholars, artists and other visitors from abroad interested in better understanding among peoples. In the course of its subsequent development this Committee in a single recent year provided hospitality and cultural contacts to as many as 391 women from 110 countries who were referred to it by 58 other NCWs or by the US Department of State, Bureau of Educational and Cultural Affairs.

The Committee as a whole then undertook a study of the Science of Human Relations, particularly as exemplified in the Exchange of Persons Programmes, and made every effort to assist Technical Assistance Programmes then being organized by intergovernmental bodies.

Mrs DeWitt Stetten became Acting-Convener in 1956 and was elected Convener at Montreal in 1957. At Istanbul in 1960, she recalled the basic preoccupations of the Committee by recapitulating resolutions passed since 1947: Peace and Liberty, Control of Atomic Energy, Support of U.N., Promotion of Technical Assistance, Limitation of Nuclear Test Explosions, and Protection against Radiation. While all these major questions inevitably still preoccupied the Committee, it had recently turned its attention to certain points of immediate practical interest such as the extension of hospitality to U.N. and Specialized Agency Technical Assistance Experts by National Councils in those countries to which they were sent, and an evaluation of the benefits of international exchange among women. On a different level, the Committee undertook an investigation as to the extent to which women are affected by the divergent ideological trends in the world today and on present concepts of democracy. It also undertook a study of movements towards world community by investigating the function and interrelationship of the UN family (including the Regional Commissions) and of other regional intergovernmental bodies.

At Washington in 1963 this Committee put forward one resolution supporting the ECOSOC Draft Declaration on the right of asylum and another appealing to the governments of advanced industrialized states 'to devote more intensive efforts to the needs of the less-developed countries and to divert to this great constructive endeavour a substantial part of the resources presently spent on military purposes'.

The 1963–66 work programme includes renewed efforts to facilitate and further the work of Technical Assistance personnel in all countries, and to study methods for ICW participation in the UN Year for International Cooperation.

PRESS AND PUBLIC RELATIONS

This Committee was set up in 1899 to make known the work of the ICW and to act as liaison between ICW Headquarters and the Press Committees of National Councils. The Committee plays an important rôle during ICW meetings when it is responsible for public relations, organizations of press conferences, etc.

The *Press Committee* has co-operated with the Editor of the ICW *Bulletin*, of which a few experimental issues were published in the early years of the century, to be followed by regular issues in English (1922) and French and German (1925, the latter appearing until 1940). Miss Harper (US) was first Convener (1899), followed by: Mrs Willoughby Cummings (Canada) 1904–09; Mrs Johanne Naver (Netherlands) 1909–14; Mrs Kate Waller Barrett (Great Britain) 1914–19; Miss Frederike Mørck (Norway) 1920–25; Mrs William MacCloy (Great Britain) 1925–30; Mrs Wynaendts Francken-Dyserinck (Netherlands) 1930–36; Miss E. Zellweger (Switzerland) 1936–38; Miss A. Christitch (Yugoslavia) 1938–47; Miss D. M. Retchford (Great Britain) 1947–51; Mrs Betty Barzin (Belgium) 1951–62.

The Committee has supported resolutions on freedom of access to correct information as a means of promoting understanding between peoples and the UNESCO International Convention on Free Circulation of Publications.

The Committee stresses the importance of exchange of information between Councils, and from 1954–60 has issued a Monthly News Sheet. It urges the importance of informing the press in all countries of UN and ICW activities as well as of those of women in general. It has also concerned itself with the status and training of women journalists. Recent studies have concerned children's periodicals and their possible effect on juvenile delinquency.

In 1962, Mrs Barzin relinquished the Convenership shortly before her death in the same year, and was replaced by Miss Lily Marx (Italy), Doctor of Political Science of the University of Rome, journalist and Honorary Vice-Recording Secretary of the ICW.

At Washington in 1963 Miss Marx was elected Convener of the Committee which decided to change its name to *Press and Public Relations* and to increase its activities in the latter sphere. The Convener recommended that particular attention should be given to ways and means of assisting new Councils in obtaining the right kind of ICW news and to establish, locally, good collaboration with the press and other information media. Within the framework of the UN Decade of Development, the Committee will follow up the UNESCO Survey of Mass Media in developing countries and encourage NCWs to support all government and other initiatives aiming at the development of adequate information for all peoples.

RADIO AND TELEVISION

At Dubrovnik in 1936—just ten years after the Press Committee of the ICW first voted to recommend maximum use of that 'most powerful instrument for mutual understanding'—radio—urging Councils to make every effort to secure broadcasts devoted to questions of concern to women, the Broadcasting Committee began its separate existence under the Convenership of Dr Maria Castellani, a pioneer of the early days of broadcasting. The first few years were devoted to familiarizing the 35 countries affiliated to the ICW with the necessity of bringing into effect a comprehensive programme for women covering their fundamental problems and at the same time improving international relations.

In 1947 Miss Elizabeth Long (Canada) who had wide professional experience of radio programmes directed to women was elected Convener (re-elected in 1951, 1954 and 1957). Broadcasting had made tremendous strides and women, even if not in policy-making positions, were frequently behind the microphone. Though it was now evident that radio constituted a powerful means of mass communication, and a tool for peaceful and educational purposes, free access to information remained an unsolved problem. In 1951 the name of the Committee was changed to *Radio and Television* to indicate the vast expansion in radio in the preceding four years and the fact that television was operating regularly in several countries. Programmes had improved in variety, depth and richness and listening panels had been set up to survey children's programmes. Women's programmes had developed from fashion, cooking, child care and beauty talks to a balanced fare devoted to home and family questions, and the homemaker's duties and activities as a citizen.

Miss Elise Sprott, Vice-Convener of the Committee, reported in 1952 on a survey of audience reaction to television conducted at a time when few countries could speak with authority on the effects of television on the family. Mrs Kerstin Axberger (Sweden), the other Vice-Convener, conducted a survey of homemaking programmes. National Councils inquired of women as to what type of programmes they wanted; made a psychological survey of audience reaction to radio programmes; suggested that broadcasts to housewives be included in a five-year plan of social improvement; and requested that women be appointed to broadcasting boards. Progress in placing women in policy-making bodies was reported at Helsinki in 1954, but it was pointed out that the struggle would have to be repeated for television which by now was rapidly gaining ground: 21 countries were telecasting. Since television was very accessible to children from 6 to 12 years of age, it was the responsibility of women to use their influence for good programmes.

The Committee works for and defends freedom of speech on radio and television and fair comment, nationally and internationally. While its recommendation concerning the setting up of national listening panels has not yet been adopted in all Councils, several have encouraged member organizations to establish listening and viewing groups to submit reactions to the National Council.

Since 1957 attention has been increasingly focused on television: its effect on children, the place of women in the conception and execution of its programmes. Members reported active participation by their National Councils in panel programmes, as well as in government or independent inquiries into listening habits and audience reaction.

Meanwhile the Committee is keenly conscious of the tremendous technical needs of the 70% of the world's population still inadequately served by any mass communication media. The rôle of radio in the UNESCO Major Project on the mutual appreciation of cultures in East and West has been studied, and an inquiry conducted into the place of broadcasting in the education of Afro-Asian women. The *Radio and Television Committee*, since 1960 under the Convenership of Mrs Schmidt-Kreis (Switzerland), holds itself ready to supply informational material requested by broadcasters of women's programmes in Eastern and African countries.

In 1960 the Committee began a study of what radio and television can do for aged and ill persons, together with three regional studies: Radio at women's service (Africa), news and current events broadcasts (Asia) and the effects of the modification of the number of working hours on listening and viewing habits (Europe).

At Washington in 1963 the Committee decided to concentrate the programme of the next triennial period on civic education by radio and television. Committee members are also undertaking a regular exchange of information on successful national programmes in this and other fields, with the aim of stimulating where appropriate, the international exchange of outstanding programmes.

SOCIAL WELFARE

In 1904 the ICW formed the *Committee on White Slave Traffic* with the intention of keeping in the forefront of its programme the suppression of this evil. All women were urged to fight against state regulation of tolerated vice in their own countries as constituting 'an insult to every woman' and encouragement of 'the idea of a double moral standard for men and women'. In 1909, the scope of the Committee was widened and its name became '*Standing Committee on Equal Moral Standard and Traffic in Women*'. The Committee worked for many years with the International Bureau for the Suppression of Traffic in Women and the International Abolitionist Federation, and at the insistence of Mrs Avril de Sainte-Croix (France), elected Convener in 1904 and serving for thirty-two years, the Association voted in 1911 to make inquiries as to whether state regulation had helped or hampered traffic in women.

In 1919 the Paris Peace Conference received an ICW deputation who spoke, among other subjects, against slavery, licensed houses of prostitution and traffic in women. In 1922 the League Council established a Consultative Committee on Traffic in Women and Children on which Mrs Avril de Sainte-Croix served as representative of international women's organizations until 1936. The reports presented to the League Committee were of vital importance in its work and the support of the League greatly assisted women's organizations in their fight against state regulation of vice. After 1936, when women's organizations were no longer given a place in the Committee, Mrs Avril de Sainte-Croix was recognized by the League's Consultative Committee as an International Expert on social questions, and continued to work through this channel.

In 1936, Lady Nunburnholme (Great Britain) became Convener and the Committee endeavoured to achieve three main objectives:

1. The recognition in both law and custom of equal moral responsibility by both sexes.

2. The fullest possible legal protection of minors of both sexes from sexual interference or seduction.

3. The suppression of third-party exploitation of the immorality of others, including the abolition of tolerated brothels.

The Committee also studied the rehabilitation of adult sexual offenders and the best methods of protecting all minors.

In 1938 Miss Alison Neilans (Great Britain) succeeded Lady Nunburnholme as Convener and after her death in 1942 the work was carried on by Mrs Grabinska (Poland), a former judge of the Juvenile Courts of her country, who organized unofficial discussion groups on Moral Welfare in London during the war with outstanding women who had fled to that city from a number of countries.

In 1947 the Committee changed its name to *Moral Welfare Committee*. As an aftermath of the war, reports from many countries emphasized lowered morality in relations between the sexes, an increase in juvenile delinquency and in the number of illegitimate children. Defence measures against venereal diseases were based on national regulatory systems and it was felt that the Committee must redouble its efforts in making it known that infection was spread by both sexes and not women alone and that regulation of brothels was no solution to the problem of venereal disease.

By the time of the Athens Conference in 1951, when Mrs Leroy-Boy (Belgium) succeeded Mrs Grabinska as Convener, the United Nations had (in 1949) adopted the 5th Convention on the Suppression of the Exploitation of the Prostitution of Others. Non-governmental organizations, which had played an important part in the seventy-five year struggle for such international legislation based on abolition, were now helping the United Nations to plan action against traffic in human beings while also fighting discrimination against women sex offenders. The WHO, in its struggle against venereal disease, had recommended the method of compulsory naming of the source of infection, but as this was liable to result in new discrimination against women, the ICW reaffirmed its own belief in free, voluntary and confidential treatment.

In 1954 the Committee again discussed the question of women police and also the social readjustment of prostitutes; the problem of unmarried mothers; alcoholism as a cause of prostitution; pornographic literature; preparation for marriage and sexual education; mental hygiene; the carrying out of maintenance obligations in other countries. This last question had been studied at a joint meeting with the Child Welfare Committee in Geneva in the preceding year.

A resolution was adopted at Venice in 1956 to request the UN to approve the draft Convention on the Abolition of Slavery and Servitude for 'the matter of the prompt eradication of these customs is most urgent if women everywhere are to be given that dignity and worth which the UN Charter recognizes'. Extensive reports on family education and the social status of unmarried mothers were presented at Montreal.

In 1957 Mrs E. Droin de Morsier (Switzerland) was elected Convener (re-elected 1960 and 1963).

Under her guidance, the Committee concentrated its energies on furthering the progress of the 1949 Convention, with particular reference to certain articles of vital importance to women, while continuing its work on the social readjustment of prostitutes. The Committee congratulated the Secretary General of the UN on the Report presented by this Organization in 1959 on the problem of prostitution, and at the Executive Meeting in Vienna, in that year, the Committee decided upon a detailed study of this Report and a corresponding work programme by all National Councils. In 1960, while keeping on its programme the problems of family education and of prostitution, and, in particular, the encouragement of further ratifications of the 1949 Convention, the Committee decided to undertake a new study of the present condition of women in prisons. This resulted in an important resolution presented to the 1963 Conference in Washington on the need for new methods of rehabilitation and education for women prisoners, stressing in particular the desirability of a transition period between imprisonment and the resumption of community life, as recommended by the Second UN Conference on the Prevention of Crime and Treatment of Offenders. In preparation for the third meeting of this body, special studies are currently being made on the question of freedom under supervision and parole, and the training of social assistants and prison personnel.

At Washington the Committee decided to change its name from Moral to Social Welfare, and sponsored the joint resolution on education for responsible parenthood. It undertook to collate information on the legal situation regarding family planning in individual countries, and to conduct an inquiry into existing documentation on sexual education and preparation for marriage.

TRADES AND PROFESSIONS

Although the *Standing Committee on Trades and Professions* was set up when the ICW met in Rome in 1914, under the Convenership of a distinguished economist, Professor E. Altmann-Gottheiner (Germany), the Committee was unable to start its work until after the First World War. Miss Anna Polak (Netherlands) was elected Convener after the war and presided over interesting studies on the position of women in trade unions, the physical welfare of the worker, and many obstacles that still beset the path of the woman worker. In Washington in 1925, the Committee brought forward resolutions affirming the principle of equal pay for equal work, and the right of a married woman to work. It recommended that any prohibition to work before or after confinement should be accompanied by a maintenance allowance. Professor Altmann-Gottheiner was once more elected Convener in 1925, Miss Cecile Matheson (Great Britain) taking her place after the Vienna Conference in 1930 when ill health caused her retirement.

At Vienna the Committee urged that no action regarding protective legislation for women's work be taken without first consulting working women's and other organizations. It asked the Council to study minimum wage machinery and its application in combating the evils of sweatshop employment. During the depression the Committee investigated the effects of unemployment on women workers, especially married or middle-aged workers. Women were urged to join mixed organizations for their protection as workers, but they were seldom allowed a proportionate share in the administration of such organizations and their membership seemed a soporific rather than a bulwark against unequal pay, restrictions, etc. Studies were also made of conditions in domestic service and in agricultural work, and the work of indigenous women workers insofar as this question was investigated by the International Labour Organization.

When the Committee met after the Second World War, with Mrs K. Gloerfelt-Tarp (Denmark) as Convener, it was noted that employment of women had greatly increased, as during the First World War (especially in the countries which had been at war) with the difference that women had obtained more skilled work and responsible posts in industry, the armed forces and administration. Although women were still considered as a reserve labour market, their ability had increased in value and some barriers had fallen, e.g. women could now enter the foreign service in an increasing number of countries and the bar to employment after marriage had been temporarily abolished in many cases. Women's wages had increased more than men's during the war and there was some progress towards equal pay.

The Committee felt that when advocating equal pay it should also combat women's greater absenteeism by urging the development of family allowances and the easing of domestic burdens of women with family responsibilities. The Committee was convinced that the right to work, irrespective of sex, was a development which would prove in the long run to be in the interest both of women and of production.

In 1947, Mrs A. Murset (Switzerland) was elected Convener and in Athens in 1951 Miss J. J. Th. ten Broecke Hoekstra (Netherlands) succeeded her. The Committee studied how to combine work and domestic duties, joint taxation of husband and wife, part-time work for women, and the problems of the older woman worker, and noted a change in women's work, i.e. the trend away from unskilled manual labour towards public services and office work. It also drew attention to the need for trained women to work on job-assessment committees. It supported the International Convention on Equal Pay adopted in 1951.

At the Helsinki Conference in 1954 an exhibition of Finnish handicraft was arranged. There was some discussion of cottage industries and the status of domestic employees. It was recommended that maternity leave before confinement should not be compulsory. During the following triennial period 1954–57 the Committee studied the progress made in women's education and their vocational (technical) training; the part played by women in production and in the economic life of countries in the process of industrialization; the rôle played by women in trade unions and professional organizations; access to all positions, especially in public service; working women with family responsibilities; the necessity of influencing public opinion in favour of women's work through the newer methods of publicity, i.e. radio and television.

In 1956 Miss ten Broecke Hoekstra resigned and Miss Adèle Hauwel (Belgium) became Acting-Convener until the Council Meeting in Montreal in 1957 when Miss Frieda S. Miller (US) was elected Convener. Two pieces of work were then undertaken at the request of the UN Commission on the Status of Women: inquiries into the age of retirement for women, and on the access of women to liberal professions. Other subjects investigated were opportunities for the vocational training of girls and the participation of women in professional organizations and in trade unions. On the resignation of Miss Miller in 1958, Mrs Eulambio of Italy took over as Acting-Convener until the election (1960) of Mrs A. Hosia of Finland under whose leadership the Committee undertook a survey of the possibilities of part-time work for women. Shortly after her election Mrs Hosia was appointed Minister of Education of Finland and could not complete her term of office. The Acting-Convener, Mrs Ledrus of Belgium was, however, able to prepare a most comprehensive synthesis of national reports concerning the advantages and disadvantages of part-time employment.

At Washington in 1963, under its new Convener, Miss Margaret Barnard (US), Deputy Commissioner for Family Services in the New York State Department of Social Welfare, decided to concentrate its programme on the theme of 'Women Workers in a Changing World'—selected for the ILO Conference in 1964. Special studies were planned on the potential rôle of NCWs in:

1. Promoting vocational training or guidance in newly-developing occupations.

2. Promoting the social facilities needed both by women with family responsibilities and by girls migrating to cities from rural areas.

WORKING METHODS OF STANDING COMMITTEES

Relations between International Standing Committees and other organs of the ICW—Council Meeting, Executive Committee, Board of Officers, International President and Headquarters staff —as well as the rules governing the election of Conveners and Vice-Conveners are determined by detailed regulations set out in the ICW Constitution and Standing Orders. It has, however, been thought useful to include here a brief outline of the way in which the work of these Committees is conducted from one Council Meeting to another.

ESTABLISHMENT OF WORK PROGRAMME

On the occasion of any given Triennial Council, meetings of individual Standing Committees are held to establish and submit for Council approval the Programme of Work to be undertaken by each Committee during the next three years. This does not necessarily involve an entirely new programme; further study of subjects on the current programme may well be considered necessary, or again, it may be decided to return to some problem examined in previous years and now once more requiring attention. Men and women experts in the special field of any Committee may be invited to take part in these meetings.

INTER-COMMITTEE COLLABORATION AND *ad hoc* COMMITTEES

Meetings attended by the Conveners of all Standing Committees are also scheduled at the time of the Council meeting in order to facilitate inter-Committee collaboration. Naturally from time to time subjects of urgent interest to the ICW call for joint study by two or more Committees, and arrangements are made for joint meetings on the occasion of the Council meeting or for joint study of a problem of mutual importance to two or more Committees. When necessary *ad hoc* Committees are established to work on longer term problems which are outside the scope of any single Committee.

ICW COMMITTEES: RÔLE OF CONVENER, VICE-CONVENERS AND MEMBERS

The rôle of Conveners and Vice-Conveners (elected at the Council Meeting) is to organize the work of their Committee for the next three years, providing members with a concrete plan of work and establishing, usually in the form of circular letters or of question-naires, an order of priorities and date lines for reply. The Convener works in continuing contact with her Vice-Conveners, each or any of whom should be ready to replace her at any time in case of necessity. Once Conveners have circulated their plan of work, it becomes incumbent upon Committee members in the various National Councils to do their utmost to see that this programme is imple-mented on the national level. These members—normally Conveners of corresponding National Standing Committees—act as liaison between the International and National Committees and attend ICW Council meetings as delegates of their Council.

RÔLE OF NATIONAL STANDING COMMITTEES

Like the National Councils themselves, the methods employed to collaborate with the ICW Standing Committees vary considerably from country to country. Some National Councils have long since established a series of fifteen Standing Committees corresponding exactly to those of the ICW. Others have established National Committees not only on these subjects but also on additional sub-jects of immediate interest to their own particular Council; others again restricting the number of Committees to those most relevant to their own problems. In National Councils where for any reason no National Standing Committee has been formed in any given field, the President may appoint a specialist member of her Council as the national member of the International Committee. In newly-formed Councils where no such member has yet been appointed, the President of the National Council receives all documents and questionnaires circulated by Conveners with the object of keeping such Councils fully informed of the work of the ICW Committees, and of encouraging collaboration and the eventual establishment of National Committees where appropriate.

Whatever the number of Committees established and methods of work adopted, the composition of these National Committees is founded everywhere on the same principle—that of individual competence in specialized fields. The Housing Committee in any given country, for instance, may comprise all or any of the following: women architects, building contractors, town planners, municipal or local councillors, housewives, as well as specialists in problems such as rural welfare, housing of the aged, family relations, home economics, etc.

WORK OF EXECUTIVE MEETINGS AND COUNCIL MEETINGS

Progress accomplished on the work plans of each Committee is reviewed at the Executive Meeting of the ICW (held approximately eighteen months after each Triennial Council Meeting) to which the Convener submits an interim report, based on information supplied by her Committee members. Modifications to Committee work plans may, if urgent, be introduced at this time. When necessary, meetings of Standing Committees may also be called on the occasion of the Executive Meeting.

After the Executive meeting, Convener and Vice-Conveners inform Committee members of the work programme that remains to be completed before the next Triennial Council Meeting. Several months in advance of this meeting, the Convener, aided by her Vice-Conveners, prepares from further information supplied by her Committee members, a Triennial Report which constitutes a synthesis of the work of her Committee on each of the subjects under study by her Committee during the past three years.

At the Council meeting itself, meetings of Standing Committees are held to discuss and adopt these reports and to consider resolutions placed on the agenda of the various Committees for approval and eventual submission to the Council Meeting.

COLLABORATION WITH INTER-GOVERNMENTAL ORGANIZATIONS

The reader will already have seen from the history of the ICW concerning the period 1914–38 how closely many ICW Standing Committees worked with the League of Nations, the Institute of Intellectual Co-operation, the International Labour Office and the Public Health Organization of the League, the Conveners of several Committees serving as experts on the corresponding Consultative Committees of the League. Since 1946, the ICW has collaborated with the United Nations and its Specialized Agencies on a rapidly increasing number of subjects entering the field of inter-Governmental action. The rôle of the International Standing Committees in this collaboration is, of course, vital, and every effort is made by ICW Liaison Officers and Consultants to co-ordinate the work of these Committees with that of the corresponding bodies within the United Nations family. The following list shows roughly where the work of certain ICW Committees corresponds with that of these Organizations:

UN Organ or Specialized Agency	ICW Standing Committees
United Nations Economic and Social Council Status of Women Commission Human Rights Commission Trusteeship Council Regional Economic Commissions, etc. Office of Public Information	Peace and International Relations Laws and Suffrage, Education Trades and Professions, Social Welfare
Food and Agriculture Organization	Education, Home Economics, Housing, Health
International Labour Organization	Trades and Professions, Laws and Suffrage
United Nations Educational, Scientific and Cultural Organization	Education, Peace and International Relations, Arts and Letters, Press, Radio and Television, Cinema, Home Economics
United Nations International Children's Fund	Child and Family, Health, Social Welfare, Home Economics
Office of the United Nations High Commissioner for Refugees	Migration
World Health Organization	Health, Home Economics, Child and Family

As an International Non-Governmental Organization in Consultative Status with the United Nations and three of the Specialized Agencies, the ICW is frequently asked to supply information—essential because complementary to that supplied by Member States—in response to inquiries initiated by the United Nations and its Agencies. In such cases the inquiry is, with the approval of its Convener, circulated to members of the relevant ICW Standing Committee, and the Convener subsequently collates replies into a report for the initiating body.

ICW Liaison Officers and Consultants at the headquarters of the UN and its Specialized Agencies (as well as ICW representatives or observers to meetings held away from these headquarters) find Reports from, and Resolutions initiated by Standing Committees of great value in preparing any intervention or written statements they may be called upon to make on behalf of the ICW. Similarly continuous contact with these Inter-governmental Organizations makes it possible for Liaison Officers and Consultants to suggest on occasion subjects or aspects of subjects suitable for inclusion in the work plan of the various ICW Standing Committees.

IMPLEMENTATION OF UN CONVENTIONS

More important perhaps than all such day-to-day collaboration is the effort of the ICW, through its Standing Committees and National Councils, in working towards the ratification and implementation of those UN Conventions and Resolutions relevant to their objectives. In many cases the adoption of such Conventions by an inter-Governmental Organization represents the culmination of years of patient effort on the part of Standing Committees and National Councils (for example, Conventions concerned with Slavery, Genocide, Nationality of Married Women, Discrimination in Employment and in Education, Equal Pay and Recovery of Maintenance Abroad). After the adoption of such Conventions by the Inter-Governmental Organization concerned, it remains the duty and reward of International Standing Committees to bring to bear through National Councils the greatest possible weight of public opinion in each country, to ensure that such Conventions are not only ratified but scrupulously observed by their respective governments.

Histories of National Councils
of Women

HISTORIES OF NATIONAL COUNCILS
OF WOMEN

Introductory note

The histories of National Councils of Women which follow in chronological order of their affiliation to the ICW are from information presented by the Councils themselves. Although compiled in response to an identical questionnaire circulated by the ICW in December, 1960 (see Appendix 12, p. 351) they naturally display considerable variety in length and treatment; some having been condensed by the Councils from readily available histories, others involving deeper research among their archives.

In the case of a few Councils, marked with a double asterisk (**) and mostly recent affiliates of the ICW the histories were prepared from documentation available at Headquarters, in libraries, etc., in the absence of material expressly provided for this volume by the Councils concerned.

Those NCWs marked with a single asterisk (*) are, for a number of different reasons, no longer affiliated to the ICW. The histories of these Councils, here included in their appropriate places in chronological order by the year of their affiliation to the ICW, have been condensed by Miss L. C. A. van Eeghen from the *Histories of Affiliated Councils* published by the ICW in 1938. Even this brief glimpse will show that many of these former Councils, particularly those in Central and Eastern Europe, in addition to extensive work in the fields of health, education, culture and social welfare, played a major rôle in the improvement of the status of women in their respective countries and made important contributions to the work of the ICW during the period of their affiliation.

In addition to the twelve disaffiliated NCWs whose history is included here, the ICW has worked with Councils affiliated for shorter periods in the following countries: Uruguay (1916), Mexico, Russia and Ukrainia (all 1920), Cuba (1923), Guatemala (1924), the former mandated territory of Palestine (1925), China (1925, and again in 1942) and Japan (1936).

UNITED STATES OF AMERICA

NATIONAL COUNCIL OF WOMEN OF THE UNITED STATES
COUNCIL ESTABLISHED IN 1888
Affiliated to ICW in 1893

History of the Council

The National Council of Women of the United States and the International Council of Women were organized simultaneously in March 1888.

'We are strongly in favor of such a federation—national and international,' the Committee on Organization headed by Frances E. Willard reported, 'believing that it will incalculably increase the world's sum total of womanly courage, efficiency, and *esprit de corps*; that it will widen our horizon, correct the tendency to an exaggerated impression of one's own work as compared with that of others, and put the wisdom and experience of each in the service of all. . . .'

Thus was presented a plan for organization, timeless and workable, whose structure has proved a model and inspiration to women throughout the intervening years. The occasion was a meeting—an 'International Council of Women'—called by the National Women Suffrage Association and held in Albaugh's Opera House, Washington, DC, USA, from March 25th to April 1st, 1888, to celebrate the fortieth anniversary of a similar assembly convened in 1848 at Seneca Falls, New York. The Seneca Falls gathering was the first convention organized to demand equal educational, industrial and professional, as well as political rights for women.

At the time of the March 1888 meeting, Elizabeth Cady Stanton was president of the National Women Suffrage Association, Susan B. Anthony was first Vice-President, and May Wright Sewall was Chairman of the Executive Committee. These women had visited England and France in 1882 and had conceived the idea of an International Council of Women. They had corresponded with organization leaders in this country and abroad. As a result, 53 different organizations were represented at the Washington, DC meeting by 80 speakers and 49 delegates from England, France, Norway, Denmark, Finland, India, Canada and the United States.

Included in the original founding group were the National Women's Temperance Union, the National Women's Relief Society and the Young Women's Mutual Improvement Association of the Church of Latter Day Saints, whose continued membership in the National Council of Women of the United States has been of great value.

The report of the Committee on Organization was unanimously approved and on March 31st, 1888, constitutions for the United States Council and for the International Council of Women were adopted. The Constitution of the National Council of Women of the United States began with the following preamble: 'We women of the United States, sincerely believing that the best good of our homes and nation will be advanced by our own greater unity of thought, sympathy and purpose, and that an organized movement of women will best conserve the highest good of the family and the State, do hereby band ourselves together in a confederation of workers committed to the overthrow of all forms of ignorance and injustice, and to the application of the Golden Rule to society, custom and law.'

The preamble to the Constitution of the International Council of Women was identical except for the opening words, 'We women of all nations . . .'

The first officers of the National Council were: President, Frances

204

E. Willard; Vice-President-at-Large, Susan B. Anthony; Corresponding Secretary, May Wright Sewall; Recording Secretary, Mary F. Eastman, and Treasurer, M. Louise Thomas.

Officers elected for the International Council were: President, Millicent Garrett Fawcett of England; Vice-President-at-Large, Clara Barton of the United States; Corresponding Secretary, Rachel G. Foster of the United States; Recording Secretary, Kirstine Frederiksen of Denmark; Treasurer, Isabelle Bogelot of France.

These courageous, farsighted and able women who founded the International and National Councils of Women have been eulogized often since 1888. Clara Barton, the ICW's first Vice-President, is typical of the American women who saw the value of the Council idea. She had founded the American National Red Cross and her biographers record: '... At the age of seventy-four she was in the thick of war in Turkey; at seventy-seven she came to Cuba to bring medicines and service to those who suffered from malnutrition; at seventy-nine she was still in the front line of her own private war against pain and fear as she rode her horse through the flood waters of Galveston, Texas.'

Frances E. Willard, the great American temperance leader and reformer, wrote in her book entitled *Glimpses of Fifty Years—An Autobiography of an American Woman*: 'The greatest movement ever undertaken by women is the outgrowth of that unparalleled International Council held in Washington, March 26th to April 1st, 1888, of which Susan B. Anthony was the central figure. By her invitation I made five speeches there, and through her generous partiality was chosen president of this national federation of women when the office would naturally have gone to her.'

Elizabeth Cady Stanton was a noted leader of women suffrage. Lucretia Mott organized the Female Anti-Slavery Society, and her home was a station on the 'underground railroad' through which slaves escaped. It was the refusal of the London Anti-Slavery Convention in 1840 to admit women which led Miss Mott and Miss Stanton to organize the first Women's Rights Convention in 1848.

Fields of activity and achievements

From its inception, the National Council of Women of the United States concerned itself with problems affecting women and their responsibilities to home and country. Subjects covered at its first Triennial Meeting included the care of dependents; the need of women in public institutions; women's status in the church; modern charities and church work; and women's progress in higher education. Committees on education, health, peace and arbitration and fine arts, etc., were established and have gained in importance through the years.

Perhaps the only committee which flourished in those early days of the Council which did not survive was that advocating 'dress reform'. In 1891 a committee was set up whose duty it was to report, within a year, suggestions for a business costume for women which would meet the demands of health, comfort and good taste. Women by the thousands throughout the country signed pledges to give their support towards an improvement in women's dress 'which shall be in the line of more freedom for the body and shall possess more artistic beauty'.

As early as 1895 the United States Council was vigorously protesting 'against persecution of any people on account of religious belief or unbelief, or because of race or condition, as contrary to the spirit and civilization of our time'. The Council deplored 'the outrages committed upon the Armenians', and demanded that 'we protest against the Russian persecution of the Jew'. The United States Council also expressed disapproval of the injustices towards the colored people and the Indians which were permitted by 'our people and our Government'. In 1904 the Council was lending its influence towards the establishment of juvenile courts in the United States and urging the International Council of Women to promote their establishment in other countries.

Laws concerning the legal position of women, equal moral standards and traffic in women, and the problems of emigration and immigration were carefully studied by the experts the Council enlisted to head committees in these fields. A new Department of Civics as well as Home Economics were created in 1910. The Council greatly influenced many major reforms in these areas.

The Council played its part in the First World War and in the reconstruction period which followed. During the Disarmament discussions in 1925, the Council stated: 'Mere expression of good will and of friendly regard for other nations will not carry us far towards our goal. All the world has agreed that war is barbarous, but all the world is not agreed on the definite measures by which war is to be prevented.'

In the same year the ICW accepted the invitation of the American Council to hold its 7th Quinquennial Meeting in Washington, 37 years after its foundation in that city. The Council was happy to be able to extend a welcome to 300 delegates from 35 National Councils. In addition to the normal ICW business, three Public Sessions were organized and delegates were received in the White House by President and Mrs Coolidge.

'Our Common Cause—Civilization' was the theme of an International Congress of Women organized by the American Council of Women in Chicago, Illinois, in 1933, an important conclave seeking to plan ahead for a new era. Its findings were published in a book with the same title as the conference which was sold in large quantities to schools and universities throughout the country where it was for many years used as a textbook in Sociology classes. This book received the following published comment: 'This book is a record of the vision, the courage and the fidelity of the National Council of Women and the five million American women comprising its membership.'

In 1933 the National Council published a book by Inez Hayes Irwin called 'Angels and Amazons' which told the story of American women through the preceding one hundred years. This book still continues to serve as a ready reference to the lives of women who pioneered in civic affairs.

Housed in the Deering Library at Northwestern University in Evanston, Illinois, is the Biblioteca Femina. This 'World Women's Library' consists of a large number of books written by women in the various countries represented in the International Council of Women.

A mural, painted for the Council by the internationally famous woman muralist, Hildreth Meiere, depicts the emergence of woman from the early confines of her home into the wide world of opportunity. It is now permanently hung in the library of Smith College in Northampton, Massachusetts.

The concern of the Council with world problems has grown in accordance with the increased complexity of the world situation. Consultative status for the ICW and observer status for the National Council of the US in the United Nations gives both organizations a voice in world affairs. Mrs L. Dreyfus-Barney, who has served for many years as the International Council's liaison with the National Council of the United States, officially represented the International Council first at the League of Nations and later at the United Nations.

In 1938 the National Council created a Committee on Human Relations. Although the Constitution of the Council might in itself be considered a directive for a human relations programme, the Committee was especially set up 'to gather and exchange information on the promotion of fundamental relationships, without discrimination as to race, creed, color or culture'.

The Second World War saw the isolation and repression of many National Councils throughout the world and the necessity for concentration on home politics. After the war the American Council eagerly seized the earliest opportunity of helping to re-establish the links between its sister councils by inviting the ICW to hold its First Post-War Conference in Philadelphia in 1947, centered on the vital and timely theme of 'Power and Responsibilities of Freedom' in the post-war world.

Today the Council can look back along trails blazed by its founders and count many milestones in higher education for women, as well as in the fields of laws and suffrage, child welfare and human relations. But the Council today, as in 1888, is looking to the future.

Mrs Sophia Yarnall Jacobs, President of the National Council of Women of the United States, in her 1961–62 annual report, stressed the Council's work in the following areas:

1. The still-untapped resources of American women.
2. Cultural exchange with women of other countries.
3. The history and problems of the Inter-American countries.
4. Old and new approaches to the handling of foreign students in America.
5. Ways and means of re-training teachers, nurses and social workers.

Under the tireless leadership of the chairman of the International Hospitality Committee, said Mrs Jacobs, a particularly energetic programme had included a wide variety of individually planned and rewarding events for foreign visitors referred to the Council by the ICW, the UN and its Agencies and by US government departments. In addition, the Council had given its annual reception for women delegates at the opening of the Fifteenth General Assembly of the UN, a reception honoring women appointees of the Kennedy Administration, and a luncheon to introduce the President of the ICW to leading American women. Council officers had participated in many national and international conferences, including the US President's Committee on National Goals, briefings of the US Department of Labor and of the Department of State, and of UN Committees and Agencies. The Council's official observer to the UN had fulfilled the arduous task of attending and reporting on the numerous UN meetings vital to women and to civilization. Three Council officers had travelled to Paris to participate in the meeting of the ICW Board of Officers. Many friendships with members of sister councils had been established by Council officers and members travelling to various parts of the globe.

Regarding the publications of the Council, the *Bulletin* had been circulated widely outside the US in so far as the budget permitted; it was in frequent demand by women in newly developing nations for its information on what American women are like, what they think and do. The Council's UN *Calendar and Digest*, listing meetings of the UN and its Agencies and including a regular bibliography, had been circulated to the 45 other National Councils of the ICW as well as to Council members at home.

An important innovation had been the beginning of the compilation of a *Survey of National Women Leaders* by the Council, with the ultimate goal of establishing a permanent, up-to-date register of American women qualified for non-salaried appointments to state, national and international committees, etc. It was hoped that this might prove increasingly useful to federal and state governments, to business and industry as well as to other national organizations.

As a voluntary non-profit organization, the National Council of Women of the United States maintained its national headquarters, its professional staff and additional professional services in the areas of finance and public relations, on dues from its members and its member organizations, and on generous grants from a small group of philanthropic women. Operating within its budget, for any special project the Council continued to solicit outside additional grants from Foundations and from individuals. At present for example, a survey on hospitality for the foreign student was being conducted by the Council as a result of a special grant from the New World Foundation. The Council was presently seeking grants for other important projects—a part of its credo of looking to future needs of the country and its citizens.

The usual fund raising feature of the annual programme had been a successful studio tour arranged by the Chairman of the Arts Committee by courtesy of a group of outstanding artists. This had proved a cultural event of considerable importance, as well as a means of contributing to the Council's funds.

In concluding her report, the President voiced the conviction that ' . . . the Council must continue to build with strength and speed. We must surround ourselves with wise leadership, drawing from all our members and find new young women to join in our work. . . . As I see the immediate future, the Council should continue to enlarge its programme of hospitality to foreign visitors. It should, while continuing the study of other parts of the world, concentrate for a year on the American scene, on our assets and liabilities, our strengths and weaknesses. It should search for answers to our unsolved problems in human relations, in housing, child welfare, women's rights and responsibilities.

'It is seventy-three years since Susan B. Anthony and her little band of courageous women set the Council on its course. If we allow the complexities of the modern world, the discouragements and tensions to deflect us from the conviction that each one of us has an individual responsibility in the vast scheme of life, we are lost. In his Inaugural Address, the President of the United States said: "Ask not what your country can do for you; ask what you can do for your country." It is my earnest hope that the Council will not only ask this question of itself but will be able to find some answers which will give us courage to face the dangers ahead, resourcefulness and flexibility in dealing with them, and a new belief in the power of men and women to control their destiny.'

March 1962

CANADA

NATIONAL COUNCIL OF WOMEN OF CANADA
COUNCIL ESTABLISHED IN 1893
Affiliated to ICW 1897

Fields of activity and achievements

Inspired by the founding of the ICW in 1888, Canadian women organized the National Council in Canada on October 2nd, 1893, with three national organizations in federation.

Canada is a vast country and then was sparsely populated and largely undeveloped. It had become a nation of federated provinces and territories only 26 years before the Council was organized. The Council grew up with Canada and played an important rôle in the merging of the divergent interests of many races, cultures and economies into a united country.

In 1893, shortly after election as President of the ICW, Lady Aberdeen came to live in Canada upon the appointment of her husband as Governor-General. Canadian women, working on the formation of the Council, petitioned her to take the presidency. She consented and remained in office until her departure from Canada in 1898. A review of her work indicates she had at least four objectives: the development of Canadian leaders; the setting up of committees to work on long-range projects such as immigration, health, education, housing and town planning;

209

creation of a deep interest in the ICW and international affairs; and the formation of many Local Councils. In regard to the last objective she said: 'From my experience in the Canadian Council and watching its development through a chain of local councils from the Atlantic to the Pacific, I began to understand this idea of bringing diverse people together to work for a common cause.' She personally organized 25 local councils before she left Canada.

When Lady Aberdeen returned to England, Canadian women must have had doubts of their own ability to measure up to the great responsibilities she had pointed out to them. Fortunately there was tremendous latent talent and an indomitable spirit in the pioneer women, and the Council was at hand as an instrument through which they could mobilize public opinion.

'Day by day strangers come to this beautiful land. Are they to be a source of strength or of weakness?' asked our first president. With each wave of immigration, the Council was on the alert to correct injustices, unsatisfactory placement in employment and to safeguard living and working conditions. Many improvements in procedures were made and, as a result, the post-war influx was well managed, with the Council and other national organizations co-operating with the government.

The crusade for health was long but rewarding. It was waged on many fronts: through the training and registration of nurses; the founding of the Victorian Order of Nurses for home nursing; the increasing number of hospitals, sanitation, filtration plants; improved handling of food; lowering of infant and maternal mortality. The plight of the insane with respect to accommodations, treatment and public attitude concerned the Council as early as 1897 and continues to do so to the present time, although immense gains have been made.

Education, social welfare, in fact the whole field of human welfare and relations, felt the impact of the Council.

Lady Aberdeen re-visited Canada several times after her term was completed. She also welcomed Council women to her home and wrote many letters concluding always with the word 'Altior'. The last words spoken to the Canadian Council by its first president were: 'You have entered into a goodly heritage and I pray you to hold it in high honour.'

In these days, when the whole world is shocked and bewildered with threats of total destruction, it is difficult indeed for a voluntary organization, even of great strength, to chart a course which will help to take us forward on the road to world peace. It may be that maintaining the stability of our groups, keeping free of emotional prejudice and striving to understand the forces developing in the world, we may have influence to mould it more nearly to our desires.

Through the Council, Canadian women have become students, speakers and advocates of all that is worthy, and the names of many Council women are interwoven in the history of Canada.

Composition and functions of the Council

Over the years the Council developed its operational pattern. It is organized on National, Provincial and Local levels.

In 1960 the Council was composed of 22 national organizations, 8 provincial councils and 55 local councils. Its function is to take action on national matters and to inform and serve its membership. The Provincial Council is composed of local councils within its boundaries and provincially organized societies in membership. It takes action upon provincial matters. The Local Council is composed of organizations within its community and is responsible for action in respect to the welfare and progress in its area.

Projects may be initiated and resolutions introduced by federated organizations, special or standing committees, committee officers or executive committee, but not by an individual. After study and a majority vote of the Council, action may be taken on a project or resolution. Resolutions may be presented by letter or delegation to a Municipal Council; to the Provincial Government through the Provincial Council of Women; to the Federal Government through the National Council of Women.

Many resolutions require action either by Federal or Provincial Governments for implementation. The parliamentary committees of the National Council and Provincial Councils request and are accorded interviews with the Prime Minister of Canada and the Provincial Premiers and members of their Cabinets. With rare exceptions such interviews are required each year. Local Councils meet frequently with their Mayors and City Councils.

Financing

Formation of new Councils is a continuing project of the Canadian Council and some money is allocated for this purpose each year, with the result that we have more than doubled the number of Local Councils.

Affiliation fees from Local Councils and assessments based on membership were found insufficient to maintain a national headquarters or pay various other expenses. Therefore, gradually, with work and sacrifice, a trust fund has been built up, the income from which has met many outstanding needs, including assistance in travelling to national meetings.

Service on government boards

Council has been invited to serve on the following Government Boards:
Advisory Council, Canadian Vocational and Technical Training National Advisory Committee, Unemployment Insurance Commission, Canadian National Commission for UNESCO.

The collaboration of the Council is sought by the following Non-Governmental Agencies

United Nations Association of Canada
Health League of Canada

211

Canadian Association of Consumers
Canadian Safety Conference
Conference on Education
National Housing Design Council
World Refugee Year Committee
Freedom from Hunger Campaign Committee

Briefs are invited and presented to Royal Commissions dealing with any matter of particular interest to the Council.

New organizations were needed, and the Council proposed and assisted in the formation of the Victorian Order of Nurses, Children's Aid Society and Canadian Association of Consumers. Today the Council supports mental health programmes, the education of retarded children, the Elizabeth Fry Society, United Nations Associations and all who need its strength.

Publications:

History of National Council
Annual Year Book
Newsletter (activities of Councils)

Standing Committees

At the outset the Council set up committees on Health, Welfare, Education, Economics and Taxation, Trades and Professions for Women, Peace and Arbitrations, Housing and Town Planning, Natural Resources, Laws, Immigration, Arts and Letters. From time to time standing committees have been added to provide for new situations but a few years ago, consolidation of committees brought conformity with international committees. The Council has administrative standing committees, Foundation Fund, Finance, Parliamentary, Resolutions, Constitution, International Council of Women, Public Relations, Newsletter and Public Safety. The committees established in the early days are essential even now. The problem may change, a new emphasis be required, but the work is not yet finished.

Participation at the international level

Throughout the years Lady Aberdeen, as President of the ICW, undoubtedly stimulated the active participation of the Canadian Council in the ICW and in international affairs generally, and this continues. Many Canadian women have been officers and executive members of the ICW.

In the broader field of international affairs, the Canadian Government has included Council women in the official delegation to the United Nations. Miss Winnifred Kydd (President) was a delegate to the Conference on Control and Reduction of Armaments at Geneva in 1934. Mrs Cora Casselman, MP, was delegate to the founding convention of the United Nations at San Francisco; Mrs R. J. Marshall, LLD (President)

1951 delegate to the United Nations; Mrs H. H. Steen (Vice-President) in 1960.

Other women have represented Canada at meetings of the League of Nations, of the ILO, and of the Commissions and Agencies of the UN. Among them are Mrs Charles Fremont, Senator Josie Quart, OBE, Senator Muriel Ferguson, Mrs Rex Eaton, OBE, LLD, Dr Charlotte Whitton, CBE. The Council has been invited to serve on the Canadian National Commission for UNESCO.

As a result of the reports from these and other women, Canadian women have enriched their knowledge of world affairs and their interest in the UN and UN Associations has been deepened.

July 1961

GERMANY

DEUTSCHER FRAUENRING
COUNCIL ESTABLISHED IN 1895
Affiliated to ICW 1897–1933. Reaffiliated 1951

Fields of activity and achievements: 1895–1913

The *Bund Deutscher Frauenvereine*, the predecessor of the *Deutscher Frauenring*, was established in 1895. It was joined by numerous women's organizations such as the *Allgemeiner Frauenverein*, founded as early as 1865, which aimed at the civic education of women, and the *Allgemeiner Deutscher Lehrerinnen-Verein*, which represented teachers of all types of schools. At first its chief concerns were educational and professional questions, to which were soon added universal suffrage and the amelioration of the legal status of women, especially with regard to marriage laws.

At the beginning of the nineteenth century women had gradually gained admission to all universities. Grammar schools for girls were established and, to a certain extent, run as private schools by women's organizations. There was a bitter struggle for the headship of girls schools which the women have not as yet completely won. Helene Lange and Dr Gertrud Baümer were the leaders in this movement. A 'Votes for Women' movement, formed under the leadership of Marie Stritt, was consolidated in 1904. At the same time women became active in local government by being elected to urban councils. The Evangelical Church also started to draw on women as experts and to give them a share in practical work.

1914–1933

When the First World War broke out, Dr Gertrud Baümer, Dr Marie-Elizabeth Lüders and Mrs Hedwig Heyl founded the *Nationaler Frauendienst* whose chief objective was to help wives of men who were called up by means of an information service and to support the local authorities in their welfare work and assume a share in it. The National Auxiliary

P

Service law of 1916 integrated women into the war economy. The authorities set up organizing committees headed first by Dr Lüders and later by Dr Agnes von Harnack. Women's organizations representing all political parties and religious denominations co-operated in the National Service of Women and in war work, gaining useful experience for the future.

In 1919 German women were granted the right to vote and to run for office. To prepare women for their new responsibilities the main women's organizations, in particular the *Bund Deutscher Frauenvereine*, organized non-partisan educational classes. There were women members in all parties represented in the Reichstag, in State Parliaments and in urban councils as well as in provincial and rural districts. Laws such as those concerning the Protection of Children and Young People, National Health (abolition of state registration of prostitutes and substituting hygienic regulations) and the appointment of women as jurors and in various legal professions and office were passed by the Reichstag and rank among those initiated by women.

Women members of Parliament worked closely with their organizations: Dr Baümer and Dr Lüders in the Reichstag; Martha Dönhoff in the Prussian and Dr Gertraud Wolff in the Bavarian State Parliaments; Mrs Luise Kisselbach on the Munich Urban Council, were among women pioneers in Parliament.

The National Socialist government which came into power in 1933 put an end to all these activities. The *Bund Deutscher Frauenvereine* and its 50 affiliated societies disbanded as they were not prepared to adhere to the principles of National Socialism.

1949 to the present

The *Deutscher Frauenring*, established in 1949, continues the tradition of the *Bund Deutscher Frauenvereine*. Its founder and first president was Mrs Theanolte Bähnisch, succeeded in 1952 by Dr Else Ulich-Beil. In 1955 Dr Emmy Engel-Hansen became President and, since 1958, the president has been Mrs Bertha Middelhauve. The *Deutscher Frauenring* has 13 state branches and 140 local branches, and 8 societies have affiliated. After 1933, several professional and trade women's organizations had amalgamated with similar men's organizations and their loss to the *Deutscher Frauenring* is sorely felt.

The Bonn Constitution, i.e. the Constitution of the Federal Republic, of 1949, stipulates that 'Men and women are equals'. Bundestag discussions on draft bills concerning family and marriage laws indicate that this may be interpreted in various ways, but the fact remains that the acceptance of the principle of equality is a great advance. First and foremost, women are now admitted to all professions. At present there are approximately 7,000 women doctors and 1,000 women in the legal profession; women have greater access to headships and to teaching in co-educational schools. The Evangelical Church has relinquished its resistance to the ordination of women, even though women are rarely appointed as vicars, but rather as curates. It is still exceptional for women to be appointed as University or Technical College professors, though many are readers (assistant professors) and private University teachers. The German Federation of University Women devotes much attention to this problem and can rely on the creative work of women in science and the arts as the best proof of its arguments.

The protection of women workers is being improved and, with the exception of agriculture, all employers have introduced an 8-hour working day.

Attempts to introduce a *national* (auxiliary) *service for women* analogous to male conscription have foundered on the article of the Constitution assuring free choice of work for all nationals, but churches and voluntary societies have been successful in persuading women and girls to undertake voluntary service, for instance, as nurses. German women take a lively interest in politics and are represented in all parliaments but will always form a minority because of their tasks as mothers and home-makers. The opinion that these tasks are as important as men's professional work both in general estimation and in independent economic value, is gaining ground and has nothing in common with the sentimental idealization of former times.

Women mayors, secretaries of state, and Foreign Service officials are by no means rare. Following the 1961 General Elections the first woman was appointed Minister in the Federal Government.

During the Berlin blockade the *Deutscher Frauenring*, like other women's organizations, requested help from the UN Commission on Human Rights, but the matter was referred to the US government to be dealt with by the occupying powers. The *Deutscher Frauenring*'s requests regarding illegitimate children of men serving in the occupation armies was, however, satisfactorily dealt with by the UN.

The Deutscher Frauenring does its best to help alleviate the distress of people in need and to repair war damage inflicted on other peoples as, for example, in Greece. It is most anxious to participate in all forms of international co-operation.

Standing Committees

The Deutscher Frauenring is represented on all ICW Standing Committees. Of the present 19 Standing Committees, some correspond to those of the ICW while others deal with contemporary German problems such as refugees and expellees, exclusively German questions, and with Help-to-Greece.

Organizations affiliated with the Council

The 13 State branches and 8 societies affiliated with the Deutscher Frauenring have more than a million members. The State branches represent the policy of the Deutscher Frauenring and implement its decisions. The affiliated societies have, in addition, their own objectives: these are: the Associations of Expellees and of Disabled Civilians, Service Men and Dependents of those killed in the war, including respectively

500,000 and 400,000 women; professional and trade women's groups such as midwives, civil servants, artists, agricultural and domestic workers; and the Women's Christian Temperance League.

Relations with the UN and Specialized Agencies

Dr Baümer always represented her Department in the Reichs Ministry of the Interior at the Conferences of the League of Nations. The Ministry of Foreign Affairs delegated various women of different organizations and political parties as experts. The permanent representative to the International Labour Office was Mrs Hannah, trade union leader and a member of the Prussian Parliament. Dr Lüders was one of the delegates to the Economic Conference at Geneva in 1927–28 and to the International Law Conference in the Hague in 1930.

Dr Maria Schlüter-Hermkes, who is a member of the German National Commission for UNESCO and one of the leaders of the Catholic German League of Women was elected to the Executive Board of UNESCO on which she served from 1954–60. Many women are active members of local UNICEF committees, among them members of the Deutscher Frauenring. Problems of the international organizations are very often discussed at meetings, classes and training courses of the Deutscher Frauenring.

May 1961

SWEDEN

SVENSKA KVINNERS NATIONALFÖRBUND
COUNCIL ESTABLISHED IN 1896
Affiliated to ICW in 1898

Fields of activity and achievements: 1896–1913

Council built up its organization and the number of member associations grew rapidly; undertook many important initiatives, in some cases in collaboration with other organizations.

1897: Arranged the first Inter-Scandinavian Conference of Women's Organizations to be held.

1902: Endeavour to establish factory inspection resulted in the Swedish Factory Inspection Law which was revised in 1912 to permit women appointees as inspectors.

1905: Appointment of Police Matrons: at present women serve not only as matrons but also in ordinary police work.

1907: Admittance of women to Civil Service posts. It was not, however, until 1918 that the first women teachers were appointed to Civil Service posts; by 1923 practically all such posts were legally open to women.

1908: Formed Committee for Film Censorship, superseded in due course by State Censorship.

Advocated formation of ICW Standing Committee on Domestic Economy.

216

1911: In the international field, helped Greek women and children made destitute by the Greek–Turkish war. Welcomed ICW Executive Board in Stockholm.

1914–39

Intensive activity in social work and education of women to take up posts in various fields opened to them by the Law of Women's Rights; also urged women to make use of the new possibilities to enter into professions hitherto looked upon as belonging to men only.

1914: Supported passage of Old Age Pension Law; worked for betterment of women's position under the law. A revised law was passed in 1935.
Associated with other women's organizations to set up the Women's Levy which did useful work in wartime; dissolved in 1920.

1918: Passage of Abolition of Prostitution Law on which Council had initiated action in 1913.

1921: Attainment of women's full political franchise and revision of the Marriage Law after considerable time and work by the Council.

1925: Achieved passage of Swedish Nationality Act whereby a Swedish woman married to an alien retained her nationality until she took up abode in the country of her husband. During the Second World War this right was extended so that she can retain her citizenship even after leaving the country. This proved to be of the greatest value during the war.

1929: A committee was set up, on the Council's proposal, to investigate the possibilities of an amalgamation of the ICW and the Alliance of Women. This has not yet been achieved.

1930: At the proposal of the Council, ICW Assembly periods were changed from 5 to 3 years' interval and it was also proposed that no President should keep the office for more than three consecutive periods.

1933: Council welcomed ICW Executive Board in Stockholm.

1937: Together with other organizations, achieved passage of Maternity Aid Act by Parliament.

Another problem occupying the Council and other women's organizations during this period was the revision of the Vagrancy Law. The result is that young female vagrants are now treated by the Child Welfare Board up to the age of 21 years.

1939 to the present

The Second World War and its sequels determined the work of the Council during the 1940–50 period. Many studies were made of what the future might hold for women and society as a whole in order to clarify what was needed and to assess the new possibilities opened up by the coming of peace.

At the same time constant effort was required to deal with the many problems of everyday life in wartime in a neutral country, faced with shortages in manpower and all kinds of utilities. All the Council's member associations did relief work for suffering people, particularly those in neighbouring countries. The Council appealed vainly to the dictators expressing the hope that Madame Plaminkova and other victims of their policy might be saved.

Throughout this period the Council has directed its efforts towards the education of women for their rôle in the post-war world. Thus vocational guidance and training, youth problems, child care, etc., have been given great attention.

The Council has continued to encourage women to educate themselves for higher Civil Service posts as well as for nationally and internationally responsible posts.

Especially gratifying to the Council, working together with other organizations, is the outstanding event of the last few years: the ordaining of women in the Church of Sweden on an equal basis with men.

During the war the Scandinavian peoples were brought to realize their affinity more closely than ever before. This has resulted not only in collaboration on the governmental level, but also on the non-governmental plane such as the work of the National Councils. Annual Scandinavian meetings have become a very important part of our work and valuable discussions on common problems are held. We are also interested in the new situation that the organization of European markets may bring about. Above all, we are aware of what a changing world may bring to us, and of its claims on our participation and responsibilities.

In 1946 the Council celebrated fifty years' of existence with a three-day festival meeting attended by the ICW President and other guests from abroad.

Standing Committees

All ICW Committees are represented in the Council.

Organizations affiliated with the Council

At present 12 organizations form the Council. Some work for the status of women (e.g. The Fredrika Bremer Förbundet and The Open Door Group); some are professional groups, such as the Housewives Association, the University Women's Club; some are social workers, e.g. World's Women's Christian Temperance Union, Women's Auxiliary Military Corps, etc. Other groups are at present preparing to affiliate with the Council.

Relations with UN and Specialized Agencies

Relations of the National Council with UN and its Specialized Agencies are generally conducted through Affiliated Associations, the work of the Council in this domain being mainly to keep Council members informed of the work of the various bodies of UN by means of lectures, films, etc. The Council appeals to the government whenever the status of women or children are concerned in UN programmes.

The government often consults the Council and asks it to propose candidates as women delegates to UN meetings.

The Council has several times asked the government for better representation of women at meetings of the UN and Specialized Agencies and these requests have given satisfactory results. For many years, Miss Hesselgren, former president of the Council, took a most active part in the work of the International Labour Office and regularly represented Sweden at the League of Nations. She was also a prime mover in the formation of the Swedish United Nations Association.

The Swedish delegation to the 1962 UN Assembly included two women, Mrs Rössel and Mrs Lindström, the latter a member of the National Council Board of Officers. Other Council members have served as delegates to Specialized Agencies or as experts on Commissions set up by these Agencies or their regional offices.

On the initiative of the Swedish Council, the ICW passed a Resolution (Athens, 1951) in favour of the establishment by UN of an international documentation centre on housing and the building industry: a Resolution subsequently implemented by the creation of the International Council for Building Documentation.

UN Conventions are generally taken up immediately by the Swedish government. When necessary, the Council approaches the government directly to press for ratification.

April 1961
November 1962

GREAT BRITAIN

THE NATIONAL COUNCIL OF WOMEN OF GREAT BRITAIN
COUNCIL ESTABLISHED IN 1895
Affiliated to ICW in 1898

In 1895 a gathering of women in Nottingham 'moved by an earnest wish to do what they could for the cause of mankind, by helping the cause of women' established the National Union of Women which affiliated to the ICW in 1898. In 1918 it became the National Council of Women.

Fields of activity and achievements

The Council's influence has been mainly as an educational and pressure group. Speeches on current problems by eminent women were the chief feature in the early years of the Council. Present practice is discussion of resolutions sent up from branches, affiliated societies and committees. These resolutions form the basis of representations to the government and other interested bodies. Thus over the years the Council has a fine record of achievements.

Apart from independent organizations[1] which have arisen from the Council's Committees, the Council shared the responsibility for such reforms as compulsory co-option of women to County Education Committees; official registration of Registry offices by the London County Council; appointment of women medical officers in schools; alterations to the National Health Insurance Act; inclusion of more women on the Ministry of Health's Rural Housing sub-committee; powers given to local education authorities to assist boys and girls in the choice of employment; appointment of women jurors; equal compensation in civilian air raid injury; institution of Family Allowances and their payment being made to the mother.

The Council's recommendation that British children should not be taken out of the country for adoption without a magistrate's licence was later incorporated in the National Children Adoption Act. In 1956 the Sexual Offences Act consolidating previous laws on this subject including offences against children was passed. The NCW had urged the need for such consolidation. A deputation to the Minister of Labour urged the right to transfer pension rights on change of employment. This was incorporated in the National Graduated Pension Scheme.

The Beveridge Committee on Social Security requested evidence from the Council and printed the memorandum submitted in full in the Beveridge Report whose influence was so great in the development of Britain's social insurance.

A very important category concerns direct relations with the government when deputations are received or evidence before a Royal Commission or Departmental Committee is accepted, even requested, as in 1952, by the Royal Commission on Marriage and Divorce, and in 1960 by the Home Office on the welfare of foreign girls in Britain.

Largely based on evidence from the branches, the Council prepares memoranda such as: Design of Dwellings 1942; Domestic Workers 1943; Reconstruction in Education 1943; Population 1944; Adult Education 1944; Equal Pay 1945; Housing 1949; the Criminal Justice Bill 1961; reports on children and young persons and on adoption of children; Broadcasting and Television for the Pilkington Committee 1961.

Status of women

The Council gave continuous support to the great campaign for Votes for Women from its first Conference to final victory for universal suffrage in 1928. The outstanding campaign of later years for equal pay has also been strongly supported and has met with success in the case of teachers in the national system of education and civil servants (for non-industrial workers). In other aspects of the struggle for full citizenship the Council has steadily played its part and continues to do so. Resolutions on the

[1] National Organization of Girls' Clubs (1911) which became the National Association of Youth Clubs in 1961; National Women Citizens' Association (1918); Women's Engineering Society (1918); Association of Teachers of Domestic Subjects (1937).

220

right of women to vote and act on local councils, to become magistrates, to retain their nationality on marriages have opened more doors, e.g. the Nationality Act of 1948 gave women the right to retain their nationality on marriage, a right which the Council had claimed since 1914.

Women police

The important standing of women police today stems from the early weeks of the First World War when the Council inaugurated a movement for the training and enrolment of women patrols to work among girls living near military camps. Later the Home Office's proposal to disband the patrols was strongly resisted by the Council and eventually 20 patrols were retained on which a new force could be built, if necessary.

The movement for permanent employment of women police continued for some 24 years with the Council always in the forefront through its active Committee on Women Police which joined in 1940 with 20 other organizations to form the Women Police Campaign Committee, thus securing the widest possible influence. By 1945 the objectives stated by the Council in 1929 were achieved and in the words of the Home Secretary at a Council Conference in 1948: 'The law does not know policemen and policewomen, but only police officers.'

Moral welfare

In 1900 a 'Preventive and Rescue Work Committee' was formed to care for friendless girls. The need for higher moral standards in all aspects of community life has been in the forefront of the Council's thinking. The Criminal Law Amendment Bill of 1922 was enacted without the clause enabling a man prosecuted for criminal assault to shelter behind the plea that he had 'reasonable cause to believe' that a girl was over 16. Repeal of this clause had been demanded by the Council in 1895 and 1913. The Council has urged the removal of the words 'common prostitute' in clauses relating to protection from procuration. Strong support was given the Criminal Law Amendment Act of 1951.

Evidence was given on prostitution to the Wolfenden Committee. Support has been given for many years to international work on Suppression of Traffic in Persons and the Abolition of State Registration of Prostitution.

Education

1895: Formation of education committee proposed and one of the chief topics at Conferences was the Higher and University education of women.
1903: Registration and training of teachers.
1909: Urged teaching of science, especially home economics.
1941: Education Committee held unique conference in Edinburgh when Protestant and Roman Catholics met to discuss 'religion in public education, the dynamic force of the future'.

1944: Education Act passed—deputation to the government demanded certain amendments.

1960: At the request of the Ministry of Education, the Council's Education Committee carried out a survey on the reasons why married women were reluctant to return to teaching.

Peace and arbitration—international affairs

Since 1908 the Council has been concerned with these questions. In 1919 the Council's support for the League of Nations was expressed by the formation of the Committee on Peace and the League of Nations Work. In 1920 a new organization was formed to try to secure appointment of appropriate women on the League's committees and staff and this practice has been repeated in the case of the United Nations. The Committee on International Affairs and for the Promotion of Peace added to its terms of reference 'to collect and distribute information from national and international sources regarding the work of the UN'. This aim is followed nationally and locally with the help of international groups in the Branches.

After the Second World War the Council strongly supported the revival of the *Frauenring* in Germany and invited leading members to Britain. Return visits also contributed greatly to a better understanding. Later, hospitality was arranged for German students coming to work in Britain and special interest was shown in students sent for training under Technical Assistance schemes.

In 1960 the Council helped to entertain a party of Soviet women who were given a comprehensive programme during their two weeks' visit to Britain. The following year three representatives of NCW paid a return visit to the Soviet Women's Committee. The Council co-operated for some years with the Help to Greece Consultative Committee.

The Council has been specially sensitive to the problems of refugees displaced on account of war or political upheaval. Branches all over the country helped in local schemes before, during and after the Second World War and in emergencies such as the influx of Hungarian refugees. Strong support was given to the British Council for Aid to Refugees and substantial sums were raised on behalf of World Refugee Year.

Health, Child Welfare and the Home

In 1916 the Ministry of Food asked the Council to co-operate in a food economy campaign. The Scottish Standing Committee organized the first travelling exhibition on maternity and child welfare, followed by two in England financed by the Carnegie Trust, to encourage local authorities to set up clinics. This developed into a nation-wide campaign from which grew the official maternity and child welfare organization. A deputation on maternal mortality went to the Ministry of Health in 1936. In 1960 a report was prepared on parental responsibility and juvenile delinquency based on information from the Branches.

The Council's connection with the Declaration of Geneva of the

'Children's Charter' is of interest. At the ICW meeting in Oslo after the First World War it was agreed to draw up a document embodying the minimum rights of the child. A special committee was set up by Lady Aberdeen for this purpose which completed its work in 1922. The ICW circulated this report to the National Councils to adapt to national needs and to bring to the attention of their governments. In 1924 the Council and the British Save the Children Association drew up a joint charter which was published in the name of the ICW and the Save the Children Fund International Union. In 1942 the Charter was revised for changed conditions by representatives of 19 nations and many societies, including the Council and the Save the Children Fund at a London Conference.

Several leaflets were produced on household matters and a special research sub-committee in 1932 helped to run a London exhibition on household equipment. In 1940 an exhibition organized on Food and Fitness, with a leaflet of the same title, aided housewives in making the best of wartime rationing.

Safety in the home was discussed at conferences and safety regulations regarding heating apparatus and inflammable materials were urged. This helped to bring into being the Heating Appliances (Fireguards) Act. Home safety committees were initiated by the Council in a number of towns.

The Council set up a Women's Advisory Committee to advise the British Standards Institution regarding consumer goods. The first Consumer Protection Conference in Britain was organized by the Council, followed by a deputation to the government which resulted in a grant being allocated for consumer protection. Two consumer organizations later began to exert a beneficial influence.

The country's growing recognition of responsibility for the welfare and housing of old people is due to a considerable extent to Council efforts.

Cinema and broadcasting

In 1924 the Council started a Cinema Committee whose interests have included the relation of children to the cinema. A special Enquiry Committee studied conditions of censorship, etc. The results were published in pamphlet form in May 1931. This was widely circulated, helping to draw public attention to the need for closer supervision of films shown to children.

In 1946 the Committee and the British Film Institute organized one of the first public conferences on children's films and cinema clubs. Evidence was given to the Departmental Committee on Children and the Cinema set up in 1946. The Council is represented on the Advisory Sub-Committee (Children and the Cinema) of the Cinema Consultative Committee set up in 1951.

The Council has protested against excessive violence in films, bad matching of programmes, undesirable posters and trailers and, in the case of broadcasting, against curtailment of external services.

Migration

Questions concerning migration have been largely linked with the British Commonwealth. In 1931 a committee began the study of the long-standing custom of employing 'Mui Tsai' which prevailed in Ceylon, Hong Kong and Malaya. Young Chinese girls, transferred from their parents to be brought up as domestic servants, though often treated as members of the family, were completely at the mercy of the employers. In 1936 a leading Council member was on the government Committee to investigate the question and her minority report recommending more drastic control was accepted by the government the following year and steps were at once taken to put her suggestion into practice. A booklet published by the Council was widely influential in drawing attention to the problem.

From 1954 on a study was made of the '*au pair*' situation and in 1960 a deputation went to the Government.

The Arts

Poet's Choice, an anthology published by the Council recalls a notable Poetry Reading in London in the middle of the Second World War. This was an early recognition of the demand for the reading of poetry in public.

An exhibition showing the work of contemporary women painters and sculptors was held in London in 1945.

Christmas Holiday lectures at London Galleries and Museums were started at the Council's request.

A special study of Children's 'Comics' resulted in a deputation to the Home Secretary on the Children and Young Persons (Harmful Publications) Bill 1955.

Publications

The Council's aims and achievements have been publicized by various methods. A journal has been continuously issued, not even interrupted during the war years, first as a quarterly *The Occasional Paper*, then a monthly *Council News*, later *Women in Council*. Since 1960 *Women in Council* is issued as a quarterly magazine. A comprehensive Handbook is published annually.

Examples of other publications:

Historical Sketch of the National Council of Women of Great Britain, by Dame Maria Ogilvie Gordon, DBE, LL.D, D.SC, JP 1937.

Women in Council—the Jubilee Book of the NCW of Great Britain. Edited by H. Pearl Adam, Oxford University Press, 1945.

Women Police, by Edith Tancred 1950.

A Milk-White Lamb, on the Legal and Economic Status of Women, by Florence Earengey, 1st ed. 1949, revised 1953.

During Six Reigns—Landmarks in the History of NCW Great Britain, by M. E. Alford.

The First Sixty Years (1956).

A number of leaflets on household questions, including Law and Custom regulating Domestic Service, Training in household matters as part of the school curriculum; *The Convenient Kitchen* 1935, the forerunner of many kitchen planning schemes.

Also leaflets on Committee Procedure; Control of the Cinema in England and Wales (in conjunction with the Mothers' Union and the Public Morality Council); frequent memoranda on special subjects of the moment, such as Race Problems, Widowed Mothers' Earnings.

Branches

A very important aspect of the Council's work is that done by the Branches. By 1900 these numbered 28 and in 1961 there were 102; with their locally affiliated societies they repeat the national pattern and are linked together through the Scottish Standing Committee and twelve Regional Committees. They implement the Council's policy in practical as well as academic ways and initiate reforms according to local conditions. The steady educational and social work trains members for the responsibilities of citizenship and public service. Regional conferences also play a large part in creating an informed public opinion. Many Branches show a lively personal interest in the ICW.

Standing Committees

The Council has permanent committees covering the work of the ICW's Committees though not always with identical titles. In addition the newest (1957) is on Science and Technology. Members are drawn from all over the country, appointed by Branches and Affiliated Societies with a few co-opted members with specialized knowledge. Another committee deals with the Humane Treatment of Animals while *ad hoc* committees on subjects of topical importance are appointed as the need arises.

Organizations affiliated with the Council

From 1900 the Council affiliated national voluntary societies in order that as a co-ordinating body they could present a broad and comprehensive view of women's opinions on matters of public interest. In 1961, 86 such societies covered all types of voluntary work. They included women's organizations representing the Protestant, Catholic and Jewish faiths; the Conservative, Liberal and Labour Parties; professions, moral, social and educational work and the status of women; the arts; animal welfare.

Headquarters

The Council became an incorporated society in 1951. In the same year it bought the lease of a London house, 36 Lower Sloane Street. A generous flow of gifts from regions, branches, societies and individuals soon transformed the house into a centre, not only for members but where office, committee work and social functions can be carried out under one roof and friends from other Councils may be welcomed.

Relations with UN and Specialized Agencies

See Appendix 3, p. 335 for an account of the extensive work of this Council with UN and Specialized Agencies.

November 1961

DENMARK

DANSKE KVINDERS NATIONALRAAD
COUNCIL ESTABLISHED IN 1899
Affiliated to ICW in 1899

Fields of activity and achievements: 1899–1913

Worked for the cause of peace in connection with the conferences in the Hague in 1899 and 1907. Worked for municipal suffrage which was granted in 1908. The following year 126 women were elected to town councils.

1914–38

1914: Suffrage procession before the King and Parliament which led to political franchise for women in 1915. Courses and centres for unemployed women as well as courses for housewives.

1918: Nine women elected to Parliament.

1919: Equal pay for men and women in public administrations and appointment of women to state employment in the following year.

1920: President of the Council (Henni Forchammer) appointed member of delegation to the Assemblies of the League of Nations, working mainly with social problems and problems concerning women. First woman member of delegation to the Conference of the International Labour Organization.

1921: Post-war services for Armenians (Karen Jeppe) German and Austrian children suffering from war and post-war conditions received in Denmark.

1922: Married mothers given authority over their children on equal basis with fathers.

1925: Proposed introduction in schools of subjects such as peace and the League of Nations.

1926: New law concerning equality for men and women in marriage.

1934: To assist women on the labour market with questions about their right to work, the Council founded a special body: Danish Women's Council for Trade and Industry.

1936: Another special organization was founded: Danish Women's Political Conference, whose object is the strengthening of women's interest in and understanding of politics and to secure greater influence for women in politics.

Proposals for maternity aid, increased facilities for anaesthesia during deliveries and facilities for gynaecological treatment were drawn up and submitted to the Minister of Social Affairs. Efforts made to create understanding of the activities of the Institutions

226

for Assistance to Mothers and a collection was started on 'Mother's Day' for the benefit of these organizations.

A special body, 'Our Children's Health', was founded and support was given to the adoption of schemes to provide health advisers, social physicians and trained nurses for schools.

Humanitarian international work of a special nature also conducted.

1938: A collection for the support of the work of Elise Thomsen for Spanish children during the Civil War.

1939 to present

1939: A collection for the benefit of Jewish children in Central Europe. A number of children came to Denmark with a view to later conveyance to Palestine.

From 1938 on the Council in various ways and through different statements made public its sympathy with those persecuted because of their race.

1940: Through the Danish Women's Community Service founded in 1940, Danish women contributed to the preservation and utilization of Danish values, material as well as cultural.

1945: By taking the initiative to form 'Save the Child' (which became affiliated with the International Union for Child Welfare), the Council contributed to making it possible for Denmark to stand ready to take part in post-war relief work and to work for the fulfilment of the rights of children as expressed in the Geneva Declaration.

1947: Greenland women were granted the franchise.

The Council took the initiative of convening and organizing a Danish Housewives' Consumer Council to protect the interests of the home and women by securing representation on all committees, councils and panels dealing with supplies.

A 'Committee on Widows' concluded its work with a report which should lead to a number of useful measures to ease the condition of widows. Another committee continued to work for the improvement of the position of mothers without providers.

1948: Together with the Danish Red Cross, the Council invited a group of leading German women to Denmark for a four-week stay to give them a thorough knowledge of Danish democratic social conditions. This first visit was followed up in the next two years with courses for other German women.

1949: Committee appointed to examine position of single mothers. For the first time we had our yearly daisy button-holes flag day during which the affiliated organizations sell in order to collect funds for the social, humanitarian and educational work. A small percentage of the fund goes to the Council funds in general.

The first of a series of regular annual Inter-Scandinavian Council meetings took place with representatives from Finland, Norway,

Sweden and Denmark. Mutual problems, co-operation and international questions were discussed.

The president of the Council, Bodil Begtrup, was nominated ambassador of Denmark to Iceland.

1950: Our next president, Helga Pedersen, was nominated Minister of Justice.

Many large meetings were held. Mrs Roosevelt spoke about 'Human Rights' and American lawyer, Edith Sampson, spoke about the condition of the Negroes in the USA.

1953: Report on position of single mothers was distributed to the Danish Parliament. Press and radio gave large coverage to this report and a film was made on this subject.

1954: A lecture followed by discussion on 'Where Responsibility for Sex-Education Should Rest'. This theme has been followed up in recent years with requests to the ICW, the Danish government and Parliament.

Vocational guidance has been another important aim. By means of meetings, discussions and requests and also a pamphlet edited by the Council and distributed to the pupils in public schools and other educational institutions, we drew attention to the necessity of vocational guidance for girls as well as for boys.

Our work for mothers and children has been one of our guiding principles and has been followed in various ways, asking for more kindergartens, more playgrounds, etc.

1955: A project worked on for several years became a reality: we received four Indian nurses, invited to attend a one-year special training course on treatment of tuberculosis. It was a wonderful experience to meet them and we know that all the nurses, after returning to India, were placed in better and more responsible positions. We hope that this contact may contribute to better understanding among nations.

Henni Forchammer, the Council's president from 1900–04 and 1913–31, died and left a legacy to be administered by the Council's Board; part of the interest of this bequest is to be used to finance an annual grant to a woman wishing to study peace, social or educational work abroad. The first grant from this legacy was made in 1957.

1956 ⎫ A large collection of clothes and money for the benefit of Hungarian
1957 ⎭ refugees. The Council worked with affiliated organizations and the result obtained clearly showed what co-operation can achieve.

1958: A big meeting on 'Better Housing Conditions' where the problems were discussed by architects, engineers, women members of the Danish Parliament and the Community Councils and representatives from the Ministry of Housing. This was followed up by another meeting, dealing especially with the housing problems of single persons.

1959: During World Refugee Year the 'Danish Refugee Help' organized a nation-wide collection of money. Danish schoolchildren as well as the women's organizations displayed much initiative and interest and a remarkable sum of money was collected.

1960: Our Council requested the Minister of Foreign Affairs to inform the Danish representative on the Council of Europe that in our opinion it is contrary to the best interests of working women to institute measures for their protection by forbidding performance of night work, because this would place women in an unfavourable competitive position on the labour market.

In collaboration with 24 affiliated organizations, the Council held a meeting on 'Family Planning' as seen from an international point of view. An Indian film *In Your Hands* and a Japanese film on this theme were shown. The speakers were: the president of the Council, the director of a Mothers' Help Organization, the Minister of Church Affairs, the inspector of civil teaching in the army and several doctors and nurses.

The first course on economics, arranged by the Council, was given on subjects such as 'Women and Taxes' and 'The Economic Position of Women at the time of Marriage and Divorce'.

Standing Committees

All 15 ICW committees are represented in the Council. One member of our Board is the responsible link with each committee.

Organizations affiliated to the Council

Sixty-three organizations and 150 individual members (without voting rights) are affiliated to the Council. Any organization working for social, artistic, scientific, philanthropic and vocational purposes may join the Council which includes housewife organizations, nurses, women doctors, teachers, women's sports organizations and women's unions of all political parties, as well as women's and youth organizations with different religious bases. In recent years women's labour organizations have joined the Council.

Relations with the UN and Specialized Agencies

Henni Forchammer, president of the Council, was a member of the Danish Delegation to the Assemblies of the League of Nations from 1920 until 1937. In 1946, Bodil Begtrup became the representative of Danish Women on the Danish Delegation to UN and Chairman of the UN Status of Women Commission. Every year since, the Council has been asked to propose a woman delegate to the UN. Furthermore, the Council has representatives and delegates to FAO, UNESCO and ILO. In 1962, Gudrun Relfslund Thomsen, President of the Council, was a member of the Danish Delegation to the UN General Assembly.

Council members have been representatives to the Danish Consultative Committee for UN, The National Commission for UNESCO and to UNICEF in Denmark, as well as to the Danish Refugee Council.

The Council follows up Conventions supported by the ICW at the UN Assemblies and urges the Danish Government to ratify the Conventions, calling on affiliated organizations to take necessary action.

April 1961

AUSTRALIA

AUSTRALIAN NATIONAL COUNCIL OF WOMEN
COUNCIL FEDERATED IN 1934
Affiliated as separate State Councils between 1899 and 1911.

Six State Councils—New South Wales (1896), Tasmania (Hobart–1900), Victoria (1901), South Australia (1902), Queensland (1903) and Western Australia (1911)—federated in 1934. Launceston (Tasmania) and Canberra (ACT) have joined since. There are now eight Councils embodied in the ANCW which operates on a national and international level.

Fields of Activity

1888–1913: Suppression of white slave trade, control of narcotics, franchise for women, equality for women.

1914–38: Family allowances, old age pensions, equal pay for women, world legislation of League of Nations.

1939 to the present: Nationality of married women, raising of marriage age, genocide convention, obscene literature, children's films, immigration, welfare of aged, rehabilitation of handicapped migrants, imports, old people's councils, housing, infant welfare acts, equal pay and wage cases.

Successful achievements

Establishment of Children's Courts; raising of age of consent for girls.

Improved laws on prostitution and punishment of those living on the degradation of women.

Removal of discrimination against employment of women in certain government departments.

By the end of the nineteenth century some of the states had granted the franchise to women. After Federation of the States in 1900, this was extended to all adult British subjects.

Increased allowances to foster mothers, help for deserted wives, establishment of mothercraft homes, crèches and kindergartens.

Uniform divorce law for all states.

Acceptance by the Commonwealth of a quota of handicapped migrants.

Intervention with other interested parties in the Arbitration Court to prevent the reduction of the female basic wage from 75% to 54% of the male rate.

Nationality of married women.

Membership of anti-inflation conference.

Representation on Import Advisory Council and the Annual Citizenship Convention.

Representation on Commonwealth Advisory Immigration Council.

Equal pay for equal work has been an aim for sixty years. Some success has been obtained. The 'marriage bar' in public service may soon go.

Between 1960–62 1½ tons of school books were sent to South Africa and handwork materials to Papua, New Guinea. In August 1962, the Australian government sent two observers from New Guinea (one of them indigenous) to the Biennial Conference of the National Council of Women. During the same period New South Wales, South Australia, Victoria and Launceston each staged successful large-scale educational exhibitions.

Standing Committees

National Standing Committees parallel to all those of the ICW have been established, as well as a Civic Affairs Committee.

Organizations affiliated with the Council

Seven hundred organizations form the Council: philanthropic, religious, political, professional, educational, such as: St John Ambulance Cadets, Girl Guides Associations, British and Foreign Bible Society, Women Graduates, Liberal and Labour Women's Groups, Salvation Army, Women's Christian Temperance Union, Soroptimists, etc.

Relations with UN and Specialized Agencies

Dame Elizabeth Couchman and Miss M. Williamson were alternate delegates to the League of Nations.

The following women who were members of the Council or of its affiliated societies represented Australia on the UN Status of Women Commission: Mrs Jessie Street; Mrs G. L. Byth; Miss Isabel McCorkindale; Mrs Jean Daly; Miss Ruth Gibson; Mrs J. G. Norris. Mrs Mary Tenison Woods was for many years Chief of the UN Secretariat Section on the Status of Women Commission.

Council maintains contact with UN, WHO, FAO, UNICEF, UNREF and UNESCO.

The Council has supported the following UN Conventions:

Abolition of Slavery and Slave Trade and Institutions and Practices similar to Slavery
Prevention and Punishment of the Crime of Genocide
Nationality of Married Women
Narcotic Drugs
Status of Refugees
Suppression of the Circulation of Obscene Publications
Convention of the International Atomic Energy Agency.

July 1961
September 1962

NETHERLANDS

NATIONALE VROUWENRAAD VAN NEDERLAND
COUNCIL ESTABLISHED IN 1898
Affiliated to ICW in 1899

In 1898 women of the Netherlands organized an exhibition of women's work. This collaboration of women of different standing, denominations and political opinions proved so successful that they wondered whether a way could be found to continue this temporary collaboration after the close of the exhibition by forming a national women's organization which could become a permanent link between the existing women's associations in the Netherlands. The organizing committee of the Women's Exhibition invited Mrs May Wright Sewall, Vice-President of the ICW, to give a talk about the ICW. As a result, the National Council of Women of the Netherlands was founded in Utrecht on October 29th, 1898.

A few months later, in March 1899, the Constitution was approved. The first elected president was Mrs M. Klerck-van Hogendorp and the secretary was Miss Martina Kramers. In the first years the Council tried to find its way. This did not prove to be easy. In the beginning it looked as if the Council would become an Information Bureau only but as more organizations joined the Council, the aim of providing a link between these different associations became clearer in the common effort for better social measures. It is difficult now to realize how much courage was necessary for women to become affiliated with the Council since the woman's movement was still considered an assault on man's authority.

Already in 1899 the ties with the ICW were strengthened by the visit of the President and the Secretary to London to attend the Quinquennial Meeting. Members of Standing Committees on Press, Finance, Laws and Suffrage had also been appointed.

Fields of activity and achievements: 1898–1938

The Council was very active in the first years of its existence and most of the ideals of those first members have been accomplished. In 1904 and 1908 congresses were held to discuss the problems involved in protection of children. The appointment of women to the Police Force was attained in 1912.

Other activities included: Propaganda for women's right to vote, and a survey of questions concerning the legal rights of husbands and wives to their property. The Council asked for the appointment of women to government Committees and other official bodies. A study of emigration problems was made. Copies of reports resulting from such studies were forwarded to the government.

Official recognition by the government came in 1914 when the assistance of the Council was sought during the First World War.

Women's right to vote was achieved in 1914, and since that time there have always been women members in Parliament. These women, often working members of women's organizations, have done whatever they could to further the interests of women.

Three times the NCW welcomed the ICW to the Netherlands: in 1907, 1913 and 1922 meetings of the Executive Committee were held in The Hague.

During the 1920s the Council requested the appointment of a woman to the official delegation of the Netherlands to the League of Nations and suggested that the government ratify the important Conventions of the League.

1939 to the present

During the occupation (1940–45), the Council, as most of the women's organizations, ceased to function, but this did not mean a cessation of contact and collaboration among women. In 1944, a number of outstanding women met to study the question of the organization of women after the war. Before the war some of the big women's associations had not wished to affiliate with the Council, but during the war it was felt that contact with these associations would be necessary to further the cause of equal rights in all fields for women. It was therefore decided to form the Netherlands Women's Committee of which the presidents of 14 big Women's Associations would be members.

This Committee was not to be affiliated with any international organization. The President of the NCW was one of the Vice-Presidents of the new Committee.

After the war a division of tasks between this Committee and the Council became necessary. The Committee assumed the more active rôle, that of supporting women's rights and possibilities in official circles. The Council became a forum to which women's organizations came with their troubles and interests. Since 1946 many interesting questions have been raised at the Council's meetings. From the discussions at these meetings arose the actions which have led to achievements:

The question of nursery school teachers and the need for better nursery schools were often discussed. After years of protest regarding the conduct of these schools, Parliament has passed a law that provides for better schools and more adequate education and payment for teachers.

There were frequent discussions on the unequal rights of husband and wife with regard to possession of joint properties. A law was passed in 1957 according them both the same rights.

Many discussions have taken place on the right of women to equal educational possibilities and access to higher police functions. This has not yet been settled as the Council desires but the situation has been improved.

Discussions are now going on concerning the danger to which children and women may be exposed from mentally diseased persons and how to lessen this danger.

For some years now the question of nutrition of adolescents has been brought to the attention of women.

Discussions have been held on films for children and the elimination of films dangerous for children. The National Censorship Committee does not work to the satisfaction of many women and various attempts have been made to have more women belonging to women's organizations appointed to the Committee.

International questions are also brought to the attention of the Council's members and meetings and resolutions of the ICW are discussed.

Standing Committees

The Council is represented on all Committees of the ICW.

Organizations affiliated with the Council

About 50 organizations are affiliated to the Council. These are not only the general women's organizations as the Housewives Association, the Dutch branch of the Alliance, but also women's trade unions such as nurses, nursery school teachers, women executives and business and professional women.

Relations with UN and Specialized Agencies

At the request of the Foreign Office the Women's Committee suggests the name of a woman to serve on the delegation of the Netherlands to the General Assembly of the UN and as a member of the Status of Women Commission. These delegates often speak at the Council's meetings on their work at these international gatherings.

Contact with the regional offices of the Specialized Agencies is maintained through specialist organizations of men and women whose object is to bring the work of these agencies and their aims to the attention of the people.

With regard to UN Conventions, it is again these specialist organizations as well as the Women's Committee which press the government to ratify and support these Conventions.   *July 1961*

ITALY

CONSIGLIO NAZIONALE DELLE DONNE ITALIANE
COUNCIL ESTABLISHED IN 1898
Affiliated to ICW in 1900; reaffiliated 1951

Fields of activity and achievements: 1898–1913

The Council was established by an active and capable group of women who were able to bring the attention of public authorities to social problems by initiating solutions which could serve as examples outside any political influence. Branches were set up in Rome, Florence, Turin,

Milan, Bologna, Naples and Ancona which united various women's associations under the guidance of the National Council and encouraged participation in the work of specialized welfare agencies.

Turin and Florence: founded an institution for unmarried mothers, women's workshops, home economics courses, health and civic education for working women, restaurants for female sales personnel and office workers, schools for domestic personnel, small libraries for elementary classes. *Rome:* founded a large popular circulating library; obtained the organization of a Women's Office for the Protection of Migratory Women and Children which was given the task (by the Government Emigration Administration) of inspecting factories abroad employing young Italian women. In 1908 its proposal was accepted to establish homes near each factory providing cheap and decent lodgings. Reception centres were also set up in the railroad stations of Rome, Florence and Milan to assist migratory workers.

1908: First National Congress of Council held in Rome, attended by the Queen and State officials. A 700-page report put forth the programme demanded by the women of this period:

—Increased professional, agricultural and adult education.

—Assignment of women members of press associations to management to combat sensational journalism.

—Establishment of paternity; administration of dowry and other property; equality of sentence for adultery; right of women to guardianship; study of divorce; problem of sanctions for crimes committed in the name of family 'honour'.

—Started co-ordination and classification of welfare agencies; insisted that welfare workers be engaged on educational and not a charitable basis; provided social assistants to work in the migratory services and welfare institutions.

1911: Presented to public opinion the problem of reversibility of women's pensions.

—Organized workshops for women after the disaster caused by earthquake in Avezzano and Calabria.

ICW General Assembly elected in Toronto Countess Spalletti Rasponi as second Vice-President and Countess Danieli Camozzi as President of the Standing Committee on Migratory Workers.

1914–38

Received ICW General Assembly in Rome in 1914. As a result of discussions at this meeting, the Council insisted on government regulation of work performed at home (asking for the same health, welfare and minimum wage benefits as in industrial enterprises) unions and for co-operatives for production and sale of products, as well as training schools.

Supported equal pay and pay increases for women, eight-hour day, paid holidays, aid for working mothers, cantines and crèches in factories, kindergartens and after-schools surveillance for children in industrial centres.

Supported legislation to: (a) establish a Children's Bureau to protect the rights of the child to education, physical and moral health; (b) to create placement bureaus and professional schools for migratory women workers; (c) to assign women inspectors and social workers to correctional institutions (prostitution and corruption of minors); (d) to provide social insurance and public loans. In the combat against poverty, provided first catalogue of existing charitable organizations in Italy.

During the First World War the Council was ordered by the Ministry of War to collaborate in replacing male workers by women, and to participate in local committees set up to relieve suffering among civilians and soldiers. In 1917, the Council founded in Rome a model hospital for unmarried mothers which is still in existence.

After the war, the Council supported the demand for the right to vote; in 1919, government granted equality to women in the administration of their paraphernal property and earned income.

In 1924, the Council was invited by the government to collaborate (together with the Union of Catholic Women) in preparing a law creating a National Bureau for Mothers and Children. These were the only two women's organizations recognized by the authorities.

From 1925 on, political events dispersed the constructive and liberal forces in the Council. Of its works there remained only the Circulating Library in Rome which was dismantled in 1938.

1938 to the present

During the Second World War the Council practically disappeared, its archives first dispersed, then destroyed. The Council's history was re-constituted on the basis of the archives kept by the Florence Branch.

In 1951 the ICW Executive Board meeting in Lugano re-admitted the new Council created at the Milan Congress in 1949, after which a great effort was devoted to bringing to the Council the greatest possible number of women's organizations, and to adapt programmes to post-war realities.

1948: Italian Constitution granted equal franchise. However, conflicts exist between the Constitution and the Codes so that the Council must co-ordinate the efforts of its affiliated associations to implement effectively the statutory regulations.

1951: Adopted a programme against the state regulation of prostitution and inadequate sentences for crimes committed in the name of 'family honour'.

1955: Worked for establishment of female police; evaluation and classification of women's work to arrive at equality of wages; civic education in secondary schools as well as in vocational training schools (where it was already taught). Presented a proposal for legislation and a report on female police; made a study on working women recognized as extremely valuable by public authorities; succeeded in having civic education presented by the TV Schools Programme, viewed by millions.

1956: Demanded a Bureau for Women's Work to follow up all problems arising from the law regulating women's work and international conventions, but this has not been entirely achieved due to lack of governmental flexibility in organization.

Council's IVth Congress held in Milan presented valuable studies as follows:

—part-time women's work based on suitable occupations for working mothers;

—teaching of home economics from primary school on, a subject now limited to technical and professional schools;

—juvenile delinquency research showing responsibility falls principally on ill-adapted mothers and on loose family ties.

1957: Council organized a large study group on the application of the ILO's Convention 100, ratified by Italy: Equal pay for equal work. Twelve of the largest women's associations have rallied to the 'Committee of Women's Organizations for Equal Pay' of which the Council is the co-ordinator. Satisfactory results and solutions have been reached, stimulated by inter-group meetings and contacts. On this occasion the President of the Council since 1953, Mrs Fonda Salvio, offered a generous prize for the best publication on 'Technological Progress and Women's Work with regard to Equal Pay' which was won by Mme Ines Pisoni. Based on the principle of unanimous decision this Committee serves to alert public opinion and the authorities to problems concerning women workers and its published studies and proposals are widely recognized as juridically valid and of the utmost usefulness. The Committee organized two other study groups: 'professional preparation of women' 1959; 'discharge of women workers for reason of marriage' 1961.

1958: Supported ratification of the Convention for alimony payments; the creation of a Bureau for Women's Work; reform of the National Bureau for Mothers and Children; professional training of migratory women workers; artistic education of youth; creation of courses for parents; participated in a study group to find solutions permitting working mothers to handle their double duties; formulated proposals to amend the recent domestic work law.

In the field of legal status of women, the Council's best advisers have always been those affiliated organizations specializing in the legal profession; together or separately, they have achieved some measure of success (sometimes for political reasons) in co-ordinating all aspects of family law; gaining access to all public careers; real application of the principal of equality to the status and work of women; better distribution of the cost of maternity allocations (this being the main cause of discharge of women at the time of their marriage). The Council has tried to direct women towards a more active and conscious participation in the political life of the country and to encourage their confidence in their ability to conduct active investigations and to influence public opinion.

1959: Legalized prostitution abolished, women's police constituted, some women judges assigned to minors' courts. Greatly reduced disparity of pay has been achieved in many productive sectors. The Fifth Congress of the Council supported equal rights for women over their children, the application of International Conventions and laws whose object is the equality and dignity of working mothers and the active participation of women in the economic life of the country, with full recognition of their contribution.

1960: The Council called for participation by women in the Centenary Celebration of Italian Union (Turin, 1961). It organized study group in Naples on food education within the framework of the World Campaign against Hunger.

The many real achievements of the Council of Women of Italy, all carried out in the spirit of the ICW, in which qualified members of Italian Council continue to play a valued rôle, have made this Council a true and dynamic expression of Italian women.

Standing Committees

Arts and Letters, Child Welfare, Cinema, Education, Finance, Health, Home Economics, Housing, International Relations and Peace, Laws and Suffrage, Migrations, Social Welfare, Press and Publicity (Radio and Television) and Women's Work.

Organizations affiliated with the Council

Council has 40 women's and mixed organizations:

Cultural: Lyceum Club, Parents–Teachers Association, 'Les Quatre Arts', VAL (lecture agency), Feminine Section of Press Associations.

Professional: Federation of University Women, Women Jurists, Women Writers, Health Assistants and Nurses, Artisans.

Social Work: National Association for the families of persons killed or dispersed by war, Refugee Assistance, National Association for Emigrants' Families, Assistance to Abandoned Mothers.

Recreation: Federation of Italian Recreational Activities.

Italian sections of the YWCA and the WIZO.

Relations with UN and Specialized Agencies

The Council follows UN activities carefully through the intermediary of those of its affiliates represented on its Executive Board whose activities lead them to concern themselves closely with the work of one or other of the UN bodies. Whenever a Convention or Resolution taken by inter-governmental organizations is esteemed useful to the status of Italian women and children, in the family or in the community, the National Council takes the necessary steps to encourage its ratification by the Italian government, to suggest appropriate legislative action and to propose suitable experts and delegates from among its members.

Council members have recently participated as experts in the preliminary study of a proposed international Convention concerning the adoption of minors. Countess della Gherardesca (Vice-President of the ICW since 1954) was a member of the Italian delegation to the United Nations General Assembly in 1961 and 1962, Miss L. Corcos and Countess della Gherardesca both represented Italy at the meetings of ECOSOC in 1961 and 1962.

The National Council is represented on the Education Section of the National Commission for UNESCO. Close relations are maintained with FAO headquarters in Rome and with the Italian Association for the UN.

An affiliated society—the National Union for the Eradication of Illiteracy—is collaborating closely with UNESCO. Its activity—of which women and girls are the main beneficiaries—is serving that organization as a guide to efforts to be promoted in other countries in connection with the proposed World Campaign for the eradication of illiteracy.

The National Council is working actively for the ratification of Convention on the Recovery of Maintenance Abroad and has participated in the *ad hoc* Committee set up on the subject in the Ministry of Foreign Affairs. Constant steps are taken to ensure the implementation of other UN conventions concerning the status and welfare of women and children.

May 1961

NEW ZEALAND

NATIONAL COUNCIL OF WOMEN OF NEW ZEALAND
COUNCIL ESTABLISHED IN 1896
Affiliated to ICW in 1900

Fields of activity and achievements

New Zealand women were granted the franchise as early as 1893 and one of the prime movers in that momentous event was Mrs K. W. Sheppard who already in 1894, when a delegate to the World Convention of the Women's Christian Temperance Union in England, discussed with Mrs McLaren, the ICW Corresponding Secretary, the idea of forming a Council in New Zealand.

On her return home in 1896 she found the formation of such an organization under discussion at a meeting convened in Christchurch by the Canterbury Women's Institutes' Executive. One of the papers for consideration at that meeting concerned 'The Advantages of Establishing a National Council of Women' delivered by Lady Stout who had also been inspired by discussions with Mrs McLaren in London. Following the presentation of that paper, a motion requesting that the meeting resolve itself into a National Council of Women was carried unanimously and there came into being, on April 13th, 1896, the first National Council of Women of New Zealand. Mrs Sheppard was elected the first President, with Lady Stout as one of the Vice-Presidents, Mrs Wells the Honorary Secretary and Miss Sherriff Bain the Honorary Treasurer.

A wide range of subjects received close and careful consideration, such as the need for amendments to the Marriage Laws, economic independence for married women, equal conditions for divorce. Among the social reforms advocated were listed the classification of criminals, indeterminate sentences for sexual offences against women and children, the abolition of capital punishment, and the right of women to serve on juries. The need for legislation was stressed regarding industrial conditions, hours of work and rates of pay, the extension of technical education in primary and secondary schools and the establishment of free kindergarten schools.

As many of the societies affiliated with the Council had been formed primarily to work for suffrage, it was almost inevitable that, once their objective had been achieved, they would disband. Unfortunately, this is what happened and, as a consequence, the Council ceased to function in 1906.

In 1900 the Council had affiliated with the ICW and from cessation of activities until 1909 the very capable Secretary, Miss Henderson, kept the ICW informed of the progress of women's affairs in New Zealand. At the Conference of the ICW in Canada in 1909 it was resolved that the link between New Zealand and the ICW should be maintained by the appointment of Mrs Sheppard as Honorary Vice-President—so it can be rightly claimed that the Council has had close liaison for more than 60 years.

In 1916 a small group of women led by Mrs Sheppard, Miss Henderson and Miss Mackay met in Christchurch to discuss the need for arousing women to a sense of their responsibilities, and as a result personal letters and circulars were sent to women in various centres urging the reconstruction of the National Council. So well was this suggestion received that in 1917 local councils (under the title of branches of the National Council of Women) were formed in Wellington, Auckland and Christchurch and the following year in Hamilton and Dunedin. In 1961 there were 33 such branches comprising more than 150 affiliated societies. Some ten years ago societies with a National Executive and National Policy were admitted to membership of the Council at Dominion level and the present strength of those societies on the Dominion Executive of our Council is twenty-four. Today our Council is representative of approximately 250,000 women.

Many of the legislative amendments and improvements in social and economic conditions, advocated in the earlier life of the Council, are now law: the marriage age for boys and girls has been raised from 14 and 12 years respectively to 16 years for both; old age benefits are now payable under the Social Security Scheme; indeterminate sentences have been written into the New Zealand Crimes Act; technical education has been introduced; free kindergarten schools subsidized by the government have been established in practically every city and district.

After years of dogged persistence we now have a splendid body of police women as an adjunct of the Police Force and they are performing excellent work, particularly among our young people. Equal pay for equal work will be an accomplished fact in 1963 in Public Service employment and the Council will continue to press for its implementation in every industry and profession and the removal of sex discrimination in every facet of our economic life.

After almost sixty years of continued representations to successive governments, the Council persists in its claim for full citizenship, as for the right for women to serve on juries on equal terms with men.

In all matters affecting the welfare of the community, the Council is ever vigilant and never hesitates to approach the government when improvements are considered necessary or when it is apparent that anomalies should be removed.

As always, the main plank in the policy of the Council is to work unceasingly for peace by fostering goodwill, friendship and good relations between the nations of the world and by the abolition of racial, sex, religious and economic discriminations.

July 1961

ARGENTINA

CONSEJO DE MUJERES
COUNCIL ESTABLISHED IN 1900
Affiliated to ICW in 1901

Fields of activity and accomplishments

The Council acts directly through a number of different sections, each of which assumes a share of the work to be done.

Library Section. Established in 1903, at the permanent headquarters of the Council, the Library directs all cultural and educational matters and serves more than 1,000 external students who follow general and commercial secretarial courses, book-keeping, languages (English and French), Spanish, Argentine and world literature, interior decoration, etc. From 3 to 5 p.m. every Saturday free courses are offered to office employees and working women.

Social Welfare Section. Established in 1910. Affords protection for women doing various types of piece work—children's clothing, etc.—in their own homes and maintains an exhibition room for the public sales of these goods. The aims are:

1. To aid women's work in every way possible.
2. To provide work for women of proven ability.
3. To obtain a qualitative and quantitative improvement of the articles offered for sale.

4. To improve the welfare of the working women by raising the standard of living.

In addition, the Council provides layettes for babies which are distributed to municipal hospitals.

Legislation Section. Established in 1915. Composed entirely of experienced women lawyers, this section plays an important rôle through its activity and decisive influence on the juridical and legal status of women and children. Its action has influenced the acceptance of many laws relating to women's civil and political status, work, maternity, etc. Although Argentine women now enjoy wide civil and political rights, its present work consists in obtaining certain changes in the Civil Code which still requires improvement. Eminent jurists also give educational talks on juridical subjects of concern to women.

Special Voluntary 'Godmothers' Section. Established in 1922. Its work began with the distribution of books to teachers and pupils in national schools far from urban centres. Over the course of the years this work has developed and taken on an extensive social aspect through the periodic distribution of clothing, food, medicines, seeds for student gardens, teaching materials, work tools, etc. The work is performed by individual voluntary 'godmothers' and this section also undertakes any necessary additional work.

White Cross Section. Established in 1926. Its essential aim is 'to save the Child through science, love and understanding of his problems'. It organized in 1932 the first Congress of Social Service for Children ever held in the country. Since its inception it has endeavoured to extend its action to help children needing help on a moral plane and to deal with the problems of juvenile delinquency.

Inter-American Section. Established in 1936 and formerly entitled 'Peace and Arbitration'. Its principal aim is to contribute to the union of the countries of the continent and to gain accurate knowledge of other countries through the study of geographical, historical, artistic conditions, etc. Lectures are given by ambassadors, cultural attachés and other prominent people in Argentina and other American countries.

Home Economics Section. Established in 1943. Studies home problems, makes information on home economics available through special short courses, and maintains practical courses on subjects such as dressmaking toy-making, etc.

Press and Propaganda Section. The Council's official Bulletin contains information about all of the activities of the Council, the Divisions and the Organizations associated with the Council.

Standing Committees. The Council is represented on 11 of the 15 ICW Committees.

Organizations affiliated with the Council. Cultural, charitable and social welfare organizations, working independently in their own fields, are affiliated with the Council.

Relations with UN and Specialized Agencies. The Council does not maintain direct relations with UN, but its rostrum is open to any request made of it from UN and all delegates and representatives are welcome at headquarters. Mrs Ana de Figueroa, Assistant Director of the International Labour Office, has given a conference concerning World Refugee Year and the Council was honoured to receive the women attending the 7th Regional Conference of the American States organized by the ILO in Buenos Aires in March 1961.

May 1961

FRANCE

CONSEIL NATIONAL DES FEMMES FRANÇAISES
COUNCIL ESTABLISHED IN 1901
Affiliated to ICW in 1901

French women have associated themselves with the work of the ICW from the time of its foundation. In 1888 Mme Isabelle Bogelot (who was working on behalf of women discharged from St Lazare, a detention hospital for prostitutes) went to the United States to attend the ICW's foundation. Since that time the cause of peace has been one of the main interests of the French National Council which has been represented at all the principal conferences whose aim was to further this cause. Mme Avril de Sainte-Croix was one of the two ICW delegates sent to the 1907 Hague Peace Conference at which the ICW and the Salvation Army were the only groups allowed representation.

Former Council Presidents have been: Mlle Sarah Monod, Mme Jules Siegfried, Mme Avril de Sainte-Croix, Mme Pichon-Landry, all of whom have played an important part in the evolution of the status of women in France from a political and social point of view. Mme Marie-Hélène Lefaucheux was elected President in 1954.

The Council's fiftieth anniversary was celebrated in 1952 during which speeches were made by the President of the Senate, by M. André Siegfried (son of one of the founders of the Council), Mrs Eleanor Roosevelt, Baroness Boël, Mrs Eder and Mme Lefaucheux. A brochure entitled *Fifty Years of Action* contains these speeches and a resumé of the work accomplished during this period.

Fields of activity and achievements: 1901–39

During this period the NCW worked steadily and methodically for better social justice for everyone and for equality of the sexes in family matters and in the professions. However, the Council's outstanding women, who had succeeded in gaining the support of many French men, were unable because of the opposition of the Senate to obtain the right to vote or equality of the sexes until after the Second World War when this was incorporated into the Constitution of 1946.

Principal reforms obtained in this period:

Women's right to be guardians and members of *Conseils de Famille*.
Penal sanctions for abandonment of family.

Paternity investigation.

Women allowed to keep their nationality in case of marriage with a foreigner.

Equality of salary for men and women school teachers.

Admission of women to Competitive Examination for entry into Ministries.

Equality of secondary teaching programmes for girls and boys.

Admission of women to equality with men in University faculties.

Regulation of remuneration of work performed at home.

Prohibition of under-age labour in unhealthy industries.

1929: States-General meeting on the Status of Women: delegates of 250 associations and of women executives at all levels demanded the right to vote for women.

1931: States-General second meeting on the Status of Women in the Overseas Territories.

1934: Organization of a Defence Committee for Women Workers to protect women's right to work, freedom of choice and equality of remuneration.

1937: Congress of Women's Activities to demonstrate the value of women's contributions in all fields.

1938: Mme L. Brunschwicg, Under-Secretary of State for Education, and the first woman to hold Cabinet rank in France, addressed a meeting on New Careers for Women on the occasion of the ICW Golden Jubilee Council Meeting in Edinburgh.

War of 1914–18: Creation of a Bureau of Women's Activities and an Information Office for Dispersed Families.

War of 1939–45: Creation of a Recruitment and Placement Bureau for Voluntary Workers. During the occupation of France many members of the Council, then forbidden to hold meetings, participated in the organization of resistance.

1945 to the present

The main work of the Council in this period has been:

To have equality of the sexes written into the Constitution by fighting against discrimination which persists in practice as in private law.

To provide political and civic education for women.

To further the evolution of women in French Overseas Territories.

At the time of the 1950 and 1955 elections the Council campaigned (1) requesting the parties to include women in their lists and reminding them of the urgent reforms which women wished to achieve; (2) requesting women to study the programmes of the parties, to register their candidature, and to vote for women.

The principal reforms for which the Council has worked in latter years:

1949: Law for the Censorship of Children's Publications.

244

1945–58: Decree improving children's courts and changing the methods of control and retraining of delinquents.

1957: Law prohibiting the sale of alcohol to children.

1960: Repeated demands by the Committee on Moral Welfare finally achieved the promulgation of decrees harmonizing French legislation with the International Convention on Female Prostitution.

1951: Creation of the Consumers Federal Union. The Council took an active part in its work. Mme Pichon-Landry, its Vice-President, has contributed to the creation in 1956 of the Association for Information on Home Economics.

Mme Elie Chevalley, President of the Committee on Migration, worked with the Ministry of Labour on a contract for the protection of foreign girls working *au pair* (without salary) in French families. The Committee on Social Welfare, in liaison with the British National Council of Women, worked on the protection of young girls working *au pair* in England in families or as student nurses.

Since 1958 the main activity of the Council has been the campaign against the disadvantageous Reform of Marriage Laws proposed by the government. Due to this energetic action the proposal has not yet been passed.

Work on behalf of women in overseas countries

During the Fiftieth Anniversary celebration Mme Lefaucheux, recently elected Vice-President of the *Assemblée de l'Union Française* (then the legislative body for Metropolitan France, its Overseas Departments and Territories) requested the Council to employ the same zeal on behalf of French women in overseas countries as on behalf of those in France.

From 1948 to 1960, the date on which the former French overseas possessions became independent, the Council obtained outstanding reforms either by its own action or through its specialized affiliated associations:

1952: Application of the Labour Laws to Overseas Territories: equality of payment, maternity leave, family allowances.

1953: Right to choose the Metropolitan (mainland France) decrees concerning marriage.

1956: *Loi Cadre* granting women equality of political rights.

Action on behalf of Algerian Moslem Women

1957: Guardianship rights for Moslem women. Proof of marriage by registration in Civil Register.

1958: Right to vote accorded to Algerian Moslem women.

1959: Requirement of personal and verbal consent for a valid marriage to take place.

1960: The Departmental Council of Women of the Gironde (section of the National Council) established in Bordeaux a reception centre for Moslem families.

R

Collaboration with the ICW

Up to 1938

Mlle Sarah Monod, Mme Jules Siegfried, Mme Avril de Sainte-Croix and Mme Pichon-Landry have been ICW Vice-Presidents. The presidents of ICW Standing Committees have included Mme Avril de Sainte-Croix (Moral Welfare, 1904-36); Mme Maria Vérone (Laws and Suffrage, 1927-36), Comtesse de Pange (Letters); Mme Germaine Dulac (Cinema); Mme Dreyfus-Barney (Radio, and later Peace); Mme Thuillier-Landry (Health).

1932-34: ICW Headquarters established in Paris
1934: Triennial Council Meeting of ICW held in Paris at the Head-quarters of the International Institute of Intellectual Co-operation.

Since 1939

Mme Marie-Hélène Lefaucheux elected ICW President at Triennial Meeting in Montreal, 1957.

Members of ICW Board of Officers: Mme Pichon-Landry, Vice-President from 1938 to 1947; Mme Majorelle, Honorary Recording Secretary from 1947 to 1960, Honorary Vice-President since 1960.

Conveners of ICW Committees: Mlle F. Dissard (Housing 1954-66); Dr. S. Laborde (Health, 1938-51); Mme E. Chevalley (Migration, 1938-60); Mme J. Barbizet (Child Welfare, 1947-57).

Standing Committees

All ICW Committees are at present represented in the Council except that of the Cinema.

Organizations affiliated with the Council

Forty affiliated associations. Among these are French Federation of Girl Guides, War Widows Association, Civilian Widows Association, Social Workers Association, Women Physicians Association, Association of Women in the Legal Professions, Association of Women Executives in Small and Medium Businesses, Movement of Solidarity of Algerian Women.

Relations with League of Nations, UN and Specialized Agencies

1927: Mme Dreyfus Barney was appointed to the Sub-Committee of Experts of the League of Nations Committee for Intellectual Co-operation.

1936: Mme Malaterre-Sellier was appointed by the French government to the French delegation to the League.

1938: Mme P. Bastid was named by the French government to the League Committee of juridical experts on the Legal Status of Women. Mme Dreyfus Barney and Mme Puech were appointed to the French Committee to the Institute of Intellectual Co-operation. (Mme Dreyfus-Barney was then of French nationality.)

246

Mme Lefaucheux is the Permanent Delegate of the French Government to the Commission on the Status of Women. She was President of this Commission from 1947–51 and also represents the government at the Social and Economic Council of the UN.

Mme Bastid is President of the UN Administrative Tribunal.

Dr Sérin has performed missions for the UN in Morocco, Yemen and Iran.

The Council welcomed the establishment of UNESCO in Paris and has collaborated with this organization from the very outset.

Representation at UNESCO Meetings

Mme Puech 1947; Mme Pichon-Landry 1950–60; Mme Majorelle 1950–   ; Mme Delavenay 1959–   .

In addition, the Council is represented at the Council of Europe by Mme de Pange.

Mme Saunier is on the staff of the Information Service of UNICEF for Europe and the Near East.

Ratification of International Conventions

In recent years, the Council has been very active in the ratification of the following:

1956: Convention on Refugees.
1957: Convention on Equality of Political Rights.
1960: Convention on Suppression of the Traffic in Women and Children.
1961: UNESCO Convention against Discrimination in Education.
Convention concerning the Recovery of Maintenance Abroad.

December 1961

AUSTRIA

BUND ÖSTERREICHICHISCHER FRAUENVEREINE
COUNCIL ESTABLISHED IN 1902
Affiliated to ICW in 1903–38. Reaffiliated 1951.

In 1899 the ICW invited Austrian women's associations to unite in a National Council and subsequently to join the ICW, and in the same year asked these organizations to send a delegate to the Second Quinquennial Council Meeting held in London. This invitation inspired action and Mrs Marianne Hainisch was chosen to attend the ICW meeting where she was elected Honorary Vice-President.

1902–13

1902: Organization of the Federation of Associations of Austrian Women under the courageous leadership of Mrs Hainisch in the face of great obstacles in that period which were set up to oppose collaboration among the different nationalities and parties in Austria-Hungary. Nineteen groups joined together at this time.

1904: The Federation, now consisting of 35 associations, was accepted as a member by the ICW and as such took part in the Third Quinquennial Council Meeting in Berlin. The first action of the Austrian delegation was formulation of a petition to the Sultan of Turkey to abolish white slavery. Mrs Hainisch and Mrs Berta von Suttner also spoke at the Peace Meeting held on this occasion.

1905: Mrs Berta von Suttner was first woman to receive Nobel Peace Prize.

1906: The first statistical monograph on 'Schools for Austrian Women' was prepared by Mrs Eleonore Jeiteles and presented to the ICW Special Council Meeting in Geneva in 1908.

1907: A special inquiry was made into problems of public health.

Mrs Berta von Suttner presented the Federation's resolution favouring pacifist aims to the President of the Second Peace Conference at The Hague.

1909: Mrs Hainisch, President of the Federation, was elected third Vice-President of the ICW.

1910: The ICW Executive Committee held its meeting at Innsbruck.

1911: Dr Dora Teleky, member of the International Committee for Public Health, reported on the prevention of tuberculosis at the ICW Executive Council meeting in Stockholm.

1912: The Federation opened the first public office in Vienna for professional orientation for young girls in collaboration with the Union of Working Women. Until 1913 the Federation ran 4 professional orientation offices with the unpaid collaboration of teachers, women doctors and committee members.

Juridical Committee studied the status of women under Austrian civil law as compared to men.

1913: One of the last reports prepared before the First World War concerned the status of aid to young people and the treatment of juvenile criminals.

1914–38

1914: After the Fifth Quinquennial Council Meeting held in Rome the ICW delegates visited Vienna. The 70th birthday of Mrs May Wright Sewall, one of the founders of the ICW, was cordially celebrated by Viennese women.

At the beginning of the war it was generally believed that hostilities would be of short duration. Thus the Federation received many letters from neutral countries containing various proposals for future world peace and for a federation of European states. Suggestions for continuing peace efforts as soon as war should end came even from enemy countries.

1915: In spite of strong opposition, four Austrian women attended the

International Women's Congress for Peace, the first in the history of the world, which was held in The Hague.

1918: After the Armistice, Mrs Hainisch, then President of the Federation, urgently requested other national councils to start a pacifist movement with the aim of preventing a future war of revenge.

Austria had been profoundly affected by the war: the middle class was impoverished and the women from whom the Federation obtained its most active elements and financial support, were cut off from their cultural and spiritual aspiration by the difficulties of daily life. Thus the magazine *Der Bund* had to stop appearing as well as the sending of delegates to international meetings.

1923: A Peace Assembly was held for the first time in Vienna.

1924: The Federation inquired into a proposed law on protection against venereal diseases on the basis of equal treatment for men and women and presented a petition to the National Council for rapid passage of the law.

The Federation was represented at the Congresses of the Society against White Slavery and the International Abolitionist Federation which were held every two years at Graz.

The Federation proposed that the Austrian Emigration Service establish contact between international organizations of local women and immigrants. Mme Avril de Sainte-Croix, Vice-President of the ICW and delegate to the League of Nations, personally supported the Federation's efforts to obtain a woman official for feminine emigration.

With the aid of other national women's councils the Federation created 'Women's Aid' for the control of tuberculosis by providing a consultation service for mothers and placement of sick children.

The Federation's professional guidance service passed under the administration of the City of Vienna.

A detailed report was prepared on Austrian school reform with emphasis on the teaching of girls.

The Juridical Committee reported on the Austrian Civil Code concerning deliberate abandonment of the family and formulated its demands for improvements.

1925: The Legislature considered a petition prepared by the Juridical Committee on the keeping or re-obtaining of Austrian nationality by Austrian women married to foreigners.

1930: The outstanding event for the Federation in the period between the two wars was the welcoming to Vienna of the Eighth Quinquennial Council Meeting of the ICW, of which Lady Aberdeen was President and Marianne Hainisch, then 90 years old, was Honorary President.

1931: The Austrian Committee on Public Health reported on the expulsion of non-Austrian prostitutes.

1933: Inquiry made into attitude of the press regarding disarmament and the question of nationality in marriage.

1934: Mrs Marie Hoheisel and Mrs Henriette Hainisch represented the Federation at the Triennial Council Meeting of the ICW in Paris.

The Federation's proposal to recommend the holding of peace rallies was taken up. Mrs Hoheisel wrote the first article for a new column entitled *Peace* in the ICW's publication.

1936: After the ICW Triennial Council Meeting in Dubrovnik at which Marie Hoheisel represented the Federation the delegates met in Vienna at the Federation's invitation. A public meeting was held at which delegates reported on the status of the women's movement in their countries.

At the suggestion of Lady Aberdeen, the Federation, together with all national councils, sent to the League of Nations a message expressing women's desire for peace and their willingness to collaborate in the work of reconciliation.

1938: The last work done before the Second World War was on the political, civil and economic status of Austrian women which was to have been reported to the League of Nations.

During the years of crisis preceding the occupation of Austria by German National Socialism, the Federation had to fight against measures taken to the detriment of the workers, especially married women. Shortly after the occupation of Austria the Federation was banned.

1947 to the present

1947: The Federation was re-established.

1949: Dr Grete Laube sent as a delegate to the ICW Executive Council in Lugano.

Work continued on the problem of prostitution and also on relations between Parents Associations and the schools.

1951: Mrs Henriette Hainisch, present President of the Federation, was sent to the ICW Triennial Council Meeting at Athens during which the Federation was reinstated in the ICW. The efforts made by Austrian women to obtain compulsory household education for young girls were enthusiastically received and all Council members were urged to contact their governments to suggest that home economics be made compulsory.

1952: Reports made on aid to old people and on the professional rights of teaching personnel and the need for a civic pacifist education.

1953: The Federation organized an exposition for its fiftieth anniversary.

1956: The Federation was represented at the ICW Executive Council meeting in Venice.

1959: The Federation welcomed the delegates to the ICW Executive Council meeting where the questions of emigration and the juridical status of women in Austria were discussed. The ICW trimestrial review published the Federation's report on its efforts to obtain amendment of the family law and the social insurance law.

Relations with UN and Specialized Agencies

The Federation is represented in the Women's Section of the Austrian Association for the United Nations. This Section works in contact with the Status of Women Commission and with UNESCO, UNICEF, ILO, etc. Qualified members are designated as representatives, observers or experts to these organizations on the national or international level.

The Federation obtained ratification of Convention 100 of the ILO and is working on ratification of: (1) the UN Convention on the Political Status of Women; (2) Convention against Discrimination in Employment and Occupation; (3) Convention against Discrimination in Education.

April 1961

SWITZERLAND

ALLIANCE DES SOCIETES FEMININES SUISSES
COUNCIL ESTABLISHED IN 1900
Affiliated to ICW 1903

Fields of activity and achievements

From its foundation the Council's work has consisted of the following:

1. Represented women before the federal authorities.
2. Informed women on all present-day problems of particular interest to them.
3. Kept the public informed on questions concerning women.

Maintenance of press service, publication of pamphlets, brochures, organization of and participation in seminars and conferences.

From the beginning the Council has given special attention to major legislation of the Swiss Confederation. As a sign of high recognition the authorities submit to the Council all proposed legislation of particular interest to it, on juridical, social, economic and cultural questions. Moreover, the Council's delegates often take part in the work of non-parliamentary federal commissions of experts which are set up to study proposed laws and their regulation. Council delegates also take part in administrative federal commissions. Since 1907 when for the first time a woman was nominated to a federal commission (revision of the factory-work law), this collaboration has steadily increased, and it is not unusual now to find several women taking part in the same commission. This participation in the work of federal commissions affords the Council a direct rôle in the creation of laws.

On the other hand, the Council's constant attention is given to certain fields: status of women, political rights, labour problems, professional orientation and education of women, economic problems, social insurance, public health, the problem of prostitution, the sexual education of young girls, education (particularly civic education).

Following are some highlights in the Council's history:

1900–13

1903: Became member of the ICW. Followed closely the elaboration of the Swiss Civil Code and published a commentary directed to women.

Active rôle in the revision of the factory law, creation of the medical and accident insurance law, and obligatory home economics instruction.

Tried (unsuccessfully) to have a Buyers League established.

1914–38

1914: Participated in the Swiss National Exhibition.

1921: Participated in the 2nd Congress for Women's Interests.

1922: Created the Central Bureau for Women's Professions.

1928: Collaborated in the establishment of SAFFA (Berne), the first women's exhibition, which was an outstanding success.

1933: Created the Swiss Association for Domestic Help.

Requested amendment of the Federal Constitution to grant political rights to women.

Took part in action towards creating a place for women in the police force.

Demanded the creation of film censorship.

Took part in the proposal for old age and survivors' insurance.

Supported legislation on home work.

Supported legislation concerning alcoholism.

Defended the economic interests (professional) of women affected by the economic crisis.

1939 to the present

1939: Became member of the Consultative War Economics Committee.

Participated in the Swiss National Exhibition.

1944: The Central Bureau for Women's Professions became the Swiss Women's Secretariat (extension of activity to all women's problems).

1946: Participated in the Third Women's Congress.

1949: Received the ICW Executive Board.

Joined with the Swiss Women's Secretariat which became its administrative branch.

1952: Took initiative in the foundation of the Swiss Association of Family Aid Organizations.

Took part in working out laws concerning warrant and guarantee, old age and survivors' insurance, nationality, female suffrage in federal matters, agriculture, labour, professional education, revision of the law concerning the family, medical and maternity insurance, traffic, cinema, civil protection, hire purchase transactions.

Special effort was made to have the authorities sign ILO Convention No. 100 concerning equal pay for equal work.

1958: Initiated and played a leading part in the 2nd SAFFA Exhibition 1958: Women of Switzerland, their life and work. Like the first SAFFA, it was a remarkable success.

Standing Committees

The Council is represented on all ICW Committees. It also has National Standing Committees on: Insurance, Social problems, Economic problems, Women's Status in Federal Administration, Professional activities of mothers, Family allowances, Civil protection.

Organizations affiliated with the Council

As follows: 46 Swiss associations; 18 cantonal liaison centres; 186 local associations. These represent all fields: protection of women's interests—political, economic, religious; public service; professional; cultural and sports.

UN and Specialized Agencies

Various members of the Council (or of its member-associations) represent international organizations with UN:

Miss M. Zwahlen	Associated Country Women of the World
Mrs P. Bugnion-Secretant	The World Association of Girl Guides and Girl Scouts
Miss Alice Arnold and Mrs H. de Mestral	World YWCA
Miss Travelletti, Miss F. Ehni and Miss Elisabeth Feller	International Federation of Business and Professional Women
Mrs Marie Fiechter	International Federation of University Women
Mrs J. Brunschwig	Women's International Zionist Organization
Mrs Droin de Morsier and Mrs A. Rochedieu	ICW
Mrs A. Wiblé	Liaison Committee of Women's International Organizations
Mrs Y. Leuba and Mrs N. Chaix	World's Women's Christian Temperance Union

The Council is represented on the Swiss National Commission for UNESCO, and on the Swiss National Commission for FAO. A member of the Council (President of the Swiss Federation of Girl Scouts) is a member of the Swiss Commission for UNICEF.

Switzerland is in a special position due to the fact that it is not a member of UN. Nevertheless, the Council recently recommended that the Federal authorities sign the International Convention for the Recovery of Maintenance Abroad, as well as Convention No. 100 of the ILO concerning equal pay for equal work. The Council will soon support the ratification of the 1949 Convention concerning the abolition of human slavery and the exploitation of prostitution. It recently requested the Swiss Government to support the International Red Cross Committee in charge of establishing regulations regarding dangers faced by civilian populations in time of war.

May 1961

*HUNGARY

Affiliated 1904

The National Council of Women of Hungary was founded in 1904 with 52 affiliated organizations. This number grew to 104 in 1913. Countess Lajos Batthyany was its first President. In 1910 she was succeeded by Countess Albert Apponyi, who was to direct the activities of this Council with unfailing energy for more than 30 years.

In 1905, and during the following years, the NCW was active in promoting anti-alcoholic instruction in the schools, in regulating the sale of liquor and in establishing temperance hostels in slum areas. It urged the eligibility of women to the Council of Public Instruction and the admission of girls to High Schools, Commercial Colleges and the University. It participated in the fight against pornographical literature and the white slave traffic and collaborated with the government in its Office for the Protection of Youth.

The NCW tried to raise the level of education among domestic servants by founding homes and schools for their training. From 1904–14 it worked for equal conditions for workers of both sexes and the establishment of minimum wages, investigating the deplorable conditions of those employed at home on piece work. It also advocated the introduction of old age insurance for domestic servants.

The Peace Committee, led by Mrs Zipernovsky, strove for peace through arbitration.

A Reference Library of the NCW was created, and from 1909–14 the Council published a periodical edited by Augusta Rosenberg.

In 1909, the National Council obtained from the Minister of Home Affairs: (1) compulsory notification of tuberculosis cases; (2) compulsory disinfection; and (3) the creation of dispensaries and similar welfare institutions.

From 1909 onwards the Council worked for women's suffrage (Mrs Rosika Schwimmer) and in 1912 asked for the vote on an 'intelligentia census'.

In 1914 the full attention of the Council was concentrated on war work. Over 2,000 nurses received their training through the NCW, which organized a special office for the protection of the families of soldiers and assisted in the exchange of letters between prisoners of war in Russia and their families. The Council organized a national collection to rebuild schools in war-stricken areas, one of which was dedicated to the memory of Countess Alexander Teleky. During the war the regular activities of the NCW continued and contact with the ICW remained unbroken.

In 1918, new Committees were formed: Press, Letters, Laws, and Arts and Crafts. The civic, political and economic rights of Hungarian women were investigated and the rights of married professional women defended in a series of public lectures. Thanks to the NCW, women were appointed to the official committee for the censorship of films.

In 1927, Miss Augusta Rosenberg was the first Hungarian woman to be a delegate to the League of Nations Assembly, and from 1928-33 she was also a delegate to the Conferences of the ILO.

From 1928, Countess Apponyi was a delegate of Hungary to the League of Nations Assembly and in 1930, 1935 and 1937 was elected Chairman of its Fifth Commission.

NORWAY

NORSKE KVINNERS NASJONALRÅD
COUNCIL ESTABLISHED IN 1904
Affiliated to ICW 1904

Fields of activity and achievements: 1904–13

Fights against white slavery and for the abolition of prostitution.
Woman suffrage (partially granted in 1907, for parliamentary elections since 1913).
Equal guardianship rights (granted in 1927).
Women factory inspectors (granted in 1910).
Schools for teaching home economics to girls (done in 1909).
Equal pay for equal work.
Revision of marriage laws.
Family education.
Maternity rights and insurance.
Increased prison sentences for crimes against morality.
Access to all employment by women (granted in 1912 except in the religious, military and diplomatic fields).
Requested women members of the Board of Censorship for the Cinema (granted).
Women members of provincial commissions (granted).
Better education and salary increases for midwives.
Revision of wages for child labour (granted).
Anti-alcoholism.
Minimum age of consent (marriage) set at 20 and 18 years.
Betterment of legal status of illegitimate children.
Equal inheritance rights for widows (granted).

1914–38

Equal rights to matrimonial property.
Obligatory home economics education for boys and girls (granted).
Divorce laws.
International peace programme.
Requirement of three years' instruction for nurses before obtaining diploma (granted in 1948).
Right of women to enter the ministries (granted in 1916; first and only woman minister in 1945).
Foundation of Council school for social workers, the first of its kind in Norway until 1950.
Right for women members of tribunals dealing with crimes against morality (granted).
Raising of age of minors from 16 to 18 years (granted 1934).
Women jailers in women's prisons (granted).
Animal protection.
Greater control of food production.
Clinics for female alcoholics.
Two-year apprenticeship requirement for midwives (granted).
Nationality of Norwegian women married to foreigners (granted).
Abortion laws.
Women members on Executive Board of the Norwegian Radio (granted in 1935).
Obligatory manual training in primary schools (granted).
Equal promotion rights (Government posts).
Foundation of a Home Economy Information Bureau (granted in 1939).
Marriage laws: right of wife to her share of property acquired during marriage (granted).
Equal access to education.

1939 to the present

Social security (partially granted).
Child insurance (granted).
Women ecclesiastic ministers (granted in 1961).
Maintenance allowances for illegitimate children.
Improved legislation for insane and mentally deficient persons.
State subsidy for kindergartens.
Obligatory home economics instruction for girls and boys.
Maintenance allowances abroad.
Fight against atomic warfare and experimental nuclear explosions.
Rehabilitation of 'hard core' refugees.
Traffic teaching in the schools.
Guardianship of minors.
Taxation of married women.

Standing Committees

All ICW Committees are represented in the Council.

Organizations affiliated with the Council

Anti-Poliomyelitis Association.
Social Hygiene Association.
Mother and Child Association.
White Ribbon League.
Union of Associations for Public Health.
Union of Associations for the Protection of Animals.
Christian Union for Young Girls.
Social Service Association of the Women of the Salvation Army.
Missionary Union of School Teachers.
Women's Association for Civic Service.
Association of Housewives.
Association of Rural Women.
Association of Soroptimist Clubs.
League for Women's Rights.
Association of Women Judges.
Association of State Nurses.
Association of Social Workers (Women).
Association of Women School Teachers.
Association of Home Economics (Women) School Teachers.
Association of Women Employees of the Telegraph and Telephone.
Union of Midwives.

UN and Specialized Agencies

Council members as delegates: in 1919 Mrs Kjelsberg and Mrs Aarum
to the International Labour Organization; Mrs Wicksell and Mrs Dan-
nevig to the Mandate Commission of the League of Nations; Mrs Dalen
to the 1st session of the United Nations. NC President Astri Rynning,
Judge of the Oslo Tribunal, was elected member of the Norwegian
National Commission for UNESCO (1961). Council has brought pressure
on the Government to obtain implementation of ICW-supported UN
Conventions.

April 1961
November 1962

BELGIUM

CONSEIL NATIONAL DES FEMMES BELGES
COUNCIL ESTABLISHED IN 1905
Affiliated to ICW in 1906

Fields of activity and achievements: 1905–13

Supported the campaign for compulsory education.
 Fought for: entry of women in Public Welfare Commissions; guardianship rights of mothers and sisters; accession of women to the electorate
and eligibility to 'Conseils de prud'hommes'; revision of the Civil Code

regarding the nationality of married women; legislation against alcoholism; creation of nurses' schools and nomination of women inspectors in girls' schools; creation of mutual benefit organizations for female domestic personnel; improvement of the status of illegitimate children; child welfare.

Participated in international manifestation for peace.

1914–38

1914–20: Action suspended. When resumed, the Council reorganized and enlarged its activities.

1920–21: Women received the right to vote in municipalities; became eligible to enter municipal, Senate and provincial administration and finally the House of Representatives. This was achieved as a result of a steady campaign carried on for the extension of women's suffrage.

Defended the right of women to studies at all levels on an equal basis with men.

Successfully defended women's right to work, especially that of married women. Worked towards the improvement of the juridical status of married women and for the safeguarding of their savings.

Participated increasingly in international meetings.

1939 to the present

1939: Published a pamphlet entitled *Practical Advice During Mobilization*.

1940–45: Once more obliged to suspend activities. Work continued underground.

1946–61

Resumed the fight for women's suffrage and succeeded for the first time in 1949 in having Belgian women participate in legislative and provincial elections.

Succeeded in obtaining access of women to the magistrature and declared determination of obtaining access of women to all professions.

Succeeded in ending the civil inferiority of married women.

Combated sex discrimination regarding teaching and studied technical education of girls in view of the new job outlets created by new techniques (two publications: *Trades, Professions and Careers for Our Girls* and *The Future of our Daughters*).

Protested against sex discrimination in employment, promotion, social security, unemployment insurance and pensions.

Obtained suppression of the regulation of prostitution and the creation of a female police force.

Studied social questions for the promotion of family welfare.

Created the following new committees to correspond to current needs:

Ad hoc Committee for Gerontology—all problems concerning old-age.

Ad hoc Committee concerning a National Military–Civil Women's Force.

Ad hoc Committee on Production and Consumption—studies in particular the possibility of counting housework in the national income.

A Liaison and Watch Committee of women's organizations whose task is to make urgent representation to public authorities.

Reception Committee (within the Committee for International Relations) which organizes international gatherings, welcomes foreigners and helps Council members to participate in European and international meetings.

Since 1946 published a bi-monthly pamphlet, *The National Council of Belgian Women*, together with index. In addition has published:

The Vote for Women, by M. Verneire-Jadot.

Juridical Status of Native Women in the Belgian Congo, by G. Cyfer-Diderich.

Feminism in Belgium, by Baroness Boël and C. Duchêne.

In 1955 organized 'Friday Tribune'—a series of luncheon lectures.

Standing Committees

All ICW Committees are represented in the Council.

Organizations affiliated with the Council

There are 28 organizations affiliated with the Council:

Professional organizations such as the National Federation of Belgian Nurses.

Teaching Institutions such as the State Institute of Social Studies.

Social organizations such as the National Council of Hospital Libraries.

Social and educational organizations such as the YWCA.

Political organizations such as the National Federation of Liberal Women.

Relations with the UN and Specialized Agencies

1952: Mlle L. Joly attended meetings in Washington of the FAO Consultative Committee on Rural Life, and in 1957 attended the European Congress organized by FAO and ILO in Bad Godesberg.

1950: Mme Lehouck-Gerbehaye was a member of the Belgian Delegation to the UN General Assembly.

1951: Mme de Bray attended the European Cycle (medico-psychologic and social examinations of delinquents) organized by UN and WHO.

1952: Mme Georgette Ciselet attended as Belgian delegate meetings of ECOSOC and the UN General Assembly.

1959: Mme Ciselet presided the Third Committee of this Assembly and in 1962 again represented Belgium at the General Assembly.

1958: Mme Cyfer represented the government at the 12th Session of the Status of Women Commission in Geneva.

1953: Mme de Bray was sent by UN to Vienna as an expert on Penitentiary Social Service.

1953: Mlle Bromham and Mme Pelemans attended an International Music Congress organized by UNESCO.

1954: Mlle L. Talloen was placed in charge of a technical assistance mission to Turkey.

Mmes de Wergifosse and Preaux Van der Elst have represented the Council at meetings of the Sub-Committee of Non-Governmental Organizations in the Belgian National Commission for UNESCO.

When the UN adopted the Convention for the Prevention and Repression of the Crime of Genocide, the Council issued the following statement to the public authorities:

'Gratified to note that the UN General Assembly has unanimously adopted on 9 December 1948 a Convention for the Prevention and Repression of the Crime of Genocide which outlaws acts committed with the intention of destroying a national, ethnic, racial or religious group.

'Certain that Belgian women, who witnessed such acts during the last war, desire that everything be done to outlaw genocide.

'The National Council of Women of Belgium requests the Belgian Government and Parliament to sign and ratify as soon as possible the Convention proposed by the UN to which already 21 countries have agreed.'

Through its Liaison and Watch Committee, the Council brought pressure on the Ministry of Foreign Affairs resulting in the signature and ratification by Belgium of the Convention on the Political Rights of Women.

The Committee for Social Welfare campaigned for the signature and ratification by Belgium of the International Convention for the Repression of Human Slavery and Exploitation of Prostitution.

The Council follows closely all international conventions and takes the necessary action, either directly or through its Liaison and Watch Committee.

July 1961

*BULGARIA

Affiliated 1908

The National Council of Women of Bulgaria (Union of Bulgarian Women) was created in 1901. By 1938 it consisted of 126 associations with a total membership of 15,000 women.

The earliest organization was founded in 1857, and many others between 1860 and 1870. Their aims were mainly educational and humanitarian, but in 1901, the principal object of the Council was the emancipation of women.

The Council organized conferences, meetings and petitions: for thirty-five years it published its activities in the daily press and in its own monthly *Jenski Glas (Woman's Voice)*.

The Council campaigned for equal political rights, based on liberty and equality for all persons, without distinction of sex, party or class, for disarmament and for peace.

In November 1937 a law accorded married women the right to vote and when, in the following year, Bulgarian women voted for the first time, the NCW urged women to vote for candidates supporting women's claims for (1) full and equal franchise; (2) equal legal rights; (3) the admission of women to all professions and occupations and (4) full legal protection of mothers and children, safeguarding the position of the family.

The perseverance and social work of the Council obtained the confidence of the government, and in recognition of the successful efforts of the Council to promote the technical training of girls, Mrs Ivanova, who succeeded Mrs Malinova as President in 1926, was awarded the Cross of the Order of Civic Merit.

Late in 1940 the NCW held an important Congress in Sofia to consider the situation of women in law and in the nation.

GREECE

NATIONAL COUNCIL OF WOMEN OF GREECE
COUNCIL ESTABLISHED IN 1908
Affiliated to ICW in 1908

Fields of activities and achievements: 1908–13

Between 1908 and 1912 the Council endeavoured to make known its aims and to affiliate member organizations. Its activity was suspended during the period of the Balkan wars.

1914–38

1. *Equal civic and political rights*

1920–30: First proposal for equal rights submitted to Parliament in 1920; right to vote granted in 1930 to women of 30 years of age who fulfilled certain educational requirements.
1934: Women first voted in 1934, but numbers were very limited due to registration restrictions and difficulties.

2. *Education and protection of women and children*

1921: Council maintained legal services to aid women unable to pay court charges, lawyers, etc.

S   261

1924: Obtained establishment of first association for the protection of minors in moral danger.

1925–26: Obtained prohibition of entry to films of children under 12 years of age; the establishment of the Educational Films Office under the Ministry of Public Education; and open-air projection of films under the auspices of the municipality of Athens.

Obtained insertion of special clause in revised Greek Constitution of 1926 prohibiting immoral publications and spectacles.

Participated in the State Commission on the proposed law for the establishment of paternity and the legitimation of children born out of wedlock. The Council's views were accepted.

1926–40: Organized and maintained evening classes for women and children.

Requested government to reform public education system with regard to duration of compulsory elementary and professional education.

1928: Council's proposals adopted for law regulating the function of courts for minors.

1930: Council established in a working-class neighbourhood the first large children's playground and sports field. This served as a model.

3. Working women

1923: To develop outlets and professions for working women and to assure refugee women the means of earning their livelihood, the Council opened a workshop, which functioned until 1952, where women did bookbinding, lingerie making and embroidery. This work was sent to various international expositions and in 1930 the Council organized a large Balkan exposition in Athens, thus contributing to the development of women's handicraft.

4. Public health and welfare

1921–40: Published monthly review entitled *Hellinis*.

1932–34: Published various brochures on public health and welfare.

1936: Published a guide to social welfare institutions.

5. Participating in international assemblies

From 1920 on, the Council attended all ICW assemblies and was also represented at 18 meetings of various international organizations.

1939 to present

Because of the dictatorship 1936–40, the war years 1940–45 and the struggle against the Communist attack, it was only in 1949 that the Council's efforts began to achieve satisfactory results.

1. Equal civic and political rights

1949: Equal voting and eligibility rights in communal and municipal elections: two women councillors elected to Athens City Hall.

1951: Large feminine vote registered in municipal elections; several women elected as municipal and communal councillors.

1952: Equal right to vote and eligibility to parliamentary elections under equal conditions.

1953: Election of first Greek woman deputy (Salonika).

1954: Right of women to participate in juries, act as witnesses and become notaries and judges.

1955: Election of first woman mayor (Corfu).
Right of women to enter all public posts on equal basis, except for the ecclesiastic and military fields.

1956: Appointment of first woman Minister: Ministry of Health and Social Welfare.

2. Education and protection of women and children

Evening classes for women and children continued to function until Greek participation in the Second World War.

1939: Maintains and continues to develop the installation of its playground and sports field.

1941: Organized and still maintains Education Centres for girls from 10 to 18 years of age in several working-class districts of Athens, teaching them home economics, hygiene, sewing, embroidery; recreation also provided.

1941–47: Maintained two boarding schools for children of orphaned soldiers and war victims.

1943–47: Organized child psychology and kindergarten courses and maintained a Montessori kindergarten.

1948–50: Organized a series of lectures for parents on family education.

1952–57: Reform of Education Law based on Council's proposals.

1948–51: Addressed appeals to ICW, International Red Cross and other international organizations regarding the repatriation of Greek children abducted to countries behind the Iron Curtain by Communist groups. The Executive Board meeting of the ICW in Lugano supported this appeal to the UN. The ICW repeated its request in a resolution adopted during the 1951 General Assembly in Athens. Following this movement, the UN passed a resolution supporting the repatriation. Unfortunately, the number of children repatriated and returned to their families was very limited.

1960–61: Obtained registration of illegitimate and adopted children without indication of their origin on their birth certificates.

3. Public welfare

1952–55: Created Office for the Moral Protection of Unmarried Mothers; worked for the establishment of an unmarried mothers home.
Council backed ratification of UN Convention of 1949 for the suppression of white slave traffic and exploitation of prostitution. This Convention was not ratified in its entirety but a special law

was passed in 1955 closing all houses of prostitution. In 1959 a proposal was made to annul this law because of public reaction but the Council's report on prostitution proved effective in leaving the law unrevised.

4. Publications

Since 1948, the Council has published (in collaboration with the Lyceum Club of Greek Women, Girl Scouts and the Greek Association of University Women) *Hellenia* in English, which gives news of women's activities in Greece.

1953: In collaboration with the Liaison Committee for Women's Organizations, the Council edited a booklet entitled *Reasons Why You Should Vote.*

Standing Committees

All ICW Committees are represented in the Council.

Organizations affiliated with the Council

Ninety-nine organizations are affiliated with the Council in the capital, the provinces and abroad, covering social welfare, cultural, professional and educational organizations.

UN and Specialized Agencies

Some of the Council's members are named by the government as official delegates to General Assemblies as well as to the UN Commission on the Status of Women.

Some members of the Council participate in the National Commission for UNESCO.

The Council has always supported ratification and application of UN Conventions to which the ICW has given its support.

April 1961

FINLAND

SUOMEN NAISJÄRJESTÖJEN KESKUSLIITTO
COUNCIL ESTABLISHED IN 1911
Affiliated to ICW in 1911

Fields of activity and achievements: 1911 to the present

The Council was founded, with 7 member organizations, in May 1911, by Mrs Alexandra Gripenberg, who had already been long associated with the International Council and was a firm believer in its policy of national and international collaboration. Her death, only three years later, was a great loss to the Finnish Council.

Shortly before the First World War Mrs Tilma Hainari was elected President and worked energetically and untiringly in this post for twenty-three years. Miss Alli Wiherheimo was President from 1937 to 1938, Miss Helle Kannila from 1938 to 1947, and Mrs Margit Borg-Sundman from 1947 to the present.

The Council has always worked for more effective use of women's suffrage (granted in 1906) and for women to become more conscious of their responsibilities as citizens.

When the new Marriage Law and the law qualifying women for the Civil Service came up for decision at the end of the 1920s, the Council strongly appealed to Parliament and the Cabinet, thus helping to obtain the passage of these bills.

An example of one of the many practical social activities undertaken by women is the Women's Police Committee which has done pioneering work in Finland.

A very important event from the point of view of the co-operation among Finnish women was the meeting in 1941. Twenty-seven organizations were invited. It was the first time that women representing different views, political parties and both the Swedish and the Finnish language groups had come together under one roof. The significance of the victory attained by women through such common action is the measure of their mutual understanding. The number of women's organizations affiliated to the Council, e.g. the Social Democratic Women, Kalevala Women and Agrarian Party Women increased as a result of this meeting.

New times have brought new tasks and methods. Emancipation and independence of women have created new problems which will be solved by mutual understanding. For example, the problem of working mothers outside the home, is receiving close attention. The Council arranges lectures and discussion days for young housewives and negotiates with employers and employees, emphasizing the importance of part-time jobs.

In this connection the Council desires to mention with gratitude the full co-operation of the press in publicizing the Council's work.

Moreover, meetings, discussions, and study groups are arranged for members of affiliated organizations and the public at which questions concerning the community, housing, economics, civic education and the aims of the modern feminist movement are dealt with. Questions concerning young people have always played a significant rôle at Council meetings. The problems of part-time jobs, women's duties today, education and the problems of the aged have been discussed after speeches by three women ministers (two Finnish, one Swedish).

In addition to its national activities, the Council carries on a number of international activities and through its representatives among ICW office-holders tries to make known Finnish problems and aims.

In 1954 the Council organized the Triennial Council Meeting of the ICW in Helsinki and welcomed 240 visitors. It published the booklet, *Women of Finland,* to provide information on Finnish history, culture and the activities of Finnish women. In the same year was celebrated the fiftieth anniversary of women's right to vote and the next year the fiftieth anniversary of the first General Election in which women participated.

The Council provides Finnish women both with a window open to the changing world and a wide field of activities in their own country.

Standing Committees

Housing, Trades and Professions, Education, Laws and Suffrage, Moral Welfare, Women Police, Press.

Organizations affiliated with the Council

At present, 52 women's organizations are affiliated with the Council, totalling an overall membership of 415,000 women. The following are examples of the type of organizations:

Housewives (e.g. the Finnish–Swedish Martha Association).
Political women's associations (e.g. Coalition Party, Agrarian Party, Union of Social Democrats).
Professional (e.g. The Association for Teachers in Handicrafts, Federation of Teachers in Home Economics).
Sport (e.g. Swedish–Finnish Women's Gymnastic Association).
Cultural (e.g. Kalevala Women).
Social (e.g. Women's Temperance Union, Prevention of Blindness Association).
Educational (e.g. The Finnish Women's League, Finnish Federation of University Women).

Relations with UN and Specialized Agencies

From 1927 to 1930 Finland appointed a woman—Miss Armi Hallsten Kallia—as substitute delegate to the Assembly of the League of Nations.

At present there is a women representative—Mrs Helvi Sipilä, a lawyer—on the UN Commission on the Status of Women.

Mrs Armi Hosia, with Mrs Marjatta Väänänen as alternate, is on the Finnish National Commission for UNESCO.

Mrs Elizabeth Beaurain-Pickhala is a member of the Finnish National Commission for FAO.

September 1961
March 1962

*YUGOSLAVIA

Affiliated 1911

The National Council began in 1906 and after 1909 functioned regularly as the NCW of Serbia. In the early days of the Council organizers were greatly helped in their difficult task by the ICW and the International Women's Suffrage Alliance. Originally working for the improvement of women in general, the Council added political rights to its programme in 1909.

From 1911 it organized conferences on equal pay, pension rights, the right of women to administer their own property and to obtain the same inheritance rights for children of both sexes. In 1912 a Memorandum calling for women's suffrage was sent to Parliament.

After the First World War, a large Meeting convened by the NCW of Serbia, united delegates from women's organizations in Serbia, Croatia and Slovenia and founded the NCW of Serbia, Croatia and Slovenia, which in 1928 became the NCW of Yugoslavia.

Until 1933 the NCW was administered from Belgrade (Serbia); after that date it divided its work into regional sections in accordance with regional requirements, giving more initiative to the branches. Headquarters, however, remained in Belgrade.

The Council organized Peace Days and Mother's Days, and worked for the protection of the married and unmarried mother and their children. It also campaigned in favour of complete equality of the sexes, of equal pay, and of the appointment of women judges. It protected against discrimination towards women in high posts in education; it supported a bill for the control of venereal diseases and called for the abolition of government regulation of prostitution.

The Council spread its principles by means of a regular radio programme and through its Bulletin. It also edited two brochures: *The Literary Work of Yugoslav Women*, and *Activities of Women's Societies in Yugoslavia*, and contributed financially to the publication of a Bibliography of works written by Yugoslav women, edited by the Federation of University Women.

In 1936, the Council acted as hosts to the Triennial Assembly of the ICW held in Dubrovnik; and in 1938 it organized in Belgrade, Zagreb and Ljubljana a travelling Exhibition of works by women artists from the states of the Little Entente.

In January 1939, Mme Lepossava Petkovitch was re-elected President and under her continued leadership the Council played an important part in the national and social life of Yugoslavia. Through its Standing Committees the Council acted as a clearing house for information concerning sociological and educational problems affecting the nation as a whole.

In 1940, the Council again made an effort to obtain the vote for women. Two million women demonstrated. In 1941 the NCW was hard at work sending parcels to prisoners of war.

SOUTH AFRICA

NATIONAL COUNCIL OF WOMEN OF SOUTH AFRICA
COUNCIL ESTABLISHED IN 1913
Affiliated with ICW in 1913

The foundation of the National Council of Women of South Africa was laid in 1909 in Cape Town when a branch of the National Council of Women Workers was formed as a result of contacts made and fostered by Lady Aberdeen during the preceding ten years. In 1912 a second branch was established in Johannesburg, rapidly followed by others in Port Elizabeth, Bloemfontein and Pietermaritzburg. All four provinces of the Union were thus represented and enabled the formation of a National Council which applied for and was granted affiliation with the ICW in 1913. The first National Conference was held in 1914. Today the Council numbers approximately 2,500 private members and 700 societies affiliated with its 36 branches and 3 outposts. It has been estimated that the Council is in touch with nearly 195,000 persons. At the national level the Council does not affiliate with other national organizations but the closest co-operation is maintained with over 50 other national bodies whose branches are in many cases affiliated with those of the Council in towns where both function.

From its inception the Council has modelled itself on the ICW pattern and elected members serve on each of the ICW Standing Committees. Its International Standing Committee member has, upon election, become the Convener of a National Standing Committee in her subject with Corresponding Members in each of the branches and outposts. This provides a closely-knit and efficient administrative framework which facilitates dissemination and collection of information on a national scale. Close co-operation with the ICW has been maintained since affiliation in 1913, and the Council has steadfastly furthered the policies and aims of the ICW throughout the years. It has constantly promoted the work of the 15 Standing Committees and, in order to deal with local conditions, set up in 1934 an additional Standing Committee on African Affairs and in 1939 further Committees on Coloured Affairs and Indian Affairs. In 1946 a Committee on Soil Conservation was added.

Against the background of wide and varied activity and the immense amount of work undertaken, both nationally and locally, it is difficult to point out major issues nor is it easy to list achievements for which the Council may claim sole credit. Locally the 39 branch councils and outposts play a prominent part in civic affairs where practical achievements are attained. On the national level, however, the Council works in fields less productive of recognizable achievement. The Council's views are consolidated and presented by deputation, memoranda and letters to the appropriate authorities. It holds national conferences on vital issues and influences public opinion and activates other groups to do the same. Thus, achievement cannot solely be claimed by the Council but its contribution towards final success is worthy of its efforts.

Persistent effort to remove the legal disabilities to which South African women were subjected resulted in the appointment of a government Commission in 1946. Its report led to the passage of the Matrimonial Affairs Act in 1953 which was piloted through Parliament by one of the Council's members, Advocate Mrs Bertha Solomon. Unfortunately this act did not provide for equal guardianship of children but it removed or ameliorated certain other disabilities.

The Council actively engaged in suffrage work until the franchise was granted in 1930. It was also tireless in its vigilance to obtain for women increasing opportunities to sit on Boards, Commissions and Advisory bodies of all kinds and to encourage women to offer themselves for election as Members of Parliament, Members of the Provincial Councils and of Local Municipal Councils.

Under the system of Roman/Dutch Law in South Africa marriage can be contracted either in or out of community of property and the Council has always worked to bring to the attention of all South African women the disadvantages and benefits of both forms of contract. Its work from 1919 onwards regarding the nationality of married women culminated in the South African Citizenship Act in 1949. On all possible occasions the Council affirmed the political, legal and economic equality of the sexes and pointed out the inequalities in laws between black and white. Success crowned the Council's efforts by the obtaining of provincial unity on the age of consent (16 years) and on domiciliary qualifications of women suing for divorce. Attention has been given to the detention of women prisoners, preventive and after-care treatment; jury service for women; women as assessors and payment of maintenance to divorced and deserted wives. Only recently has the long struggle for the introduction of women police in suitable branches of the Police Force shown the first small sign of qualified success in the opening of some clerical posts in the Force to women.

The Standing Committee for Moral Welfare is very active in a wide field: against prostitution and the double moral standard; education of the public about venereal disease and provision of appropriate treatment; penal reform; restrictions on pornographic literature; protests against lotteries, pin-tables and gambling games (declared illegal in 1939) and dog racing (abolished in 1940); liquor and alcoholism have been constantly under review and great efforts have been made to obtain a State Retreat for inebriate women (achieved on a small scale in 1958). The government has been urged to undertake a vigorous policy in regard to dagga traffic (Indian hemp or hashish). Care of the aged has taken a leading place on the Council's agenda together with various aspects of juvenile delinquency. The Council directs its efforts to improving economic and social conditions of all races, obtaining subsidies for crèches, soup kitchens, etc., and provision of an increased number of subsidized social welfare posts for all races. It welcomed the establishment of a National Council for Marriage Guidance and Family Life in 1954 and a National Council for the Welfare for the Aged in 1956 and continues to work in these fields in close co-operation with the newly-formed organizations.

From the beginning the Council, through the constant activity of the Standing Committee for Trades and Professions, has advocated equal pay for equal work; the opening to women of higher posts in the Civil and Diplomatic Services; and the right of married women workers to be considered as permanent staff, in particular married women teachers who at present are forced to become temporary staff members, subject to twenty-four hours' dismissal notice. In the early 1940s the Council achieved the creation of 6 new permanent posts for Women Industrial Inspectors in the Department of Labour. Work for the registration of the unemployed of all races resulted in the passage of the Registration of Employment Act of 1944. In addition, the Council has requested the regulation of wages in shops and offices, the limitation of overtime, compulsory provision of seating accommodation, a shorter working week, annual leave with pay, provision for sick leave pay, the issue of protective clothing and a contributory pension fund to be operated without a means test.

The Council has always stressed education: continuation classes for boys and girls; establishment of Departments of Social Studies in all Universities; inadequacy of rural education. Establishment of crèches and free primary and vocational education for non-whites in urban areas was requested in the 1940s, such primary education to become compulsory as facilities permitted. In opposition to the policies of the present government of South Africa, the Council has consistently urged that white children of both language groups be educated together in dual medium instead of in separate schools. Some other problems dealt with by the Council are: overcrowded primary school classes; technical and vocational training; technical colleges for the Coloured people; additional schools for Africans; increased recruitment and training of African teachers and the insistence that no bars of colour, race or creed shall be imposed on students entering the universities.

African, Coloured and Indian peoples' housing needs have been burning questions for years, particularly in the urban areas, and the Council has pressed for removal of slums and shocking living conditions. Recently a campaign was carried on for control of air pollution as well as for better and more comprehensive health services for all races in both urban and rural areas, and in particular the deplorably inadequate health and hospital services for non-whites.

Other major points in the Council's programme have been care of expectant mothers, the integration into the community of the physically handicapped and the care of the mentally defective adult and child of all races, together with the training of the necessary suitable staff.

In co-operation with the National Council for Child Welfare constant attention has been paid to the needs of the child and the family. The Council has fought to retain school feeding, particularly for needy non-white children and has requested regulation and compulsory inspection of all institutions for children, including nursery schools, and comprehensive and scientific investigation into the caning of juveniles.

In the field of Arts and Letters, constant watch has been kept on censorship and the banning of books.

Due to the Council's work initiated in 1952, the National Federation of Consumer Associations was formed in 1957.

For the African, Coloured and Indian peoples: the Council has requested the franchise for women on the same basis as men; compulsory education; adult education, the establishment of crèches and nursery schools, community centres, the feeding of needy schoolchildren, technical and vocational and university education; opening and widening of fields of employment; training of doctors, nurses, midwives, social workers, teachers, probation officers, etc.; better housing, amenities and transport; removal of discriminatory laws; better distribution of food and all social welfare measures designed to ease poverty and ill health; a realistic increase in the amounts paid in Disability Pensions; increase in wages of unskilled labourers; provision of suitable hostels for African women.

The Council has protested against the principle of the Group Areas Act (allocation by the government of specified areas of land for living space to each racial group which has already entailed the moving of vast numbers of non-European people) and the removal of the Cape Coloured people from the Voters' Roll.

The Council maintains contact with the National Council of African Women both at the national and branch levels and with organizations of Coloured and Indian women, now more than ever valuable in view of the increasing separationist policies of the government.

The Council protests vigorously against the principle of Job Reservation (a government policy of reserving certain occupations or classifications of work for certain race groups with a view to the protection of white workers).

The work of the Council proceeds steadfastly. Long may each succeeding generation continue to build on the sure foundations which have been laid down!

Relations with UN and Specialized Agencies

Miss Hansi Pollak worked with UNRRA in Europe in 1947.

Miss L. M. Mackenzie, at present ICW Convener of Child Welfare Standing Committee, was assigned to the UN Department of Social Affairs in 1948 and again in 1949.

Mrs Chapman Handley, then ICW Convener of the Standing Committee on Home Economics, attended the FAO meeting of 1949 as ICW representative.

April 1961
December 1961

*PORTUGAL

Affiliated 1914

The National Council of Women of Portugal was founded in 1910 by a group of women led by the well-known Doctor of Medicine, Adelaide Cabete.

This group worked for the advancement of feminism in Portugal and organized several cultural congresses aiming at the elevation of the moral, civic and social position of women. The Council also worked for the improvement of the conditions of mothers and children and for social welfare.

After a difficult campaign the Council obtained women's suffrage and the admission of women to posts in the Administration and Public Offices, in which many women performed admirable work.

A major part of the activities of the Council was dedicated to the cause of peace, and it participated in women's congresses in Rome, Paris and Washington. It also organized special meetings for children, in the conviction that it was on them that the future must be founded.

The Council aimed at rousing the interest of Portuguese women by defending their interests, directing their attention to social questions, and developing their sense of solidarity.

In 1938 the Council expressed the hope that new conditions would enable it to realize its ambitions: recognition of the dignity of women and equal rights.

*ICELAND

Affiliated 1920

The National Council of Women of Iceland was founded by the affiliation of seven women's organizations in Reykjavik on May 30th, 1917. At the first post-war Quinquennial of the ICW held at Christiania (Oslo) in 1920 it affiliated to the ICW.

Activities included the establishment of a women's club and convalescent home, child welfare work and the distribution of clothing to the needy. During the period 1920 to 1925 the NCW was busy in international relief work to countries still suffering from the after effects of war and by 1925, 12 associations were affiliated.

The next Quinquennial period (1925–30) witnessed a slackening of the activities of the NCW of Iceland. Most of the affiliated associations were in Reykjavik, and the Rural Women's organizations had not joined the Council. In 1930, these separate organizations formed a second group which was gradually joined by nearly all the women's organizations in the country, and the membership of the former National Council declined, so that it retained only individual members. In 1934 it discontinued its affiliation with the ICW and joined the new Federation of Icelandic Women.

*ESTONIA

Affiliated 1921

The Estonian National Council of Women was founded in 1921, under the presidency of Mrs Marie Reisik. One of its principle activities was to work for the acquisition of political and civil rights and to ensure that such rights, once acquired, were put into practice. The Council worked specially for legal obligation for the payment of alimony, and for the prevention of ill-treatment of minors. Under continual pressure from the Council, the question of Youth Tribunals was taken up by the government, and a Youth Council established to inform and aid young people in every way.

After 1923, the Public Health Committee organized travelling courses through the country to instruct mothers on how to take care of their babies. Children's Health Centres were opened at the request of the Council, which also urged reforms with respect to venereal disease.

In 1935, important progress in the women's movement was made by the creation of the Chamber of Home Economics, an official institution representing the NCW and its many affiliated societies, and consulted by government Commissions whenever questions concerning women and home economics were involved. At the request of this Chamber, the NCW opened in 1935, at Talinn, a school for home economics, followed in 1938 by a school for social work, numbering 80 pupils. In 1936 a hostel for schoolgirls was opened in Talinn and the intention of the Council was to extend this activity and to add a hostel for schoolboys.

For many years the Council organized study courses in handicrafts. It also established a series of special courses for the instruction of leaders of women's organizations, and a large number of societies for rural women were formed throughout Estonia.

Thanks to the NCW many women were appointed to high positions in public office in the Ministries of Labour, Education and Health, and also in the police. In 1938 two women were sitting in the Estonian Parliament.

The NCW at this time consisted of 62 women's organizations. Its Standing Committees covered the fields of public health, legal questions, trades and professions, administrations of hostels and of schools for home economics and social work.

In October 1939, the NCW paid tribute to the combined talents of a remarkable trio of Estonian women artists: Anna Haave, poetess, Niina Harma, composer and Aino Tamm, singer.

*RUMANIA

Affiliated 1921

The National Council of Women of Rumania was founded and affiliated to the ICW in 1921. It united almost all the women's associations in the country.

In 1925, under the Presidency of Princess Alexandrine Cantacuzène, the Council created a Horticultural School in order to help to prevent the exodus of peasant girls to the city. Theoretical and practical instruction was dispensed to 70 pupils, and the school was highly appreciated by the Ministry of Agriculture.

In 1928, a *Casa Femeii*, or centre of women's activities, was established, including a secretariat, library, restaurant, dispensary, etc. In nine years the restaurant served nearly 2 million inexpensive meals, while the dispensary gave 20,000 free consultations and the legal section 9,500.

From the beginning the Council fought to obtain in the Rumanian

Constitution equal political and civil rights for men and women. After 30 public meetings in different towns, the NCW obtained the right to vote and to stand for election for the following categories of women:

1. Those with secondary school and professional certificates.
2. Municipal and state functionaries.
3. War-widows.
4. Those decorated for war service.
5. Directors of cultural, educational and social institutions.

In 1932, Rumanian women acquired the right to exercise a profession without marital consent; married women could dispose of their own fortune and keep their nationality if they married aliens.

The Council obtained the creation of Children's Tribunals, with a woman attached to each Tribunal.

The Council formed Committees on Education, Emigration, Trades, Peace, Arts, Letters, Equal Moral Standard and Child Welfare. Under the chairmanship of Princess Caradgea, the Child Welfare Committee fought successfully to reduce infant mortality.

The Peace Committee instituted in all schools annual competitions on peace, the League of Nations and the position of minorities. Later these competitions were continued by the Government under the auspices of the Council.

In 1938, the Council was largely instrumental for the insertion in the new Rumanian Constitution of full voting rights and the eligibility of women to serve in the Rumanian Senate. In 1939 Mrs Marie Popp, Chairman of the Association for Juridical and Political Emancipation of Women, was elected to the Senate.

In 1940, the NCW did all in its power to help the Polish refugees, housing many in the *Casa Femeii*.

Princess Alexandrine Cantacuzène, Vice-President of the ICW, and President of the NCW of Rumania for many years, served on several occasions on the Rumanian delegation to the League of Nations. In 1928 she represented the ICW at the Congress of Popular Arts held in Prague under the auspices of the League.

*LATVIA

Affiliated 1922

The National Council of Women of Latvia was founded in 1917. When Latvia obtained independence, the new Constitution sanctioned the equal rights for men and women which had long prevailed in the custom and the family life of Latvia. For centuries Latvian women had worked as equal partners with men and shared in the creation and preservation of Latvian culture and folklore.

The Juridical Section of the Council prepared drafts on Civil Rights,

Property, Inheritance and Family Laws, which were submitted to the Minister of Justice and accepted.

Representatives of the NCW were nominated to serve on Parliamentary Commissions concerned with the rights of the unmarried mother and her children, and their views were sought concerning the Washington Convention on night work for women.

As a member of Parliament, Mrs Pepin, President of the NCW, obtained the passage of a bill requiring divorced men to pay alimony. In 1932–33 during debates on the wages of married women, she obtained for NCW representatives the right to state their views before Parliament, and this question was finally settled to the satisfaction of the Council.

In 1928 the NCW opened a school for handwoven carpets and textiles. Diplomas granted by this school were officially recognized by the government and many women were enabled to earn their living at this craft. In order to popularize aesthetic and practical housing, the NCW organized a Housing Exhibition in 1936 which proved so successful that the NCW was subsequently asked to undertake the decoration of many new buildings and private homes.

Although the Latvian Constitution guaranteed full rights to women, it was sometimes difficult for them to reach high positions. The NCW asked for the appointment of Women Police, and took measures to ensure work for women prisoners on their release. It obtained the same curriculum for boys and girls in some of the State High Schools, and administered a number of Mother and Child Welfare clinics, in which the health of some 150,000 children was followed up during fifteen years. This work was highly valued by the government. Thanks mainly to the NCW, unsuitable films were forbidden to children under 16.

In 1937 the Council organized a big Exhibition on the participation of Latvian women in the fields of science, education, arts, journalism, literature and music. In the following year an Exhibition on the work and aims of the ICW was organized to celebrate the 20 years of the work of the NCW of Latvia.

**CHILE

CONSEJO NACIONAL DE MUJERES
COUNCIL ESTABLISHED IN 1919
Affiliated to ICW in 1923

Fields of activity and achievements: 1919–39

Under its first President, Mrs Amanda Labarca, the earliest activities of this Council were:

1. The promotion of an active campaign to obtain from Parliament the introduction of a law on compulsory primary education.

2. The foundation of a Students' Home to provide a centre for girls coming to the capital to study.

3. The successful promotion of a law on civil and juridical rights for women.

During the 1930s the Council conducted much relief work among the unemployed, particularly by the provision of free medical attention to the wives and children of those without work. It also collaborated with the government on such subjects as prison reform, the protection of minors and adult education.

In 1930 a draft bill on women's rights was presented to both Houses of Parliament and in 1935 a second bill concerning the legal capacity of women was presented. By 1938, the Council was able to report that almost everything the NCW has asked for in 1920 had been granted to women by the Chilean government.

1938 to the present

In 1949, the formal celebrations of the decree granting suffrage rights to Chilean women were marked by a speech by Mrs Amanda Labarca, then Hon. President, stressing the active part of the NCW in the early stages of this legal struggle. In 1951 the Council celebrated the twenty-five years of the presidency of Mrs Elena Oliveira and many tributes were paid to her pioneer work in organizing and maintaining the Homes for University Students which form such an important branch of the work of the Chilean NCW. Round the original Home, founded in 1919, have been added others, while the *Centro Femenino* (founded in 1940) constitutes a lively centre for Chilean girls and young women from the provinces studying in Santiago. This Centre also houses the offices of the NCW and a restaurant for women workers. In 1959, in the course of a visit to South American NCWs, the ICW President, Mrs Marie-Hélène Lefaucheux, was received in the *Centro Femenino* and was greatly impressed by the scope and utility of this undertaking.

Under its President, Mrs Victoria Nora de Lira, teacher in biological sciences and dietetics at the University of Chile, the Home Economics Committee has been particularly active in pressing for the teaching of nutrition in Chilean primary, secondary and special University schools, teachers' training colleges and training schools for nurses.

Standing Committees

Art and Letters, Child Welfare, Education, Home Economics, Housing, Moral Welfare and Press.

Relations with UN and Specialized Agencies

Members of this Council have represented the ICW at meetings of the UN and its Specialized Agencies in Chile, notably at the ECOSOC meeting held in Santiago in 1951, and at the UNESCO-sponsored Conference for Economic Development and Education in Latin America held in the same city in 1962.

Mrs Amanda Labarca represented Chile at the first General Assembly of the United Nations in 1946 and has subsequently represented her country on the Status of Women Commission of the ECOSOC and at other international meetings.

Between 1950 and 1955, Mrs Ana Figueroa represented Chile at the UN General Assembly, on the ECOSOC, the Commission of Human Rights and the Status of Women Commission. She was the first woman to preside one of the main Committees of the UN Assembly (1951). Since 1955, Mrs Figueroa is Assistant Director General of the ILO.

November 1962

*CZECHOSLOVAKIA

Affiliated 1924

In 1901, Mrs F. Plaminkova and Mrs Tumova founded the 'Women's Club' which became the centre of the Czech women's movement. From the very beginning Professor Masaryk strongly supported the women's claims for equal civil, educational and political rights. After the First World War, Mrs Plaminkova obtained the acknowledgment of these rights and in 1923 she founded the NCW of Czechoslovakia, comprising 39 organizations, which increased to 80 by 1938. Committees corresponded to those of the ICW; they worked locally and were represented by their chairmen at weekly meetings.

As early as 1905 Mrs Plaminkova had formed a Committee for women's suffrage. In 1912 Mrs Vikova-Kuneticka was elected to the Bohemian Parliament, and in 1925 Mrs Plaminkova became Senator of Czechoslovakia.

In 1929 the Arts Committee founded a 'Painters and Sculptors Club', which organized exhibitions in Buenos Aires, Milan, London and Paris. The Press Committee edited a Revue entitled *Zenska Rada* and the Cinema Committee produced several films: Women in Industry, shown at the ICW Council Meeting at Dubrovnik in 1936, Life and Work of Czechoslovak Women, and Model Housing. The Peace Committee worked for the deletion from school books of hostile expressions towards other countries and urged the nationalization of the armaments industry.

The Legal Committee worked hard to secure the necessary reforms in Family Law and also obtained for women married to aliens the right to keep their nationality. Dr Milada Horakova served as a delegate to the Hague Conference on the Codification of International Law in 1930.

In collaboration with government Factory Inspectors, the Trades Committee studied conditions of women workers in the textile, glass, chocolate, porcelain and chemical industries and worked to safeguard the right of women to paid employment. They also obtained equal life annuity premium rates for men and women, and maternity allowances.

The Committees on Home Economics and Education achieved many reforms in housing and in teaching conditions, and the Equal Moral

Standard Committee obtained the ratification of the 1921 Convention against the Traffic in Women and Children. It also worked for the organization of women police, and the adoption of laws concerning the bad influence of sensational journalism and films on young people.

In 1930, the NCW founded a Brno Branch which, with the aid of teacher organizations succeeded in attracting young people by means of its artistic and cultural programmes. In 1933, local clubs were created all over the country uniting local organizations and individual members. These Clubs formed a meeting ground where men and women met and organized social activities, conferences on feminist questions, etc.

Under the inspiration and unfailing leadership of Senator Plaminkova, assisted throughout her long presidency by Dr Milada Horakova, the NCW of Czechoslovakia had by 1938 achieved remarkable progress in the elevation of the status of women throughout the country.

At the Council Meeting of the ICW held in Philadelphia in 1947, tribute was paid to Senator Plaminkova, Vice-President of the ICW for many years, who had been imprisoned and executed by the Nazis in 1942.

In 1950 the ICW appealed to the Secretary General of the United Nations in an attempt to prevent the execution of Dr Horakova, condemned to death by a Czech court. Despite this appeal and the direct intervention of many NCWs with the Czech government, Dr Horakova too was executed in June 1950.

*IRELAND

Affiliated 1924

The National Council of Women of Ireland was formed and affiliated to the ICW in 1924. Much early work of the Council was for reforms which were later adopted as government schemes: e.g. Widows' Pension Bill. The movement for Women's Police Patrols, initiated during the First World War, developed into a demand for a recognized and uniformed Women's Police Force.

As the Irish Free State enfranchised women in 1922, the Council subsequently worked for the full participation of women in economic and professional life. It took an active part in such reforms as: equal guardianship of children, separation and maintenance laws, adoption of children, inspection and registration of maternity homes and the legitimization of children born out of wedlock.

In 1926, the NCW organized a Conference in Dublin on 'Like conditions of work for men and women'. When in 1928 the Irish government, in spite of concerted action from the women's organizations, abolished compulsory jury service for women, the NCW continued to work for the removal of this restriction.

Resolutions passed by the ICW in London in 1929, protesting against the proposed examination of women in ports, were brought to the attention of the government and of delegates to the ILO. The NCW repeatedly brought before the Irish Free State government the names of suitable women as delegates to ILO conferences and Miss B. Stafford was appointed full delegate in response to these requests. The Council was also able to have a woman lawyer (Miss K. Phelan) included in the delegation to The Hague Conference on the Codification of International Law, 1930. The NCW also strongly supported the interventions of the Joint Committee for the representation of women on the League of Nations.

The year 1933 was marked by a number of meetings arranged in Dublin and Belfast for the Association for Moral and Social Hygiene. A Standing Committee for Legislation concerning women and children was established in 1935, and a memorandum of women's work and status sent to the Secretariat of the League of Nations.

In 1938 the NCW grouped 10 important societies, both national and local. In 1939 it again requested the Ministry of Justice to appoint women police in Dublin and other cities, and co-operated in relief work for refugees from central Europe.

*POLAND

Affiliated 1924

Organized and affiliated to the ICW in 1924, the National Council of Women of Poland was composed of 12 important organizations and its first President was the Polish Senator Josephine Szebeki.

The first two aims pursued by the Council were the co-ordination of the activities of its affiliates and direct participation in social welfare work by means of its committees.

The Child Welfare Committee studied the laws and statistics concerning children and young people, founded a Consultation Centre and drew up model rules for child welfare institutions. An annual Mother and Child Week was organized from 1927 onwards.

The Committee on the Status of Women worked for the maintenance of women's rights in all new laws and organized debates on current problems. The Public Health Committee inquired into the conditions of hygiene in factories employing women workers and published a booklet on rational nutrition. The Committee against white slave traffic and for the protection of emigrants participated in the work of the international organizations concerned with these problems. The Trades and Professions Committee fought against restrictions applied to women in certain branches (e.g. the magistrature) and helped to organize the work of married women so that they could combine professional work with family duties. The Education Committee worked for higher education for girls and the Press Committee spread the activities and principles of the ICW as well as those of the NCW.

The majority of women Members of Parliament and Senators were members of organizations affiliated to the NCW. In many cases, the

Council contributed to the adoption of laws concerning the protection of women and children, alcoholism, etc.

The Council was re-organized in 1936; the new Constitution laid stress on the representative and co-ordinative character of the Council. In 1937, 26 societies (100,000 women) belonged to the Council, which obtained that year a reform in vocational schools for girls. Headquarters published an Information Bulletin, often quoted by important newspapers.

In December 1937, Dr Regina Fleszarova, President of the NCW, was a member of the Directing Board of a Housing Congress in Warsaw. On the motion of the NCW, this Congress recommended the construction of low-rent lodging houses for single women.

In 1938, several Polish Women were appointed to posts in the University, and in November NCW members were invited to serve on the National Nutrition Committee.

The invasion of Poland in September 1939 brought about the disruption of the Council's work and the subsequent imprisonment and death of many members. Mrs Grabinska, an eminent judge of the Children's Court, and Vice-Convener of the ICW Standing Committee on Moral Welfare, took refuge successively in Rumania and Switzerland, finally reaching the US, where she served in settlement work before receiving an official appointment in a State Reformatory (New York). Mrs Grabinska served as Convener of the Moral Welfare Committee of the ICW until 1957.

INDIA

NATIONAL COUNCIL OF WOMEN OF INDIA
COUNCIL ESTABLISHED IN 1919
Affiliated to ICW in 1925

During the First World War, very valuable work was done by the Bombay Women's Branch for the War Relief Fund under the Presidency of Lady Willingdon. At the end of the war this organization was converted into the Bombay Presidency Women's Council out of which developed the National Council of Women in India.

In 1918 Lady D. J. Tata and Mrs R. M. Gray formed the first Interim Committee and in 1919 a public meeting of women was held under the Presidency of Lady Lloyd, wife of the then Governor of Bombay. At this meeting the Bombay Presidency Women's Council undertook to co-ordinate and direct all social work concerning women and children in the Presidency of Bombay and a programme covering every aspect of social, educational, health and infant welfare questions was drawn up. The Association of University Women, the Girl's Athletic Society, the Catholic Ladies Association and the League of Mercy were affiliated with the Bombay Council.

In 1919 five National Councils were formed: in Bengal, Bihar, Orissa,

Delhi and Burma. Mrs R. M. Gray, one of the founding members of the Bombay Women's Council, and Miss Cornelia Sorabji became members of a provincial committee in England to organize the formation of a National Council of Women in India. In 1925 Miss Sorabji, organizing Vice-President of the NCWI sent greetings to Lady Aberdeen, then President of the ICW, at the Seventh Quinquennial Conference in Washington at which India was formally admitted as a member of the ICW.

The NCWI grew subsequently into the All-India body it is today. In 1927 the original State Council in Bombay affiliated formally and the first representatives to a meeting of the International Council from India, were Lady D. J. Tata, Mrs Palmer and Miss Gedge. Since then NCWI members have attended ICW Conferences and Mrs Maneklal Premchand has served as Vice-President of the ICW.

Fields of activity and achievements

Questionnaires and Papers received from the government of India, the State government and the International Council are sent to the various councils for their opinion and for information, as well as to the Sectional Committees to gather the necessary information and replies.

The NCWI was one of the pioneers—if not the pioneer—in turning the attention of women social workers to village welfare and city labour problems. These questions were taken up with enthusiasm and a labour conference was held under the auspices of the NCW in 1933.

The Council was instrumental in the agitation against brothels and helped in procuring the Prostitution Act in Bombay. It also did intensive propaganda in favour of the Sharada Act by which child marriages are banned. The Council was requested by the government to investigate the possibilities of reform in the Hindu marriage and inheritance laws and public interest in these questions was aroused. The Council organized in Bombay a very successful conference on the Legal Status of Women where eminent legal dignitaries gave talks on the prevailing laws in India as they affect women of various communities.

During the unfortunate famine of Bengal in 1943 the Council collected a large sum of money to relieve the miseries of starving millions. Whenever calamities like floods, famines or earthquakes have occurred, the Council has come forward to help.

After the attainment of independence in 1947–48, the partition of India brought new problems. The Council gave meritorious service by helping the government and the population concerning the various refugee problems.

The women's suffrage movement was one of the main activities of the Council when the new Constitution of India was being written in 1935. Jointly with other all-India women's associations, a stand was taken for unqualified adult suffrage for both men and women and reservation of seats for women was decried.

After the first ten years of work, the Council began to expand into new fields of activity. The *Bulletin* began its publication during the Sixth

Biennial period. Public health, nutrition, legal matters, women police were some of the problems taken up. The Council took the initiative in the idea of establishing a children's library and in 1943 had organized a Holiday Library and Reading Room in Bombay. This scheme has now been adopted by other councils in different states including Bombay.

Since its inception the Council has given its attention to many problems concerning the welfare of women and children, and especially to education. The Council has fought for the increase of women's wages in various fields of work; maternity benefits; women's inheritance rights; provision of better facilities for nurses; reforms in women's wards in jails; medical aid; slum clearance; reforms in the Hindu Code bill. The Council has always been alert to the growing problems of the country and has rendered yeomen service.

Standing Committees

The Council has Standing Committees in almost every field covered by those of the ICW, plus Committees on:

Delinquency and Rehabilitation.
Handloom and Small Scale Industries.
Khadi and Village Industries.
Prison Reform.
Small Savings.
Arts and Crafts.
Village Welfare.
Welfare Work for Harijans.
Welfare Work for Adivasis.
Women's Co-operatives.

Organizations affiliated with the Council

The Council has 11 Councils and 3 all-India associations federated with them:

Bombay State Women's Council.
West Bengal Council of Women.
Bihar Council of Women.
Delhi State Council of Women.
Orissa Nari Seva Sangh.
National Council of Women in India, Jamshedpur.
National Council of Women in India, Lucknow.
National Council of Women in India, Allahabad.
National Council of Women in India, Nagpur.
National Council of Women in India, Simla.
Assam Provincial Mahila Samity.
Association for Moral and Social Hygiene.
YWCA
Trained Nurses Association of India.

Each of these councils, and associations carried on social work in their own part of India, particularly for the betterment of conditions for women and children.

Relations with UN and Specialized Agencies

The Indian National Commission for UNESCO having recently invited NGOs to apply for admission as Associate Members, the NCW has applied for such membership.

September 1961
October 1962

**PERU

CONSEJO NACIONAL DE MUJERES
COUNCIL ESTABLISHED IN 1923
Affiliated to ICW in 1926

Affiliated Organizations

Fifty-three Women's Associations which dedicate themselves to projects of a social, professional, educational, cultural or religious nature.

Activities and achievements

Earliest activities, under its first President, Mrs Gallagher Parks, included a concentrated effort at improving the standards of the daily press and of the cinema and the institution of a co-operative sickness insurance for teachers, as well as help for delinquent and abandoned children.

The Council has had forty years of work towards the individual and collective betterment of the Peruvian women in the moral, intellectual and social aspects. The NCW favours campaigns to eradicate illiteracy and to create new educational centres for women. It has created fellow-ships and offers prizes on a competitive basis to students and artists, as well as organizing historical and literary competitions. The NCW holds conferences in its headquarters and also through the national radio.

The Council has helped to secure the passage of important social laws such as the *Codigo de Menores* and a law assuring retirement with full benefits for women working in public administration after twenty-five or more years of service. Members of the NCW also members of the Senate and House of Representatives have succeeded in having the government adopt a Law for the Protection of the Family containing specific penalties for those guilty of abandoning their families.

In 1959, the President of the ICW, Mrs Marie-Hélène Lefaucheux, visited the NCW of Peru in the course of a visit to a number of Latin American Councils.

In an effort to promote the prosperity of the family and to help to solve the housing crisis in the capital city of Lima, the Council is planning to create a special housing development for the families of workers on land donated by its President, Señora Anita Fernandini de Naranjo.

November 1962

**BRAZIL

CONSELHO NACIONAL DE MULHERES DO BRAZIL
COUNCIL ESTABLISHED IN 1927
Affiliated to ICW in 1927

Fields of activity and achievements
Housing, home economics, child welfare, education (including special interest in modern methods of teaching, such as film and radio, essential in a vast country with relatively small and scattered population). Under its President, Mrs America Xavier de Silveira, the Council took a special interest in the fight against leprosy. In the course of a visit to Latin American NCWs in 1959, Mrs M. H. Lefaucheux, the President of the ICW was able to appreciate the remarkable work of the present President, Mrs Romy Medeiros da Fonseca, lawyer and senator, which lies behind many of the recent legal gains achieved by the women of Brazil.

Standing Committees
Arts and Letters, Child Welfare, Cinema, Finance, Health, Home Economics, Housing, Laws and Suffrage, Migration, Press and Trades and Professions.

November 1962

*LITHUANIA

Affiliated 1930

The National Council of Women of Lithuania founded in 1929 by Mrs Ona Masiotiene was affiliated to the ICW in 1930. The Council worked for women's rights, for equal pay and for access to all professions. It also fought for censorship of films, and supported efforts for peace. As a result of Council work an annual Mother's Day was established, and at the request of the NCW the President of Lithuania granted freedom to a number of imprisoned mothers on this occasion.

The NCW took an active part in the improvement of social conditions throughout the country and collaborated with several public institutions.

The Council's Club House was a cultural centre, where public debates, conferences and concerts were held and important foreign visitors received.

The NCW ran a weekly radio programme of information on women's problems and another on parent education. In 1937 the Council founded a successful monthly Review.

On December 11th, 1937, a Congress of women met in Kaunas to commemorate the thirtieth anniversary of the First Lithuanian Women's Congress held in that city in 1907.

From 1935 to 1938 Mrs Sofija Ciurlionis, Professor of the University of Kaunas, was a delegate to the Assembly of the League of Nations.

In 1940 the Council helped in the reception of 30,000 Polish war refugees arriving in Lithuania.

**SOUTH WEST AFRICA

COUNCIL OF WOMEN OF SOUTH WEST AFRICA
COUNCIL ESTABLISHED IN 1937
Affiliated to ICW in 1938

Branches in Windhoek and Walvis Bay. The Council has 10 affiliated societies, is non-political and aims at harmony between man and man, regardless of race, colour or creed.

Fields of activity and achievements

Social welfare, adult education, children's playgrounds, representations to authorities concerning native questions, road safety measures, hygiene, etc.

November 1962

NYASALAND

NYASALAND COUNCIL OF WOMEN
COUNCIL ESTABLISHED IN 1932
Affiliated to ICW in 1945

Two branches: the Blantyre/Limbe Branch and the Cholo Branch. Quarterly meetings of the Council are held at which both Branches and affiliated associations present reports.

Fields of activity

Branches meet each month, usually holding a business meeting followed by a talk or other activity.

The Council has established a Home for Elderly Europeans and a Hostel for Coloured Working Girls.

The President or other members of the Council serve on the National Council for Social Service, Educational Advisory Board, Advisory Board for Health, etc.

July 1962

SOUTHERN RHODESIA

NATIONAL COUNCIL OF WOMEN OF SOUTHERN RHODESIA
COUNCIL ESTABLISHED IN 1946
Affiliated to ICW in 1946

Some time before 1946 the formation of a National Council of Women in Southern Rhodesia was raised by the Federation of Women's Institutes, but the idea was not immediately realized as existing organizations did not see the need for further co-ordination. Many women in the Colony, however, continued to feel that if maximum progress was to be achieved, all women's organizations should speak with one voice and to this end co-ordinating committees were formed, first in Bulawayo and Gwelo and then in Salisbury, with the aim of bringing to the attention of Rhodesian women the *modus operandi* of National Councils of Women working with the ICW.

These Committees later became Councils and for four years worked for the formation of a National Council. Warm tribute must be paid to the work of Mrs Blanche Gordon of Bulawayo, to the late Mrs Winifred Tumner and to Dr Olive Gumprich both of Gwelo. During 1944 and 1945 a committee was instructed by the Bulawayo and Gwelo Councils to draw up a constitution to submit to the ICW with application for recognition as the National Council of Women of Southern Rhodesia. This application was accepted and in 1946 the National Council came into being.

Fields of activity and achievements

Headquarters

Memoranda, resolutions and recommendations have been submitted to government departments on all matters affecting women and children and other aspects of the Council's work. The government has accepted members recommended by the Council for service on Commissions, etc.

In 1960 the Council first attended an ICW Triennial Council Meeting —that held at Istanbul. A resolution proposed by the Council was adopted by the ICW in plenary session.

Bulawayo Branch

1949–52: After-care of cripples. Survey of working conditions of African domestics. Request for appointment of women to Board of Film Censors (granted).

Foundation of crèche and day nursery in the Bulawayo African Location with a Committee comprising representatives of nine other organizations and private citizens. Soup kitchen opened and run by Union of Jewish Women for under-nourished African school children.

1953–54: Formation of first non-European Councils of Women, both African and Indian. Organization of Home Economy Week, together with a publication of cookery book of economical recipes.

1955–61: Organized Festival with affiliated societies in aid of Rhodesia University. Street collection in aid of Hungarian Refugees. Formed first Coloured Council. Inaugurated Domestic Science Training Centre for African Women. Reported on conditions at Bulawayo Memorial Hospital, as a result of which a new hospital was erected.

Initiated the formation of a Mental Health Association.

286

Gwelo Branch

1950–55: Opening of the Winifred Tumner Hostel for Working Girls. Collaborated with the Child Welfare Society and the Women's Institutes to establish a Child Welfare Clinic. Opened a Mother-craft Clinic for African mothers in the Native Village Settlement. Formed first African Women's Council in Gwelo.

1956–61: Formed second African Council. Opened Children's Home.

Salisbury Branch

1955–61: Assisted in setting up a committee to investigate juvenile delinquency. Responsible for the formation of the Salisbury Youth Council. Research work on the need of providing sheltered employment for those unable to work in normal channels, and on the need for rehabilitation centres to assist persons recovering from physical and nervous disorders. Represented on Committee on Alcoholism. Formed Coloured Council.

All three branches have assisted charitable organizations with fund raising and have made gifts in kind to various institutions. All three assisted in relief for the Belgian Refugees from the Congo in July 1960.

Standing Committees

All ICW Committees are represented, plus committees on African Affairs, Food and Agriculture and the Office of Parliamentary Officer.

African Affairs

1950–55: Investigation of malnutrition among African schoolchildren; African housing conditions in Bulawayo; needs of African women and children in urban areas; training of African women as domestic workers; need for women's social centres in urban areas. Municipalities urged to encourage vegetable growing in urban locations. Recommendations made to the Kerr Commission on African Education. Protest against proposed discriminatory Education Tax on Africans (proposed tax later withdrawn). Comprehensive survey of work being done for the African throughout Southern Rhodesia.

1955–61: Instruction given to African women in homecrafts, hygiene, child care and use of electricity. Exhibition of work done by members of African Councils. Survey of professions and trades open to African girls. Formation of kindergarten for African children by Salisbury branch. The National Convenor for African Affairs is the first women elected to serve on the Institute of African Affairs.

Arts and Letters

Survey of current work in Southern Rhodesia in art, music, drama and letters. Close liaison maintained with the National Arts Council of Southern Rhodesia.

287

Child Welfare

Committee worked on the Child Protection and Adoption Act, on the disabilities of women with regard to the guardianship of their children, and on the need for a works colony in this country.

Cinema and Broadcasting

Production of a series of women's broadcasts. Memorandum presented to the Broadcasting Commission (1955). Evidence submitted to Commission of Enquiry into Censorship. Watch kept on films undesirable for children and regular reports made to the National Executive on this question (1956–61).

Education

This Committee has studied and reported on the following subjects: Technical education for girls; lack of schools and classrooms; education of handicapped children; conditions of service of women teachers; standard of teacher training; children's playgrounds in densely populated areas; registration and inspection of nursery schools; Commonwealth exchange of teachers; classroom lighting; corporal punishment; school leaving age; civics instruction; raising retirement age of teachers; bringing together of children of all races for greater understanding; standards of English teaching.

Food and Agriculture

Investigations made on need for grading and marketing of fruit, vegetables and eggs; refrigeration; bad effects of hormone-produced poultry.

Health

Committee stresses need for measures to counteract the increase in preventable diseases among Africans and for education of Africans and Europeans on the subject of nutrition. It has participated in anti-bilharzia and anti-malaria campaigns, helped to form the Rhodesian Association for the Prevention of Tuberculosis and to introduce African women to the use of dried milk.

Home Economics

Organized meat display, showing grades and cuts and recommended methods of cooking (in collaboration with Women's Institutes). Presented evidence to government Commissions on Cost of Living and on Cattle Marketing. Protested against the lifting of price control on beef (control re-imposed), against supply stoppage to retailers who cut prices, against proposed change in Shop Hours Act, against new railroad rates. Organized free distribution of cookery books on the use of milk and cheese. Advocated weekly wage system. Deplored indiscriminate credit.

Housing

Survey of building programme for housing, hospitals, schools and other essential buildings. Supported housing projects for all races; improvement of poor housing conditions for coloured people. Is represented on Committee of Rhodesia Children's Home.

Laws and Suffrage

1950: Joint memorandum presented on the subject of the Child Protection and Adoption Act by Federation of Women's Institutes, the League of Business and Professional Women and the NCW. Certain recommendations were incorporated into the law.

1952–61: Investigation into legal disabilities of women in Southern Rhodesia resulted in the setting up of a Commission to study the matter; some proposals accepted by government investigation of conditions of service of women in the Public Service. Protested deletion of names from voters' roll of people in reduced circumstances (old age pensioners). This was remedied.

Migration

Represented on Bulawayo Advisory Committee for European Migration. New Settlers Club formed in Salisbury.

Parliamentary Officer

Constant study of Acts and Bills, municipal by-laws, government notices, etc., and reports made to NCW.

Press and publicity

Keeps press-cutting book. Publishes periodical newsletter, also brochures on *History of NCW, 1946–1956* and *Women in Central Africa* for the Rhodes Centenary Exhibition in 1955. In the same year organized a successful United Nations Exhibition.

Social and Moral Welfare

Memorandum on Immorality and Indecency Act submitted to government. Investigation of sale of undesirable literature and records. Efforts to obtain ban on such sales. Protested successfully against wording of law governing sale of Indian hemp; also on subject of Credit Control for Minors. Close liaison with Social Welfare Department and Prisoners Aid Society. Helped establish home for care of women alcoholics.

Organizations affiliated with the Council: 26 in all, among them:

Baptist Congregational and Presbyterian Women's Associations.
Catholic Women's League.
Girl Guide's Association.
Union of Jewish Women.
British Red Cross.
Southern Rhodesia Nurses Association.
YWCA.
African Welfare Society.
Nursery School Teachers Association.

League of Professional and Business Women.

Retarded Children's Aid Society.
Salvation Army.

UN and Specialized Agencies

No members have served as representatives to UN or Specialized Agencies. There is no regional office of UN in Southern Rhodesia. The Council has, however, received beneficial visits from UN personnel on mission in Africa. It receives all UN documentation relevant to its work, contributes to studies and inquiries on request by the ICW, and has organized an Exhibition of UN work (1955).

The NCW draws the government's attention to UN Conventions by sending them to the government with its comments and recommendations.
March 1961

**DOMINICAN REPUBLIC

CONSEJO NACIONAL DE MUJERES
COUNCIL ESTABLISHED IN 1948
Affiliated to ICW in 1951

During the first years of its existence the National Council set up Headquarters in the capital and founded 20 local branches.

Fields of activity and accomplishments

The principal activities of the Council are in the fields of social and child welfare, by means of its Committee of Social Assistance and Hygiene and Welfare which operate throughout the country. The Education and Library Committees collaborate actively with the Women's University in a moral and civic training programme. Since 1958 the Council has operated a model Girls Home which lodges 20 girls of small means, both students and employees, who have left the provinces to come to the capital.

Standing Committees

Education, Home and Family, Social Assistance, Hygiene and Welfare, Library.

Organizations affiliated to the National Council

The Council has 20 local branches and 3 Affiliates.

Relations with UN and Specialized Agencies

The National Council has broadcast radio programmes on UN activities and its President, Mrs Amada Nivar de Pittalunga, who has represented the ICW at regional meetings of UN organizations, has contributed a series of Articles on the UN to *La Nacion*.

290

As Delegate of the Dominican Republic to the San Francisco Conference in 1945, Miss Minerva Bernardino, Vice-President of the ICW 1951-57 was one of those who fought hardest for the inclusion of equal rights for women in the UN Charter. Miss Bernardino has also been President of the UN Status of Women Commission and in 1950 was appointed Minister Plenipotentiary of her country to the UN.

November 1962

**EGYPT

UNION BENT-EL-NIL
COUNCIL ESTABLISHED IN 1949
Affiliated to ICW in 1951

The declared aims of this organization were the improvement of the status of all the women of Egypt and the granting of full and unconditional rights to Egyptian women. Headquarters in Cairo, branches throughout the country.

Fields of activity and achievements

The strenuous work of this Council under the Presidency of Mrs Doria Shafik, during the years immediately preceding and following its affiliation to the ICW contributed greatly to the gains made towards the emancipation of the Egyptian woman during this period.

With the collaboration of the various Ministries concerned, the Union-Bent-el-Nil (Daughters of the Nile) was extremely active in the field of adult education for women. Starting in Cairo, Alexandria and the main cities of the Nile valley, schools for adult literacy were established in villages throughout Egypt. In 1953 a large-scale experiment in this domain was carried out by the Union Bent-el-Nil, practising its own visual method of teaching literacy (instructions for which were published in their periodical publication) by which a single volunteer could in three months teach ten illiterates basic reading and writing. Examinations conducted by the delegates of the Ministry of Public Education at the conclusion of the first three months showed that $78\frac{1}{2}\%$ of the pupils were literate. The Union Bent-el-Nil also pressed for the use of television in the fight against illiteracy in Egypt.

November 1962

**HONG KONG

HONG KONG COUNCIL OF WOMEN
COUNCIL ESTABLISHED IN 1947
Affiliated to ICW in 1951

Fields of activity and achievements

In addition to social welfare work such as free legal advice to those in need, the sponsoring of beds in hospitals and children's Convalescent

Homes, the activities of the Hong Kong Council of Women since 1947 have included the formation of a Family Planning Association, and the organization of two clinics. The Council has successfully urged the government to take steps for the training of women probation officers; has intervened in regard to various forms of film censorship; has advised on the institution of a social science course at the University.

The Council has also recommended government consideration and adoption of the revision of Ordinances pertaining to the laws of marriage, divorce and inheritance. Since concubinage is a recognized factor in Hong Kong, women are faced with particularly difficult problems. Although a British Colony, Chinese Marriage Law still applies, and the Council has been working on the problem since 1948. The government has recently circulated a Draft Report on Chinese Marriages in Hong Kong and in May 1961, the Council submitted its comments. It is gratifying to note that the government is now taking steps to amend these laws.

The Council is represented on many public committees such as the Price Control Committee, the Social Welfare Committee. A special women's programme was inaugurated by the Hong Kong Radio at the request of the Council.

The President represents the Council at the meetings of the Hong Kong Government Social Welfare Advisory Committee and the Hong Kong Council of Social Service.

Since the Council's Headquarters opened in 1960, both men and women have been in to seek assistance: appeals for free legal aid, maintenance, free education for children, marriage counselling and other family problems. Assistance has been given whenever possible. At regular and well-attended luncheon meetings talks are given by experts in various fields of interest to the women of Hong Kong.

Organizations affiliated to the Council

Nine women's organizations are affiliated to the Council of Women: including Chinese, Indian and European Women's groups.

November 1962

LEBANON

NATIONAL COUNCIL OF WOMEN'S ASSOCIATIONS IN LEBANON
COUNCIL ESTABLISHED IN 1922
Affiliated to ICW in 1951

Fields of activity and achievements

Its purpose is to unite and co-ordinate the activities of the various member organizations. Its work is carried out through monthly meetings, annual conferences and frequent contacts with the authorities to press for the implementation of its programme.

Through such contacts the Council has achieved a large measure of

292

success, such as the recognition of full franchise and equal inheritance rights for women.

The Council has played an important part in the evolution of the General Federation of Arab Women's Organizations, and has participated in conferences on an international as well as regional scale.

The Council is determined to press for free and compulsory education, for prison reform, higher civic standards and community development. It is committed to combat vagrancy, juvenile delinquency and white slave traffic.

Organizations affiliated with the Council

The member organizations, 110 in number, are engaged in various social, cultural, civic and charitable activities; a number of them are taking an active part in the development of rural areas.

A few typical organizations are: the Young Women's Christian Association, Village Welfare Societies, Child Welfare Societies, Prison Reform Society, University Women's Organization, in addition to a large number of charitable and educational societies.

Relations with UN and Specialized Agencies

The Council has participated in the work of UNESCO and of the UN Status of Women Commission. Mrs L. Tabet (Vice-President of the ICW 1954–60) has served for several years on the latter Commission.

August 1961

UGANDA

NATIONAL COUNCIL OF WOMEN OF UGANDA
ESTABLISHED IN 1948 AS COUNCIL OF WOMEN, BECOMING NATIONAL COUNCIL IN 1962
Affiliated to ICW in 1951

Fields of activity and achievements

Monthly meetings are attended by women of all races. Discussions are held on matters of common interest and concern and all work together on projects to raise money for causes benefiting women and children.

Hostel for Working Girls. One of the Council's first preoccupations was to provide hostel accommodation for girls who wished to work in Kampala in non-residential occupations. Successful negotiations with the government ended in a substantial grant being made for the erection of a hostel in Kampala. Simultaneous negotiations with the World YWCA resulted in the establishment of this movement under American sponsorship. It has extended its work far beyond the initial objective of running a hostel.

Appointment of Woman Probation Assistant. Protracted negotiations with the government led to the appointment in 1953 of the first African Woman Probation Assistant, a nominee of the Council. A few years later she was the only African delegate to the Associated Countrywomen of the World Conference on Juvenile Delinquency in Northern Rhodesia.

Improved Status of Women. In 1960 a conference on this subject was held, attended by African women delegates from all over the country and by visitors who chanced to be in Uganda at the time. Work is proceeding on the findings of the conference, especially regarding the clarification of the marriage laws. Asian women subsequently instituted an investigation into their legal status in marriage, having received strong support from leading women of their own communities all over the world.

Care of orphaned and deprived children

The Council was active in making known the plight of such children and gave full support to the scheme for the establishment of what is now the Sanyu Babies Home. Branches of the Council make financial contributions to Sanyu and give personal service in money-raising activities.

The need for elementary instruction for nursery nurses (ayahs) was met in the early years by classes in Kampala. Candidates were later transferred to the Sanyu Babies Home for training and put on a full-time basis.

UNICEF: Milk distribution is done by branch members.

Maternity Hostel. Until recently adequate facilities for the confinement of European women were available only in Kampala and they were obliged by government regulations to enter hospital there. The Council maintains a small hostel for expectant mothers. With the establishment of improved medical facilities in other centres, progressively less use is being made of the hostel.

Home Nursing Service. This is a scheme planned and put into operation by the Kampala Branch for the assistance of families who need part-time or temporary professional nursing.

Broadcasting

The Council prepares and broadcasts monthly programmes in English and Luganda devoted to the interests of women. They give special prominence to overseas visitors and subjects of a topical or controversial character.

Education

Members of the Council sit on Advisory Committees and Boards of governors of all kinds including many educational institutions.

Council branches provide classes in domestic subjects: health, child care, cookery, needlework, history, civics, English, public speaking. Successful negotiations with the Department of Education have resulted in Council-sponsored classes in English being financed by the government. The demand for English is countrywide and growing daily. Application has been made to UNESCO through the Associated Countrywomen of the World so that this need can be filled on a broad permanent basis.

Education for Citizenship. In view of the franchise granted to a majority of women and their participation in the approaching and subsequent elections, the Council has planned a series of citizenship leaflets each of which will contain a study scheme. The first—*A Guide to Women Voters*—is already in circulation.

Help to Newcomers. A booklet introducing Uganda was written and published by the Council in the mid-50s and revised and reissued in 1959. It is on sale in the United Kingdom and Uganda. It has also received official recognition and is issued by the government to newly-appointed officers.

Employment of Women

Council plans for an employment agency have reached an advanced stage.

Women's Handicrafts: When the Council was established there was little outlet for women's handicrafts and women were beginning to drift to the towns in search of more lucrative employment with unsatisfactory results. The Council incorporated a small shop where women's work was offered for sale. Increased trade outlets for such work have recently made this shop redundant.

Council as Unifying Agency

Energetic efforts are made to bring all women's organizations into closer touch through affiliation, consultation and joint activities. Considerable and encouraging progress has been made in this field.

Standing Committees. The Council aims at appointing corresponding members for each ICW Standing Committee.

Organizations affiliated with the Council. Council consists of 14 branches, roughly one in each main district of Uganda. Organizations comprise: (*a*) African women's rural clubs which form the greatest bulk of membership of rural groups—these usually take up membership as county associations; (*b*) some groups of the Indian Women's Association; (*c*) the Muslim Women's Society; (*d*) some of the Mothers Union groups; (*e*) the Forward Society.

UN and Specialized Agencies

The Council first learned about ICW/UN collaboration through its delegates to the ICW Triennial Council Meeting in Istanbul in 1960, when Mrs Pumla Kisosonkole became a Vice-President of the ICW. In 1961 Mrs Kisosonkole was invited to represent the ICW at the UN Commission on the Status of Women in Geneva. Unfortunately lack of funds made this impossible. She was however able to represent the ICW at the UNESCO Conference on Education in Africa held in Addis Ababa in May 1961, where the value of her participation was the object of an official letter of congratulation to the ICW. In 1962 two Council members, Mrs Kalema and Mrs Mulira represented Uganda at the UNESCO General Conference.

The Council has done much work on the status of women and adult education and is confident that the government will be disposed to consider requests to support at least UNESCO programmes and those of the Commission on the Status of Women.

March 1961
November 1962

TANGANYIKA

NATIONAL COUNCIL OF WOMEN OF TANGANYIKA
ESTABLISHED IN 1951 AS COUNCIL OF WOMEN, BECOMING NATIONAL COUNCIL
IN 1962
Affiliated to ICW in 1952

Fields of activity and achievements: 1951–62:
Inter-racial social group holds monthly meetings for discussion and lectures. Until 1956 Council operated African Nursery School. Council also organizes clinics for mothers and babies and classes of sewing, knitting, homecraft and swimming. The Council operates a Hostel for African girls run by a voluntary committee of African, European and Asian women providing accommodation for students following the clerical course run by the Ministry of Education and other working girls coming into the capital. This has twice been extended but demand far outruns accommodation and a further important extension is planned. Council helps in the Prime Minister's self-help building scheme and maintains an arts and crafts shop with the object of keeping alive the decreasing number of old crafts. An important arts and crafts exhibition was organized in connection with Independence Week Celebrations, which was visited by thousands of visitors from all over Tanganyika and overseas. The Council helps in the literacy campaign in hospitals and other centres.

In addition to headquarters activities, the Council has 15 active up-country branches which aim to supply any need within their power—organizing clinics, for instance, where there is no Red Cross.

1962: With the independence of Tanganyika a new National Council was organized to include a wide range of women's groups including the former Council of Women. This new National Council is participating in national building schemes, and in village development programmes. It has requested the government for a community centre in every village and has itself begun on the construction of a nursery school.

October 1962

PAKISTAN

ALL PAKISTAN WOMEN'S ASSOCIATION
COUNCIL ESTABLISHED IN 1949
Affiliated to ICW in 1953

Fields of activity and achievements: 1949 to the present

Arts and letters. The All-Pakistan Women's Association's activities aim mainly at reviving traditional cultural patterns in all spheres of life. Emphasis is put on the need for development of talent in the younger generation and supporting professional talent. Regular classes are given in the fine arts and handicrafts. Periodic programmes of music and dancing have been organized to encourage amateur talent. The Association has sponsored exhibitions of arts and handicrafts done by women and children, and Essay Competitions among school and college girls on subjects of interest to women. The Association supports the wide observance of all religious functions.

Child Welfare. This is carried out mainly through rehabilitation of mothers to enable them to provide suitable homes and support for their children. Character-building, social education, health education and recreation programmes are organized for children in the Association's combined Mothers' and Children's Clubs. The Association works together with the Pakistan Council for Child Welfare for the enactment of suitable legislation for children and for implementation of child labour legislation. As an incentive for the achievement of better standards, regular competitions in art, music, handicrafts and sports are sponsored among children. The Association joined with the Pakistan Council for Child Welfare in pointing out to the government the need for a separate Child Welfare Section in the Directorate of Social Welfare. This has now been established.

Cinema. The cinema has been used as a medium for educating the public in social problems and for publicizing the work being done for women and children through special films made in co-operation with the government.

Education. The Association has given priority to education, for the percentage of literacy is low and the demand very great. It runs 61 Primary and Secondary Schools, 2 Arts and Science Colleges, 70 Adult Literacy Centres as well as Religious Education Centres. In addition, it has carried out research as to the type of education and the curricula required for different groups to re-orient the educational system of the country and this has been presented to the National Commission on Education. At present it is working with the government on a scheme for fundamental education. It plans to establish Training Schools and Colleges for Women Teachers.

Finance. The Association has a Fund Raising Section which is responsible for organizing fund raising campaigns. Most of the funds are raised through voluntary contribution. Grants are received from the government for its formal educational institutions.

Health. This covers public health education, diet and nutrition, short health courses for volunteers, family planning, maternity and child health and the establishment of clinics, dispensaries and hospitals. Because of the extreme shortage of nurses, this section started its constructive project of filling up this shortage as rapidly as possible by initiating the training of nursing-aides. Thirty girls completed the training in the first batch. This very successful project has now been taken up by the government. This Section is running approximately 8 Clinics, Dispensaries, Maternity and Child Health Centres, and 1 sixty-bed Maternity Hospital in Karachi. Health Education and Family Planning Guidance are given at Mother's Clubs and Industrial Homes as well as at the Clinics and Dispensaries.

Home economics. The Association's initiative brought into existence the College of Home Economics, Karachi, and the Home Science Departments in the universities at Dacca and Lahore. Homecrafts are taught to women through the Mother's Clubs.

Housing. The Association has two housing projects, one in Lahore for housing widows and one in Karachi for housing craftsmen. Accommodation provided is usually the minimum consisting of a one-room quarter with a courtyard, kitchen, bath and toilet, with provision for building one other room. This is in line with the type of housing provided for lower income groups. In addition to living accommodation the projects include; schools, health centres, industrial homes and playgrounds.

International relations and peace. One of the aims and objectives of the Association is 'The promotion of international goodwill and the brotherhood of mankind'. This is done through personal contacts with people of other countries, by sending delegations abroad to international conferences, by welcoming foreign guests, through affiliation with international agencies and co-operation with national agencies in other countries. The Association is affiliated with the Associated Country Women of the World, the General Federation of Women's Clubs, the International Alliance of Women and the International Council of Women and has Consultative Status, Category B, with the United Nations Economic and Social Council and representation on the UNICEF Board in New York.

The Association tries to send either an observer or statements to meetings of the UN and its Specialized Agencies whenever possible. It participates in conferences sponsored by international organizations. It welcomes foreign guests and organizes programmes for them.

It provides information on Pakistan to international bodies and to foreign visitors.

Together with UNESCO the Association sponsored a Regional Seminar in Karachi in October 1958 on the 'Rôle of Women in the Preservation and Development of Culture'.

Laws and suffrage. Women have enjoyed the right to vote since the inception of Pakistan (1947). The Association's work in this field has been to educate women to understand and make proper use of their political rights. It also seeks to bring about necessary legislative enactments. For a number of years now, the Association has been demanding reforms in Marriage and Family Laws and the promulgation of the Muslim Family Laws Ordinance 1961 may well be considered the Association's crowning achievement.

Migration. The formation of Pakistan (1947) resulted in a large influx of refugees from India many of whom were widows and orphans. The Association came into being in order to meet this challenge. Its main work for the first few years was the rehabilitation of refugees through provision of housing, means of livelihood, health and education facilities.

298

Moral welfare. This is promoted through religious education, public meetings and emphasis on moral values, by social action for banning unsuitable films and literature, and by calling upon its members to set an example of simple living and the practice of Islamic principles.

Peace. At the Fourth Triennial Conference of the Association held in 1961 it passed a resolution banning the use of nuclear warfare. The Pakistan Ministry of External Affairs has taken cognizance of this resolution.

Press and Publicity. The Association receives excellent coverage in the press for all its programmes. Space is also provided for special features, particularly those concerning project work.

Radio and Television. There is no television in Pakistan, but radio facilities are provided to the Association for publicizing its work and focusing attention on vital issues concerning women. A regular Woman's Programme is conducted over the radio.

Trades and Professions. The Association has set up industrial centres for training women and girls and assisting girls in obtaining admission in professional colleges. It sponsored the formation of the Business and Professional Women's Club. It has taken up with the government authorities cases of discrimination against women and is pressing for the employment of women in all services.

Organizations affiliated with the Association

The Association has 58 branches in all parts of the country and 4 affiliates which are: The Gul-e-Raana Nusrat Club, the Gul-e-Raana Nusrat Industrial Home, the Pakistan Cottage Industries and the Women's International Club.

Standing Committees

The work of the Standing Committees of the International Council of Women is carried out through the following sections of the Association:

Conference.
Cultural.
Education.
Fund Raising.
Health and Social Welfare.
Industries.
International.
Legal Advice and Assistance.

Membership.
Publicity (English and Urdu).
Relief.
Rights and Responsibilities (Civil, Economic and Political).
Rural Reconstruction.
UN Affairs.
Youth.

UN and Specialized Agencies

One member of the Association is on the Commission for UNESCO and two members on the Commission for UNICEF. Members of the United Nations Information Service and the United Nations Specialized Agencies are represented on the United Nations Affairs Standing Committee of the Association.

February 1962

NIGERIA

NATIONAL COUNCIL OF WOMEN'S SOCIETIES OF NIGERIA
ESTABLISHED IN 1954 AS COUNCIL OF WOMEN, BECOMING NATIONAL COUNCIL
IN 1962
Affiliated to ICW in 1954

The Nigerian National Council of Women's Societies was officially inaugurated in Lagos in 1959, although a branch of the Council had previously been functioning at Ibadan and was affiliated to the ICW as a Council of Women in 1954.

Fields of activity and achievements

The first years of the Council's life have been devoted almost entirely to work of consolidation, i.e. aiding member societies with their programmes. At a convention held in 1961, it was resolved that the Council should adopt Adult Education for Women as its main project for the next two years. This work has been carried out with varying success throughout the country. The Baptist Women's Union of the Lagos Branch has been particularly successful in running four lively centres, and one of the Directors has been awarded by UNESCO a six-months' study grant for an Adult Literacy Course in Europe. The Women's Co-operative and Thrift Society has been helped in programmes to extend trading facilities to women and to plan the establishment of Laundrette Services and small-scale Self-Service Stores.

As a national body, it has acted as hostesses to women visitors from other countries, participated in disaster relief work, and campaigned for adequate welfare services for children. Grants were made available for the founding of 8 scholarships, known as the Eleanor Roosevelt Scholarships at the Queen's College for girls in Lagos, under the aegis of the Council, by the National Council of Women of the United States. The Committee of Correspondence (U.S.A.) financed a two-months' Leadership Training Workshop held in all the 4 regions of Nigeria in January and February. The Women's Africa Committee of the African–American Institute has financed and sponsored a project by which 16 members of the National Council, selected from all parts of the country on the basis of a wide scale of interests and skills, are at present taking a ten-weeks' Leadership Course at Columbia University. It is anticipated that these women will make a stimulating impact on the future work and growth of the Council on their return.

In August 1960 the Council participated in a Seminar sponsored by UNESCO and the International Alliance of Women at Ibadan. The Theme of the Conference was 'The African woman designs her future' and was attended by women from both English- and French-speaking West African countries.

Organizations affiliated with the Council

Owing to the immense size of Nigeria, in terms of territory and population, it has been found necessary to operate the Council in four Regional Branches: East, West, North and Lagos. Each Regional Branch is composed of member societies of non-political women's organizations.

July 1962

**PHILIPPINES

CIVIC ASSEMBLY OF THE WOMEN OF THE PHILIPPINES
COUNCIL ESTABLISHED IN 1947
Affiliated to ICW in 1957

Founded in 1947 with the active encouragement of President Roxas, first President of the Republic, who wished the women of the Philippines to organize for reconstruction as they had already done during the war.

Fields of activity and achievements

Under its first President, Mrs F. Benitez, President of the Philippines Women's University, the CAWP drew up a basic platform for endorsement by candidates to national elections and successfully campaigned for the election of a woman senator. The influence of the CAWP became evident in the increasing place given to women in the political parties, in municipal and provincial elective office, on National and School Boards, as delegates to international conferences, judges in municipal and juvenile courts, etc. The CAWP has also campaigned for peace, for social welfare, rural development, adequate basic and adult education and consumer education.

Standing Committees

Family and Home, Moral and Spiritual Welfare, Education and Culture, Recreation, Agriculture, Industry and Professions, International Relations, Public Affairs and Legislation, Health and Social Welfare, Planning, Information and publications.

Affiliated Organizations

Over 40 women's groups including:

Associacion de Damas Filipinas, Batangas Province Ladies Association, Catholic Women's League, Philippine Constabulary Women's Club, Girl Scouts of the Philippines, National Federation of Women's Clubs, National Young Women's Christian Association, League of Women Voters of the Philippines, Philippine Association of University Women, Philippine Association of Women Writers, Home Economics Association, Rural Improvement Club.

Relations with UN and Specialized Agencies

Miss H. Benitez has represented the Philippines on the Status of Women Commission of the ECOSOC.

Senator G. Pecson was the first woman member of the Executive Board of UNESCO (1950–56) and was re-elected for a second term in 1960. She has represented the Philippines at the UNESCO General Conference on many occasions and has also served as National Chairman of the UNESCO National Commission for the Philippines. Other Council members also serve on this Commission.

November 1962

ISRAEL

COUNCIL OF WOMEN'S ORGANIZATIONS IN ISRAEL
COUNCIL ESTABLISHED 1939
Affiliated to ICW 1957

Fields of activity and achievements

The Council is composed of 7 separate organizations and has a membership of over 500,000 including both Arab and Jewish women; it works through its 15 Standing Committees. The practical work of the Council is concentrated on three points: hospitality, study of special problems relating to women and children (in particular, legislation), and practical welfare work (social and educational). The main function of the Committees is collecting and disseminating information. The Moral Welfare Committee initiated a scheme to train volunteers for preventive work among girls and women likely to become victims of prostitution.

Contact is maintained with all women members of parliament on questions of particular interest to women, children and the family unit. Bills presented to the House have included those concerning the adoption of children, and the protection of young persons.

The greatest efforts of the Council are concentrated on the problems of education and practical welfare, in particular the education of refugee women arriving from foreign countries so that they may be on an equal footing with their husbands and maintain the respect of their children. The courses and classes which have been organized have a general attendance including Arab women and girls. Mrs Zena Harman has represented Israel on the International Council for Social Service.

Standing Committees

Nine of the Council's 15 Standing Committees correspond to those of the ICW: Status of Women, Child Welfare, Migration, Moral Welfare, Literature and Arts, Work and Professions, Home Economics, Housing and International Relations and Peace.

302

Organizations affiliated to the National Council

Moetzet Hapoalot (Women Workers' Council).
Wizo (Women's International Zionist Organization).
Equal Rights Organization.
Association for Equal Rights.
Religious Women.
Liberal Women.
University Women.

Relations with UN and Specialized Agencies

Mrs Tamar Eshel has represented Israel on the UN Commission on the Status of Women.

A Representative of the Council of Women's Organizations of Israel is an observer in the Israel National Commission for UNESCO. A Council member, Mrs Sonia Diener, has been the beneficiary of a UNESCO Study Tour Grant for adult education leaders, attending courses and programmes arranged for her by the National Councils of Great Britain, Denmark and Sweden.

May 1961

BURMA

UNION OF BURMA COUNCIL OF WOMEN'S ASSOCIATIONS
COUNCIL ESTABLISHED IN 1956[1]
Affiliated to ICW in 1958

Fields of activity and achievements

Burma being a Buddhist country, the religion teaches equality among all humanity. There is no discrimination between man and woman and equal work receives equal pay. Women are encouraged to form their own societies for religious, social and cultural work, so there have been local women's social welfare organizations in the country for many decades. When the country became independent in the year 1948, these organizations in the field of health, moral, maternity, infant and youth welfare were raised to the national level and the Union of Burma Council of Women's Associations was formed in 1956. The Council took immediate steps to be affiliated to the ICW and became affiliated in 1958.

[1] A number of women's organizations in Burma were affiliated to the National Council of Women of India under the British joint administration of the two countries. In 1937, when the administration of Burma was separated from that of India, these organizations affiliated directly to the ICW as the National Council of Women of Burma and worked actively with the ICW for a number of years before the establishment of the Union of Burma Women's Associations.

Standing Committees

Education, Health, Radio, Cinema, Moral Welfare, Home Economics.

Organizations affiliated with the Council

Seven member associations:

National Council of Maternity and Infant Welfare Societies. Mothers cared for during confinement; pre- and post-natal care have greatly reduced infant mortality.

National Young Women's Christian Association. Opened working girls' hostel; does local community service for adults and youth, giving educational and language classes; periodical training is given for leadership and professional secretaryships; also rural leadership.

Burma Girl Guides. Teenagers and younger members are trained for citizenship service. Summer camps during school vacations.

Burma Nurses and Midwives Association. Provides nurses with good contact with the public they serve during ill health; has greatly enhanced the standard of nursing since independence.

Burmese Women's League. Engaged in moral welfare work since pre-war days, this is the oldest social organization in the country. By running a home for girls it helped the government to suppress widespread post-war prostitution. It will soon start a Home Economics class for girls.

Women's Christian Temperance Union. Provides information on the disadvantageous effects on women, men and children of drinking and smoking.

Kachin Women's Association. The only association as yet formed by a State of the Union of Burma composed of primitive rural hill people. Education, health, cultural and welfare work have been started in this State and women are doing their part by running maternity and infant welfare centres and homes for girls. As a member association of the Council, every possible aid is given for their advancement.

Relations with UN and Specialized Agencies

Specialized Agencies in Burma are: UN, UNESCO, UNICEF and WHO. Each has its regional and local offices in the country.

Burma is an agricultural country and has many rural areas which are difficult to reach, so that these agencies all find it necessary, in order to reach the far corners of the country, to approach the Union Council of Social Service (which is the chief voluntary social organization providing co-ordination between the State and the public) to effect adequate distribution.

July 1962

**BOLIVIA

CONFEDERACION NACIONAL DE INSTITUCIONES FEMINAS
COUNCIL ESTABLISHED IN 1958[1]
Affiliated to ICW in 1960

The National Federation of Women's Institutions was founded in La Paz on July 11th, 1958, for the express purpose of grouping existing women's national organizations, and to educate the woman citizen to obtain, enjoy, promote and defend her civil and political rights as granted by the laws of the Republic. Assembly meetings are scheduled for every month and the Board meets every two weeks. The Federation was affiliated to the ICW in 1960.

Fields of activity

The National Council has worked in co-operation with the Association for the Orientation and Protection of young girls and women. Free courses, lasting three months, are given under the supervision of the Council. Subjects have included: manual industries, sewing and dressmaking, toymaking and applied arts. Courses in civic education are also given and have proved very popular. The Council participates in the campaign begun by the National Adult Literacy Administration of the Ministry of Education. It has also concerned itself with spreading information concerning the legislation in force and the situation of working women, in order that the next generation of women, for which the Council feels responsible, be more enlightened than the preceding one. These courses are carried on keeping in mind the goal of manual, cultural and intellectual training and the elimination of hate, envy, ignorance and fear.

Projected activities include the creation of schools, study centres, seminars, exchange of persons, the sponsoring of publications including theses and scientific and legal works by Bolivian women in keeping with the purposes of the Federation.

Standing Committees

The Council is divided into the following Committees or sub-Committees: Civic education, Study and vulgarization of national history, Folklore, Initiation to Common Law, Human rights, Alphabetization and adult education, Moral welfare, and International relations.

[1] In 1927, the Ateneo Femenino of Bolivia, in association with several other women's groups affiliated with the ICW as the NCW of Bolivia. Local Councils were formed and a periodical publication issued. Unfortunately political circumstances made collaboration with this Council short-lived and no reports were received after 1930.

Organizations affiliated with the Council

At the time of its foundation, the Federation was composed of 23 Affiliated Institutions active in the cultural, professional, and social welfare fields: among them The Women's Athenaeum of Bolivia, The Association of Women Librarians, The Catholic Teachers Association, and the National Association for the Protection of Youth.

Relations with UN and Specialized Agencies

One of the specific aims included in the Constitution of the Federation is the study of the organization and functioning of the United Nations, of the Organization of American States and of the Inter-American Women's Commission.

November 1962

COLOMBIA

CONSEJO DE MUJERES DE COLOMBIA
COUNCIL ESTABLISHED IN 1959
Affiliated to ICW in 1960

In April 1959, immediately before the Seminar on the Participation of Women in Public Life organized in Bogota by the UN Commission on Human Rights, and at the suggestion of ICW Vice-President Mrs W. Barclay Parsons, and Mrs DeWitt Stetten a group of highly qualified Colombian women was convened by Mrs Cecilia Hernandez de Mendoza with the purpose of founding the Colombian National Council of Women. The ICW President, Mrs Lefaucheux, twice attended these meetings to explain the ICW aims and to offer guidance in orientation. Mrs Hernandez de Mendoza became the Council's President, Maria Isabel de la Vega its Vice-President and Mrs Maria Teresa Samper de Samper its Secretary.

Fields of activity and accomplishments

This recently-founded Council has not yet achieved significant results, but its members work with considerable enthusiasm towards the extension of its programme throughout the country.

Statutes. Prepared by Mrs Blanca Gnecco de Samper, they have been approved at subsequent Council meetings and may serve as models for councils in other Latin American countries. These statutes were approved and the Council admitted to membership of the ICW at Istanbul in 1960.

Publicity. Mrs Ofelia Romero de Wills directs a weekly programme on the radio, and Mrs Amparo Gomez de Palacios directs another for the newspaper *El Espectador*. A television programme has also been offered.

Studies. Prepared for the ICW and presented at Istanbul a report on 'The Woman and the Family in a World in Evolution' based on inquiries made of various social and professional groups in Bogota and most especially in Cali; report in ICW Bulletin on Political Rights of Women in

Colombia; report on the results of the UN Seminar held in 1959 in Bogota on the 'Participation of Women in Public Affairs' comparing conclusions with the previous seminar on the same subject held in Bangkok.

Representation and appointments

Mrs Cecilia Hernandez de Mendoza: appointed to the Consultative Commission of the Ministry for National Education; chosen by the Academy of History to speak on the Women of the Independence Movement in July 1960. Mrs Carmen Ortega Ricuarte was invited to give a course on Contemporary Civilization by the US State Department and was chosen to represent the Council as delegate to the ICW Council Meeting in 1960. Mrs Blanca Gnecco de Samper was invited by the US State Department to study US institutions for the prevention of delinquency and rehabilitation of juvenile delinquents. Mrs Maria Victoria Franco de Jaramillo was invited by US State Department to visit education, social service and home economics centres. Mrs Ofelia Romero de Wills was chosen by the ICW as Vice-Convener of the International Standing Committees on Radio and Television and on the Cinema. Mrs Gabriela Paláez has been appointed President of the Inter-American Committee for Women in the Organization of American States in Washington. A successful exhibition of the paintings of Miss Judith Marques was organized in Washington.

Standing Committees

All ICW Standing Committees are represented, with the exception of Housing, Health, and Trades and Professions.

Organizations affiliated with the Council

Pan-American Women's Round Table.
American Women's Club.
Guides and Scouts of Colombia.
Union of Colombian Citizens.

The Council has collaborated with the Union of Colombian Women by aiding activities on civic education, attending its meetings and participating in the organization of study groups in Bogota.

Relations with UN and Specialized Agencies

The Council has sent observers to the following: UN Seminar on the Participation of Women in Public Life, May 1959; UN Regional Conference, June 1959; UN/Office of American States Seminar on Educational Planning, September–October 1959.

The Council has requested admission in the National Commission for relations with UN and several Council Members are in the National Commission for UNESCO.

February 1962

307

HAITI

NATIONAL COUNCIL OF WOMEN OF HAITI
COUNCIL ESTABLISHED IN 1958
Affiliated to ICW 1960

The President, Mrs Fortuna Guéry, has given the following account: In August 1956 I received a letter from Zürich from the President of the International Council of Women, Mrs Jeanne Eder: 'We take the liberty of writing to you on the advice of our Vice-President and the President of the French National Council of Women, Mme Marie-Hélène Lefaucheux, a former colleague of yours on the Commission of the Status of Women. We are very anxious to establish closer contact with Haitian women and to see a National Council established in Haiti which could later be affiliated with our world-wide organization. The next Triennial Council Meeting of the Council will be held in June 1957, in Montreal, Canada, and we should be honored if you could attend on behalf of the women of Haiti.'

I was greatly tempted by this adventure, for it is indeed an adventure to plan an overall movement in my country, especially if one is aware of the miracles performed by existing associations to remain operative.

I went to Montreal and returned from the ICW Triennial Council Meeting greatly impressed by the intelligent, serious, extensive and thorough work performed by the International Council of Women with the appreciable aid of the various National Councils. I felt myself under obligation to add my own efforts, however insignificant they might be, to carry forward this important international work.

On my return to Port-au-Prince I published a full account of my trip in the *Nouvelliste*, a daily newspaper, and in the *Haiti Sun*, a weekly English-language paper. At the end of these reports I made an appeal to Haitian women who might be interested in the formation of a National Council. It was necessary to reach those women whose healthy ideas, moral courage, silent devotion and competence I knew from having seen them at work. It has been difficult—and it still is—to persuade them to add to their already numerous family, professional, social and administrative duties. I believe I have convinced them, in the course of the past three years, of the importance for Haitian women to know what has been accomplished in other countries and particularly in milieus with geographic, racial and economic conditions similar to our own.

We were informed by telegram dated May 17th, 1959, of the unanimously favourable acceptance of the candidature of our Council by the Executive Council.[1] Moreover, we did not wait for affiliation before answering all requests and questionnaires coming from the ICW. We produced articles for the ICW *Review* and a novel for the Literary Prize Contest. We have

---

[1] This NCW was formally affiliated to the ICW at the Council Meeting held in Istanbul in 1960. It is responsible for the education and welfare of 150 young girls sent from rural areas to the city to work in urban families.

faithfully passed on to the competent authorities of our country the various documents pertaining to their particular fields and have tried to obtain official response which is not always forthcoming. We also keep informed on the needs of women in our country and of the notable events in women's activities.

Almost all members of the Haitian National Council of Women are educators, facing difficult situations every day, for each human being is a world to explore and to form with the goal of making each one more fit to play his or her part in the universal concert. The strength and nobility of this profession are nourished by optimism and faith in perfectibility, both of which are pledges of the quality and the durability of our co-operation with the International Council of Women.

November 1961

IRAN

HIGH COUNCIL OF WOMEN'S ASSOCIATION OF IRAN
COUNCIL ESTABLISHED IN 1960
Affiliated to ICW in 1960

In 1960, 20 different Women's Associations in Iran decided upon the establishment of the High Council of Women's Associations of Iran, under the Presidency of HRH The Princess Ashraf Pahlavi.

Fields of Activity

Status of Women and Political Rights. Regardless of their various objectives and activities, these associations unanimously strive to attain one single aim: the promotion of the social status of women. With due regard to national traditions, and with an ardent inclination—felt in every walk of our social life—towards modernization and the acquisition of new branches of science, women have achieved a characteristic, and new, position in our society. Their new responsibilities demand that the social status of women should be based on more up-to-date rules and regulations and an aim is to study such rules with the object of improving the basis of society, and to encourage the Iranian woman to adapt herself to the new order of society.

Legal Problems. Proposals submitted by Legal Committees or member Associations are discussed with the competent authorities. Although we have not yet attained full political rights, public opinion and the opinion of governmental authorities are to a great extent on our side. By virtue of a law passed in 1949, women were able to vote and did vote extensively in municipal elections in Resht and Zahidan. In 1950, when municipal elections were being prepared in Teheran, the names of nine women were put forward by the Women's Associations as candidates for election, and their candidatures were accepted. Unfortunately municipal elections subsequently fell into abeyance in Teheran. A law ordaining such elections has, however, now passed the Senate, though still on the agenda of the

Lower House, and women will run for office and vote in Municipal elections in Teheran as soon as these take place. It is hoped that this may pave the way towards participation in Parliamentary elections.[1]

Activities covered by the Member Associations include: improvement of the level of public education and organization of an anti-illiteracy campaign; establishment of vocational schools for delinquent girls and women; provision for the welfare of mothers and children by co-operation of Municipal Public Nurseries and recognized charitable institutions; the improvement of public health through the establishment of Medical Centres by Member Associations; the encouragement of the education of girls by the provision of scholarship grants; the protection of women prisoners, through rehabilitation centres and by following cases through the law courts; the provision of legal advice and the protection of women whose rights have been violated by others; the study of juvenile life and delinquency; supervision of the curriculum of girls' schools; a woman elected to the High Council of Education; improvement in the living conditions of rural women; co-operation with the press in propagating the objectives of the Council and Member Associations.

Organizations affiliated with the Council

Some of the twenty Associations affiliated with the High Council are professional unions, such as Women Doctors, Nurses or Educators; others work mainly for charitable purposes; others again are primarily concerned with women's suffrage, or the education and welfare of Iranian girls.

Relations with UN and Specialized Agencies

In the field of international relations, some of our Women's Associations (particularly those of a professional nature) have representatives on various international organizations. Activities in this field have recently been concentrated within the High Council and the Council has obtained government authorization to delegate an observer to the United Nation's Commission on the Status of Women.

The Women's Organizations of Iran are in close and friendly contact with sister organizations in most countries of the world. A step towards the creation of better understanding between women of different nationalities was the opening of a successful International Exhibition of Women's Activities in Iran in January 1961, with the participation of 27 nations from Asia, Europe and America.

June 1962

---

[1] On February 27th, 1963, the Shahinshah announced his decision to grant to Iranian women the rights recognized in the Constitution, but not so far realized in fact. On March 3rd of the same year the former electoral law was modified to allow women to participate in the forthcoming elections. Six Iranian women were subsequently elected to Parliament.

**KOREA

NATIONAL COUNCIL OF WOMEN OF KOREA
COUNCIL ESTABLISHED IN 1959
Affiliated to ICW in 1960

Under the presidency of Dr Helen Kim, President of the Ewha Women's University in Seoul, this young Council has grouped associations active in many fields and, despite unsettled political conditions in Korea, has made a strong start.

Reports have been made to the government and National Assembly on concubinage, prostitution and other urgent problems, public opinion being aroused through radio and newspapers.

The Korean Council has also organized a special committee for Family Planning through the Mothers' Association. A Clinic for Mothers has been opened and adminsters medical consultation and treatment. Information on child spacing is made available to parents (particularly women) in both urban and rural areas.

The Council has also recommended the establishment of a Domestic Court and the improvement of the laws of inheritance. It has strongly emphasized the importance of the Women's Bureau of the Ministry of Health and Social Affairs.

The Council proposed to the government to render financial assistance for building a Women's Centre that can be used by all women's organizations. Thanks to an anonymous gift, the Women's Centre Building at Nam San Dong in Seoul has now been completed.

Affiliated Associations

Korean Association of University Women.
Korean Mothers' Association.
National Committee of Korean YWCA
Han Yang Women's Club.

Women's Welfare Association.
Korean Women's Association.
Research Institute of Women's Associations.
Institute of Student Counselling.

Relations with UN and Specialized Agencies

Dr Helen Kim headed the Korean Delegation to the UNESCO General Conference in Paris in 1962.

November 1962

311

**SINGAPORE

SINGAPORE COUNCIL OF WOMEN
COUNCIL ESTABLISHED IN 1951
Affiliated to ICW in 1960

Objects. To further the cultural, educational, economic, moral and social status of women in Singapore, to ensure justice to all women and to further their welfare as embodied in the Declaration of Human Rights, and to facilitate and encourage understanding among women of all races, religions and nationalities in Singapore.

In 1959, the President, Mrs Shirin Fozdar, reported that the granting of full political rights had been followed by elections resulting in the introduction of a new and greatly improved Marriage Law. Now that their eight years of struggle for political rights had brought victory, the women of Singapore were prepared to play an important rôle in bettering conditions for themselves and for their families.

November 1962

THAILAND

NATIONAL COUNCIL OF WOMEN OF THAILAND
COUNCIL ESTABLISHED IN 1959
Affiliated to ICW in 1960

In 1952 a group of members of the Siamese Association of University Women and the Association of Women Lawyers of Thailand urged the wife of the former Prime Minister, Than Phuying Laiad Pibulsonggram, then President of the Women's Institute of Culture, to bring together all the women's organizations of Thailand and form the National Council of Women. A constitution was drafted and the Council was legally registered in 1954, but owing to changes in the political situation, the Council was held in abeyance until 1958, when a group of representatives from various women's organizations was called to elect a committee for the following year of which Princess Prem Purachatra was elected President for a two-year term (since renewed). The National Council applied for membership in the ICW and was accepted at the Triennial Conference in Istanbul in 1960, when Princess Prem Purachatra was appointed a Junior Member of the ICW Board.

Fields of Activity

The Thai NCW has been especially active in community development, i.e.: (1) community club pilot project; (2) promotion of home industries; (3) safeguarding the welfare of young girls; (4) organizing regional workshops to support community development projects. It has received full

312

co-operation from the public and the government through both governmental and non-governmental organizations.

Standing Committees

The Council has 5 sectional committees: arts and literature, home economics, law, education and culture, and health.

Organizations affiliated with the Council

Eighty different organizations constitute the Thai NCW, including the Association of Women Lawyers, the Association of University Women, the Nurses Association, the Women's Medical Association, the Pan-Pacific and South East Asian Women's Association, the YWCA, Alumnae Associations, provincial women's associations, the Thai Women's Association, the Thai Women's Culture Club, the Home Economics Association.

Relations with UN and Specialized Agencies

Council members serve as experts, consultants or delegates to the UN and the Specialized Agencies in Bangkok and elsewhere in their capacity as government officials or have served as ICW observers at the latter's request. The Council is prepared to give strong support to campaigns for the ratification of UN Conventions.

June 1962

**TUNISIA

UNION NATIONALE DES FEMMES DE TUNISIE
COUNCIL ESTABLISHED IN 1956
Affiliated to ICW in 1960

Fields of activity and achievements

Political rights. In Tunisia the granting of civic rights for women in 1956 was coincident with the organization of the Union Nationale des Femmes. Tunisian women are now eligible to vote and to stand for office in municipal and parliamentary elections and a major task for the Council—whose President was elected a member of the first Tunisian Parliament—is to prepare women to exercise these new rights. The meaning of the Constitution and voting procedure have been explained in lectures and open meetings and the participation of women as voters, candidates and election officers is being successfully encouraged.

Social Welfare and Education. Political rights achieved, Tunisian women are taking stock of all the social tasks to be accomplished in order to meet the new aspirations of the Tunisian people. The Council has already been able to establish centres on vestimentary, household, sanitary and moral education. With the co-operation of the appropriate governmental or municipal authority, 100 anti-illiteracy centres have been opened, catering for 5,000 women. Four centres dispense shoes, clothing, and food to needy girls in Tunis, where 61 girls have been trained as social welfare visitors. Two hundred girls attend the training centre opened at El Ouardia in 1959 and 500 uneducated women are supplied with paid work by machine sewing workmen's overalls cut out by Council members.

Economic Welfare. In order to provide money for their social services and to participate in the economic expansion of Tunisia, the Council has opened a knitting factory which now functions as a limited liability company. The machines and initial capital—gift of the President and of the Directorate of the Plan—constitutes the Council's capital. The work of girls and women from this and other sections of the Council have been exhibited at the International Fair of Tunis, at the Anniversary Celebrations of the Foundation of the Republic, and at various local fairs. Stock-breeding and gardening centres are also planned.

Youth Welfare. Since 50% of the population of Tunisia is under 25, youth welfare is naturally a primary concern of the Council. Work has included the encouragement of nursery schools, care for abandoned children and young girls. With government and municipal aid, a re-education centre for girls has been opened in Den Den and the Council has recruited monitors for the Association for 'Colonies de Vacances'. Schoolgirls and students are encouraged to participate in voluntary work for women and sections of the Councils have been created for them, as well as one for government employees.

Organizations affiliated with the Council

The 300,000 members of the Union Nationale are sub-divided into 116 sections, and frequent seminars are held to train leaders in various fields. Co-operating organizations are the 'Vestiaire National'—a society encouraging women to cease wearing the veil—the cultural 'Club Aziza Othmana' and 'Le Nourisson' which facilitates the adoption of abandoned children.

Relations with UN, Specialized Agencies and other international organizations

The Council is actively promoting the formation of women's organizations in other African countries and would like to see a federation of North African women's organizations. It has been represented at a number of inter-African conferences and at the White House Conference on Children and Youth in 1960. In 1959 UNESCO consulted the Council on the basic education of women and on reading material for new literates.

November 1962

**TURKEY

NATIONAL COUNCIL OF WOMEN OF TURKEY
COUNCIL ESTABLISHED IN 1959
Affiliated to ICW in 1960

Following the foundation of the National Council on July 29th, 1959, at Ankara, the first General Assembly was held in December of the following year. The Board of Officers elected at this Assembly holds a weekly working session, and full monthly meetings are attended by all Affiliated Groups.

Fields of activities: 1960—

The first step taken by the new Council was to invite the ICW to hold its 1960 Triennial Council Meeting in Istanbul. This entailed a major effort on the part of a new Council, both as regards the organization of the Council Meeting itself, and also as regards the reception and entertainment of delegates and observers from forty countries. Arrangements were made for a special commemorative issue of Turkish stamps to mark the occasion. The Council Meeting was well attended by Turkish delegates and Committee members. Two members of the Council were elected to international office: Mrs Adela Ayda as Vice-Convener of the International Standing Committee on International Relations and Peace, and Mrs Selma Erzen as Hon. Vice-Recording Secretary. The Council entered a novel by Halidi Edip Adivar in the Eder Literary Prize competition and is organizing, in collaboration with other National Councils, the publication and translation of children's literature and the exchange of educational and documentary films for children. It is hoped that a Parents' School will soon be opened in Ankara. In Turkey the Council has supported the campaign for the election of Mrs Firdevs Mentese to the Council of State. A campaign is under way for the greater participation of Turkish women in political life. On the occasion of various national anniversaries, the Council has voiced gratitude to Ataturk who granted Turkish women their civic and political rights.

NCW items are often printed in the weekly newspaper *Woman* and in the daily press of Ankara and Istanbul. Press Conferences have been held and lectures and radio talks given on subjects such as the social aspects of women's work in Turkey, alcoholism, and the psychological effects of hunger.

During the Freedom from Hunger Campaign food, clothing and medicines were distributed in three villages.

Two provincial branches have been established—Istanbul and Izmir. The work of the Istanbul branch is directed principally to the following subjects: Moral and Social welfare, legal aid to needy women and the establishment of a rest home for single women.

Standing Committees

Standing Committees parallel to all those of the ICW have been established.

Affiliated Councils. Four.

Relations with UN and Specialized Agencies

The Convener and Vice-Convener of the Standing Committee on Education have been appointed observers on the Turkish National Commission for UNESCO. The Turkish Council was happy to have been able to arrange for the ICW/UNESCO seminar on the rôle of women in

315

UNESCO's Major Project on the Mutual Appreciation of Eastern and Western Cultures, at the conclusion of the Istanbul Council Meeting.

November 1962

**CAMEROONS

CONSEIL NATIONAL DES FEMMES CAMEROUNAISES
COUNCIL ESTABLISHED IN 1962
Affiliated to ICW in 1962

The National Council of Women of the Cameroons is a non-political co-ordinating body grouping a number of separate Women's Associations and Movements of all kinds working for the advancement of women. By July 1962, 18 legally constituted Women's Associations were affiliated to the Council.

Fields of activity

Several of the main women's Associations affiliated to the National Council conduct adult literacy classes in local schools after regular school hours. In some centres pupils have advanced as far as the 'Certificat d'études primaires élémentaires/(76 in 1962). Others provide classes in cookery, practical home management, hygiene and child care. The successful participation of pupils in the National Competition for the best housewife has proved a particularly effective stimulant.

The National Council takes an active part in combating juvenile delinquency, and in the protection of young people from bad films and literature. A member of the National Council sits on the official Film Censorship Board. Other concerns are school hygiene (vaccination, effective medical inspection, etc.), the decentralization of girls' boarding schools in a number of centres in order to ensure better moral protection for pupils and the reform of boarding conditions in such schools. Recommendations made on these subjects to the Ministries of Education and of Public Health are being considered. A recommendation by the Social Affairs Committee of the National Council has led the government to consider establishing an orphanage, and a memorandum has been submitted to the Ministry of Public Health on the problem of the rational redistribution of maternity hospitals throughout the national territory. A beginning has been made in the organization of Study Groups for the examination of key problems such as marriage dowries, status of widows, and polygamy.

Organizations affiliated with the National Council

These fall into two categories: the principal Women's Organizations actively engaged in the education of the women of the Cameroons, and those engaged in activities such as social welfare, folklore, the defence of public morality, etc.

November 1962

**CONGO (BRAZZAVILLE)

CONSEIL DES FEMMES CONGOLAISES
COUNCIL ESTABLISHED IN 1961
Affiliation to ICW 1962

The Council of Women of the Congo, with headquarters at Pointe Noire, was founded in January 1961 on the initiative of Madame Tchitchell, wife of the Vice-President of the Republic.

Fields of activity

The aim of the Council is to further the progress of the women of the Congo by encouraging the development of basic instruction, education and morality, and to promote all other activities susceptible of reinforcing the individual character of African women. For this purpose members of the National Council have undertaken the conduct of classes in fundamental education (to combat illiteracy), cookery, child care, sewing and embroidery. Work executed in these classes was exhibited at the 6th International Fair at Pointe Noire. The Council has already acquired the land for a permanent Headquarters, and is hoping to obtain official help in building. Meanwhile a drive is being made to organize local branches elsewhere than in Point Noire, and Propaganda Committees have been formed to visit other centres and to hold information meetings.

Organizations affiliated with the Council

An effort is at present under way to encourage the women's Associations already in existence in the Congo, most of them based on ethnic groupings, to affiliate with the National Council and thus benefit from the affiliation of this body to the ICW.

November 1962

KENYA

NATIONAL COUNCIL OF WOMEN OF KENYA
ESTABLISHED IN 1961 AS A COUNCIL OF WOMEN, BECOMING NATIONAL COUNCIL IN 1963
Affiliated to ICW in 1962

The Kenya Council of Women grew out of a Convention of Women's Societies in East Africa which held its first annual meeting early in 1957 and included among its members the Uganda Council of Women and the Tanganyika Women's Service League. Towards the end of 1959, a proposal was circulated to members of the Convention that they should consider forming a Kenya Council of Women with a view to eventual affiliation to the ICW. A trial Constitution was formally adopted at a meeting of the member societies in February 1961.

317

Fields of activities and accomplishments

The Kenya Council has so far been engaged mainly in finding its feet, an informal survey of the problems of 'Single women in Employment' was, however, undertaken, and revealed the need to safeguard and improve the status of women in Kenya and in particular to examine the position of marriages under customary law. After adopting the final Constitution in February 1962 the second plenary meeting of the Council decided to undertake a further investigation of 'Marriage and Inheritance in Relation to Customary Law'.

Another activity is the promotion of home and cottage industries, with special emphasis on the development of traditional handicrafts, for which markets are being sought both at home and abroad. In addition the promotion of pottery, bee-keeping and screen-painting on fabric is being actively considered, all with a view to helping our women to increase their spending power and thereby raise their standard of living.

Organizations affiliated to the Council

Eighteen Associations including:—

Asian Women's Association
East Africa Women's League
Kenya Girl Guides Association
Maendeleo ya Wanawake Organization
Young Women's Christian Association.

East African Central Muslim Women's Association.
Indian Women's Association, Mombasa.
Kenya Women's Society.

October 1962

ORGANIZATION OF NATIONAL COUNCILS

'THE INTERNATIONAL COUNCIL is a republic composed of National Councils. . . . The National Council is a republic composed of national organizations.' When May Wright Sewall spoke these words, at the close of the World's Congress of Representative Women at Chicago in 1893, only one National Council was in existence, and the ICW itself was only 5 years old. Seventy-five years is a long time in the life of an international organization, yet her words are as true today of the 56 National Councils of Women spread over every continent in 1963 as they were at Chicago in 1893.

The preceding pages, in which something of the history of National Councils has been told, will have shown the reader how, while all subscribe to the Council Idea and pursue the same objectives, there is considerable variation in the structure and working methods adopted by the different Councils.

From the very beginning of the ICW great insistence has been placed on the complete autonomy of Affiliated Councils. To quote the ICW Constitution of 1888: 'No society voting to become an auxiliary of this Council shall thereby render itself liable to be interfered with in respect to its complete organic unity, independence or methods of work.' For a new Council to be accepted as an Affiliate of the ICW, the Constitution of 1888 (as also that of 1963) stipulates only that it 'shall be composed of constituent national associations, representative societies and institutions', and that its Constitution (a copy of which must accompany its request for affiliation) must be 'in harmony with the basis of the Constitution of the ICW'.

Current lists of National Affiliates of National Councils show that in many cases the nucleus of each Council, old or new, is still formed by associations entering into one or other of the original categories. On the one hand, however, the attainment of objectives has terminated the affiliation of some societies, while, on the other, many

319

new associations, with new objectives, have naturally been added through the years.

The general pattern of affiliation is as follows:

Social Welfare and Health. Child, youth and moral welfare organizations. Associations for the protection of the family, the housewife, the consumer, the mother; also for the prevention of disease and for the promotion of hygiene, sport, etc.

Educational. Teachers' organizations (particularly pre-school, primary, technical, vocational, home economics, dietetics, handicrafts) as well as numerous Alumnae associations.

Professional. Associations of professional women, foremost among them the medical and para-medical professions: doctors, nurses, midwives, physiotherapists, dentists, laboratory assistants. Associations of women lawyers, architects, civil servants.

Civil Rights. Societies for women's rights still figure prominently in many councils. In an increasing number of countries women's citizenship societies and leagues of women voters are now affiliated, as well as societies for the defence and promotion of Human Rights.

Trades Unions. Representation of organized labour is more sporadic than that of professional groups; among those represented are telephone workers, small business, shop and commercial employees, domestic workers.

Political. In a number of countries the women's sections of various political parties are affiliated.

Cultural. Organizations concerned with the arts and handicrafts are represented in almost every council: cultural clubs, library associations, societies of women artists, writers, musicians, painters and sculptors; associations for the promotion of national arts and crafts; for the preservation of natural beauty spots, monuments, etc.

Deviations from the general pattern, doubtless attributable to special geographical conditions or to strong national traditions, are also interesting. For instance: Finland—Association of Forestry Officers' Wives; Switzerland—Club Suisse des Femmes Alpinistes; Nigeria—Market Women's Associations; Great Britain—6 of the 86 affiliates of this Council, are concerned with animal welfare.

In some countries practically all important women's organizations are affiliated to the National Council; everywhere National Councils maintain excellent relations with other women's organizations in their country whose principles conform with those of the Council, co-operating closely whenever important action of concern to all is required.

SOME TYPICAL STRUCTURES

Many of the oldest councils, particularly those with anglo-saxon traditions of administration, still mirror with remarkable fidelity the blueprint sketched by Mrs Sewall at Chicago in 1893: that is to say the National Council groups National Affiliates, while Local Councils throughout the country group the local branches of these Affiliates. In such cases the National Council operates largely as an educational and progressive action group, occupying an important position in the public life of the nation, often representing all organized groups of women in the country and speaking in their name before government authorities and public alike. In some such Councils, established on a regional basis, State or Provincial Councils serve as intermediaries between Local and National Councils.

Countries in continental Europe have sometimes preferred a rather different pattern, concentrating on the affiliation of strong National Associations, with action at the local level being carried out by the local branches of these Affiliates, rather than by local branches of the National Council. These Councils act as a permanent 'clearing house' for information and action on all problems that concern women, approaching government and parliament, informing public opinion, and mobilizing the co-operation of their National Affiliates in support of campaigns of mutual concern. Many Councils of this type are highly influential with national authorities, and it is to the National Council that the governments turn for consultation on issues of importance to the women of the country, and for the representation of women on government boards, commissions, etc.

No picture of the different types of National Councils can be complete without reference to the powerful Councils of Central and Eastern Europe affiliated to the ICW for varying lengths of time between 1904 and the end of the Second World War, which saw the disappearance of 9 such Councils. Grouping large numbers of National Affiliates, these Councils served not only as focal points for influencing public opinion and governments, leading in many cases to notable advances in the status of women in these countries, but also as centres of active work in the fields of education, social and moral welfare and culture. This type of Council was adopted by a number of Latin American countries, where the National Council itself undertakes the active work elsewhere organized by Local Councils or by the local branches of National Affiliates. This means a highly centralized permanent headquarters, from which radiate the various activities of the Council, including direct enterprises in educational, child or social welfare.

RECENTLY AFFILIATED COUNCILS

Most Councils affiliated since 1946 have followed one or other of the patterns established by earlier NCWs. Largely for reasons of geography or administrative tradition, certain Asian or African Councils have organized mainly on a regional basis, others—more densely populated or with longer traditions of centralized organization on the national scale—have preferred the type of Council operating mainly through its National Affiliates. Perhaps because in certain countries the foundation of the National Councils has coincided closely with national independence and the granting of extensive civil rights to women, a somewhat original type of Council has recently arisen. Particularly in predominantly Moslem countries, both in Asia and North Africa, new Councils have been formed, which, rapidly becoming powerful bodies in themselves and with only few affiliates have, in close collaboration with government agencies and municipal authorities, assumed important and large-scale tasks in the field of social welfare and of education.

In certain regions of Africa the formation of new Councils has been hindered by the inevitable lack of existing Women's Organizations of sufficient strength and experience to federate into a National Council. The system of 'Councils of Women' (in contrast to 'National Councils'—which can be formed only in independent countries) established with the affiliation of South West Africa in 1938, has served the useful purpose of enabling women in such countries to make a practical start with a minimum of Affiliates and few local branches. From such small beginnings, and limited activities in the field of inter-racial co-operation, welfare and education, several such Councils of Women have found themselves, with the achievement of national independence, well placed for expansion into full National Councils.

In other African Countries, where the formation of a Council has awaited independence, the initiative has, in several cases, been taken by a very small group of women's organizations, which, after forming a National Council and applying for affiliation to the ICW, endeavour to stimulate the creation and affiliation of other women's groups. Particularly characteristic of the women of such Councils, now coming for the first time into touch with the international field of women's organizations, is the intense feeling of loyalty and responsibility to their own organizations and to the women they represent.

REGIONAL CO-OPERATION

While close contact has always been maintained between Councils in geographically adjacent countries such as Canada and the US, France and Belgium, and National Councils everywhere have long made it a practice to invite representatives of neighbouring Councils to important congresses, jubilees, etc., more systematic efforts have also been made to establish regular regional consultation on matters of mutual interest. A Conference of the women of Sweden, Denmark Norway and Finland was first called as early as 1897, and the Councils of these four countries have met regularly and with useful results for many years. A permanent Centre of all NCWs in Europe has recently been established in Brussels and has received Consultative Status I with the Council of Europe. At Washington, in 1963, the ICW Council Meeting was informed of initiatives in the direction of further regional groupings of NCWs within the framework of the ICW in the Middle East and the Western Hemisphere, while Australia announced plans for a regional meeting of NCWs in Brisbane in 1964.

HEADQUARTERS AND STAFFING

The management arrangements of National Councils vary as much as do the NCWs themselves. Most Councils have a permanent secretariat, some with paid staff, some with voluntary workers only, some with both. Smaller Councils have no permanent secretariat, but an elected secretary who deals with all documentation and correspondence in her own home, handing over the position to a new secretary whenever one is elected. Elected officers are, of course, everywhere voluntary. Some Councils have spacious accommodation, large enough to serve as club rooms, lecture halls, etc., as well as for the reception of visiting individuals and delegations. Others are still in the stage of raising funds to house the secretariat of the Council. A few receive government assistance in acquiring premises, but the majority rely exclusively on their own resources.

Appendices

APPENDICES

1. Preamble and first two Articles of the ICW Constitutions of 1888 and 1963.
2. Examples of Declarations and Resolutions adopted by the ICW.
3. An example of the work of a National Council of Women with the United Nations and its Specialized Agencies.
4. ICW Archives Project.
5. Some of the principal libraries which contain ICW documentation.
6. Some scarce ICW publications of historical importance.
7. An account of the ICW Delegation received by the Committee for the League of Nations at the Paris Peace Conference in 1919.
8. Publications of National Councils of Women.
9. Note on finances of the ICW.
10. List of ICW Council Meetings.
11. National Councils affiliated to the ICW, June 1963.
12. ICW Questionnaire addressed to National Councils concerning their history.
13. Board of Officers of the ICW, 1963–66.
14. ICW Consultants with the United Nations and Specialized Agencies (1963).
15. Abbreviations.

Preamble and first two articles of the
CONSTITUTION OF THE ICW
adopted in Washington, 1888

Preamble

We, women of all Nations, sincerely believing that the best good of humanity will be advanced by greater unity of thought, sympathy and purpose, and that an organized movement of women will best conserve the highest good of the family and of the State, do hereby band ourselves in a confederation of workers to further the application of the Golden Rule to society, custom and law: DO UNTO OTHERS AS YE WOULD THAT THEY SHOULD DO UNTO YOU.

Article I Name

The Federation shall be called the International Council of Women.

Objects

(a) To provide a means of communication between women's organizations in all countries.

(b) To provide opportunities for women to meet together from all parts of the world to confer upon questions relating to the welfare of the commonwealth and the family.

Article II General Policy

This International Council is organized in the interests of no one propaganda, and has no power over its members beyond that of suggestion and sympathy; therefore, no National Council voting to become a member of the International Council shall render itself liable to be interfered with in respect to its complete organic unity, independence or methods of work, or shall be committed to any principle or method of any other Council, or to any utterance or act of this International Council, beyond compliance with the terms of this Constitution.

Preamble and first two articles of the
CONSTITUTION OF THE ICW
as amended in Washington, 1963

Preamble

We, women of all Nations, sincerely believing that the good of humanity will best be advanced by greater unity of thought, sympathy and purpose and that an organized movement will serve to promote the highest good of the family and of the State, do hereby band ourselves in a federation of women of all races, nations and creeds to further the application of the Golden Rule to society, custom and law: DO UNTO OTHERS AS YE WOULD THAT THEY SHOULD DO UNTO YOU.

Article I Name, Headquarters and objects:

The Federation shall be called the International Council of Women . . . The objects shall be:

(*a*) to broaden the minds and mutual sympathies of women through international contacts.

(*b*) to bring together in voluntary association women's organizations from all parts of the world for free consultation on action to be taken to promote the welfare of mankind, of the family and the individual.

(*c*) to work for the removal of all discrimination against women.

(*d*) to encourage women to recognize, and to train them to fulfill, their responsibilities as citizens.

Article II Policy

1. The International Council of Women is pledged to promote:

(*a*) Recognition and respect for human rights.
(*b*) Equal rights and responsibilities for both sexes in all fields.
(*c*) Peace through negotiation and arbitration.

2. The International Council of Women is established in the interests of no one particular social, political or religious propaganda. Political and religious questions of a controversial nature affecting the interrelationship of two or more countries are excluded, excepting those affecting fundamental rights and freedoms.

3. The International Council of Women shall not intervene in the internal work of its affiliated councils, beyond making suggestions for common action.

4. A Council shall not be committed by its affiliation to any principle or method of any other Council, or to any utterance or act of the International

Council of Women, beyond compliance with the aims and rules set down in this Constitution.

5. Affiliated Councils shall not communicate with any intergovernmental or international authority without first referring the matter to the Councils of the countries that may be concerned and to the President of the International Council of Women.

EXAMPLES OF
DECLARATIONS AND RESOLUTIONS
ADOPTED BY THE ICW

Declaration

A declaration is a broad statement of principle made in the name of the ICW. An outstanding example is the Declaration on Peace and Liberty adopted by the Council Meeting held in Athens in 1951.

'The ICW, since its foundation in 1888, has constantly worked for conciliation and for peaceful settlement of disputes. It reaffirms its intention to continue on this path, on which each generation must work out its needs, both between nations and within each national society.

'The ICW recognizes that to live in peace and to live in liberty (national and individual) are fundamental needs for nations and human beings. It therefore condemns all intents and actions of aggression as endangering peace and liberty.

'It records its conviction that to protect peace and liberty armament for defence today still remains necessary. It recognizes in the light of terrible experience that the once widespread belief in disarmament as a means to peace is a fallacy, unless the UN has both the moral authority and the material and physical power to maintain peace and protect human liberties.

'The ICW voices the need, felt by thinking and suffering people everywhere, that wholehearted service be given to the principles of the UN Charter and of the Declaration of Human Rights. It welcomes the recognition by the General Assembly in the Resolutions adopted at its 1950 session, of the close connection to be made between striving for social and economic justice and striving for a lasting peace.'

Resolution

Resolutions call for action by NCWs, Intergovernmental Institutions, governments or other responsible national authorities, and are referred to the appropriate ICW International Standing Committee for study and endorsement before presentation to a Plenary meeting of the Council or of the Executive Committee for adoption as an official Resolution of the ICW.

Examples:

Resolution on *Genocide* adopted by the Council meeting held in Philadelphia in 1947:

'The International Council of Women in conference assembled in Philadelphia, September 5th to 12th, 1947, unequivocally supports the principle of the proposed international agreement to be presented to the UN General Assembly at Lake Success later this month for a Convention on the Prevention and Punishment of Genocide by an International Criminal Tribunal.

'With the adoption of this Convention it urges its National Councils of Women to work in their respective countries for prompt signature and ratification.'

Resolution on the *Rights of the Child* adopted by the Council meeting held in Athens in 1951:

'The ICW welcomes the draft Declaration of the Rights of the Child. It notes that while special emphasis is laid on the physical, intellectual and social rights of the child, the vital importance of spiritual and moral training is not equally developed.

'It accordingly urges all National Councils of Women to work through their legislatures and through the voluntary organizations of their countries for a comprehensive scheme of development for the child's whole personality.'

Resolutions adopted by the Council Meeting held in Helsinki in 1954:

The International Council of Women urges its National Councils to collaborate efficiently with the vital effort that the United Nations Food and Agriculture Organization is making for the improvement of nutrition, domestic economy, rural life, and the safeguarding of natural resources, in order to better the lot not only of under-developed countries, but also of countries struggling with economic and social problems.

The International Council of Women urges the National Councils in countries where the danger of drug addiction exists to help the authorities in every way in their power to combat this peril.

The International Council of Women, in Conference assembled in Helsinki in June 1954, urges that measures be taken in all countries in order to do away with illiteracy equally among both sexes.

Resolution on *The peaceful and beneficial use of outer space* adopted by the Council Meeting held in Istanbul in 1960:

'Noting with great interest the efforts now being made to explore outer space, noting also with appreciation, that under the aegis of the International Geophysical Year scientists of the world have worked together in furthering efforts to explore outer space, realizing the great prospects for the advancement of human knowledge which will result from the exploration of outer space, recalling that the question of peaceful use of outer space was discussed by the General Assembly of the United Nations at its thirteenth session and that favourable consideration was given by the Assembly to the possibilities of international co-operation in the field of outer space, the ICW expresses the conviction that:

'(1) the community of nations has an overriding interest in the peaceful and beneficial use of outer space;

'(2) this interest of the community of nations requires that the uses of space are made by nations acting in co-operation,

'(3) the interest of the community of nations requires that outer space and the celestial bodies therein, should not be considered capable of being appropriated by any state, but should be regarded as a *res communis* open to all nations for peaceful and beneficial exploration.

'The ICW in pursuance of this conviction would urge upon governments its hope that:

'(1) satellites or other bodies placed in orbit in outer space will not be used to carry weapons of any kind;

'(2) governments will co-operate through some international agency to set up a system of security measures so that satellites may be used without endangering the safety or infringing the rights of any nation . . .

'(3) benefits obtained from the exploration of outer space will be placed at the disposal of all mankind . . .

'Further, the ICW

welcomes the proposal to call a conference sponsored by the United Nations on the peaceful uses of outer space, and requests that the conference consider setting up some permanent body within the framework of the United Nations to deal with the exploration of outer space.'

AN EXAMPLE OF THE WORK OF A NATIONAL COUNCIL OF WOMEN WITH THE UNITED NATIONS AND ITS SPECIALIZED AGENCIES

NCW of Great Britain

Relations with UN and Specialized Agencies

UN Status of Women Commission. In 1948, the NCW set up a Consultative Conference to compile lists of women suitable for appointment by the government to UN Commissions and Specialized Agencies, particularly with regard to the Status of Women Commission. Various recommendations submitted. On several occasions letters expressing satisfaction with appointments sent to the government. Requests also made to the government to instruct its delegates to take certain action on such questions as ritual operations on girls and Age of Marriage.

UNESCO. Government urged to instruct UK representatives to express dissatisfaction with inadequate provision for educational facilities for girls and women in the 1957/58 programme. NCW is taking part in the UNESCO Study Tour and Gift Coupon Schemes.

FAO. NCW is supporting the FAO Freedom from Hunger Campaign and is represented on its National Committee. A one-day conference was organized by NCW and branches are actively supporting local programmes.

UNICEF. Interest in UNICEF has continued since the UN Appeal for Children in 1948. Branches help local Committees in the UNICEF campaign and in sale of Greeting Cards. Government urged to give further financial support.

UNHCR. Keen interest and support given to work of the Office of High Commissioner for Refugees from its early days to present date, when NCW is urging government to support recommendation of the High Commissioner's Committee regarding future activities and to give generously to appeal for increased contributions. Branches throughout the country took prominent part in World Refugee Year.

Relations with Regional Offices of UN and Specialized Agencies

UNESCO. Since 1946 to present date, the NCW has endeavoured unsuccessfully to obtain representation on the National Commission for UNESCO, which has not adopted co-operative attitude towards the representation of NGO's.

FAO. The NCW has been represented on the National Committee for FAO and is represented on the Freedom from Hunger Campaign Committee. It is considered that the work of FAO is not sufficiently known.

UNICEF. The NCW is represented on the UK Committee for UNICEF.

UN. Within the NCW the work of the UN and its Agencies is made known chiefly through the International Affairs and the Scientific and Technological Committees, where, at each meeting, reports are given of UN activities and of international literature. Reports are also given by members attending UN and NGO Conferences and Seminars, and by NCW representatives on the Standing Conference on the Economic and Social Work of the UN and of the Women's Advisory Council of the United Nations Association.

Action taken regarding UN Conventions

UN Conventions ratified by the UK. Nationality of Married Women, 1958; Status of Refugees, 1954; Status of Stateless Persons, 1960; Supplementary Convention on the Abolition of Slavery, the Slave Trade and Institutions and Practices similar to Slavery, 1957. In each case the NCW had urged ratification.

UN Conventions not yet ratified by the UK. Prevention and Punishment of Crime of Genocide, 1951. Political Rights of Women, 1954; Recovery Abroad of Maintenance Obligations, 1957; in all cases the NCW has repeatedly pressed for ratification of these Conventions. With regard to the Convention on the Suppression of Traffic in Persons and Exploitation of the Prostitution of Others, the NCW has taken a very active part for many years on the various Conventions on this subject. Government unable to ratify Convention owing to Colonial Application clauses and to omission of the words 'for purpose of gain' in Article 1.

Recent Convention on Marriage, Consent, Minimum Age and Registration: the government has been urged to support and ratify this Convention.

NCW is also actively supporting the UK policy regarding the Slavery Conventions; it has also recommended the setting up of a UN Committee of Experts in this connection.

ILO Conventions not ratified by UK. Equal Remuneration Convention, 1953. The NCW has approached the government many times on this, so far unsuccessfully.

Convention concerning Fee-charging Employment Agencies. NCW has repeatedly urged the Government to introduce legislation in this country to provide for system of licensing and supervision of private employment agencies. Until this is done, UK is unable to ratify this Convention.

UNESCO Conventions. The following have been ratified by the UK: Agreement on the Importation of Educational, Scientific and Cultural Material, 1952. Convention against Discrimination in Education, 1962. In both cases the NCW approached the government to urge ratification.

December 1962

ICW ARCHIVES PROJECT

The destruction of so many libraries, both public and private, during the Second World War, and the consequent irretrievable loss of many valued publications and much historical documentation, led the ICW to undertake in 1947, an informal inquiry to ascertain what ICW documentary material still existed, where and in what condition.

At the meeting of the Executive Committee held in Reading, England, in 1952, a formal Archives Project was adopted, aimed at locating and surveying existing material, at providing ICW headquarters with as complete a collection as possible and at distributing duplicate copies to appropriate libraries in different parts of the world interested in possessing such material.

At the Council Meeting held in Helsinki, Finland, in 1954, an Archives Project Advisory Group was formed, on which the following ICW officers were asked to serve:

Baroness Boël	President
Miss Henni Forchammer	Hon. Vice-President
Lady Nunburnholme	,, ,,
Miss I. Palme	,, ,,
Mrs. Pichon-Landry	,, ,,
Miss van Eeghen	,, ,,

Mrs. L. D. Barney was designated to give direction to this project during its formative period and to report to subsequent ICW meetings on progress achieved.

A number of National Councils and individual Council members co-operated in this project. Special thanks are due to the NCW of Great Britain and in particular to its Archives Committee—Mrs K. M. Cowan, Miss D. M. Retchford and Miss A. M. Rienits. Exemplary efforts were made to collect, classify and preserve the many ICW publications and records of historical importance in the possession of this Council which include the valuable collection of Lady Aberdeen's extensive personal correspondence, the gift of her daughter, Lady Pentland. In the NCW of South Africa Mrs E. E. Monro and Miss Thelma Gutsche also rendered notable service to the Archives Project. Valuable work in cataloguing existing collections was performed by Miss Duchêne (Belgium) who was charged with classifying documents in the possession of Baroness Boël, and by Mrs Coleman, librarian, who, while working at the ICW office in Zürich was able to make a complete classification of ICW documentation then at headquarters. Both these collections were subsequently sent to Paris. At the NCW of the US the extensive classification of ICW material was undertaken by Frances W. Cummings, Director of Education and Assistant to the President of the National Federation of Business and Professional Women's Clubs, and Research Consultant to many well-known US organizations including the National YWCA.

By 1959, Mrs Barney was able to report to Councils (*Résumé of Activities: Archives Project, 1946/58*) that much of the work of recording ICW material so far located in public and private collections had been completed and that duplicate copies of certain publications had been sent to appropriate permanent depositories on their request. Expressions of appreciation for ICW material thus donated to augment existing collections were received from the important libraries concerned, foremost among them the UN Library in Geneva and the Library of Congress in Washington.

In the permanent Headquarters for the ICW in Paris, an office has been set aside for use as an Archives and Study Room. Under the direction of Mrs Coleman, classification of all the ICW archives is now being undertaken (1965).

Appended is a list of the principal libraries where those wishing to undertake research on or study of the women's movement will find ICW material of interest (see Appendix 5).

Also appended is a list of a number of ICW publications of historical importance which appear to have become rare (See Appendix 6). NCWs are asked to continue to notify headquarters when additional copies of these or other scarce ICW or NCW publications are located, so that existing major collections of ICW material may be augmented.

Steps remaining to be taken in the Archives Project are:

(1) To complete and maintain collections of ICW publications at Headquarters;

(2) to continue to encourage NCWs to set up or maintain Archives Committees and to keep accurate records of ICW documentation available in their respective countries;

(3) to augment and keep up-to-date existing collections in important libraries in different parts of the world, and

(4) to establish new collections in suitable libraries in areas where none so far exist.

NCWs are asked to collaborate by continuing to notify headquarters of libraries in their respective countries which wish to acquire ICW documentation, or to increase that already in their possession.

1965

SOME OF THE PRINCIPAL LIBRARIES WHICH CONTAIN ICW DOCUMENTATION

UNITED NATIONS LIBRARY, GENEVA (Switzerland)

This library, in which is incorporated that of the League of Nations, contains a remarkably complete record of ICW activities from 1888 to the present, including Quinquennial and Triennial Reports. Particularly rich in material covering the period 1919–38, it also comprises such ICW items as the *Report on the International Congress of Women on the Legal Position of Women, Paris, 1913*, edited by Mrs Avril de Sainte Croix, and the *President's Memorandum of ICW activities 1914–1920*. In 1959, through the ICW Archives Project, the librarian, Mr Breycha Vauthier, welcomed an ICW gift of scarce documentation on the work of the Committee and Institute of Intellectual Co-operation, expressing particular appreciation for the gift of records of the Sub-Committee of Experts on the education of youth in the spirit of peace, on that of the Institute of Educational Cinematography in Rome and on the activities of the ICW Standing Committee on the Cinema.

LIBRARY OF CONGRESS, WASHINGTON, DC (US)

An extensive collection of ICW material from 1888 to the present is to be found in the Library of Congress. To the remarkable collection of documents on the early period of the women's movement in America (including the newspaper cuttings and photographic records of the period) the NCW of the US (through the ICW Archives Project) was able to contribute a number of contemporary documents such as *The College, the Market and the Court, or Women's Relation to Education, Labour and Law*, Caroline H. Dall, 1863; the *Records of the World Congress of Representative Women, Chicago, 1893*; an account of the work of the Indianapolis Local Council of Women founded by May Wright Sewall in 1892; as well as ICW material referring to later periods such as *Women's Position in the Law of the Nations*, compiled by Mrs d'Abbadie d'Arrast (1912). The Library of Congress was also pleased to receive from documents formerly in the possession of Baroness Boël, the records of the work of the Special Committee of Women's International Organizations in Support of the Limitation and Control of Armaments, 1931–37. The Library itself arranged for the packing and shipping of their selections from the NCW-US to Washington.

UNESCO ARCHIVES, PARIS (France)

The archives of UNESCO include documentation on the International Institute of International Co-operation (1925–39). In 1959, through the good offices of Mr Opučenski, Chief of the Archives Section, and of his Assistant Mrs M. Fawtier, the ICW Archives Project was able to enrich this documentation by the donation of 60 out-of-print documents on the pioneer work of the *Comité d'Entente* or Joint Committee of Major International Organizations working in collaboration with the Committee and Institute of Intellectual Co-operation.

LIBRARY OF INTERNATIONAL ARCHIVES FOR THE WOMEN'S MOVEMENT, AMSTERDAM (Netherlands)

This collection comprises a number of ICW books and publications including Annual, Quinquennial and Triennial Reports since 1899. Handbooks on the Quinquennial Council Meetings of 1899, 1904, 1914 and 1920 are also included.

SOPHIA SMITH LIBRARY, SMITH COLLEGE, NORTHAMPTON, MASS (US)

The important specialized Sophia Smith collection of works on the social history of women, while primarily American, deals also with the history and status of women in many countries from ancient times to the present. The ICW Archives Project has been able to contribute material welcomed as 'greatly enhancing' this collection, which comprises documentation on the organized international activities of women from the foundation of the ICW to the present, including the published proceedings of the ICW and publications of the NCWs of the US, Greece, India and Pakistan. *Note:* Also in this library is a large mural by Hildreth Meiere, presented in 1943 by the NCW of the US, described by Mrs Mary S. Grierson, Director of the Sophia Smith Collection as follows:

> 'The first section is a stylized presentation of women in the home, behind bars, and then of women at schools, where the bars gradually lessen in number as she emerges, through education. The second section shows three real women, Harriet Beecher Stowe with the slave, Clara Barton with the Civil War soldier, and Susan B. Anthony with the suffrage flag . . . Underneath is an interesting little frieze which pictures the development of the position of women through the centuries, decade by decade, e.g. the banquet of the pioneer women's club Sorosis, the first women working at the typewriter, etc.'

FAWCETT LIBRARY, LONDON (Great Britain)

A long-established collection of works on the history of the women's movement in which documentation on the ICW is included.

MARGARET COUSINS MEMORIAL LIBRARY, NEW DELHI (India)

A recently created library now building up a collection on the international history of women.

WOMEN'S ARCHIVES, RADCLIFFE COLLEGE, CAMBRIDGE, MASS (US)

This comprehensive collection includes material in both published and manuscript form on the ICW (and on the NCW of the US) dating from 1888.

DEERING LIBRARY, NORTHWESTERN UNIVERSITY, EVANSTON, ILL. (US)

The *Biblioteca Femina* consists of works written by women in various countries where the ICW is represented: many volumes were the gift of Mrs Grace Seton, former Convenor of the Letters Committee of the NCW of the US.

BIBLIOTHÈQUE HISTORIQUE DE LA VILLE DE PARIS, PARIS (France)

Historical documentation of the NCW of France is included in this library.

PUBLIC ARCHIVES, OTTAWA (Canada)

The records of the NCW of Canada, including the diaries and personal correspondence of Lady Aberdeen from 1893 to 1898, are preserved in these government archives.

LADY ABERDEEN MEMORIAL LIBRARY (Canada)

Information Librarian: Miss Elizabeth Long, of the NCW of Canada.

OTHER COLLECTIONS

In addition to the libraries listed above, significant ICW records are held by certain National Councils and by private individuals, notably Mrs Henriette Hainisch (Austria), Miss Ingegerd Palme (Sweden) and Miss L. C. A. van Eeghen (Netherlands). The NCW of Great Britain possesses 100 Letter Files of the correspondence of Lady Aberdeen, donated by her daughter, Lady Pentland.

SOME SCARCE ICW PUBLICATIONS OF HISTORICAL IMPORTANCE

Records of International Congress, ICW, Washington, D.C. March 28th, 1888 (Notebook bound in cloth).

Report of the International Council of Women Assembled by the National Woman Suffrage Association, Washington, D.C. March 25th to April 1st 1888. National Woman Suffrage Association. 471 pages. (Washington, D.C., Rufus H. Darby, Printer, 1888.)

Report of Women's Conference on Women's Work, held in the Music Hall Buildings, Aberdeen, October 9th, 10th, 11th, 1888. Paperbound. 104 pages. Under the auspices of the Aberdeen Ladies Union (Aberdeen: D. Wyllie & Son, 1888).

Report of the Progress of the ICW during the Past Four Years. Submitted by Teresa F. Wilson, Corresponding Secretary of the ICW. July 1897. (Typewritten, 5 pages.)

ICW Memorandum sent to Presidents of National Councils of Women, by May Wright Sewall, Vice-President-at-large of the ICW. Indianapolis, August 22nd, 1898. Paperbound. 14 pages.

Executive Committee of the ICW: Report of Meeting held at 3 Tilney Street, London, W, March 23rd, 1899. Paper. 15 pages.

International Congress of Women, '99 (Second ICW Quinquennial) 7 volumes, viz: vol. 1—Report of Council Transactions, 363 pp; vol 2—Women in Education, 222 pp; vols. 3 & 4—Women in Professions, 215 & 246 pp; vol. 5—Women in Politics, 152 pp; vol. 6—Women in Industrial Life, 252 pp; vol. 7—Women in Social Life. Edited by the Countess of Aberdeen, retiring ICW President. Clothbound. (T. Fisher Unwin, London.)

ICW Memorandum sent to Presidents of NCWs by May Wright Sewall. Paperbound. 20 pages. (Indianapolis: Burford, Printer and Binder, 1902.)

Bilder vom Int. Frauen-Kongress, 1904.

Constitution and Standing Orders of the ICW, 1904.

Annual Reports of the ICW, 4 vols. 1904–08. Compiled by Mrs Ogilvie Gordon. Paperbound.

Health of the Nations. Compiled by Mrs Ogilvie Gordon, 1909. Paper.

Annual Reports of the ICW, 5 vols. 1909–14. Compiled by Alice Salomon. Paperbound.

Historical Sketch concerning the ICW and the NCW of the USA, Lillian M. Hollister, 1909. 19 pages.

Women's Position in the Law of the Nations. Compiled by Mrs d'Abbadie d'Arrast (1912). Paperbound. 195 pages.

National Systems of Education. First report of the ICW Education Committee. Compiled by Mrs Ogilvie Gordon, 1913.

Juvenile Delinquency: its causes and methods of correction. Report of the ICW Education Committee. Compiled by Mrs Ogilvie Gordon, 1913–1914.

Dixième Congrès International des Femmes: Oeuvres et Institutions féminines. Droits des Femmes. Inauguré par M. Klotz, Ministre de l' Interieur, le 2 juin, 1913. Compte rendu des travaux par Mme Avril de Sainte-Croix, Paris, Giard et E. Brière, 1914. Paperbound. 590 pages.

Genesis of the ICW and the Story of its Growth (1888–1893). Compiled by May Wright Sewall, ICW, 1914. Paperbound. 75 pages.

The Children's Charter. Compiled by the Special ICW Child Welfare Committee, 1923.

The Prevention of the Causes of War: Full report of Addresses delivered at the Conference held at the British Empire Exhibition at Wembley, May 1924. Paperbound. 327 pages.

The Council Idea, by Anna Garlin Spencer, Hon. Vice-Pres. NCW of USA. Paperbound. 55 pp. (Heidingsfeld Co., New Brunswick, N.J. 1930.)

Birth of the ICW, Fernande Baetens, 1957. Paper. 12 pages.

President's Memorandum regarding the Council Meeting of the ICW held in Edinburgh, Scotland, July 11th/21st, 1938. Paperbound. 159 pages.

Golden Jubilee Conference Souvenir Guidebook, Edinburgh, 1938. Paperbound. 71 pages.

Quinquennial Reports, 1889–1930.

ICW Bulletins

Numbers of the ICW Bulletin (English, French and German Editions) published between 1922 and 1944 have also become rare, particularly Vols. I to IV and that dated July, 1934, which contains the only record of the 1934 Council Meeting in Paris. Several collections of the post-war *Bulletin* (1944–57) (Bilingual French/English edition) are complete except for Vol. XXIX, May 1951 which is very rare.

Standing Committees

Copies of the summary of the work of the ICW Standing Committees (in English, 1957 and in French, 1958) compiled by Miss F. Baetens, are still available at ICW Headquarters. A sequel, bringing the history of these Committees up to 1964, is now available.

AN ACCOUNT OF THE ICW DELEGATION RECEIVED BY THE COMMITTEE FOR THE LEAGUE OF NATIONS AT THE PARIS PEACE CONFERENCE IN 1919

From: *The Precursors of the International Bureau of Education*, P. Rossello, 1943. Chapter: The League of Nations Covenant, pp. 133 ff.

The International Council of Women, together with the League of Women Suffragists of the Allied Powers and the United States, requested an audience before the Committee for the League of Nations, whose task was to work out Part I of the Peace Treaty, i.e. the Covenant. The Hotel Crillon was the headquarters of this Committee, whose Chairman was President Wilson. The minutes of the 12th session held on March 24, 1919, recorded the following: 'The President of the United States presented a letter from the International Council of Women requesting to be heard by the Committee on several important points concerning the future of women's status. After examining this request, it was agreed that the Committee would receive the International Council of Women's Delegation at its next-to-last session.'

Were these 11th-hour demands not coming too late? The closing session is not the one most likely to make revisions.

However, fifteen days were still to pass. The 'next-to-last' session, the fourteenth held by the Committee, did not take place until April 10th. At 8 p.m. the women's delegation was introduced immediately after the opening of the meeting by President Wilson. The White House host had no other 'bigwigs' at his side although several of those in his entourage were to plan an important rôle later on in the life of the future League of Nations.[1]

---

[1] Present: President Wilson and Colonel House—US; Lord Robert Cecil and Lt-General J. C. Smuts—British Empire; Messrs. Léon Bourgeois and Larnaud —France; Mr Orlando and Senator Scialoja—Italy; Baron Makino and Viscount Chinda—Japan; Mr Hymans—Belgium; Mr Epitacio Pessoa—Brazil; Mr Wellington Koo—China; Mr Venizelos—Greece; Mr Dmowski—Poland; Mr Betalha Reis—Portugal; Mr Danielopol—Rumania; Mr Vesnitch—Serbia; Mr Kramar—Czechoslovakia.

The women's delegation, headed by Lady Aberdeen, was made up of feminists well known in international circles.[1]

With customary brevity and dryness the official minutes reveal the manner in which the session took place. In introducing the delegation, Lady Aberdeen offered to place the experience of the organization she represented at the service of the League of Nations. She begged the President to pay the greatest attention to the points the delegates would present. Then one by one the various delegates explained and supported the demands contained in the MEMORANDUM: nomination of women to posts in the League; abolition of exploitation of women and children and abolition of prostitution; women's suffrage; creation of an International Bureau of Education and an International Health Organization. President Wilson expressed his pleasure in hearing these speeches. If all these requests could not be approved, this did not mean that the Committee did not recognize their value but was due only to the fact that the League of Nations could not solve all world problems at once.

The text of the MEMORANDUM edited by the International Council of Women and the League of Women Suffragists of the Allied Powers and the US was addressed : 'To the Chairman and Members of the Preparatory Committee of the League of Nations and the Plenipotentiary Delegates of the Peace Conference'. It is divided into 4 chapters: (1) Situation of women in committees and the permanent staff; (2) Welfare; (3) Suffrage; (4) Education; (5) Health. It also contains a final statement in favour of disarmament.[2]

[1] Mesdames Andrews, Corbett Ashby, Bratianu, Brunschwicg, Brigode, d'Amelio, Margery Fry, Commandante Girard-Mangin, Grinberg, Puesch, Rublee, Schivioni, Schlumberger, Siegfried, Avril de Sainte-Croix, Vérone.

[2] This text was reproduced in Vol. VIII (Document 744) of *My Diary at the Conference of Paris with Documents*, by David Hunter Miller, p. 173.

PUBLICATIONS OF NATIONAL COUNCILS OF WOMEN

1. *Periodical Publications*

Monthly or bi-monthly
Argentine
Belgium
Canada
Colombia
Finland
Germany
India
Israel
New Zealand
Norway
South Africa
Southern Rhodesia
Uganda
United States
(*Bulletin* and UN Calendar)

Quarterly
France
Germany
Great Britain
Kenya
Pakistan
Tanganyika

Yearbooks,
Annual Reports,
Directories, etc.
Australia (every two years)
Belgium
Canada
Finland
Great Britain
Nyasaland
United States (Study Guide)

Regular Congress Reports
Philippines
Tunisia.

2. *Some Histories of National Councils*

Canada—*Proud Heritage: a History of the NCW of Canada*, Rosa L. Shaw, Toronto, 1957.

France—*Cinquante anneés d'activité 1901–1951.*

Finland—*Forty years of Women Suffrage in Finland*, Helsinki, 1947.

Great Britain—*Historical Sketch of NCW of Great Britain, 1895–1937*, Dame Maria Ogilvie Gordon, 1937.

    —*Women in Council: Jubilee book of the NCW of Great Britain*, Oxford, 1945

    —*The First Sixty Years*, 1956.

    —*During Six Reigns—Landmarks in the History of the NCW of Great Britain*, M. E. Alford.

India—*Women of India* with foreword by Jawaharlal Nehru, Government of India, 1958.

Norway—Survey of social work and kindred activities in Norway in connection with the Standing Committees of the ICW, Oslo, 1920; also histories of the National Council on the occasion of its 25th and 50th anniversaries.

South Africa—*NCW, Johannesburg, 1912–1962: an impression of 50 years of service to city, province and nation*, Mrs E. E. Monro and Dr Thelma Gutsche, 1962.

Southern Rhodesia—*The NCW of Southern Rhodesia 1946–1956.*

Sweden—*History of the ICW*, I. Palme, 1937.

APPENDIX 9

NOTE ON FINANCES OF THE ICW

1. *General*

Annual affiliation dues of National Councils (fixed at the beginning of each Triennial period).
Annual assessments of National Councils (based on the income of each Council).
Fees of Triennial Contributors and Patrons (individuals).
Fees of Life Members (individuals).
Contracts with Intergovernmental Organizations for specific purposes.
Legacies.
Donations.
Golden Book. The ICW has a *Golden Book* in which is inscribed the name of any person, institution or society who, with the approval of the ICW Board of Officers and of the National Council of Women in his or her country, expresses his or her appreciation of the aims and activities of the ICW by sending to the ICW Treasurer a sum of at least 1,000 Swiss francs. The name of any person who remembers in his or her Will the ICW with a substantial bequest is also recorded in the *Golden Book.* Donations recorded in the *Golden Book* in the past have included gifts from friends of the ICW in Asia, Africa, America and Europe.

2. *ICW meetings*

Fees paid by individuals attending Triennial Meetings (fixed for each meeting).
Contribution by the NCW of the host country in the form of accommodation for and servicing of the Board, the Executive and the Triennial Meetings of the ICW.
Contributions of International Officers of the ICW (Board Members, Conveners and Vice-Conveners of International Standing Committees) who are responsible for their own travel and other expenses when attending ICW meetings.

1962

ICW COUNCIL MEETINGS

Year	Place	President of NCW of Host Country
1888	Washington (US) (Foundation)	
1893	Chicago (US)	Mrs May Wright Sewall
1899	London (England)	Mrs Alfred Booth
1904	Berlin (Germany)	Mrs Marie Stritt
1909	Toronto (Canada)	Lady Edgar
1914	Rome (Italy)	Countess Spoletti Rasponi
1920	Christiania (now Oslo) (Norway)	Mrs Betsy Kjelsberg
1925	Washington (US)	Mrs Philip North Moore
1930	Vienna (Austria)	Mrs Hertha von Sprung
1934[1]	Paris (France)	Mrs Pichon-Landry
1936	Dubrovnik (Yugoslavia)	Mrs Lepossava Petkovich
1938	Edinburgh (Scotland)	Lady Ruth Balfour
1947	Philadelphia (US)	Mrs Ambrose N. Diehl
1951	Athens (Greece)	Mrs Elmina Pantelaki
1954	Helsinki (Finland)	Mrs Margit Borg-Sundman
1960	Istanbul (Turkey)	Mrs Edibe Sayar
1963	Washington (US)	Mrs S. Yarnall Jacobs

[1]NOTE. First Triennial Meeting. Before this date the meetings had been every five years (Quinquennials).

NATIONAL COUNCILS[1]
AFFILIATED TO THE ICW IN JUNE 1963
(in chronological order by year of affiliation)

Country	Date of Affiliation	Country	Date of Affiliation
United States	1893	Hong Kong	1951
Canada	1897	Lebanon	1951
Germany	1897	Uganda	1951
Sweden	1898	Tanganyika	1952
Great Britain	1898	Pakistan	1953
Denmark	1899	Nigeria	1954
Australia	1899/1911	Philippines	1957
Netherlands	1899	Israel	1957
Italy	1900	Burma	1958
New Zealand	1900	Bolivia	1960
Argentina	1901	Colombia	1960
France	1901	Haiti	1960
Austria	1903	Iran	1960
Switzerland	1903	Korea	1960
Norway	1904	Singapore	1960
Belgium	1906	Thailand	1960
Greece	1908	Tunisia	1960
Finland	1911	Turkey	1960
South Africa	1913	Cameroons	1962
Chile	1923	Congo (Brazzaville)	1962
India	1925	Kenya	1962
Peru	1926	Ecuador	1963
Brazil	1927	Gambia	1963
South West Africa	1938	Liberia	1963
Nyasaland	1945	Luxemburg	1963
Southern Rhodesia	1946	Niger	1963
Dominican Republic	1951	Sierra Leone	1963
Egypt	1951	Trinidad and Tobago	1963

[1] Including Councils of Women.

ICW QUESTIONNAIRE ADDRESSED TO NATIONAL COUNCILS CONCERNING THEIR HISTORY

NC/17, Paris, 1960.

History Questionnaire

The following information is requested both for maintaining a central record at ICW Headquarters, Paris, of the ICW activities of the National Councils, and also for incorporation in a short history of the ICW 1888–1963. Please make your replies as brief as you can, and specific to each of the questions. Your answer should be mailed in time to reach the ICW Headquarters office in Paris not later than April 24th, 1961. Kindly mark the envelope 'History Questionnaire'. Your co-operation is sincerely appreciated.

1. In which ICW fields have you been especially active during the 25-year periods:

   (a) 1888–1913,
   (b) 1914–38,
   (c) 1939–63,

and what have been your accomplishments?

2. Which ICW Standing Committees are represented in your Council?

3. How many organizations form your National Council, and what kinds of organizations (give sampling)?

4. (a) What contacts do your NCW members have as representatives to the United Nations and its Specialized Agencies (or did they have to the former League of Nations) as delegates, observers, experts or consultants?

   (b) What contacts do your NCW members have as representatives with the United Nations or its Specialized Agencies that have regional or local offices in your country?

   (c) What has your NCW done towards obtaining ratification and implementation of Conventions of the United Nations and its Specialized Agencies that have been supported by the ICW?

BOARD OF OFFICERS OF THE ICW
1963–66

Honorary President	Mrs M-H. Lefaucheux (France)
Honorary Vice-Presidents	Countess Flavia della Gherardesca (Italy)
	Mrs Margit Borg-Sundman (Finland)
	Mrs Saraladevi Sarabhai (India)
	Miss Ingegerd Palme (Sweden)
Treasurer of Honour	Miss Karen M. Glaesel (Denmark)
President	Mrs M. Craig Schuller-McGeachy (Great Britain)
Vice-Presidents (elected)	Mrs K. Stassinopoulo (Greece)
	Eva, Marchioness of Reading (Great Britain)
	Mrs Theanolte Bähnisch (Germany)
	Mrs Pumla Kisosonkole (Uganda)
	Princess Prem Purachatra (Thailand)
	Miss Ruth Gibson (Australia)
	Mrs Saul Hayes (Canada)
	Miss Helena Benitez (Philippines)
(co-opted)	Mrs Sophia Yarnall Jacobs (US)
	Mrs C. Hernandez de Mendoza (Colombia)
	Mrs J. Moghaizel (Lebanon)
	Miss A. Rynning (Norway)
Hon. Treasurer	Miss E. B. ten Bruggen Cate (Netherlands)
Hon. Recording Secretaries	Miss Mary Shaw (Great Britain)
	Miss Nellie Wiener (Belgium)
Hon. Vice-Treasurers	Mrs Dorothy Edwards (Australia)
	Mrs Zimmermann-Bütikofer (Switzerland).
Hon. Vice-Recording Secretaries	Miss Lily Marx (Italy)
	Mrs Kretschmer-Dorninger (Austria)
	Mrs E. Ségalen (France)
Non-voting members	Mrs Z. Harman (Israel)
	Begum Faridi (Pakistan)
	Mrs Mbono Samba (Cameroons)
	Miss Ortiz de Zevallos (Peru)
Liaison Officers with UN	Mrs L. Dreyfus-Barney
	Mrs W. Barclay Parsons
	Mrs A. DeWitt Stetten

ICW CONSULTANTS WITH THE UNITED NATIONS AND SPECIALIZED AGENCIES (1963)

United Nations Commission on Human Rights, and Sub-Commission on Prevention of Discrimination and Protection of Minorities (New York)—Mrs E. Carter.

United Nations Social Commission (New York)—Miss M. Forsyth.

Economic and Social Council (Geneva)—Miss L. C. A. van Eeghen.

Food and Agriculture Organization (Rome)—Miss L. Corcos.

International Labour Organization (Geneva)—Miss L. C. A. van Eeghen.

United Nations Educational, Scientific and Cultural Organization (Paris)—Mrs K. M. Delavenay

United Nations International Children's Fund (New York)—Miss M. Forsyth.

Office of the United Nations High Commissioner for Refugees—Mrs J. Papanek.

NOTE: With the development of opportunities for combined action on the part of the ICW and post-war inter-governmental institutions, it gradually became clear that the work of the ICW Liaison Officers with the United Nations needed to be supplemented by building up a system of ICW Consultants with certain specific Organs and Commissions of the UN, and with those Specialized Agencies with which the ICW enjoys consultative or other special status. The function of these Consultants is to inform the ICW of suitable lines of co-operation with the organization to which they are accredited, and to bring to the attention of that organization fields of action in which practical results achieved by the ICW may prove of interest.

ABBREVIATIONS

ECA: United Nations Economic Commission for Africa.
ECAFE: Economic Commission for Asia and the Far East.
ECE: Economic Commission for Europe.
ECOSOC: Economic and Social Council.
FAO: Food and Agriculture Organization.
IBE: International Bureau of Education.
ICW: International Council of Women.
ILO: International Labour Organization.
IRO: International Refugee Organization.
IWSA: International Women's Suffrage Alliance (now International Alliance of Women).
NCW: National Council of Women.
UNESCO: United Nations Educational, Scientific and Cultural Organization.
UNHCR: Office of the UN High Commissioner for Refugees.
UNICEF: United Nations Children's Fund.
UNRRA: United Nations Rehabilitation and Relief Administration.
WHO: World Health Organization.
WYWCA: World Young Women's Christian Association.

Permanent Headquarters of the International Council of Women: 13 rue Caumartin, Paris, 9e, France.

INDEX

Note—This index includes names appearing in those sections of this book dealing with the International of Women and its International Standing Committees.

It has not been thought useful to index the Histories of individual National Councils of Women, as these are self-contained. Readers are referred to the Table of Contents on page viii for a page index of these Histories country by country.